Modern American Drama: Playwriting in the 1960s

DECADES OF MODERN AMERICAN DRAMA: PLAYWRITING FROM THE 1930s TO 2009

Modern American Drama: Playwriting in the 1930s
by Anne Fletcher

Modern American Drama: Playwriting in the 1940s
by Felicia Hardison Londré

Modern American Drama: Playwriting in the 1950s
by Susan C. W. Abbotson

Modern American Drama: Playwriting in the 1960s
by Mike Sell

Modern American Drama: Playwriting in the 1970s
by Mike Vanden Heuvel

Modern American Drama: Playwriting in the 1980s
by Sandra G. Shannon

Modern American Drama: Playwriting in the 1990s
by Cheryl Black and Sharon Friedman

Modern American Drama: Playwriting 2000–2009
by Julia Listengarten and Cindy Rosenthal

Modern American Drama: Playwriting in the 1960s

Voices, Documents, New Interpretations

Mike Sell

Series Editors: Brenda Murphy and Julia Listengarten

methuen | drama
LONDON • NEW YORK • OXFORD • NEW DELHI • SYDNEY

METHUEN DRAMA
Bloomsbury Publishing Plc
50 Bedford Square, London, WC1B 3DP, UK
1385 Broadway, New York, NY 10018, USA
29 Earlsfort Terrace, Dublin 2, Ireland

BLOOMSBURY, METHUEN DRAMA and the Methuen Drama logo
are trademarks of Bloomsbury Publishing Plc

First published in Great Britain 2018
Paperback edition first published 2021

Copyright © Mike Sell and contributors, 2018

Mike Sell has asserted his right under the Copyright,
Designs and Patents Act, 1988, to be identified as author of this work.

For legal purposes the Acknowledgements on p. ix constitute
an extension of this copyright page.

Cover design: Louise Dugdale
Cover image: March in support of the Black Panther Party, Connecticut,
November 1969. Photo © David Fenton/Getty Images

All rights reserved. No part of this publication may be reproduced or
transmitted in any form or by any means, electronic or mechanical,
including photocopying, recording, or any information storage or retrieval
system, without prior permission in writing from the publishers.

Bloomsbury Publishing Plc does not have any control over, or responsibility for,
any third-party websites referred to or in this book. All internet addresses given
in this book were correct at the time of going to press. The author and publisher
regret any inconvenience caused if addresses have changed or sites have
ceased to exist, but can accept no responsibility for any such changes.

A catalogue record for this book is available from the British Library.

A catalog record for this book is available from the Library of Congress.

ISBN: HB: 978-1-472-57220-2
PB: 978-1-3502-0454-6
ePDF: 978-1-3501-5361-5
eBook: 978-1-3501-5362-2
Pack: 978-1-4725-7264-6

Series: Decades of Modern American Drama: Playwriting from the 1930s to 2009

Typeset by RefineCatch Limited, Bungay, Suffolk

To find out more about our authors and books visit
www.bloomsbury.com and sign up for our newsletters.

CONTENTS

Acknowledgements ix
Biographical Note and Notes on Contributors x
General Preface   Brenda Murphy and Julia Listengarten   xii

1   Introduction: Living in the 1960s *Mike Sell* 1
   The baby boom 3
   The golden age of capitalism 3
   Social forces, political movements 4
      The labour market 5
      The fight against white supremacy 5
      Sex, gender and sexuality 8
   Culture: From the quotidian to the extraordinary 15
      Where did we live? 15
      What did we eat? 16
      What did we watch? 18
      What did we listen to? 23
   A year of cataclysm and promise: 1968 26

2   American Theatre in the 1960s *Mike Sell* 31
   Broadway: Crisis and continuity 32
      The Broadway musical 32
      Broadway drama 36
   Off- and Off-Off-Broadway 45
      Off-Broadway 45
      Off-Off Broadway 51

The residential theatre movement: Acorns and oak trees 63
  The Guthrie Theater 66
The Black Arts Movement 67
  The Black Arts Repertory Theatre/School 68
  Ed Bullins and the New Lafayette Theatre 68
  Concept East Theatre 70
  Barbara Ann Teer and the National Black Theatre 71
Theatre collectives: The power of community 73
  The Living Theatre 74
  The Free Southern Theater 77
Gay and queer drama: Out of the closet 79
  Drama out of the closet 79
  The Theatre of the Ridiculous 82
Asian American theatre 84
  The East West Players 85
  Oriental Actors of America 86
Latino theatre 87
  El Teatro Campesino 87
  Latino theatre in New York 89
Conclusion: Into the new millennium 91

3 Edward Albee *Helen Shaw* 93
  Introduction 93
  Dawn of the 1960s 95
  The Zoo Story 96
  The Sandbox and *The American Dream* 99
  Who's Afraid of Virginia Woolf? 105
  Tiny Alice 112
  A Delicate Balance 114
  Other works 118
  Conclusion 120

4 Amiri Baraka *Susan Stone-Lawrence* 123
  Introduction 123

Beginnings 126
The Beat Period: *The Eighth Ditch* and *The Baptism* 127
The Transitional Period 129
   The Toilet 129
   A Recent Killing 131
   Dutchman 132
   The Slave 134
The Black Nationalist Period 136
   Experimental Death Unit #1 138
   A Black Mass 139
   Great Goodness of Life: A Coon Show 140
   Madheart 142
   Celebrity satires: *J-E-L-L-O*, *The Sidney Poet Heroical* and *Rockgroup* 144
   Slave Ship 145
Conclusion 148

5 Adrienne Kennedy *Lenora Inez Brown* 151

Introduction 151
Early life and career 152
Kennedy and the Black Arts Movement 158
Funnyhouse of a Negro 161
Cities in Bezique 165
A Rat's Mass 171
London plays: *The Lennon Play*, *A Lesson in Dead Language*, *Sun* 173
General response to her work 176
Conclusion 178

6 Jean-Claude van Itallie *Timothy Youker* 181

Introduction 181
'Playwright of the Workshop' 186
The 'Doris' Plays 190
America Hurrah 193

The Serpent 204
Conclusion 213

Documents *Compiled and edited by Bradley Allen Markle* 215
    Awards 215
        Obie 215
        Drama Desk–Vernon Rice 224
        Antoinette Perry Award ('Tony') 229
    Primary voices 243
        Historical and cultural context 243
        Changes to the theatre 249
        Artistic influence and criticism 256

Notes 261
Bibliography 297
Index 309

ACKNOWLEDGEMENTS

Thanks to Julia Listengarten, Mark Dudgeon, Ian Howe and the staff at Bloomsbury Methuen Drama for their support and patience, particularly as the project's deadline loomed. I'm grateful to have had the opportunity to work with each of the contributors to this volume, but especially Susan Stone-Lawrence, who joined the project at the last minute, yet crafted a thorough and insightful essay. My essay on 1960s theatre would be inconceivable without the work of the dozens of critics and historians who preceded me, but James Harding and Cindy Rosenthal were especially and personally helpful. Bradley Markle proved himself once more to be a meticulous, insightful and indefatigable research assistant. Bradley and my spouse Kate Sell put in countless hours helping me compile the index. Though I am pleased and proud of the story we tell in this volume about theatre in the 1960s, we have, inevitably, left out innumerable playwrights, performers and crew members. Their labours of heart, mind and hand are acknowledged here in spirit, if not in letter. Finally, my thanks to Kate, River, Brando and Dylan, who showed loving patience and kindness during the several weeks I spent more time with books and laptop than with them.

BIOGRAPHICAL NOTE AND NOTES ON CONTRIBUTORS

Mike Sell is Professor of English and faculty member in the Graduate Program in Literature and Criticism at Indiana University of Pennsylvania. He is the author of *The Avant-Garde: Race, Religion, War* (2011) and *Avant-Garde Performance and the Limits of Criticism* (2005). He is editor of *Avant-Garde Performance and Material Exchange: Vectors of the Radical* (2010) and *Ed Bullins: Twelve Plays and Selected Writings* (2006), and contributing editor to *The Columbia Encyclopedia of Modern Drama* (2007). His essays on modern drama, the avant-garde, the Black Arts Movement and video games have appeared in *New Literary History*, *TDR*, *Theatre Journal*, *Theatre Survey*, *Modernism/Modernity*, *African American Review* and other journals.

Lenora Inez Brown is an author and production dramaturg who specializes in new play development for audiences of all ages. In addition to articles for *American Theatre* magazine and *TYA Today*, Brown has written two texts: *The Art of Active Dramaturgy: Transforming Critical Thought into Dramatic Action* and *New Play Development: Facilitating Creativity for Dramaturgs, Playwrights, and Everyone Else* both published by Focus Publishing, an imprint of Hackett Publishing. Her chapter 'A Little Knowledge This Way Comes: The Importance of Distilling Research for the Rehearsal Hall' is in *Playing with Theory in Theatre Practice*. Brown is a reader for *Youth Theatre Journal*. She holds an MFA in Dramaturgy and Dramatic Criticism from the Yale School of Drama.

Bradley Markle is a graduate student pursuing his PhD in English Literature and Criticism at the Indiana University of Pennsylvania.

His research interests include African American literature, Caribbean literature, performativity and technology-related English studies. His previous research has investigated how West African musical and oral storytelling techniques have influenced white writers such as Faulkner. Currently he is exploring how technology can be better implemented in the classroom to improve pedagogical systems.

Helen Shaw has written about theatre for *Time Out New York* since 2005. She also writes about performance, dance and theatre for *The Village Voice*, *TheatreForum* and *American Theatre*. She has twice curated the City University of New York's avant-garde Prelude festival, and she also teaches classes in Modern US Drama and Chekhov at New York University. She wrote the introduction to *The Difficulty of Crossing a Field: Collected Plays by Mac Wellman* and is at work on her own book on Wellman's *oeuvre* and the rise of the High Weird in American playwriting.

Susan Stone-Lawrence is a Fine Arts Doctoral Program student in the School of Theatre and Dance at Texas Tech University, earning her PhD in History/Theory/Criticism and Playwriting. As a long-time admirer of Amiri Baraka, she often writes about the prominent Black Arts Movement poet–playwright, who was the subject of her master's thesis as well as subsequent papers and conference presentations. One of these, '"A Simple Knife Thrust": The Complicated Power of Purgative Ritual in *Madheart*', appeared in the 'Amiri Baraka: Revaluation and Appreciation' issue of *Continuum: The Journal of African Diaspora Drama, Theatre and Performance*, published on the anniversary of Baraka's passing. In August 2016, the Black Theatre Network selected this essay for inclusion in their thirtieth anniversary special edition.

Timothy Youker is an Assistant Professor of English and Drama at the University of Toronto and a member of the New York-based United Broadcasting Theater Company. His forthcoming book *The Document and Its Double: Documentary Theatre and the Historical Avant-Garde* traces the history of intersections between avant-garde theatre and documentary art forms from the 1870s to the 1990s, including the work of Karl Kraus, Erwin Piscator, the Open Theatre and Handspring Puppet Company. His work has been published in *Theatre Journal* and *The Journal of American Drama and Theatre*.

GENERAL PREFACE

Decades of Modern American Playwriting is a series of eight volumes about American theatre and drama, each focusing on a particular decade during the period between 1930 and 2010. It begins with the 1930s, the decade when Eugene O'Neill was awarded the Nobel Prize for Literature and American theatre came of age. This is followed by the decade of the country's most acclaimed theatre, when O'Neill, Tennessee Williams and Arthur Miller were writing their most distinguished work and a theatrical idiom known as 'the American style' was seen in theatres throughout the world. Its place in the world repertoire established, American playwriting has taken many turns since 1950.

The aim of this series of volumes is to focus attention on individual playwrights or collaborative teams who together reflect the variety and range of American drama during the eighty-year period it covers. In each volume, contributing experts offer detailed critical essays on four playwrights or collaborators and the significant work they produced during the decade. The essays on playwrights are presented in a rich interpretive context, which provides a contemporary perspective on both the theatre and American life and culture during the decade. The careers of the playwrights before and after the decade are summarized as well, and a section of documents, including interviews, manuscripts, reviews, brief essays and other items, sheds further light on the playwrights and their plays.

The process of choosing such a limited number of playwrights to represent the American theatre of this period has been a difficult but revealing one. In selecting them, the series editors and volume authors have been guided by several principles: highlighting the most significant playwrights, in terms both historical and aesthetic, who contributed at least two interesting and important plays during the decade; providing a wide-ranging view of the decade's theatre, including both Broadway and alternative venues; examining many historical trends in playwriting and theatrical production during the decade; and reflecting the theatre's diversity in gender and ethnicity, both across the decade and across the period as a whole. In some decades, the choices are obvious. It is hard to argue with O'Neill, Williams, Miller and Wilder in the 1940s. Other decades required a good deal of thought and discussion. Readers will inevitably regret that favourite playwrights are left out. We can only respond that we regret it too, but we believe that the playwrights who are included reflect a representative sample of the best and most interesting American playwriting during the period.

While each of the books has the same fundamental elements – an overview of life and culture during the decade, an overview of the decade's theatre and drama, the four essays on the playwrights, a section of documents, an Afterword bringing the playwrights' careers up to date, and a Bibliography of works both on the individual playwrights and on the decade in general – there are differences among the books depending on each individual volume author's decisions about how to represent and treat the decade. The various formats chosen by the volume authors for the overview essays, the wide variety of playwrights, from the canonical to the contemporary avant-garde, and the varied perspectives of the contributors' essays make for very different individual volumes. Each of the volumes stands on its own as a history of theatre in the decade and a critical study of the four individual playwrights or collaborative teams included. Taken together, however, the eight volumes offer a broadly representative critical and historical treatment of eighty years of American theatre and drama that is both accessible to a student first encountering the subject and informative and provocative for a seasoned expert.

> Brenda Murphy (Board of Trustees Distinguished Professor Emeritus, University of Connecticut, USA)
> Julia Listengarten (Professor of Theatre at the University of Central Florida, USA)
> Series Editors

1

Introduction: Living in the 1960s

Mike Sell

There is no decade in US history argued about as much or as passionately as the 1960s. When conservative pundits decry the 'decline of family values', when crowds gather to protest police brutality, when politicians run against 'elites' and claim to represent the 'silent majority', when college students demand 'safe spaces', they are commenting, whether they know it or not, on the 1960s and the people and events that shaped that moment and our own.

Why?

The 1960s was a decade when the 'Establishment' – the institutions, people and ideas that had dominated American society since the end of the Second World War – was challenged from every direction.

Black Americans led the charge, organizing sit-ins, freedom rides, boycotts and demonstrations to expose the nation's racial caste system and achieve landmark legal reforms across the country. The founding of Students for a Democratic Society in 1962 heralded the emergence of the 'New Left'. In 1965, Cesar Chavez and the National Farm Workers Association joined with Filipino American farmworkers to strike for higher wages. Feminism's second wave broke in 1963 when Betty Friedan published *The Feminine Mystique*. In the summer of 1969, transgendered people, drag queens and homeless youth took to the streets around Greenwich

Village's Stonewall Inn to protest police harassment, igniting the LGBTQ rights movement.

The 1960s was a momentous decade for conservatism, too. In 1960, Barry Goldwater published *The Conscience of a Conservative*, and William F. Buckley, founder of *National Review* magazine, invited a group of young people to his estate in Connecticut, helping them found Young Americans for Freedom. Yes, Presidential candidate Barry Goldwater lost by a landslide in 1964, but Ronald Reagan was elected Governor of California in 1966, and, even more momentously, Richard Nixon won the Presidency in 1968, doing so with the support of the 'great silent majority of my fellow Americans'.

Television beamed into middle-class living rooms new forms of entertainment and the gritty reality of political assassination, war and the struggle for social justice. The box office success of *Bonnie and Clyde* and *The Graduate* in 1968 put the nail in the coffin of the old Hollywood Studio System. As we'll discuss in Chapter 2, Off-Broadway, Off-Off-Broadway and regional residential, identity-based and activist theatres challenged the big producers and geriatric aesthetics of the Great White Way. African Americans founded dozens of literary and cultural journals and neighbourhood cultural centres as part of the Black Arts Movement. Robert Crumb and Gilbert Shelton wrote drugged-out, sexed-up comics that appealed to countercultural sensibilities and rejected the Comics Code Authority. *The Los Angeles Free Press* rolled off the press in 1964, the first of the underground newspapers. Meanwhile, at the Massachusetts Institute of Technology, computer scientists invented the internet and video games.

And then there was Vietnam. US military involvement in the conflict between North and South escalated precipitously in the early 1960s. Over three million Americans would eventually serve in the war, half of them in combat. Almost sixty thousand Americans would die there, and thousands came home suffering from post-traumatic stress disorder. As many as a million Vietnamese – both combatants and civilians – lost their lives. The anti-war movement drew thousands to neighbourhood meetings, public demonstrations and violent clashes with police. Opposition to the American presence in Vietnam was one of the contributing factors to the events of May 1968, when a student revolt in Paris led to a governmental crisis and uprisings around the world.

So it's not surprising that the 1960s remains a subject that is as controversial as it is compelling. But, as significant as the changes to the political system, media and the global order were, it was also a decade when everyday life, work and technology changed. Understanding all of these will help us better understand how and why the playwrights, theatre artists and performers of the 1960s did what they did the way they did.

The baby boom

As historian Landon Jones memorably put it, nine months after the end of the Second World War 'the cry of the baby was heard across the land.'[1] In 1946, 3.4 million babies were born in the US, 650,000 more than the year before; between 1954 and 1964, four million babies were born every year. By 1964, there were 76.4 million people in the US under the age of eighteen, almost 40 per cent of the population.[2] This so-called 'baby boom' reshaped education, marketing, popular culture, the labour and housing markets and much more.[3]

The boom had its downside. There was talk of a 'generation gap'. Many young people felt a sharp sense of suspicion towards their elders, captured best by the activists who warned, 'Don't trust anyone over thirty.' Indeed, so pervasive was this distrust that a veritable 'counterculture' emerged, exemplified by the 'hippies', who rejected middle-class (i.e. 'square') standards of dress and decorum, wore their hair long and embraced an ethos of anarchic joy and altruism. Mistrust of the Establishment wasn't just felt by the hippies. As historian Rebecca Klatch notes, 'While thousands of youth [joined] protests on the left, thousands of others mobilized on the right', including those who would engineer the brash, anti-establishment movement that led to the election of President Donald Trump in 2016.[4]

The golden age of capitalism

Between 1940 and 1960, the gross national product of the US grew by more than 500 per cent.[5] Low interest rates, the construction of a national highway system, the expansion of the suburban housing market, the GI Bill (which subsidized college educations for thousands of veterans) and the maturation of $200 billion in war bonds enabled unprecedented prosperity for many Americans. In 1960, the average family in the United States earned almost 60 per cent more than they did in 1950.[6] By the end of the decade, average annual income would increase 70.7 per cent to $11,419.[7] Meanwhile, the cost of food, clothing and housing dropped, increasing the amount of discretionary spending available to consumers.[8]

Prosperity wasn't evenly distributed. Unemployment among black Americans was double that of whites.[9] Blue-collar workers saw their prosperity decline, though not always in ways that were easy to detect. As Sharon Smith explains, 'During the years when wages were rising, working conditions were deteriorating.'[10] In exchange for higher wages, unions signed contracts requiring higher productivity, less vacation time and limited sick leave, alongside automation, assembly-line speed-ups and forced overtime. Thus, though the number of manufacturing jobs grew by almost a third between 1950 and 1968, workers worked more hours. Net corporate profits doubled.

If things were getting progressively worse for African Americans and skilled labour, they remained as bad as ever for the poor. As Michael Harrington showed in his 1962 book *The Other America*, 25 per cent of the nation lived in poverty, mostly concentrated in city slums and isolated rural communities.[11] The Johnson administration launched its War on Poverty in 1964, an omnibus set of policies that included Medicaid and Medicare, Head Start, an increase in the minimum wage, subsidized housing, cost-of-living increases for social security, and food stamps. As a result, the poverty rate was halved from 22.4 per cent in 1959 to 11.1 per cent in 1973.[12] But the poverty rate in the US remained two to three times higher than in European countries.[13]

Social forces, political movements

The 1960s witnessed tectonic shifts in the way people related to each other, to their communities and to their government. Indeed, historians often point to the decade as the moment when the traditional social and political structures were torn down and rebuilt, a decade when terms like 'identity politics' and phrases like 'the personal is political' signalled a new way of challenging and wielding power.

The labour market

Though the way that Americans worked – and what they did when they worked – didn't change as dramatically as other aspects of life in the 1960s, there were a number of significant trends.

In 1960, 37.7 per cent of women worked in the civilian labour force, an increase of about 4 per cent since 1950. That number would rise to 43.3 per cent by 1970.[14] But though more women worked, they didn't earn as much as men and were often relegated to jobs with fewer opportunities. They were paid less for the same work, too. The median earnings of a full-time, year-round working-woman were $13,400 less than a man's.[15] Women were systemically denied promotions, too; many companies had policies that required a woman who married or became pregnant to quit. Not surprisingly, the number of women in corporate leadership positions remained flat during the decade.[16] It was clear – at least to women – that the economic constraints determining women's lives were unacceptable and feminism was a necessity.

The number of farms in the US declined precipitously between 1950 and 1960 (1.7 million fewer) and dropped by another million by 1970.[17] At the same time, the size of those farms increased, as did the amount of workers on farms who were wage or salary workers, though the overall number of workers employed by farms dropped due to mechanization and other efficiency solutions.[18] In other words, farms grew bigger and more industrialized, one of the factors that led to the farmworkers' movement.

The information economy took off. Computer-based professions spiked starting in 1960, the first year data was collected by the Bureau of Labor Statistics.[19] That growth was due to the development and dissemination of computer and robotic technologies for use by business, industry and the military (the first large-scale, multi-use network went online in 1969).[20] Engineering jobs continued the steady growth they had enjoyed since the 1940s.[21]

The fight against white supremacy

The US Supreme Court declared racial segregation illegal in 1954, but resistance to change was fierce, particularly in the South. 'Whites only' schools and water fountains were only part of the problem. Black Americans were denied access to political office and the vote.

Property and wealth were grievously contingent. Harassment and violence were ubiquitous. Racist stereotypes saturated popular culture. As James Baldwin wrote in 1961, 'To be a Negro in this country and to be relatively conscious is to be in a rage almost all the time.'[22]

The challenge for anti-racist activists was threefold. First, they had to organize poor and working-class African Americans. Second, they had to devise forms of activism that undermined white supremacy in both its systemic and quotidian forms. And third, they had to draw the attention of the television networks, the federal government and the world.

It was in that spirit that four students from North Carolina Agricultural and Technical College took their seats at a 'whites only' lunch counter on 1 February 1960. Though their action appeared to many as spontaneous, it was the culmination of months of organization and training on campuses across the region. Their courage inspired others to devise similar tactics, pressed leaders like Martin Luther King Jr to take more decisive action, and focused media and government attention on racist terror. This would not be the only time that a younger, more energetic, more creative and more radical group of activists would accelerate the pace of action and change.

Fourteen months after the sit-ins, the first Freedom Ride departed from the nation's capital, headed for New Orleans. Testing a recent Supreme Court ruling on interstate travel, riders crossed the colour line at bus terminals across the South, meeting violence at virtually every stop. In Anniston, Alabama, one bus was firebombed; in Birmingham, infamous Public Safety Commissioner Eugene 'Bull' Connor delayed the police while Ku Klux Klan members mercilessly beat the passengers.

Connor's hard line led movement leaders to select Birmingham as the focal point of the campaign. Sit-ins, marches and other acts of protest and civil disobedience led to the arrests of dozens, including King, who wrote his now celebrated 'Letter from Birmingham Jail', a document that affirmed the strategies of non-violent resistance, excoriated those who did not join the struggle and defended the right of people to come from around the country to help the cause. 'Injustice anywhere', King wrote, 'is a threat to justice everywhere.'

Meanwhile, those who walked door to door registering black voters faced intense resistance. Medgar Evers was murdered on the front lawn of his Mississippi home on 12 June 1963, the day after President Kennedy called for the passage of a Civil Rights Act and two months before the historic March on Washington for Jobs and Freedom, where King declared, 'I Have a Dream.' The next summer, the Civil Rights Act was put into law, mere weeks after James Chaney, Andrew Goodman and Michael Schwerner were abducted and killed. National outrage provided momentum for the Voting Rights Act, signed into law in 1965.

Not all black Americans believed that equal access was the goal or non-violence the best strategy. Among them was Malcolm X, leader of the Nation of Islam's Temple 7 in Harlem. X did not speak of equality, access or the vote. Instead, he argued for the safety and security of black Americans and the right to self-determination for people of colour around the world 'by any means necessary'. His assassination in February 1965, inspired the Black Arts Movement. Community centres like Amiri and Amina Baraka's Spirit House, independent presses like Dudley Randall's Broadside Press or Haki Madhubuti's Third World Press, and arts collectives like Chicago's AfriCOBRA provided black artists with opportunities to produce work outside the expectations and demands of the white establishment. Robert F. Williams's Black Armed Guard defended the neighbourhoods of Monroe, North Carolina, from the KKK in the late 1950s and guarded the Freedom Riders in 1961. When Williams and his wife Mabel were forced to flee the US after a false kidnapping charge, they landed in Cuba where they ran Radio Free Dixie, broadcasting commentary, news and music across the Caribbean and the eastern US. The Black Panther Party was founded in Oakland, California, in the autumn of 1966, rising to national attention as a result of television-friendly demonstrations, its practice of monitoring the police with armed patrols, and its Free Breakfast for Children programmes. FBI Director J. Edgar Hoover deemed them 'the greatest threat to the internal security of the country', and launched a program of surveillance, provocation, harassment and infiltration known as COINTELPRO.

As Langston Hughes warned, if a dream is deferred, it explodes. Violent uprisings erupted in black ghettos throughout the decade, reflecting the profound frustration and hopelessness of the racialized urban poor. The first broke out in Harlem in July 1964, in response to the killing of a boy by a police officer. The next summer, Watts, a Los Angeles community, witnessed the immolation of over

$40 million in property in response to the arrest of a drunk-driving suspect. Similar events struck Newark and Detroit in 1967 and in over 100 cities after the assassination of Martin Luther King Jr in 1968. Activist H. Rap Brown viewed such uprisings as the most radical expression of popular discontent, and urged crowds to 'Burn, baby, burn!'

Meanwhile, an insidious development was occurring within the circle of advisers surrounding presidential candidate Richard Nixon. In a 1994 interview, John Ehrlichman, Nixon's domestic policy chief, explained that the decision to run on a 'law and order' platform and declare a 'war on drugs' was designed to galvanize racist Southern voters against the Left and enable the legal harassment of organizations like the Panthers.[23] That decision has given us our current prison-industrial complex. In 2014, over 2.2 million Americans were locked in federal and state prisons or local jails, an increase of 500 per cent since the early 1980s.[24] Black and Hispanic Americans constitute over half of those prisoners, despite the fact they make up only a quarter of the US population.[25]

Sex, gender and sexuality

The sexual revolution

Though calling it a 'sexual revolution' is something of an overstatement, there is no doubt that attitudes towards sexual behaviour transformed during the 'Swinging 1960s', especially among young people. And compared to the 1950s, when sex was simply not discussed in polite society, there was a lot more talk about it. William H. Masters and Virginia E. Johnson published their groundbreaking – and bestselling – book *Human Sexual Response* in 1966. Dr Benjamin Spock's *Baby and Childcare* – just as groundbreaking and popular – made the case that a child's experimentation with their body, including masturbation, was perfectly natural and should even be encouraged. Andy Warhol's *Blue Movie* was released nationally in 1969, the first film with explicit sexual content distributed on that scale, though effervescent fare like *Barbarella* (1968) and *Rosemary's Baby* (1968) had its titillating moments, too.

Surveys showed women throwing off the old rules, and having sex before marriage.[26] Spurred on by books like Helen Gurley Brown's straight-forward *Sex and the Single Girl* (1962), women embraced what may now seem a common-sense idea: that sexual pleasure was as appropriate an expectation for women as financial independence. But loosening attitudes towards sex were also due to medical advances. In 1960, 'The Pill', a general term for oral contraceptives, was approved for use by the Federal Drug Administration, though it wouldn't be legally available in all states until 1965, and wasn't legally available to single women until 1972. The Pill proved enormously popular during a time when abortion was illegal, enabling sexually active women to take greater control of their bodies and their futures. By 1962, almost two million women were taking it.[27]

Among the counterculture, criticism of 'square' lifestyles extended to sex, as well. Writers like Herbert Marcuse and Wilhelm Reich argued that sexual mores were as fundamental to the maintenance of the Establishment as the police and army. Communal living arrangements often included the sexual lives of community members, who embraced the philosophy of 'free love', sharing their bodies with multiple partners. The politicization of sex was captured in the popular slogan 'Make Love, Not War', the credo of 1967's 'Summer of Love'. But even among the most counter of the counterculture, patriarchal attitudes persisted. The epicentre of the Summer of Love was San Francisco's Haight-Ashbury district. Though peace, love and understanding were what drew thousands of young people to its ramshackle splendour, as Chester Anderson put it, 'Rape [was] as common as bullshit on the Haight.'[28]

Feminism

It's hard to overstate how restricted the lives and opportunities of American women were in the early 1960s. It was assumed that a woman would marry and find satisfaction in the work of raising a family and caring for a home. 'Head and master laws' allowed husbands to make decisions about household and property without a wife's knowledge or consent. Women had no right or claim to their husband's property or income. Professional opportunities were severely limited. Though, as we noted, the number of women in the workforce grew, they were generally limited to work as nurses, clerks and teachers. Women accounted for only 6 per cent of doctors, 3 per cent of lawyers and less than 1 per cent of engineers.[29] Medical schools had strict quotas; some admitted no women at all. Women were paid less than men for the same work. Employers assumed they did not support families and would quit when they married.

The 'second wave' of feminism can be dated to two events, one concerning the law, the other consciousness – and we might conceptualize the movement as encompassing simultaneous battles on those two fronts. In terms of the law, we look to 1962, the year President Kennedy signed an Executive Order establishing the Presidential Commission on the Status of Women (PCSW), to be chaired by Eleanor Roosevelt. The report, published in October 1963, identified sexism in virtually every aspect of US life and recommended reforms concerning work hours and wages, better counselling for female workers, affordable childcare and maternity leave. Shortly before the commission's report was released and two decades after it was first proposed, Kennedy signed the Equal Pay Act, though its protections did not extend to most professionals. Despite the ridicule of legislators, women were included in the Civil Rights Act of 1964.

The other inaugural event of second-wave feminism was the publication, in 1963, of Betty Friedan's *The Feminine Mystique*. Her exploration of 'the problem that has no name' detailed the anomie and hopelessness of suburban housewives, many of them educated in elite universities. It rejected the idea that 'fulfillment as a woman had only one definition for American women'; i.e. mother and housewife.[30] Friedan's focus on the personal lives of her subjects was one of the inspirations for the notion that 'the personal is political'. Unlike the first wave of feminism, which focused almost exclusively on political rights, second-wave feminism also focused on matters less obviously about power: sexual pleasure, appearance, the division of household labour, self-esteem and so on. The significance of these were discovered in 'consciousness-raising groups', where women would gather in small meetings and talk frankly about their lives. Carol Hanisch, a member of the New York Radical Women (NYRW), the group that developed the strategy, wrote that '[o]ne of the first things we discover in these groups is that personal problems are political problems. There are no personal solutions at this time. There is only collective action for a collective solution.'[31]

In 1966, Friedan co-founded the National Organization for Women (NOW) with Shirley Chisholm, Kathryn F. Clarenbach, Mary Eastwood and twenty-four others. Their original goal was to press for enforcement of Title VII of the Civil Rights Act of 1964

– the measure that was intended to end hiring and pay discrimination against women – but they soon expanded their platform to 'bring women into full participation in the mainstream of American society now, exercising all the privileges and responsibilities thereof in truly equal partnership with men'.[32]

Unlike their liberal (and generally middle-class) sisters, radical feminists viewed patriarchy in a more systematic, transhistorical and essentialist fashion – indeed, as the most fundamental form of oppression. Groups like NYRW, the UCLA Women's Liberation Front, the Redstockings and The Feminists (led by Ti-Grace Atkinson) challenged middle-class feminists for not questioning gender roles, pornography, prostitution, rape and violence against women. Redstockings co-founder Ellen Willis later wrote that radical feminists got the politics of sex recognized as a public issue, forced NOW to expand its platform beyond economic issues, and drove both the movement to legalize abortion and the near-passage of the Equal Rights Amendment in 1977.[33]

Even radical feminists had difficulty recognizing and engaging the way sexuality, race and class impacted the lives of women. The Lavender Menace was founded in 1970 by Rita Mae Brown, Lois Hart, Barbara Love and Ellen Shumsky in response to Friedan's remark at a 1970 NOW conference that lesbians were a 'lavender menace' to the progress of women's rights. In the early 1970s, groups like the Combahee River Collective would challenge feminists and feminism to more effectively theorize concepts like identity and embrace a more diverse set of political goals and arguments that would account for race, class and sexuality.

LGBTQ rights

If the 1960s proved momentous for women, they were earth-shaking for those who didn't conform to the norms and categories of 'compulsory heterosexuality'.[34] Homophobia and transphobia were endemic in the United States in the 1960s; indeed, they were the law of the land. Before 1962, 'sodomy' (a euphemism for homosexual sex) was illegal in all fifty states. Non-heterosexuals were considered 'security risks' and were barred from federal civil service and the military. The FBI kept files on known homosexuals and their associates. A person could be arrested for cross-dressing or approaching an undercover cop for sex. Those arrested often had their names published in newspapers, costing them jobs and friends and putting them at risk of institutionalization, since the American Psychiatric Association categorized homosexuality as a mental disorder. Immigrants with 'abnormal impulses' were denied entry and citizenship.[35] But, inspired by the civil rights movement, peace protests and the counterculture and empowered by dancers, artists and playwrights and durable community bonds in enclaves like New York City's Greenwich Village, LGBTQ activists challenged legal and cultural homophobia in court, in magazines and social clubs, on the streets and, most influentially, in spontaneous uprisings.

In 1960, Virginia Prince, a transgender woman living in San Francisco, published the first issue of *Transvestia*. In 1962, she founded the Hose and Heels Club, later known as Phi Pi Epsilon, a Greek-letter version of the acronym for 'Full Personality Expression'. Predicting one of the basic principles of queer theory, Prince asserted that the binary gender system was harmful and that gender expression should be the free choice of the individual. Though genital transformation surgery had been available in Europe since the 1930s, and despite the pioneering advocacy of trans celebrity Christine Jorgensen in the 1950s, few doctors in the US were willing to perform it. Some considered it 'unethical'. However, in 1966, Harry Benjamin, Jorgenson's doctor, published *The Transsexual Phenomenon*, which not only affirmed the procedure, but, as Susan Stryker describes it, 'initiated a paradigm shift in American medical attitudes toward transgender people'.[36]

The total number of LGBTQ activists was small at the start of the 1960s and generally quite polite, but they were persistent. In 1965, a small picket marched outside a draft induction centre in New York City to protest the violation of gay men's confidentiality rights. Later that year, protestors interrupted a lecture by a psychoanalyst who argued that homosexuality was a mental disorder. In April 1965, ten members of the East Coast Homophile Organization (ECHO) demonstrated outside the White House. The next day, twenty-nine ECHO members picketed the United Nations. And a week after that, 150 people began a sit-in at Dewey's restaurant in Philadelphia in response to the manager refusing to serve a group of young people he said 'looked' gay. The president of the Janus society (publisher of *DRUM* magazine, one of the earliest LGBTQ magazines) and three others were arrested and convicted of disorderly conduct. Pickets would continue throughout 1965. On 4 July, forty activists converged on Philadelphia's Liberty Bell to demand equal treatment for gays and lesbians. 'Annual Reminder' protests organized by the always immaculately dressed members of the Mattachine Society, Janus Society and Daughters of Bilitis would be held annually until 1969. In 1970, they gathered to celebrate the Stonewall uprising, inaugurating the annual New York Pride Parade and signalling a more activist, less strait-laced approach to LGBTQ rights.

Even as lesbian and gay Americans fought for equality, they often looked down upon the transgendered, especially those who were poor or not white. That was the case in the gritty Tenderloin district of San Francisco. The neighbourhood was one of the few places where trans women and men could afford to live, since they were ostracized by both straight and gay communities in the city and denied most jobs. The Tenderloin was by no means a safe place. Many worked in the sex trade, and police harassment was constant. Since they weren't welcome at the gay bars, the hustlers and queens would congregate at Compton's Cafeteria, a greasy spoon open twenty-four hours a day, the kind of place where one could nurse a sixty-cent cup of coffee for hours. Restaurant staff were openly hostile and often called police to report individuals breaking the city's cross-dressing laws. Members of Vanguard, a gay youth organization headquartered at the queer-friendly Glide Memorial Church, fought back, organizing a picket in July 1966 to protest their treatment. The picket failed but ratcheted up community spirit. Matters came to a head in August when a police officer grabbed the arm of a customer, who responded by throwing her coffee in his face. Tables were flipped, sugar shakers thrown through windows, the riot police called, and mayhem ensued. Ultimately a corner newsstand and a police car would be destroyed. 'We just got tired of it,' Amanda St Jaymes remembers. 'We got tired of being harassed. We got tired of being made to go into the men's room when we were dressed like women. We wanted our rights.'[37] And those rights, Stryker argues, didn't just pertain to sexual orientation, but to gender, race and class, issues often ignored by gay rights organizations of the day.[38]

These kinds of spontaneous uprisings often had long-lasting impact. This was the case in Los Angeles when undercover police raided the Black Cat Tavern late on New Year's Eve 1966, breaking up the party, arresting over a dozen patrons for 'public lewdness' – in other words, same-sex kissing – and beating several with pool cues.[39] But the patrons had had enough and fought back, the violence spilling onto the street and into a second bar, where police continued their rampage. Ultimately, the raid, the arrests and subsequent protests 'inspired the first legal argument that gay people were entitled to equal protection under the law'.[40] One of the organizers of the protest, Personal Rights in Defense and Education (PRIDE), began publishing a newsletter called *The Advocate*, which would become a leading periodical for the LGBTQ rights movement, and remains so to this day.

Though it was not the beginning of the LGBTQ rights movement in America, the uprising at the Stonewall Inn in Greenwich Village was a watershed. Like other queer-friendly bars, the Stonewall wasn't exactly a safe space, but it was a decidedly queer place. Unlike other gay-friendly businesses in the city, the Stonewall's regulars were despised not only by straights, but also the strait-laced gay and lesbian community. But the homeless kids, hair-teased transvestites and hustlers who frequented the Stonewall tolerated the cops, the malfunctioning toilets and the filth because the drinks were cheap and it was the only gay bar in the city where dancing was allowed.

At 1.20 am on Saturday 28 June 1969, the 200 or so patrons heard the familiar 'Police! We're taking the place!' For some reason, the raid didn't go as usual. Patrons dressed as women refused to go with police to the bathrooms to be inspected. Others refused to produce their identity cards. Patrol wagons were slow to show, so patrons were forced to wait in line, increasing tension and drawing bystanders who encouraged the queens to openly mock the police. By the time the first wagon arrived, the crowd had grown bigger, angrier and more demonstrative. Cries of 'Gay Power!' could be heard among the several hundred gathered, and impromptu lines of high-kicking drag queens formed. Pennies and bottles started raining down on the wagons, a scuffle broke out between an officer and a patron, and the police realized they were in trouble, retreating inside and barricading the door. Though the police escaped, the community refused to back down. Five days of violent confrontation followed, including one in front of the offices of *The Village Voice*, which had published an egregiously homophobic account of the events.

After Stonewall, the tenor and tactics of the movement changed forever. LGBTQ rights organizations formed in every major US city – and in many others around the world. And there was a palpable change in the way LGBTQ Americans carried themselves in public. Allen Ginsberg told a friend, 'You know, the guys [at

Stonewall] were so beautiful – they've lost that wounded look that fags all had ten years ago.'[41] Lillian Faderman writes, 'The Stonewall Rebellion was crucial because it sounded the rally for [the] movement ... By calling on the dramatic tactic of violent protest that was being used by other oppressed groups, the events at the Stonewall implied that homosexuals had as much reason to be disaffected as they.'[42] In 1999, the US National Park Service placed the Stonewall Inn on the National Register of Historic Places. In 2016, President Barack Obama declared the Inn, Christopher Park and the surrounding streets a national monument.

Culture: From the quotidian to the extraordinary

Like so much else, culture itself evolved and transformed during the 1960s. Whether in living rooms or city streets, in front of televisions or in an automobile, in a suburban kitchen or a communal garden, how Americans lived and how they tasted, saw and listened to their lives changed, too.

Where did we live?

The conjunction of baby boom, economic prosperity, federal investment in roads and railways, low-interest mortgages for veterans and mass-production construction techniques spurred the development of suburbs. Suburban homes were more spacious, both inside and out, boasting 'family rooms', where everybody and their friends could gather, and large, grass-carpeted yards.[43] By 1960, a third of the US population – almost all of them 'boomer families' – lived in the suburbs.[44]

The housing boom played out differently for Americans of colour. Real estate agents used techniques like 'blockbusting' and 'redlining' to segregate and isolate African American, Hispanic and Asian American communities. Despite the advances of the civil rights movement, people of colour were quite simply '[l]ocked out of the greatest mass-based opportunity for wealth accumulation in American history',[45] and they became easy targets for unscrupulous lenders.[46] Little has changed to this day.

Jane Jacobs fought to defend the rich and varied texture of city life against suburbanization and the so-called 'urban renewal' that destroyed old neighbourhoods in favour of high-speed roadways, sleek attractions like Lincoln Center and high-rise buildings for the poor. Her 1961 book *The Death and Life of Great American Cities* celebrated the organic diversity of neighbourhoods like New York City's Greenwich Village and Boston's North End. She drew attention to their varied architecture, multiple uses, pedestrian traffic and high population density. Her book directly attacked modernist urban planners like Robert Moses, who viewed such neighbourhoods as ugly and inefficient. She loved sidewalks, which she saw as a stage for an 'intricate ballet in which the individual dancers and ensembles all have distinctive parts which miraculously reinforce each other and compose an orderly whole'.[47]

Regardless, popular culture and the consumer market were dominated by the tastes and attitudes of the white, suburban middle class. They were the ideal vision of the prosperous, contented consumer.

What did we eat?

Renowned chef Jacques Pépin recalls his arrival in the United States in 1959. 'In the early 1960s,' he writes, 'food was sustenance, and the American culinary landscape was bleak.'[48]

The industrialization of food was one cause of the bleakness. In order to feed troops during the Second World War, food technologies were developed to guarantee long shelf life and those technologies were enthusiastically embraced by middle-class consumers when the war ended. In 1959, consumers spent $2.7 billion a year on frozen foods, $500 million of which was spent on so-called TV dinners, which provided protein, vegetable, starch and dessert, all on one, oven-safe, disposable aluminium tray.[49] And for those who had the dollars to spend, the American supermarket was a cornucopia of day-glo snack foods: diet soft drinks, Starburst Fruit Chews, Pringles, single-serving pudding packs, Funyuns, Pop-Tarts, Lucky Charms, Lemonheads, Razzles and ZotZ.

Fast food continued to boom, powered by convenience, intensive marketing towards children (the 'Hamburger-Happy Clown' Ronald McDonald appeared on television ads starting in 1963), the franchise model (local outlets supported by a national supply chain and marketing team) and the automobile. Iconic fast food chains spread like crabgrass: Shakey's Pizza, Pizza Hut, Domino's, Kentucky Fried Chicken, Taco Bell and Jack in the Box. By 1969, McDonald's had sold over five billion hamburgers, and by 1971 had franchises in all fifty states.[50]

But two communities resisted the siren song of day-glo convenience. The first was a small, elite group of what we would now call 'foodies'. Nationally syndicated columnist Clementine Paddleford published *How America Eats* in 1960, affirming the deliciousness and value of local foodways. Craig Claiborne took over as food editor for the *New York Times* in 1957. In addition to re-inventing the restaurant review, he, like Paddleford, delighted in all kinds of deliciousness. One day he might write a review of the latest haute cuisine hot spot; on another praise a working-class chain like Chock Full o' Nuts or a new Chinese restaurant. The ebullient, Faltastaffian James Beard was the first 'celebrity chef', urging Americans to expand their palates in a series of television shows, cookbooks, cooking schools in New York and Oregon and legendary dinner parties. But the iconic figure of the foodie revolution was surely Julia Child. Her 1961 cookbook *Mastering the Art of French Cooking* adapted the high-French tradition to the practical necessities of the home cook. It was a massive hit, going through nineteen printings by 1970. But it was her television show *The French Chef*, premiering in 1963, that brought her fame. 'She demystified French cuisine,' Pépin recalls, and she did so with an unflappable goofiness that made every viewer feel they too could prepare a perfectly acceptable sole meunière.[51] Paddleford, Claiborne, Beard and Child were a true culinary vanguard, promoting the new, valuing the traditional, and insisting that food be nothing more than authentic and tasty.

In contrast, a second group of environmental, social-justice and back-to-the-land activists addressed food in sociopolitical, environmental and economic terms. Frances Moore Lappé, Alicia Bay Laurel, the Nation of Islam, the Diggers, the Black Arts Movement and others rejected capitalist convenience cuisine. Whether they organized co-ops and communes to curate food from farm to table, provided food to the poor and oppressed, built a sustainable food economy, rediscovered ethnic traditions or spread the word about meat-free diets, they built an 'alternative food system with its own ideology, staples and supply lines, a countercuisine'.[52] Civil Rights Activist Fannie Lou Hamer, with the help of Harry Belafonte, founded Freedom Farm Corporation in 1969 to provide land for farmers to work and food to poor families. Indeed, respecting the labour that grew the food was no small part of this countercuisine. In the early autumn of 1965, California field workers, most of them Filipino, struck against grape growers to demand the federal minimum wage. A week later, the National Farmworkers Association, led by Cesar Chavez, joined the action. Through a combination of non-violent strategies, a national boycott of California grapes that cut sales by over 10 per cent, and legislative action, they were able to achieve a collective bargaining agreement that improved the lives of over ten thousand agricultural labourers. Activists and allied politicians pressed for laws to secure the safety of food and foodways. The 1962 Consumer Bill of Rights established the right to safety, information and choice, and 1966 saw the passage of the Fair Packaging and Labeling Act, which required honest and informative food labelling. In 1969, the Food and Drug Administration established oversight procedures to ensure that milk, shellfish, food service and interstate travel facilities were sanitary.

But for many in the US, the issue wasn't what they ate, but that they didn't have enough. When Joseph S. Clark and Robert F. Kennedy toured the Mississippi Delta in 1967, they discovered a region suffering from crippling poverty and endemic malnutrition. The ensuing Senate subcommittee hearings of 1967 and President Nixon's 1969 address to Congress would lead to a 500 per cent increase in federal spending on hunger relief.[53] The grassroots took action, too. In 1969, the Black Panther Party started a free breakfast programme in Oakland, California, for poor black children; by the end of the year, similar programmes were being created around the country, providing a warm meal for over ten thousand children a day.

What did we watch?

Television

The screens were small (most were about 22 inches), the sound poor (a single channel from a small speaker), and the picture was black and white and low-definition. And unlike today, when we have a veritably infinite choice of programming, most viewers could select from only three channels. That didn't matter. By 1962, over 90 per cent of homes in the US had a television.[54] Television was the national hearthstone.

The emergence of a national audience, the growing costs of television production, and pressure by conservatives to avoid anything even vaguely critical of the status quo led the industry to play it safe. The risk-averse 1960–61 season was deemed by *Time* magazine 'the worst in the 13-year history of US network television'.[55] Pundits wrung their hands over the impact of televised violence and banality on the nation's culture, particularly its youth.

One-hour westerns like *Wagon Train*, *Bonanza* and *Gunsmoke* were consistent top-ten shows. Situation comedies came by the bushel, whether sit-coms about everyday family life like *The Patty Duke Show*, *My Three Sons* and *The Dick Van Dyke Show* or the gloriously implausible *Gilligan's Island* (about seven disparate castaways on a desert island) and *The Flying Nun* (about, you guessed it, a flying nun).[56] Variety shows offered a little bit of everything to the family gathered in the set's flickering blue glow. *The Ed Sullivan Show* introduced the Beatles to the nation in 1964 (and over seventy million Americans watched), as well as ventriloquists and dancing dogs. Johnny Carson took over NBC's *The Tonight Show* in 1962, establishing the basic grammar of the late-night talk show. The incomparable Carol Burnett got her own sketch-comedy programme in 1967.

By 1963, Americans were getting most of their news from television, usually from dinner-hour national network broadcasts. News anchors like Walter Cronkite were nationally known – and trusted. The 1960 debate between presidential candidates Richard Nixon, the incumbent, and John F. Kennedy was the first to be televised and likely cost Nixon the election due to his sallow appearance. When President Kennedy was assassinated in 1963, the nation remained glued to its sets for days, watching as the investigation unfolded, their President was buried, and alleged assassin Lee Harvey Oswald was murdered on air as he was being transferred from a Dallas jail.

But the 'glaring light of television', as one historian puts it, played its most important role in bringing attention to the systemic racist violence of the American South.[57] No racist euphemism could sweeten the sight of fire hoses and attack dogs turned on peaceful protestors.[58] However, if they were regularly featured on the nightly news, black Americans weren't on television much otherwise. A 1962 study noted that 309 of the 368 half-hour units of prime-time television showed no black people at all. And the rest showed mostly athletes or entertainers.[59] Starting in 1966, though, they began to appear far more often as stars, co-stars or continuing characters, leading some to call the late 1960s the 'Golden Age of Blacks in Television'.[60]

The networks were hardly behind the cause of social justice. Walter Annenberg, publisher of the weekly *TV Guide*, the most popular periodical in the country, used his magazine and his powerful allies to pressure the networks to toe the ideological line. Among the programs he hated most was *The Smothers Brothers Comedy Hour* (1967–9). The show featured bitingly satirical sketches, courtesy of a roster of brilliant writers, which included Steve Martin, Bob Einstein and Rob Reiner. Network censors routinely demanded script revisions, and local affiliates cut to commercials during moments they deemed to be in poor taste or bad politics. CBS President William S. Paley cancelled the show on 4 April 1969. The brothers sued for breach of contract, winning the case in federal court four years later.

And then there was the war in Vietnam, sometimes called the first 'living room war'.[61] Early on, news stories were generally positive and formulaic – and the pressure against negative coverage was immense. But the reality of the situation couldn't be covered up forever. On 27 February 1968, Walter Cronkite, the 'most trusted man in America', presented a prime-time special report from Vietnam, concluding it with an editorial deeming victory impossible and negotiation necessary. President Johnson reportedly told his aides, 'If I've lost Cronkite, I've lost Middle America.' Though that may be apocryphal, it was true in fact. By August of that year, polls showed over half of Americans felt the war was a mistake.[62]

Movies

What Americans didn't watch – at least as much as they used to – were movies. Despite dazzling attractions like Technicolor, Cinemascope and 3-D, the 1950s was 'the horrible decade' for Hollywood as far as ticket sales were concerned.[63] But the bottom line wasn't just being challenged by television and suburbanization.

Viewers wanted something different, something that reflected the world around them, something that would allow them to see that world in a new way.

The studio heads wanted nothing to do with that. They figured that if epic, melodramatic fare like *The Ten Commandments* (1956) and *Ben-Hur* (1959) could bring in big profits yesterday, then it would bring them in tomorrow. Joseph L. Mankiewicz's *Cleopatra* proved them wrong. Filmed on location in Rome and starring tabloid favourites Elizabeth Taylor and Richard Burton, it went grievously over budget (Taylor's costumes alone cost over $200,000) and, despite being the top-grossing movie of 1963, almost destroyed 20th Century Fox.

For those who did want to see something new, there were the unfamiliar aesthetics and adventurous themes of foreign movies. Italian films like Federico Fellini's *La Dolce Vita* (1960) could be enjoyed alongside Japanese director Akira Kurosawa's *Yojimbo* (1961) and the Swedish Ingmar Bergman's *Persona* (1966). But French New Wave movies like Jean-Luc Godard's *Breathless*, Francois Truffaut's *Shoot the Piano Player* (both 1960) and Alain Resnais' *Last Year at Marienbad* (1961) proved especially influential. Shot on low budgets with no respect for the conventions of mainstream Hollywood cinema, they inspired the film-makers who would come to be known as the 'New Hollywood'.

The New Hollywood would be inconceivable without the 'King of the B Movies', Roger Corman. His métier was quickly produced, shoestring-budget exploitation fare like *The Little Shop of Horrors* (1960, shot in two days), the biker movie *The Wild Angels* (1966) and the psychedelic *The Trip* (1967). But his adaptations of Edgar Allan Poe were enthusiastically embraced by the French New Wave auteurs for their cinematic audacity. He was an inspirational mentor to a generation of actors, directors and producers, including Jack Nicholson, Dennis Hopper, Robert De Niro, Francis Ford Coppola, Martin Scorsese, Peter Bogdanovich, Jonathan Demme and Gale Anne Hurd, to name only a few. Corman was thus a father to both the New Wave and the New Hollywood.

But change in Hollywood was slow going. Consider the case of *Bonnie and Clyde* (1968). After Truffaut and Goddard turned it down, Robert Benton and David Newman's script about Depression-era lovers turned bank robbers found its way into the hands of Warren Beatty, who ended up producing the movie and playing

Clyde. Jack Warner's response to an early cut was unalloyed disgust. Most critics agreed – and audiences generally avoided it. But a glowing review by Pauline Kael, surprise popularity in England and a hagiographic piece by Stefan Kanfer in *Time* magazine enabled Beatty to pressure the studio to re-release it. *Bonnie and Clyde* became one of the biggest money-makers of 1968.[64]

Critics hated the other surprise hit of 1967–8, *The Graduate*, too. Many of them felt 'personally attacked by a movie that portrayed [their generation] as self-centered, materialistic and immoral, [and] hypocritical'.[65] But director Mike Nichols took risks that attracted the baby boomers, including casting the unknown and rather schlubby Dustin Hoffman instead of Robert Redford, scoring the film with the folk-rock songs of Simon and Garfunkel, and pressing cinematographer Robert Surtees, in Surtees's words, to '[d]o more things in that picture than I ever did in one film'.[66] The movie made so much money that Warner Brothers and United Artists threw out their development schedule and reoriented production towards younger audiences.[67]

Meanwhile, a very different kind of film-making was happening around the art-house cinemas, film schools and bohemian studios of New York and San Francisco. In his 1963 book *Metaphors on Vision*, Stan Brakhage writes, 'Imagine an eye unruled by man-made laws of perspective, an eye unprejudiced by compositional logic, an eye which does not respond to the name of everything but which must know each object encountered in life through an adventure of perception.'[68] For *Mothlight* (1963), Brakhage glued flower petals, insect wings and other found materials directly to the film stock. In *Maxwell's Demon* (1968), Hollis Frampton assembled abstract sequences of a posing athlete, the ocean and frames of pure colour. Yoko Ono's *Film No. Five (Smile)* (1968) took a more humanistic approach to adventurous perception. John Lennon stares into the camera for almost an hour, his face slowly changing expression. Andy Warhol also explored long-duration perception in *Sleep* (1963), *Eat* (1964) and *Empire* (1964), the latter an eight-hour continuous-footage film of the Empire State Building.

The sexism, homophobia and prudery of American society were ripe targets for avant-garde film-makers. Jack Smith's *Flaming Creatures* (1963) displayed ambiguously gendered individuals in various states of dishabille drag, alternately applying lipstick and fondling each other. In March 1964 it was screened at Jonas Mekas's

Film-Makers' Cinematheque. Police seized the film. It became a cause célèbre, with Shirley Clarke, Allen Ginsberg and Susan Sontag testifying in Mekas's defence. Kenneth Anger's *Scorpio Rising* (1963) was just as offensive, with its images of leather-clad bikers, James Dean and Marlon Brando, and icons of Catholicism and Nazism cast against a soundtrack of contemporary rock 'n' roll. Like Smith's, Anger's movie was seized, and the case ultimately reached the California Supreme Court. Though she was known primarily as a performance artist, Carolee Schneemann's films were as audacious as her live art. *Meat Joy* (1964) presents a sumptuous orgy of flesh, naked performers writhing sexually among raw fish, chicken parts, sausages, paint, ropes and other detritus.

American cinema ended the decade very differently than it began. On the night of 7 April 1970, the Academy Award for Best Picture was presented to John Schlesinger's *Midnight Cowboy* (1969). The gritty (and X-rated) story of a naïve male prostitute (Jon Voight) arriving in New York City to make his fortune and fame was the apotheosis of the radical changes in film style and audience tastes that characterized the decade.

What did we listen to?

When we think of the 1960s, we more than likely *hear* them. The 1960s were a distinctly *musical* decade. Americans, particularly young Americans, tuned their lives to the psychedelic guitar virtuosity of Jimi Hendrix, the stirring lyrics of folk singers, the meditative saxophone of John Coltrane, the sand-and-surf harmonies of surf rock, the down-home rebelliousness of Johnny Cash, the soulful yearning of Aretha Franklin, the driving funk of James Brown and Otis Redding and the infectious bubbliness of the Beatles.

Interest in American traditional music had grown since the late 1940s, particularly among political progressives, but it was the Kingston Trio who brought folk music to the mainstream with their clean-cut look and studious avoidance of politics – by 1961, they were arguably the most imitated and successful artists in any genre. Joan Baez brought folk back to its roots – and its politics. Her simple treatments of songs like 'Mary Hamilton' (1960) put her at the top of the *Billboard* charts from 1960 to 1962, on the cover of *Time* magazine in 1962, and at the front of the 1963 March on

Washington, where she led the crowd in a stirring rendition of 'We Shall Overcome'. Accompanying her were Pete Seeger, Bob Dylan, Peter, Paul and Mary and Odetta Holmes, demonstrating the vital role that folk-based freedom songs played in the civil rights movement.

Though Bob Dylan enjoyed a small and loyal following in Greenwich Village, it was a cover of his song 'Blowin' in the Wind' (1963) by Peter, Paul and Mary that brought him national attention. Dylan would be among those who scandalized folk purists when he began mixing folk and rock music, and his decision to plug in his guitar at the 1965 Newport Folk Festival scandalized purists. Though the Animals' 'House of the Rising Sun' (1964) and The Byrds' cover of 'Mr Tambourine Man' were chart-toppers, it was Dylan's album *Bringing It All Back Home* (1965) – with tracks like 'Subterranean Homesick Blues', 'Maggie's Farm' and 'It's All Over Now, Baby Blue' – that established folk rock in the American soundscape. The Mamas and the Papas, Crosby, Stills and Nash and Simon and Garfunkel kept it on radios until the end of the decade.

Folk rock was only one of the varieties to be heard on the radio or ready for purchase on vinyl singles at your neighbourhood record store. Dick Dale's 'Let's Go Trippin' (1961) launched the West Coast Surf Rock trend with its heavy-reverb instrumentals, while the Beach Boys' fresh-scrubbed, vocally complex tales of surfer girls and endless summers found appeal among the land-locked. The close harmonies and spunky attitudes of 'girl groups' were ubiquitous. The Shirelles' 'Will You Love Me Tomorrow?' (1960) and 'Tonight's the Night' (1961) and the Marvelettes' 'Please, Mr Postman' (1961) were favourites. Berry Gordy's Detroit-based Motown Record Corporation produced its first number-one record in 1960 with the Miracles' 'Shop Around', and would follow with over a hundred more top-ten hits from Detroit Soul artists like the Four Tops, Stevie Wonder, Marvin Gaye, Diana Ross, the Jackson 5 and girl groups like the Supremes and Martha and the Vandellas. In 1961, Satellite Records in Memphis, Tennessee, changed its name to Stax Records, partnered with Atlantic Records, and recorded Southern Soul hits from the likes of Booker T and the MG's, Sam and Dave, the Mar-Keys and Otis Redding.

Though it had roots in the New York folk scene, psychedelic rock was a distinctly San Francisco sound. Denizens of the Haight-Ashbury district such as The Grateful Dead, Jefferson Airplane and

Country Joe and the Fish devised production techniques and lyrical references to simulate and stimulate the experience of psychoactive drugs like LSD. Many of these were invented by sound engineer Ken Babbs at the 'Acid Tests' hosted by author Ken Kesey at his farm in La Honda during 1965 and 1966. Jefferson Airplane's album *Surrealistic Pillow* (1967) and The Doors' *Strange Days* (1967) were the apogee of the trend, though Jimi Hendrix's performance of the National Anthem at the 1969 Woodstock festival remains an iconic moment, perhaps *the* iconic moment of 1960s psychedelic rock.

The hard edge and purposefully amateurish production qualities of garage rock gave the music of Paul Revere and the Raiders, the Rivieras and the Trashmen a rebellious edge. Though the trend peaked in 1966, Detroit rockers MC5 kept the spirit alive, reading Marx, carrying rifles onto stage, aligning themselves with the most radical groups of the period and playing for the protestors at the 1968 Democratic Convention. But the essence of garage rock – and its most enduring influence – was the Stooges, fronted by Iggy Pop. Raw, confrontational, almost suicidal, the Stooges were one of the taproots of the punk and alternative rock movements of the 1970s and beyond.

But in terms of influence and impact, there is nothing that compares to the British Invasion. When the Beatles arrived at John F. Kennedy airport on 7 February 1964, they were met by three thousand screaming fans, most of them teenage girls. Two days later, 73 million tuned in to *The Ed Sullivan Show* for the first of three appearances by the Fab Four. John Lennon, Paul McCartney, George Harrison and Ringo Starr scored six number-one songs, including 'I Want to Hold Your Hand', 'I Saw Her Standing There' and 'Love Me Do'. The charts filled behind them with a slough of British acts, including the Dave Clark Five, the Kinks, the Animals, Dusty Springfield and the Rolling Stones. One of the ironies of the invasion was that the British brought back to the United States the traditions of blues it had largely forgotten.

At least for white listeners. Among African Americans, the blues was alive and well at both root and leaf. LeRoi Jones's book *Blues People* (1963) argued that the blues tradition sustained a set of values and customs extending back to pre-slavery West Africa and was at its most rebellious in the jazz and popular genres of the 1960s. Traditional blues artists like John Lee Hooker, Muddy Waters and Skip James found new audiences. Soul tracks like Sam

Cooke's 'A Change is Gonna Come' (1964) mixed gospel, blues and rich horn orchestration, becoming an anthem for the civil rights movement. 'The Godfather of Soul', James Brown moved the masses with hits like 'Papa's Got a Brand New Bag' (1965) and 'I Got You (I Feel Good)' (1965). Brown's drummer Clyde Stubblefield created the template not only for funk drumming but for hip hop, too, samples of his drumming becoming ubiquitous, if generally uncredited. Music was an integral part of the Black Power movement. Brown's 'Say It Loud – I'm Black and I'm Proud' (1968) was an anthem. Elaine Brown, Minister of Information for the Black Panthers, was also a talented composer and powerful singer. Her album *Seize the Time* (1969) set revolutionary Blackness to song. Emory Douglas, the Panthers' Minister of Culture, helped a group of Panthers form the Lumpen, who performed high-energy tracks like 'Bobby Must Be Set Free' at rallies, community centres and colleges around the country.

Jazz musicians continued to experiment, building on the stunning accomplishments of the 1950s. Max Roach and Abbie Lincoln released *We Insist!* in 1960, its cover referencing the Greensboro sit-ins, its five tracks mixing traditional and avant-garde techniques. Afro-Caribbean and Brazilian sounds were explored by Dizzy Gillespie, Xavier Cugat, Arturo Sandoval and others. The sexy, smooth sounds of bossa nova were pioneered by the Brazilian João Gilberto, but it was Stan Getz's collaboration with the sultry Astrud Gilberto that produced the evergreen 'Girl from Ipanema' in 1964. Ornette Coleman, Pharoah Sanders and Cecil Taylor explored and deconstructed the very foundations of rhythm, harmony and melody. In 1969, Miles Davis released *In a Silent Way*, inaugurating fusion jazz, which combined jazz with rock, rhythm and blues and funk, and acoustic with electric instruments. The death of John Coltrane in 1967 marked the end of an era, though it energized the poets and playwrights of the Black Arts Movement, renewing their commitment to challenging the conceptual and material constraints and assumptions of art and honouring the musicians who lived.

A year of cataclysm and promise: 1968

Time magazine's Lance Morrow captures the feeling of that tumultuous year, 1968: 'If you look at the whole year as theater, as real acts of tragedy, there's an almost poetic feeling to it. Nineteen sixty-eight was one goddamned thing after another.'[69] Indeed, like the climax of a classical Greek drama, 1968 was the culmination of disasters and the herald of changes to come. For those who want to understand the 1960s, it is a year that provides a singular perspective on the decade as a whole.

The tragic irony began on New Year's Day, when General William Westmoreland, commander of US forces in Vietnam, reported to President Lyndon Johnson on the status of the campaign to defeat the Viet Cong. 'There is a light at the end of the tunnel!' he told the President.[70] A month after Westmoreland gave his report to the President, the tunnel collapsed. The Tết Offensive – called that because it occurred during the celebration of the Vietnamese New Year – was a military failure. Though the Viet Cong took more than a hundred towns, most provincial capitals and the city of Huế, the US and its allies beat them back, inflicting heavy casualties in the process. But the Viet Cong had won the battle of hearts and minds. National Liberation Front flags flew around the world, and demonstrations against the war grew bigger, louder and more violent.

On 31 March, President Johnson gave a nationally televised speech. Though he did not speak of defeat, he admitted the war was nowhere near its end. And then he dropped the bombshell: 'I shall not seek, and I will not accept, the nomination of my party for another term as your President.' The next day, the *New York Times* headline read, 'Johnson says he won't run; halts North Vietnam raids; bids Hanoi join peace moves.' That same day, Nguyễn Văn Lém, a National Liberation Front officer, was summarily executed by General Nguyễn Ngọc Loan on a public street in Saigon. Journalists filmed the event and it became an icon of the absurd violence of the war.

By October of 1968, only 37 per cent agreed the US belonged in Vietnam.[71] More people from all walks of life opposed the war and many of them marched in the streets to express that opposition. In April, students at Columbia University went on strike and occupied five campus buildings, declaring them a liberated zone. They protested against university investment in the military-industrial complex and its plans to construct an athletic facility in Morningside Park – a facility that would evict dozens of African American and Latino residents. It was not a unified protest. Black activists occupying Hamilton Hall asked their white comrades to leave, reflecting a desire to maintain a focus on racism and not be associated with the destruction of university property. The National Mobilization Committee to End the War in Vietnam and the Youth International Party (known colloquially as the 'Yippies') planned a youth festival in Chicago to coincide with the Democratic National Convention in August. Over ten thousand demonstrators showed up, met by twice as many police and National Guardsmen and the broiling hostility of Mayor Richard J. Daley, who refused to grant permits for the demonstrators. On 28 August, demonstrators gathered in Grant Park and the police, incensed that the American flag had been lowered by a protestor, charged the crowd, batons swinging, while the crowd chanted, 'The whole world is watching.' A federal commission later judged the event a 'police riot'.

What happened inside Chicago's International Amphitheatre was almost as tumultuous. Even before Johnson's announcement that he would not seek re-election, opposition to the war and the widening gap between youth and the mainstream Democratic party emboldened Minnesota Senator Eugene McCarthy to run against Johnson on an anti-war platform. The New Hampshire Primary proved his campaign's mettle. Lofted by an impressive get-out-the-vote drive run by college students who cut their hair and put their beads away in order to 'Get Clean for Gene!', McCarthy won 42 per cent of the primary vote to Johnson's 49 per cent. Four days later, Robert F. Kennedy, brother of John F. Kennedy and former US Attorney General, joined the fray. The race between McCarthy and Kennedy came to a climax in California, where the former was feted by students for standing up against the war, the latter by people of colour in the state's barrios and ghettos. Kennedy won by four points. Just after addressing his ecstatic supporters at the Los Angeles Ambassador Hotel, he was shot three times by Palestinian activist Sirhan Sirhan. He died a day later. Thus, by the time the Democrats convened in Chicago, the party was in crisis, delegates split among McCarthy, Vice President Hubert Humphrey and Senator George McGovern. Ultimately, Humphrey would win the nomination, and the delegates refused to include a peace plank despite the fact that 80 per cent of primary voters had cast their ballots for the anti-war candidates.[72]

Meanwhile, George Wallace, two-time 'Dixiecrat' Governor of Alabama and infamous for swearing 'segregation now, segregation tomorrow, segregation forever', declared himself the candidate of the American Independent Party. Wallace struck fear in both parties. The Republicans worried that he would peel off whites with his law-and-order, segregationist message; the Democrats that he would win blue-collar voters in the North. His outrageous statements (asserting, for example, that he would happily run over a hippie if given the opportunity) won him headlines and, in the 1968 election, five Southern states, ten million votes and forty-six electors.

No group of Americans experienced the tragic irony of 1968 as acutely as African Americans – and none fought for the future more resiliently. Despite the passage of the Civil Rights and Voting Rights Acts, white supremacy maintained its cruel grip. On 8 February, South Carolina Highway Patrolmen opened fire on black protestors in Orangeburg, South Carolina, killing three and wounding dozens, most of them shot in the back while running for cover. On 4 April, in Memphis, Tennessee, Martin Luther King Jr was fatally shot while standing with friends on the balcony of the Lorraine Motel. As word of King's death spread, riots broke out in a hundred cities, the largest in Baltimore, Chicago, Kansas City and Washington DC. Dozens died, thousands were injured, millions of dollars' worth of property was destroyed and machine-gun nests were installed on the steps of the US Capitol. As one young black man put it, 'King was the only rational voice that was left in America. He stood against the war in Vietnam. He stood against violence, period. So, when you killed him, you killed everything. You killed the only rational voice that's left.'[73] Two days after King's death, Eldridge Cleaver and thirteen other Black Panthers ambushed an Oakland police patrol, leading to a ninety-minute shootout and the death of seventeen-year-old Panther Bobby Hutton. And as Panther leader Huey Newton stood trial for the murder of Oakland police officer John Frey, three more Panthers were killed in a gun battle in Los Angeles. But despite such stunts, party membership grew to almost ten thousand and the circulation of its newspaper *The Black Panther* to a quarter of a million.[74] On the morning of 16 October at the Mexico City Olympic Games, gold- and bronze-medal winners Tommie Smith and John Carlos raised leather-gloved fists while the national anthem played. In Carlos' words, they raised their fists for 'those individuals that were lynched or killed and that no-one said a prayer for, that were hung and tarred. It was for those thrown off the side of the boats in the Middle Passage.'[75] On 6 November, students at San Francisco State University, led by the Black Student Union, the Third World Liberation Front and Amiri Baraka and Sonia Sanchez, went on strike. They demanded equal access to public higher education, more faculty of colour, and a curriculum attentive to black students' needs and the racist organization of knowledge in the university. After months of violence, the resignation of the university president, the hardline stubbornness of Governor Reagan and new president S. I. Hayakawa, and the refusal of students to fold under pressure, the strike ended in March 1969, resulting in the first ethnic studies programme in the nation. More importantly, it inaugurated a wave of campus reforms and a tradition of interethnic, cross-class coalition-building that continues to this day.

One other significant event of that year: Republican Hillary Rodham was elected President of the Wellesley College Government Association. That summer, she attended the Republican National Convention in Miami. What she saw there would eventually push her to abandon the party and become a Democrat.

2

American Theatre in the 1960s

Mike Sell

To get a sense of how the American theatre scene transformed during the 1960s, we might start with 1959, a veritable *annus mirabilis*. Just after the New Year, actors took the stage at a tiny Greenwich Village coffee house called the Caffe Cino, inaugurating the 'Off-Off-Broadway movement' and gay theatre. *A Raisin in the Sun* debuted a few weeks later, the first play on Broadway written by a black woman (Lorraine Hansberry) and directed by a black man (Lloyd Richards). McNeil Lowry convened a two-day conference to share ideas about creating theatre beyond Broadway, laying 'the first planks in the resident theatre movement'.[1] In July, the Living Theatre premiered *The Connection*, a harrowingly realistic portrayal of heroin addiction set to a bebop jazz beat, courtesy of the Freddie Redd Quartet. That fall, Allan Kaprow's *18 Happenings in 6 Parts* showed that theatre did not have to be tied to narrative, character or even a shared audience viewpoint – it just had to 'happen'. In San Francisco, R. G. Davis's Mime Troupe, later known as the San Francisco Mime Troupe, presented *Games – 3 Sets* and two other works at the San Francisco Art Institute. And on 16 November, Mary Martin walked onto the stage as Maria Rainer, soon to become Maria von Trapp. Richard Rodgers and Oscar Hammerstein's *The Sound of Music* would run for over 1,400 performances before closing in 1963.

At the turn of the decade, artists were making more theatre in more ways in more places for more people. They believed that theatre had a role, a vital role, to play in day-to-day life, in the political decisions that determined how power functioned, and in the destiny of the nation and the world. And the old rules – and those who enforced them – were neither self-evident nor beyond criticism.

Broadway: Crisis and continuity

After the Second World War, the business of Broadway was as challenging as it had ever been. In the 1950–51 season, there were eighty-one Broadway productions; in 1969–70, there were sixty-two, fifteen of them play-it-safe revivals.[2] Suburbanization and television kept audiences in the comfort of their living rooms. Ticket prices were rising. And who could blame audiences for not making the trek to the city? Bridges and tunnels were irksome. Times Square was grittier. Crime was rising. And those riots?

Theatres were closing and so were opportunities for artists. By the mid-1960s, less than 3 per cent of actors working in the city earned more than poverty wages. Jack Poggi wrote at the time, 'Broadway can no more provide a steady income to most professional actors than it can to most professional playwrights.'[3] And Poggi wasn't counting the black, Asian and Latino actors marginalized by the endemic racism of the Great White Way. The situation was as dire for everyone else who worked in the theatre: costumiers, set designers, lighting technicians and stage managers. It was tough to make a living on Broadway.

And yet, as is so often the case with theatre, in the midst of crisis and hazard, excellent, durable art was created.

The Broadway musical

Historian John Kenrick puts it best: 'The Broadway musical started the 1960s with a roar and ended them with something akin to a nervous breakdown.'[4]

In the 1950s and early 1960s, the Broadway musical was *the* dominant force in commercial theatre, the pinnacle of the theatrical profession, and a taste-maker for American culture. That was abundantly evident on the evening of 31 March 1957. Rodgers and Hammerstein's made-for-television *Cinderella*, starring Julie Andrews, attracted an audience of 107 million people, a number that rivals today's Super Bowls. Original cast recordings and covers of showstoppers topped the charts: Louis Armstrong's version of 'Hello, Dolly!' reached number one on the US *Billboard* Hot 100 in January, 1964, toppling The Beatles from their fourteen-week streak at the top of the charts.

Mark Grant sums it up perfectly: 'Musicals mattered to the country. Theatre mattered.'[5]

And it looked like musicals would continue to matter. Between 1964 and 1966, six shows opened that would run for over a thousand performances, entering canon and cultural vernacular: *Hello, Dolly!* (2,844 performances), *Funny Girl* (1,348), *Fiddler on the Roof* (3,242), *Man of La Mancha* (2,328), *Mame* (1,508) and *Cabaret* (1,165).[6] And, of course, *The Fantasticks*, which opened in 1960 in the Off-Broadway Sullivan Street Playhouse, continued its improbable run towards the new millennium. But what appeared to many as the harbinger of future greatness was, in fact, a zenith.

If television was enticing the eye, rock 'n' roll was seducing the ear. But Broadway still sounded more or less the same. That was due to more than geriatric stubbornness. The modern era of musical theatre began in 1927 with *Show Boat*. *Show Boat* changed the musical in several crucial ways, but in terms of the sound of the musical, the most important change was rhythmic. Grant told Michael Dale, 'The four-beat foxtrot gave songwriters a structure that gave room for more probing and literate lyrics. It was bouncy and danceable, with a regular downbeat, and yet permitted more soaring melodies than the two-step.'[7] The durability of the foxtrot into the 1960s, he argues, wasn't a symptom of Broadway's scleroticism, but rather a sign of the bountiful flexibility of the form. But it was starting to sound all too old-fashioned, and you'd hardly know Elvis and the Beatles existed if you only read *Playbill*. Rock was kept at arm's length by producers, with the notable exception of director/choreographer Gower Champion's entirely entertaining *Bye Bye Birdie* (1960). Dick Van Dyke, playing an ersatz Elvis Presley, belted out two rock tunes ('One Last Kiss' and 'Telephone Hour'), but that bouncy foxtrot rhythm filled out the rest of the book.

As it did with Champion's *Hello, Dolly!* (1964), a brilliant example of the Broadway formula. It endured an epically rocky preview tour – David Merrick had refined the tantrum into a fine art – and was revised extensively before its premiere. Finding someone to play Dolly was almost as challenging. Ethel Merman, for whom it was written, turned it down; so did Mary Martin and Nanette Fabray. Dolly eventually fell into the hands and pipes of Carol Channing, who made it the role of her career. The show-stopping title song featured Channing descending a staircase to the acclaim of a chorus of handsome young men. The opening nighters demanded an encore, and, in Kenrick's words, 'choruses of apron-clad waiters have been escorting women of a certain age around runways ever since', including Ginger Rogers, Phyllis Diller, Mary Martin and Pearl Bailey, who starred with Cab Calloway in an all-black production in 1967 that ran for 2,844 performances.

The 1960s was a decade for divas. Barbra Streisand took the stage in *Funny Girl* in 1964, her second and last appearance on Broadway, 'bursting', in the words of *New York Times* critic Howard Taubman, 'with energy and eagerness [like an] impudent dancing doll who refuses to run down'.[8] In 1966, Angela Lansbury found her métier in *Mame*, winning her first Tony for Best Actress in the role of Mame Dennis, whose motto is 'Life is a banquet and most poor sons of bitches are starving to death.' Even Katharine Hepburn took a go at diva-dom in *Coco* (1969), Alan Jay Lerner and André Previn's musical about the life of fashion designer Coco Chanel.

But the show that captured the tension between the old and the new wasn't about big-mouthed dames, but life on a Russian *shtetl*. *Fiddler on the Roof* (1964) was adapted from the tales of Sholem Aleichem, set to the music of Jerry Bock and the lyrics of Sheldon Harnick, and starred the hammier-than-life Zero Mostel. Dairy farmer Tevye, father of five daughters, struggles to maintain his family and Jewish tradition as forces beyond and bigger than his village threaten it all. *Fiddler* broke the record for longest-running musical, surpassing 3,000 performances. But it marked the end of an era. Stephen Mo Hanan recalls, 'We didn't realize it at the time, but it was the sunset of the old-style Broadway musical ... The curtain rose on *Fiddler*, but came down on that kind of show.'[9]

Though 'Willkommen' was a 'modern show tun[e] written in a cakewalk rhythm with implied high kicks',[10] the proceedings to which Joel Grey's louche Master of Ceremonies welcomed his audiences had a decidedly countercultural vibe, from the quasi-Brechtian presentational approach devised by director Harold Prince to the play's intentionally indelicate handling of abortion, racism and homophobia. But while the raucous goings-on at the Kit Kat Club were daring, if not – gasp! – political, *Cabaret* was even more audacious in the way it explored *ideas*. The show inaugurated what Gerald Mast calls the 'concept musical', doing away with the narrative conventions of musical theatre and introducing a lithe self-reflexivity that threw into chaos old ideas about character and storytelling.[11] That was enabled in no small part by Boris Aronson's set, which brought the 'abstract, symbolic [and] fanciful' aesthetic he developed in Moscow, Berlin and Yiddish theatre to the Broadway stage, giving *Cabaret* (and *Fiddler*, which he also designed) its distinctively abstract look.[12]

As radical as *Cabaret* was, it was the 'shining, gleaming / streaming, flaxen, waxen' hair of the performers who slinked onto the stage in James Rado, Gerome Ragni and Galt MacDermot's *Hair* that precipitated Broadway's nervous breakdown. In addition to being the first bona fide rock musical, it shocked sensibilities with its integrated cast, profanity, saucy depictions of sex (one song begins, 'Sodomy, fellatio, cunnilingus') and nudity. The show deployed techniques developed by countercultural theatre collectives like the Open Theater and the Performance Group: performers mingling among the audience, emphasis on image over narrative, allusions to contemporary events. Rado and Ragni had roots in Off-Broadway, and MacDermot couldn't have cared less about the foxtrot conventions of the Broadway musical. *Hair* premiered at Joe Papp's Public Theater in 1967, then transferred to a disco for forty-five performances while a Broadway adaptation was developed. That task fell to Tom O'Horgan, long-time director at La MaMa ETC, who teased more threads out of the already threadbare plot and incorporated more nudity, improvisation games (including several used in Megan Terry's *Viet Rock* [1966]), and an 'organic, expansive style of staging' courtesy of choreographer Julie Arenal.[13] After being turned down by several theatres as too controversial, it found a home at the Biltmore Theatre in 1968 and ran for 1,742 performances.

Hair received only two Tony nominations (Best Musical and Best Direction), and critics generally refused to consider it anything but a fluke. One exception was *New York Times* critic Clive Barnes, who called it 'the first Broadway musical in some time to have the authentic voice of today rather than the day before yesterday'.[14] It ultimately proved far less influential than Barnes hoped.[15] But, as Mark Grant argues, *Hair* did change the way music sounded and stories were told.[16]

The Broadway musical found itself at a fitful end as the decade drew to a close. But while it was fitful, it was not a fatal one, though what stage composers did to break out of that fit is a story for another volume.

Broadway drama

A similar story of tradition and innovation can be told about Broadway drama. A survey of the decade's Tony Awards for Best Play is illustrative. Of the forty-five plays nominated, thirty-one utilized conventional dramatic structure, setting and characterization. But the other fourteen were something else entirely. So, while we recognize the growing influence of experimental, modernist and avant-garde aesthetics on commercial theatre during the decade,[17] the effects of that influence were far more widespread Off-Broadway.

In terms of the tradition of Broadway realism, no writer was more important than Tennessee Williams. But the 1960s were difficult for him. His addiction to alcohol and pills worsened. His partner Frank Merlo died. And he was growing impatient with classic Broadway realism. Unfortunately, plays like *Period of Adjustment* (1960) and *The Milk Train Doesn't Stop Here Anymore* (1963) were minor works and box-office duds. Kate Reed and Zoe Caldwell earned Tony nominations for their performances in the one-act plays *The Mutilated* and *The Gnädiges Fräulein* (1966). But, with the exception of Harold Clurman, the critics weren't kind. Williams's only popular success of the decade was the mostly realistic *Night of the Iguana* (1961). Though Bette Davis was miscast as the bawdy, vital Maxine (and would be replaced by Shelley Winters after four months), the production ran for 316 performances and earned multiple awards. But as Brooks Atkinson opines, 'It was as if [Williams's] basic theme had turned out to be the truth of his own experiences. He was damned, like his characters.'[18]

But the fault wasn't entirely Williams's. C. W. E. Bigsby argues that the most celebrated American playwrights of the 1940s and 1950s – Williams, William Inge and Arthur Miller – shared a focus on the 'anxious, suffering, threatened, equivocating' individual, reflecting a shared belief that the individual was 'key to social meaning and cultural achievement.'[19] That focus was of far less interest to most writers, directors and performers of the 1960s. However, while Inge and Williams's stars faded, Miller remained a writer with whom to reckon.

Arthur Miller

Miller began the decade working on the screenplay of *The Misfits*, a vehicle for his then-wife Marilyn Monroe. Though the film is now regarded as a masterpiece, at the time it was judged a flop. For Miller, it was a disaster. Monroe was awash in pills and liquor. She forgot lines (often changed by Miller the night before filming). They fought constantly, divorcing shortly before the film's premiere in 1961. Miller married photographer Inge Morath in February 1962. Monroe died six months later, likely from a drug overdose.

After the Fall opened in January of 1964 at the American National Theater and Academy (ANTA) in Washington Square, directed by Elia Kazan. Unlike the Ibsenesque realism of his earlier work, the drama here is framed by a single consciousness, 'the mind, thought, and memory of Quentin.'[20] He is a thinly veiled version of Miller, the play an expressionistic autobiographical treatment of Miller's struggle to make sense of personal and historical tragedy. Many found it distasteful. *The New Republic*'s Robert Brustein called it a 'a three and one half hour breach of taste ... misogynistic ... a wretched piece of dramatic writing.'[21] With time, the close connection of play and person has faded, and the 1990 National Theatre production, with black British actor Josette Simon as Maggie, has put to rest the ghost of Monroe.

Incident at Vichy opened at ANTA in December of 1964. Again, Miller dramatizes the struggle of individuals to make sense of staggering, seemingly irresistible violence. A group of men are detained in Vichy France during the Second World War, waiting to be interrogated by German military officers. They try to understand and accept their situation, most of them denying its reality, one attempting to get them to take a stand as, one by one, they disappear into the interrogation room. It closed after only thirty-two performances, but Howard Taubman saw it as raising an important question: 'Who can save us?'[22]

In 1965, Miller was elected president of PEN International, an organization dedicated to the promotion of cooperation and friendship among writers around the world. His work with PEN would get his plays banned in the Soviet Union in 1969. But before that happened, he wrote *The Price* (1968). It marked a return to the sentimental domestic realism of *All My Sons* (1948) and *Death of a Salesman* (1949). Victor and Walter Franz have returned to their parents' once-prosperous brownstone to divvy up their inheritance – a lifetime's worth of furniture and bric-a-brac. The conversation quickly turns from the value of possessions to the value of relationships. Clive Barnes, like the rest of the first-night audience, was 'deeply moved', even if it was 'too rigged, too pat'.[23] The show ran for 429 performances and was nominated for two Tony Awards, one for Best Play, one for Best Scenic Design (Boris Aronson).

Lorraine Hansberry

Though it closed in the summer of 1960, *A Raisin in the Sun*, Lorraine Hansberry's play about an aspiring family of black Americans contending with the death of a father and the arrival of economic opportunity, was already casting a 'long shadow', to borrow Harvey Young's figure.[24] For one, the critics took note. Hansberry received a New York Drama Critics' Circle Award and a Tony nomination for Best Play; Sidney Poitier and Claudia McNeil Tony nominations for their performances as Walter Lee Younger and his mother Lena; and Lloyd Richards for Best Direction. It is undeniably moving, evidence of the power of conventional dramatic realism.

While it also addressed to what extent a person should capitulate to the profit motive, Hansberry's *The Sign in Sidney Brustein's Window* (1964) defied expectations and was less enthusiastically embraced. The protagonists are white, the tone preachy, the structure ropey, the ancillary characters less appealing. Hansberry was fighting pancreatic cancer during the show's run, succumbing on its closing night, 12 January 1965. Her final play was *Les Blancs* (1970). Tshembe Matoseh has returned to his African homeland from England to attend his father's funeral. While there, he spars with a naïve American journalist and reunites with his two brothers, one of whom has become a Christian priest, the other an alcoholic and lover to the village's doctor, whom Hansberry models after Albert Schweitzer. Matoseh soon learns that the doctor believes colonialism to be a virtuous necessity, that Eric is the son of the occupation commander (who raped Matoseh's mother), and, perhaps most shattering, that his father was the leader of the anti-colonial resistance. After killing his Christian brother, he takes up arms against the occupiers. Hansberry considered it her most important play.

But Hansberry will be best remembered for *A Raisin in the Sun*. There are the obvious reasons: the first play written by a black woman and directed by a black director to appear on Broadway; the scintillating cast that, in addition to Poitier and McNeil, included Ruby Dee, Diana Sands, Ossie Davis (who replaced Poitier), Lonne Elder III, Louis Gossett and a young Glynn Turman; the countless translations and productions around the world. The play 'demonstrated to producers that a mainstream white audience as well as a sizable black audience would welcome a nearly all-black production'.[25]

Tiger, Tiger, Burning Bright (1962) opened shortly after *Raisin* closed. Peter S. Feibleman's play also tells the story of a black family dealing with grief, this one in New Orleans at the end of the Second World War. It too had quite a cast: McNeil, Sands, Alvin Ailey, Al Freeman Jr, Roscoe Lee Browne, Cicely Tyson, Bobby Dean Hooks, Paul Barry and Robert Macbeth. Sands found plentiful opportunities on and off Broadway, including Tony-nominated turns as Doris opposite white actor Alan Alda in Bill Manhoff's *The Owl and the Pussycat* (1964) and as Juanita in James Baldwin's *Blues for Mister Charlie* (1964). Ossie Davis played a travelling preacher in his play *Purlie Victorious* opposite Ruby Dee in a 1961 production that ran for more than 260 performances and was later adapted into a successful musical. A musical adaptation of Hansberry's play, *Raisin* (songs by Judd Woldin and Robert Brittan, book by Robert Nemiroff), won the Tony for Best Musical in 1973. Aware of Hansberry and Poitier's struggle to raise money for *Raisin*, Douglas Turner Ward, Robert Hooks and Gerald Krone applied to the Ford Foundation for funding to create the Negro Ensemble Company in 1967 (more on the NEC below).[26] Robert Macbeth followed suit and opened the New Lafayette Theatre in Harlem (also more below). Lloyd Richards continued to direct on Broadway and would be appointed artistic director of the National Playwrights Conference at the Eugene O'Neill Center in 1968 and Dean of Yale Drama School in 1979, holding both positions into the 1990s. Richards would premier six of August Wilson's plays on Broadway.[27]

The 1960s was not a prolific decade for black female playwrights, but several black women founded theatre companies, including Marjorie Moon, Cynthia Belgrave, Hazel Bryant and Vinnette Carroll, whose Urban Art Corps produced more than one hundred plays and revues, two of them (Micki Grant's *Don't Bother Me, I Can't Cope* (1972) and Alex Bradford and Carroll's *Your Arms Too Short to Box With God* (1975)) landing hits on Broadway.[28] And though *A Raisin in the Sun* was criticized at the time by black nationalists for its assimilationist politics, Amiri Baraka and Ed Bullins would later acknowledge Hansberry as source and inspiration for much of what they and their comrades accomplished in the Black Arts Movement.

Neil Simon

Though we might argue who was the most significant Broadway playwright of the decade, there is little doubt who was the most successful. In 1966, Neil Simon had four plays running on Broadway: *Barefoot in the Park* (1963–1967, 1,530 performances), *The Odd Couple* (1965–7, 964 performances), *The Star-Spangled Girl* (1966–7, 261 performances) and *Sweet Charity* (1966–7, 608 performances). These were but four of nine productions that would appear on Broadway during the 1960s, and only the beginning of a string of Broadway hits that would extend into the twenty-first century.

Yet Simon has been mostly ignored by scholars. Susan Koprince views this as a consequence of the fact that 'he appeals to the masses ... and writes comedy, a genre which some academics are reluctant to embrace'.[29] And comedy he did indeed write, honed on the television series *Your Show of Shows* (1950–54), where he worked with Sid Caesar, Imogene Coca, Carl Reiner, Mel Brooks, Woody Allen, Larry Gelbert and Selma Diamond. Also, most of his plays are domestic comedies. 'Serious' playwrights and critics were thinking about national, if not global matters. And his plays 'invariably depict the plight of white middle-class Americans, most of whom are New Yorkers and many of whom are Jewish'.[30] For critic John Lahr, Simon is best understood as the voice of the 'silent majority', the old-fashioned folks who swept Nixon to the White House in '68.[31] Regardless, the plays are charming and often laugh-out-loud hilarious.

Plaza Suite (1968) is exemplary. It tells the story of three couples in three acts: Sam and Karen Nash, returning after many years to their honeymoon suite; film producer and notorious womanizer Jesse Kiplinger and suburban housewife (and former flame) Muriel Tate; and Roy and Norma Hubley, celebrating their daughter's wedding, said daughter locked in the bathroom in a seizure of nervous regret. Clive Barnes called it 'a machine for laughing at', but admired the performances by George C. Scott and Maureen Stapleton and the deft touch of director Mike Nichols.[32] Each story ballasts the laughs with serious moments. This is also true of *The Odd Couple*, which won Tony Awards for co-star Walter Matthau, director Mike Nichols, designer Oliver Smith and Simon. It explores a genuinely serious situation: two middle-aged men are abandoned by their wives and discover they cannot get along any better with each other. But the exaggerated contrasts – Oscar Madison an archetypal snob; Felix Ungar a fastidious hypochondriac – rooted the story in a tried-and-true comic mode.[33]

The Broadway avant-garde

While realism dominated Broadway, other theatrical modes found their moments on its boards. Absurdism, for example. In the 1950s, the notion that life was meaningless, language untrustworthy and human striving ridiculous found enthusiastic disciples among hipsters and the intelligentsia. Existentialists like Jean-Paul Sartre, Simone de Beauvoir and Albert Camus were veritable celebrities. Sartre's *No Exit*, *Red Gloves*, *The Victors* and *The Respectful Prostitute* appeared on Broadway in the 1940s. The Living Theatre's 1959 production of Jack Gelber's *The Connection* was a sensation. Genet, Beckett and Pirandello appeared regularly on Off-Broadway stages during the 1950s and their influence can be traced across the Manhattan theatre scene.

So it's not surprising that producers thought there might be some profit in hopeless striving. In 1961, Zero Mostel, recently recovered from being hit by a bus and fresh from playing Estragon to Burgess Meredith's Vladimir in a middling television adaptation of *Waiting for Godot*, starred in Ionesco's *Rhinoceros*. He won a Tony for his high jinks. Joe Orton's *Entertaining Mr Sloane*, directed by Alan Schneider, closed after thirteen performances in 1965, though Sheila Hancock found admirers among Tony voters. The Royal National

Theatre's 1967 production of Tom Stoppard's *Rosencrantz and Guildenstern are Dead* was an unalloyed success. Its story was almost as absurd as the goings-on in the play. A script by an unknown writer, performed by an unpolished student company at the Edinburgh Festival Fringe, it was panned by the few critics who saw it – except the *Observer*'s Ronald Bryden, who called it 'the most brilliant debut by a young playwright since John Arden'.[34] That drew the attention of Kenneth Tynan, lead of the National Theatre. From there to New York, where it ran for 420 performances and was nominated for eight Tony Awards, winning four.

But it was Pinter and Albee who represented the Theatre of the Absurd most vividly for Broadway audiences, perhaps because of their domestic settings and more or less familiar interpersonal situations. Pinter's *The Caretaker* was staged in 1961 at the Lyceum Theatre, receiving Tony nominations for Best Play, Donald McWhinnie's direction and Donald Pleasence's performance as Davies. *The Homecoming* (1967) was a more compelling production, achieving a year-long run and Tony Awards for director Peter Hall, producer Alexander H. Cohen and actors Paul Rogers and Ian Holm. Albee's *Who's Afraid of Virginia Woolf?* (1962), *The Ballad of the Sad Café* (1963, adapted from the novella by Carson McCullers), *Tiny Alice* (1964) and *A Delicate Balance* (1966) all received nominations for Best Play; *Woolf* won. But Albee was by no means universally admired. When *Woolf* was nominated for a Pulitzer in 1962, the board refused to award it; jury members John Mason Brown and John Gassner resigned.[35] When *Tiny Alice* opened, Albee and director Alan Schneider felt compelled to meet with the press at the New School for Social Research, Albee admonishing them that a 'symbol should not be a cymbal'.[36] (The reader can consult Helen Shaw's chapter in this volume for more details on Albee's reception by audiences and critics.)

One might have predicted a Brecht craze at the start of the decade. *The Threepenny Opera* was an Off-Broadway fixture, running for six years, closing in 1961, followed by *Brecht on Brecht*, starring Lotte Lenya, which ran for two hundred performances. In 1960, the Living Theatre staged *In the Jungle of Cities* to acclaim. But Brecht wasn't an easy sell. *Man is Man* ran concurrently on and off Broadway, the former (under the title *A Man's a Man*) starring Olympia Dukakis and running for 175 performances, the Living Theatre's (with Joseph Chaikin as Galy Gay) running just a few fewer. The *Resistible Rise of Arturo Ui* was attempted in 1963 with Christopher Plummer as Ui and, in 1968, by a touring Guthrie Theater Company. Both sputtered. *Mother Courage and Her Children* ran for six weeks in 1963, though, as Marvin Carlson notes, Anne Bancroft, who had won a Tony for *The Miracle Worker* the previous year, found the role difficult. Critics found the whole 'under-rehearsed . . . flat and uninteresting.'[37]

The high-water mark of the Broadway avant-garde – and, from all accounts, the best Brecht productions of the decade – was achieved by the Repertory Theatre of Lincoln Center. Herb Blau and Jules Irving founded the Actor's Workshop in San Francisco in 1952, 'without stars, fanfare, real estate, or capital . . . convinced that the destiny of the American theatre lies as far off-Broadway as possible, in permanent companies dedicated to ensemble playing.'[38] In many ways, the Workshop was an emblematic regional residential theatre. Blau and Irving considered commercial theatre a 'pathological condition',[39] signed the first Off-Broadway contract with Equity in 1955, and received a $197,000 grant from the Ford Foundation, which enabled them to develop a rotating repertory. They staged 'more premieres of new American plays than . . . any other regional theatre of its time'.[40]

The Vivian Beaumont Theater was intended to stand shoulder to shoulder with the Metropolitan Opera, the New York City Ballet and the New York Philharmonic. If not in name, it was to be a national institution in spirit and ambition. Prior to the construction of the new building, what would be known as the Repertory Theatre of Lincoln Center did its work at the ANTA-Washington Square Theatre in Greenwich Village. Elia Kazan was its first artistic director, with Harold Clurman as consultant, Jo Mielziner as designer and Arthur Miller as writer, whose plays *After the Fall* and *Incident at Vichy* premiered there. But a series of epically disastrous productions led to Kazan's dismissal, though the core value of the group – the freedom to develop theatre relatively free of commercial pressure – survived. The board of directors searched far and wide for replacements, but finding no one willing to take the job, looked towards San Francisco.

No one was more surprised by the offer than Blau and Irving. While they 'neither leaped nor took it lightly' when the offer came in, they saw it as the 'most material certification of that Idea' – capital 'I' – of the Workshop.[41] They were overconfident and underprepared. Howard Taubman of the *New York Times* was patient with their first production, Büchner's *Danton's Death* (1965), detecting 'heartening signs of a viewpoint and a commitment'.[42] He lauded the 1967 production of Brecht's *The Caucasian Chalk Circle* as their 'best production to date, and a good production by any standards'.[43] Forty thousand subscribers didn't hurt, either. But the second season saw a drop in subscriptions, and audacious ideas lacking workable solutions. The last straw was their production of Wilford Leach's *In Three Zones*. By previews, Blau had blown the budget. The show was cancelled; so was Blau. Irving soldiered on, taking over as director of *Galileo* and achieving unqualified success. But despite maintaining quality and numbers, a lack of power and prestige put Irving and the board at a disadvantage relative to the other members of the Lincoln Center family.[44] He resigned in 1972. He would later write,

> If I've learned anything during these continuing years in Wonderland, it's that there's always room for one more at the Mad Hatter's tea party. What does it take to create and run New York's major classical theatre on $5 a day? A little madness coupled with nerves of steel, a bullet-proof directing shirt, that Ph.D. in brinkmanship, and a steady and shining dream.[45]

If the Lincoln Center was a mad tea party, the 1965 Royal Shakespeare Company (RSC) production of Peter Weiss's *The Persecution and Assassination of Jean-Paul Marat as Performed by the Inmates of the Asylum of Charenton Under the Direction of the Marquis de Sade* was a passionate, piercing cry of madness. The play takes place at the Charenton Asylum in 1808. The Marquis de Sade (played by a simmering Patrick Magee) has organized the inmates for a theatrical portraying the French Revolution and the assassination of that revolution's most incendiary voice, Jean-Paul Marat (Clive Revill), and its most anarchic and unpredictable, Charlotte Corday (the transfixing Glenda Jackson). But the inmates resist both Sade's organization and the hospital's bourgeois director. The ingenious play-within-a-play strategy enabled the company to expose the audience at one and the same time to the Artaudian shriek of madness and the Brechtian dissection of hegemony and ideology. Staged at the Martin Beck Theatre, *Marat/Sade* stands as one of the signal productions of post-war Broadway. As Carlson sums it, the production 'was in many ways perfectly suited to the times, a complex intellectual exploration of the dynamics of revolution, in one of the most revolutionary decades of the century'.[46]

Off- and Off-Off-Broadway

Off-Broadway

The term 'Off-Broadway' was originally a geographical one referring to theatres located outside, but close by the Broadway district of Manhattan. In 1949, Actors' Equity ruled that actors could perform for a lower rate in theatres that had fewer than 299 seats, at which point the term began to refer to a particular kind of theatre, regardless of its location. But for those who created art in those theatres, 'Off-Broadway' was more than seat counts and pay scale. Stuart Little calls it 'a state of mind, a set of production conditions, a way of looking at theatre at every point at odds with Broadway's patterns'.[47]

The Theatre de Lys, the Cherry Lane and Circle in the Square – all located in Greenwich Village – thrived on 'reclaiming Broadway's mistakes and . . . reviving classics that were anathema to commercial producers'.[48] José Quintero's 1952 staging of Williams's *Summer and Smoke* was the quintessential Off-Broadway production, vindicating a play regarded as a failure during its brief run at the Music Box Theatre four years earlier. But things changed in the 1960s, when Off-Broadway became a venue for new playwrights, the Black American experience, the political, the satirical, and the avant-garde – not to mention some fetching musicals.[49]

It was not the first, the last or the only successful Off-Broadway musical, but *The Fantasticks* (1960) was certainly the most remarkable. When Lore Noto first encountered this mere wisp of a musical by recent University of Texas graduates Tom Jones and Harvey Schmidt, *The Threepenny Opera* had been running for five years and Jerome Kern's *Leave It to Jane* (1959) at the Sheridan Square Playhouse and *Little Mary Sunshine* (1959) at the Orpheum Theatre were gaining momentum. It's hard to say what made the production so endearing. Jones and Schmidt tell an admittedly corny tale. Two children are tricked by their fathers into squabbling, then discover the hard facts of life and, of course, love. It opened to a tepid response. In his *Tribune* review, Walter Kerr wrote, 'It attracts you, settles back a bit limply, wakes you up again, and averages out a little less than satisfactory.'[50] But the show's combination of innocence and cynicism, its intimate staging, the suave Jerry Orbach (who had played the Street Singer and Mack the Knife in *Threepenny*) and the frisson of Greenwich Village bohemia proved perfectly charming. It closed in 2002 after 17,612 performances.

In the 1950s, only the Living Theatre (1947) regularly staged new plays by American playwrights: Frank O'Hara, John Ashbery and James Merrill during the early part of the decade and Jack Gelber's *The Connection* in 1959. But in the 1960s, Off-Broadway would introduce a generation of playwrights, including Edward Albee, Ed Bullins, Mart Crowley, Frank Gilroy, John Guare, Israel Horovitz, LeRoi Jones/Amiri Baraka, Leonard Melfi, Adrienne Kennedy (discussed in detail by Lenora Inez Brown in her contribution to this volume), Arthur Kopit, Jack Richardson, Murray Schisgal, Sam Shepard and Douglas Turner Ward. Many learned the ropes at playwriting workshops like Albee, Richard Barr, and Clinton Wilder's Playwrights Unit, which provided, Albee explained, 'something a commercial theatre cannot: the place and time to experiment and develop without the cruel pressures of the hit-or-flop syndrome'.[51]

Jean Genet's The Blacks

Off-Broadway was a wellspring for the black theatre movement – and a font of controversy. A year after Hansberry's *A Raisin in the Sun* closed, the St Mark's Playhouse staged Genet's *The Blacks*. In stark contrast to *Raisin*, Genet does not create an 'authentic' or 'moral' representation of black Americans. Further, the script stipulates that it is written for a white audience. This is no protest play, but a fantasia of white desire, hopes and fears. As Little notes, this was the first time most white viewers had ever been 'challenged from the stage, face to face, as it were, black to white, to admit their unspoken prejudices'. It was an epochal experience for the play's cast, too, which included James Earl Jones, Cynthia Belgrave, Roscoe Lee Browne, Louis Gossett Jr, Cicely Tyson, Godfrey Cambridge, Maya Angelou and Charles Gordone. Rehearsals were often interrupted by cast meetings that lasted for hours and sometimes excluded the production's white director, Gene Frankel. 'Always,' Little reports, 'the two primary concerns ... were the whiteness of the author and the whiteness of the director.'[52] But it all came together in a production that was as beautiful as it was menacing. Designer Kim E. Swados placed the action on a circular ramp, which, perched on the St Mark's arena stage, created a sense of looming, perilous intimacy.

Like Hansberry's play, *The Blacks* cast its own 'long shadow'. Indeed, with *Raisin*, *The Blacks* ignited the black theatre movement, a movement that accommodated the formally and politically radical (Amiri Baraka, Ed Bullins, Adrienne Kennedy, Sonia Sanchez) and those who, like the Negro Ensemble Company, remained committed to liberal humanism and the naturalist aesthetic.

The Negro Ensemble Company

Though preceded by Cleveland's Karamu House and Detroit's Concept East Theater and concurrent with the dozens of small, short-lived theatres inspired by Harlem's Black Arts Repertory Theatre/School, the Negro Ensemble Company's (NEC) unique position in the New York theatre scene ensured it took pride of place, but also made it a lightning rod.

In 1964, actor Robert Hooks (then starring in Jones's *Dutchman*) and Barbara Ann Teer led a free acting workshop for black youth. Their performance of Gwendolyn Brooks's poem 'We Real Cool' and Douglas Turner Ward's satirical take on white wealth and black domestic servants, *Happy Ending*, drew the attention of the *New York Post*'s Jerry Talmer, who gave it a glowing review. Confidence bolstered, Hooks staged *Happy Ending* and another Ward play, *Day of Absence*, on a double bill. That production and the *New York Times* editorial Ward wrote protesting the lack of opportunity for black theatre artists drew the attention of the Ford Foundation, which gave Hooks, Ward and Gerald Krone $1.2 million to establish an ensemble theatre that would 'concentrate primarily on themes of Negro life ... whatever the source'.[53] White money, white administrative director Krone and the use of the fusty word 'Negro' were only three of the controversies the NEC would weather. Clayton Reilly accused it of being 'white art in black face' in a 1970 *New York Times* column.[54] It was criticized almost as harshly by whites for highlighting race in its title, its policy of using black actors almost exclusively, and (after that first season) of staging plays only by black writers.

But the proof was in the pudding. Over the next two decades, the NEC produced original works by Steve Carter, Gus Edwards, Lonne Elder III, Charles Fuller, Paul Carter Harrison, Joseph A. Walker, Douglas Turner Ward and Samm-Art Williams, among others. It produced a few (all too few) women, too: Alice Childress, Pearl Cleage and Leslie Lee. Its production of Fuller's *A Soldier's Play* (1981) earned the Pulitzer, only one of many honours the NEC received. And it provided career-making opportunities for actors like Moses Gunn, Esther Rolle, Rosalind Cash, Arthur French, Cleavon Little, Richard Roundtree and Roscoe Lee Browne.[55] Perhaps most significantly, the NEC changed the way we think of African American drama: the canon of contemporary African American drama has been largely defined by the NEC.[56]

Circle in the Square

In many respects, the story of Circle in the Square (CIS) is the story of Off-Broadway. When it was founded in 1951, it was, like Off-Broadway itself, no theatre at all. They operated with a cabaret licence, so the audience sat at small tables, the company waiting tables as needed. But their 1952 production of Williams's *Summer and Smoke* established Geraldine Page as a star and the Circle as a 'theatre of respected professionals instead of a studio for out-of-work actors and hopeful theatre artists'.[57] It also cemented the paradigm of Off-Broadway theatre: provide opportunities for new actors and directors, revisit plays and playwrights that have suffered misfortune, forge a new compact between art and commerce. Like *Summer and Smoke*, O'Neill's *The Iceman Cometh* was considered a flawed work. But José Quintero's direction and Jason Robards's irresistible turn as Hickey brought universal praise for their 1956 production and renewed interest in O'Neill. The Circle's tradition of escorting actors to greatness would continue with Colleen Dewhurst, Dustin Hoffman, George C. Scott and George Segal.

The Circle executed its move to a new home in 1959, between the 333rd and 334th performances of *Our Town*.[58] Shortly after, Quintero directed Genet's *The Balcony*. David Hays's set suspended crystal chandeliers above a stage described by Atkinson as 'a rummage sale of toys – gaudy costumes, store-window dummies hanging in a circle ... a platform with a monstrous throne ... the whole paraphernalia of a ghoulish dream'.[59] Patricia Zipprodt outfitted the customers in voluminous robes and ten-inch lifts, 'emphasiz[ing] not so much their grandeur as their pathetic littleness on resuming their normal identities'.[60] The prostitutes wore sleek, severe leather. It ran for 672 performances and paved the way for the St Mark's production of *The Blacks*. Circle in the Square remains devoted to its principles to this day, presenting landmark productions of American classics and also-rans, providing break-out opportunities for actors and directors. But it does so now on Broadway, having moved in 1972 to the first new theatre built there in a half-century.

The Phoenix Theatre

The Phoenix Theatre was founded in 1953 by Norris Houghton and T. Edward Hambleton. From the start they wanted distance from Broadway in terms of both location and attitude. It was situated in the East Village, hosted a permanent company, did not honour the star system and asked its sponsors to fund seasons rather than single productions.[61] Their productions were praised. They drew directors like Tyrone Guthrie, John Houseman and Elia Kazan; and actors like Peggy Ashcroft, Montgomery Clift, Hume Cronyn, Uta Hagen, Jessica Tandy and Eli Wallach embraced the opportunity to perform there. But they had 1,200 seats to fill.[62] Their theatre's name, Little writes, 'was more prophetic ... than they could have then anticipated'.[63] It was a story of near death and miraculous comebacks. They refunded tickets to subscribers in 1959, only to pack the house that autumn with Mary Rodgers and Marshall Barer's *Once Upon a Mattress*, starring the expertly goofy Carol Burnett. That show transferred to Broadway, and they enjoyed two more seasons of success with Shakespeare (notably Donald Madden in *Hamlet*) and other classics. But then another crisis, this one as much about identity as the bottom line. Rising production costs and 1,200 seats were beginning to drive artistic decisions – the tail was wagging the dog. So, they moved to a smaller house in 1961, gave up repertory, and, once again, scored a hit with Arthur Kopit's giggly parody of the absurdists, *Oh Dad, Poor Dad, Mamma's Hung You in the Closet and I'm Feelin' So Sad*. They merged with Ellis Rabb's Association of Producing Arts (APA) in 1963, ceding 'the talent, the programming, and the artistry' to the APA and focusing on managing the theatre and audience relations.[64]

It was once again a repertory company and a very good one – Walter Kerr called it 'the best repertory company we possess'⁶⁵ – but Broadway was calling and they listened. In 1966, the company, now called the APA-Phoenix Theatre, moved to the Lyceum Theatre and gained a $900,000 general support grant from the Ford Foundation. From there, the Phoenix's story remained faithful to its name, success followed by crisis until it closed permanently in 1982.

The New York Shakespeare Festival

While Joe Papp's New York Shakespeare Festival wasn't, strictly speaking, a regional residential theatre, it had the characteristics of one: unflagging commitment to its community, sturdy relationships with leaders and tastemakers and, most importantly, 'a single, messianic leader to give it character, spirit, direction, and inspiration'.⁶⁶ That was certainly the case with Joe Papp, who Little describes as 'ambitious, animated, pugnacious', a supremely charming autocrat who had little trouble convincing his friends and rivals to commit to his unprecedented schemes, and a stalwart defender of the people's right to beauty.

The 1956 productions of *Julius Caesar* and *The Taming of the Shrew* at the East River Park Amphitheater left their audience 'astonished' and made Colleen Dewhurst, who played Katherine, a star.⁶⁷ From there, Atkinson writes, '[w]ith no encouragement from any rational person, Mr Papp moved the free Shakespeare festival into Central Park over the angry screams of Robert Moses, then the park commissioner'.⁶⁸ Moses demanded that admission be charged, a percentage of the receipts used to replace the grass. Later, he circulated a letter calling Papp a communist. Papp refused to charge admission, Moses earned a rebuke from the mayor, and the Festival found the loyalty and affection of New Yorkers, including Atkinson (influential theatre reviewer for the *New York Times*) and publisher George T. Delacorte, who provided the lion's share of funding for the 2,300-seat theatre built in 1961 that bears his name.

Without question, the signal achievement of Papp and his collaborators was the creation of excellent, accessible theatre. But the Festival is also noteworthy for the way it adapted to the changing conditions of the city. 'No group', Little writes, 'better illustrates the interplay of complex forces at work in the theatre – economic restrictions, the availability of talent, interfering political interests, the needs of the public, the spectrum of current social concern.'[69] Papp's dexterity enabled him to found the Public Theater in 1967 (reportedly, for an annual rent of one dollar). The Festival pales in comparison to the Public, which premiered *Hair* in 1967; Charles Gordone's *No Place to Be Somebody* in 1969 (the first play by an African American and the first Off-Broadway show to win the Pulitzer); David Rabe's *The Basic Training of Pavlo Hummel* (1971) and *Sticks and Bones* (1971); Ntozake Shange's *for colored girls who have considered suicide/when the rainbow is enuf* (1976); *A Chorus Line* (1975); and Larry Kramer's incendiary indictment of the failure of the nation to respond to the AIDS crisis, *The Normal Heart* (1985). Papp died in 1991, but his vision of theatre as a keystone of urban infrastructure lives on.

Off-Off-Broadway

There are many ways to tell the story of Off-Off-Broadway. It could be told as a response to the failure of Broadway and Off-Broadway to foster aesthetic audacity. It could be a story about space: coffee houses, church basements, the sacred circle of ritual, site-specific performances, environmental theatre, street-corner drama. We could focus on the reconfiguration of boundaries between text and performance, the sacred and profane, art and everyday life. There is the story of Latinos, black Americans, the LGBTQ community, and women insisting on their presence on stage and in the front office. It must be a story of playwrights: Rosalyn Drexler, Tom Eyen, María Irene Fornés, Paul Foster, H. M. Koutoukas, Charles Ludlam, Rochelle Owens, Sam Shepard, Megan Terry, Jean-Claude van Itallie, Doric Wilson, Lanford Wilson. However we tell it, the story of Off-Off-Broadway is always, fundamentally, a story of community. Michael Smith, one of its most sensitive critics and sometime participant, confessed, 'Off-Off-Broadway is decidedly clubby. To some extent it has a coterie audience; to some extent it is snobbish and self-glorifying; to some extent it is a playground. Sometimes it is despicable. But all these weaknesses are inseparable from its strength, which is its human scale.'[70]

Bottoms defines Off-Off-Broadway in terms of three criteria. First, a 'radically anti-consumerist vision'.[71] Second, a specific geography comprising 'the adjoining bohemian neighbourhoods of

Greenwich Village and the East Village', whose proximity encouraged 'a constant, freely circulating traffic of personalities and ideas around this downtown scene'.[72] The third and most important criterion is 'the centrality of the playwright to the creative process'.[73] Unlike the director-focused theatre of Richard Schechner's Performance Group, the process-centred work of the Open Theater or the aleatory 'happenings' of Allan Kaprow, the theatres of Off-Off-Broadway valued play and playwright.[74] Even so, conventional understandings of character and the 'Western notion of progress-solution, of beginnings and endings' were mostly rejected in favour of 'distilled, emblematic images or confrontations'.[75] And playwrights often composed in response to 'particular spaces, particular actors, even particular props, adopting intuitive or improvisatory writing methods'.[76] Off-Off-Broadway theatres were located on the same streets as jazz clubs and Beat poetry coffeeshops, crucibles for what Daniel Belgrad calls the 'culture of spontaneity'.[77]

There is general agreement that the story of Off-Off-Broadway is the story of four theatres (Caffe Cino, Judson Poets' Theater, Theatre Genesis and La MaMa) and two collectives (the Open Theater and the Theatre of the Ridiculous). I'll follow that convention here (leaving discussion of the Open Theatre, which Timothy Youker discusses in his chapter on Jean-Claude van Itallie, and the Theatre of the Ridiculous, discussed below). But before proceeding, a question: where are black and Latino theatre artists? Historians of Off-Off-Broadway have ignored the contribution of people of colour – Ellen Stewart of La MaMa notwithstanding. I would ask that the reader treat my discussion of the Black Arts and Latino theatre movements as two more chapters in the story of Off-Off-Broadway.

Caffe Cino

When he opened his little coffee house in December 1958, Joe Cino had no designs on a theatre that, as Wendell C. Stone summarizes, would be 'instrumental in launching and popularizing the off-off-Broadway theatre movement, in exploring new production styles, in fostering an emerging gay theatre, and in promoting the careers of numerous performers, playwrights, and directors'.[78] And though he had no managerial experience, Cino's leadership style 'influenced first experimental theatres in New York and subsequently café and small theatre managers elsewhere'.[79] It was an idiosyncratic style, for sure: the quality of the script didn't matter to him, he scheduled shows according to astrology, he didn't interfere with productions, didn't cancel poorly attended shows and provided only a pittance for production costs.[80] But he never failed to provide one priceless resource: the freedom for artists to express themselves.[81]

Like most coffee houses, the Caffe was not designed for performance. It was originally, simply and always a place for friends, especially gay friends, to gather, including actors and musicians working in Off-Broadway shows. It was a theatre of clientele, not vision. The first play 'with a set and everything' was staged in the summer of 1960.[82] It's not certain when Joe Cino began to introduce each performance, but everyone remembers what he said: 'Ladies and gentlemen, it's Magic Time!'[83]

Robert Dahdah arrived in the autumn, bringing 'a consistency of production standards and a reliable supply of new material' derived from his experience staging amateur repertory for charity.[84] Dahdah played as loose with permissions as Cino did with rent and electricity (the latter provided by his lover, a talented electrician). At first, the programme favoured gay playwrights: Truman Capote, Jean Cocteau, Noël Coward, André Gide, Inge, Williams.[85] Staging was necessarily minimalist, relying on mood and lighting (courtesy of the brilliant Johnny Dodd). The Caffe established itself as a venue for new plays in 1961. Doric Wilson's camp take on Adam and Eve, *And He Made a Her*, opened in March, followed in June by *Babel, Babel, Little Tower* (in which an actor dressed as a cop enters and demands the show be stopped), and *Now She Dances!* and *Pretty People* in the fall. Though Wilson wouldn't write another play for the Cino, he set a precedent. Jerry Caruana, Tom Eyen, Claris Nelson, Robert Patrick, David Starkweather, H. M. Koutoukas, Sam Shepard and Paul Foster premiered work there.

The brightest star was Lanford Wilson's. Nine of his plays appeared between 1963 and 1966, including *The Madness of Lady Bright* (1964), which inaugurated the gay drama movement (and is discussed below). Wilson exemplified the way that Off-Off-Broadway playwrights wrote in response to specific spaces. *Lady Bright* played with the contrast between the loneliness of its protagonist and the shoulder-to-shoulder intimacy of the audience. The six actors in *This Is the Rill Speaking* (1965) 'created a powerful image of the smothering closeness and interdependence of small-town life' by being crammed together on a bench next to patrons crammed together at their tables.[86]

Another writer who expertly staged the Caffe's space was H. M. Koutoukas. Known for his cobra rings, elaborately painted fingernails and the stuffed parrot he wore on his shoulder, he was 'the archetypal Cino playwright; his combination of whimsy, speed, camp, and insanity was precisely right for Joe's sensibilities'.[87] Michael Smith saw the characters in *All Day for a Dollar* (1965), *With Creatures Make My Way* (1965) and *Medea or Maybe the Stars May Understand* (1965) as 'people or creatures who have become so strange that they have lost touch with ordinary life, yet their feelings are all the more tender and vulnerable – the deformed, the demented, the rejected, the perverse'.[88]

Koutoukas was one of several who viewed the 1966 production of *Dames at Sea* (George Haimsohn, Robin Miller and Jim Wise's parody of 1930s Busby Berkeley backstage dramas starring the effervescent Bernadette Peters) and the revival of past hits as a betrayal of the Caffe's spirit. But Cino never sought grant funding, never accepted it when it was offered, was running both a café and a theatre, was wrestling with city authorities daily, and was developing an addiction to amphetamines.[89] The sixteen-week run of *Dames* meant steady income. At the same time it precipitated the end of Cino and his Caffe. A recent habitué, Warhol's 'superstar' Ondine, brought speed-fuelled insanity and an infectious refusal to follow any rules. Dahdah was rueful, but Dodd felt the last months of the Caffe Cino were a 'golden age' of delirious creation and conviviality. Either way, it was the end. In January, Cino's lover was electrocuted. Cino's addiction intensified, as did the atmosphere of masochistic madness. On 30 March, Michael Smith discovered him on the kitchen floor, blood spilling from self-inflicted wounds. Cino died on 2 April, and the Caffe closed shortly after. Today, a visitor to 31 Cornelia Street will find a plaque that reads, 'On this site ... artists brought theatre into the modern era, creating Off-Off-Broadway and forever altering the performing arts worldwide.'[90]

Theatre Genesis

Theatre Genesis was founded in 1964 at the St Mark's Church-in-the-Bowery as part of a pastoral programme for the East Village's population of poor, struggling, angry, immigrant and addicted.

Ralph Cook founded the theatre and was its artistic director, insisting that 'the actors, directors, and writers are members of a geographical community and we are presenting plays for members of that community not as a special gala event but as an integral part of the life of the community.'[91] Cook converted a second-floor meeting room in the parish hall into a black-box studio. After presenting an insipid show designed for churches, Cook resolved to be patient – guaranteeing an erratic production schedule and a higher level of quality than most Off-Off-Broadway theatres.[92]

Whether the result of patience or luck, the decision to stage two plays by Sam Shepard in 1964 was prophetic. *Cowboys* and *The Rock Garden* are informed equally by Shepard's passion for Beckett and the mischievous nihilism of New York's street culture. The *New York Post*'s Jerry Tallmer found little to admire, but Michael Smith found the plays 'provocative and genuinely original', especially in their control of mood and language.[93] It didn't hurt that *The Rock Garden*, a satire of bourgeois domesticity, ended with a monologue in which the boy (played by Lee Kissman) describes soaking his sheets in semen and extols small vaginas. The ensuing scandal affirmed the church's uncategorical support for its theatre, but it inadvertently amplified the atmosphere, in Cook's words, of 'almost conspicuous heterosexuality.'[94]

Genesis productions also benefited from the Monday night play-reading workshops. Cook's rigorous taste and judgement and his ability to plumb a writer's purpose allowed scripts to find their quality. Equally important was the theatre space itself, not much bigger than the Caffe Cino, which allowed writers and actors to explore subtle movement and emotional expression. It enabled lighting designer Johnny Dodd to use colour and light to magical effect – as he did with Walter Hadler's *Solarium* (1968), painting the entire space yellow.[95] It enabled the creation of intense sensory experiences like the one at the end of Shepard's *Forensic and the Navigators* (1967), in which the theatre was filled with coloured smoke, blinding the spectators while Shepard's band, the Holy Modal Rounders, reached a deafening crescendo.

The programme for the first two seasons was diverse in theme and mode – Koutoukas's *Medea*, experimental one-acts by Charles Mee, realistic works by Leonard Melfi. But by 1966, an aesthetic, 'a deeply subjective kind of realism' focusing on damaged, marginalized individuals, was established.[96] Shepard was its exemplar, 'grounding his early plays in recognizable, everyday realities ... but refracting and abstracting [them] through the application of a very personal, subjective vision'.[97] As was Leonard Melfi's *Birdbath* (1965). His depiction of an accidental encounter between a waitress and a would-be poet at an all-night cafeteria utilized dialogue to surgically excise their damaged lives, evoke a world in emotional ruin and achieve a stunning emotional climax. *Birdbath* had that distinctive Genesis sound – a 'directly emotive, densely verbal theatricality' – influenced by the St Mark's Poetry Project, which also met in the parish building.[98]

Cook generally privileged individual playwrights, but not always. *The Hawk* (1967) was developed using methods like those of the Open Theater. Like that company's *The Serpent* (1968) and *Terminal* (1969), *The Hawk* was constructed around a series of rituals defined by a set of themes: addiction, greed and obsession. True to the Genesis aesthetic, though, those rituals were anchored in a real-world setting: the cyclical violence and hopelessness of junkie culture. Michael Smith hailed it as 'the most important single achievement of Theatre Genesis'.[99]

Forensic and the Navigators premiered shortly after *The Hawk* and marked a shift in tone and politics for the theatre. Forensic and Emmett sit, smoking a pipe, the former dressed as a cowboy, the latter an Indian. They discuss a plan to break their fellow revolutionaries out of jail, but are interrupted by two Exterminators, who rain violence down upon them. The war in Vietnam and domestic protests against it were escalating, and the play addressed that, though in broad, if not ambivalent, terms. Grant Duay's *Fruit Salad* (1967) followed suit, juxtaposing film of a bourgeois housewife making, yes, fruit salad with the on-stage struggle of four soldiers hopelessly lost in the jungle. Like *Forensic, Fruit Salad* worked by contrast, shifting between a 'bitter, painful, almost despairing vision' and a 'lightness, fluidity, conciseness, and cunning' tone.[100] This tonal clash was typical of Genesis productions during its final years, which included Mednick's *The Hunter* (1968) and *The Deer Kill* (1970), Hadler's *Flite Cage* and *The Waterworks at Lincoln* (1969), and Michael Smith's *Country Music* (1971).[101]

Ralph Cook left Theatre Genesis in 1969, Mednick and Hadler picking up his responsibilities. When Michael Smith joined Mednick and Hadler as director in 1971, he put a stake through the heart of the 'boys' club' mythos, staging plays by Adrienne Kennedy, María

Irene Fornés, Ron Tavel and Jeff Weiss.[102] Even as it struggled during its final years, Theatre Genesis maintained its long-standing commitment to the playwright, its trademark aesthetic and its community (never once charging admission). It closed in 1978.

Judson Poets' Theater

Though many in the Off- and Off-Off-Broadway scenes believed that theatre was a fundamentally spiritual art form, only Al Carmines had a degree in theology (two, in fact) and an official church position. When Carmines was hired by senior minister Howard Moody to found a theatre in the sanctuary of the Judson Memorial Church, a Greenwich Village landmark, he was building on a tradition established by his predecessor, Bernard Scott, who provided space to artists like Jim Dine, Red Grooms, Yoko Ono, Robert Rauschenberg and Daniel Spoerri and, just as important, an ironclad commitment to freedom of expression.[103] Carmines would continue the church's tradition of fostering the arts, administering the seminal Judson Dance Theater and Judson Art Gallery.

The Judson Poets' Theater's first programme was shown in November 1961: Joel Oppenheimer's *The Great American Desert*, an anti-Western with Billy the Kid as 'the first juvenile delinquent' and Doc Holliday as 'the original hipster', and Guillaume Apollinaire's classic Surrealist play *The Breasts of Tiresias*.[104] It inaugurated a tradition of double bills featuring classic avant-garde texts alongside new work, and the production brought Lawrence Kornfeld, assistant director and general manager of the Living Theatre, into the fold.

The productions of Gertrude Stein's *What Happened* in the fall of 1963 and Rosalyn Drexler's *Home Movies* in March 1964, set Judson on its path. Composed in 1913, Stein's play had yet to be fully staged. For Carmines, it was the beginning of a long and storied relationship with Stein. Arguably, the peak of that relationship would come in 1968 with *In Circles*, Carmines setting Stein's motile prose to a gamut of musical styles. He would bring that same eclectic sensibility to other Stein compositions: *The Making of Americans* (1972), *Listen to Me* (1974), *A Manoir* (1977) and *Doctor Faustus Lights the Lights* (1979). Carmines's ability to find the musicality of Stein's prose was complemented by Kornfeld's commitment to collaborative process. Inspired by the text's repetition, variation and parataxis, Kornfeld 'facilitate[d] a process whereby each of the participants would be able to contribute creatively' to the overall production.[105] And, finally, there were the dancers.

The Judson Dance Theater, founded in 1962, is now recognized as a seminal postmodern dance company. George Jackson writes, 'Categories such as modern dance and ballet, professional and amateur did not apply to Judson . . . It wasn't always possible to distinguish between choreographer and performer. The dances might look like dances or like exercises, tasks or games.'[106] Five dancers joined the production – Joan Baker, Lucinda Childs, Aileen Passloff, Yvonne Rainer and Arlene Rothlein – bringing with them a quality Kornfeld admired: 'they felt no need, as most actors did, to start artificially "emoting" the moment they stepped onstage.'[107] The idea was not to unify gesture, action, vocal mode or movement, but to set them in an evolving harmony. It was a sensation. Michael Smith wrote, 'Everything that happens has the casual inevitability of great art . . . it is a divine, slight moment of joy, it is a theatrical fountain of youth, and you should go drink.'[108] *What Happened* would win three Obies: for best musical production, distinguished direction and best music. In addition to finding their musical theatre métier, the Judson had something almost as important: a hit!

Drexler's *Home Movies* shares with Stein's text humour that ranges from the wry to the bawdy; a non-linear, parataxic structure; language that twists and turns, deploying rhyme, dialect and puns; deep affection for American popular culture; and an openness to multimodal layering of music, dance and vocalization. Like most of the counterculture, Drexler viewed the bourgeois, heterosexual family as corrupt and violent. Here, we have a missing father, presumed dead, who returns at play's end; mother and daughter hating each other in the bubbly tones of detergent commercials; the exaggerated, stereotypical sexuality of the beautiful black maid (played by Barbara Ann Teer) and well-hung delivery man; a nun and priest in the kitchen flirting with each other while they corral cockroaches. Carmines sustained that spirit with music described by Tallmer as 'an extraordinary and on every occasion on-target disbursement of torch songs, Latin motets, 1890s mother melodies, Minsky motifs, ragtime penances, barbershop chorales, spirituals'.[109] Kornfeld approached the whole thing as 'a kind of homage to burlesque', if not a 'burlesquing of burlesque conventions' that emphasized the ridiculous nature of bourgeois sexuality.[110] His sharp eye for personality and his commitment to expressive autonomy allowed him, in Michael Smith's words, to 'release and use the personalities of his performers'.[111] The 'casting of personalities' would become a trademark of the JPT.[112] *Home Movies* would prove almost as successful as the Stein production, transferring to the Provincetown Playhouse for a seventy-two-show run and winning Obies for Distinguished Play and Best Music and a Drama Desk-Vernon Rice Award nomination for Teer.

The 1963–4 season draws our attention to the importance of women to the JPT, which would produce María Irene Fornés's *Promenade* (1965), Rochelle Owens's *The String Game* and *Istanboul* (1965), Ruth Krauss's *A Beautiful Day* (1965), and, of course, multiple productions of Stein. Female performers played an equally significant role. Florence Tarlow and Crystal Field were among the many women who excelled in roles beyond the usual 'wives, mothers, and other male appendages'.[113] The JPT was also a welcoming home for the LGBTQ community. Carmines was bisexual, though, David Vaughan avers, 'he regard[ed] being bisexual as a fact of which he is neither particularly proud nor ashamed.'[114] In addition to its productions of work by Fornés, Paul Goodman, H. M. Koutoukas, Ron Tavel and others, the JPT pioneered the camp aesthetic, in both its arch (Tavel's *The Gorilla Queen* (1967)) and grotesque guises (Leon Katz's *Dracula: Sabbat* (1970)). However, unlike comparable productions at Caffe Cino or The Play-House of the Ridiculous, Judson's sense of camp was essentially spiritual in focus. Kornfeld saw *The Gorilla Queen* as 'excruciatingly funny ... [but] also filled with images of metamorphosis, change, transcendence. It's a tale of spiritual transformation and a meditation on loneliness, viewed through the icons of trash culture.'[115] Similarly, Kornfeld set Katz's play squarely in the sanctuary of the church and incorporated Christian and anti-Christian rituals, positioning the climax in the area normally occupied by the church altar.[116]

As with so many Off- and Off-Off-Broadway theatres, the Judson Poets' Theater was doomed by success. Larger audiences, productions transferring to Off-Broadway venues and opportunities for grants led it astray from its original mission. In response, Carmines declared the JPT 'amateur in the highest sense' and recommitted himself and his collaborators to 'the love of doing it, period'.[117] Carmines initiated a series of choral performances with as many as sixty performers, most recruited from the church's congregation. As Bottoms explains, 'The emphasis was now very firmly on community endeavor . . . and Carmines's pastoral role . . . became inextricably intertwined with his creative leadership, as he took charge of not only composing but also writing and directing these pieces.'[118] And, of course, they continued to mount productions of Stein's work, achieving a quality 'unrivaled in American theatre history for the consistency and complexity of its attention' to her dramatic texts.[119] After suffering a cerebral aneurysm, Carmines retired his position. In 1981, Judson Memorial Church ended the theatre programme, though its collaboration with Peter Schumann's Bread and Puppet Theater in the 1980s affirmed the idea that divinity can be achieved in theatre.

La MaMa

As with Off-Off-Broadway more generally, there are many ways to tell the story of La MaMa. It is a story of space – the basements, former sausage factories, Polish ruins, international theatre festival, the space transformed by the cowbell Ellen Stewart ('La MaMa' herself) rang before every performance, or the corners of the globe into which she travelled with her 'pushcart', as she called her theatre. La MaMa is a story of artists, the hundreds adopted by Stewart as her 'kids'. But, ultimately, the story of La MaMa is the story of Stewart. 'It is no accident', Cindy Rosenthal writes, 'that she and the theatre space are inextricably bound together, sharing the legendary name.' 'A uniquely compelling and charismatic . . . woman of color,' Rosenthal continues, 'Stewart seems to have tapped into the shaman's power. Audience members experience it at every La MaMa performance she attends.'[120]

But for a woman of colour attempting to create art and community beyond the reach of convention and commerce, Ellen Stewart's story is inevitably about space. La MaMa began in a basement boutique at 321 East Ninth Street. The plan was simple, if a bit daft: sell clothing during the day; stage plays at night. The basement fostered a core group (Jim 'Mr Jim' Moore, business manager; aspiring playwrights Paul Foster and Ross Alexander; director Andy Milligan; and Stewart's foster brother Fred Lights) who proved capable of making do as they made art. They established a fruitful relationship with Caffe Cino that provided both a support network and productions.[121] Most importantly, the basement palpably celebrated the playwright. Jean-Claude van Itallie, who would work closely with La MaMa, appreciated that the space 'imposed no aesthetic, made no artistic suggestions'.[122] Finally, the period in the basement initiated Stewart's running battle with municipal authorities, and with future New York mayor Ed Koch, in particular. In 1963, fire-code and zoning violations forced La MaMa to move.

The loft at 82 Second Avenue was more spacious, though no less vulnerable to city officials. The original plan was to run the theatre as a coffee house, but zoning wouldn't permit it. So, instead, she declared it a private club – La MaMa Experimental Theatre Club (or ETC). To attend, one purchased a membership, good for one week. Though La MaMa ETC would remain in this location for only a year and a half, it made itself a place for playwrights: James Eliason, Bruce Kessler, Robert Sealy, Ross Alexander and Paul Foster were produced there.[123] Foster's *Hurrah for the Bridge* (1963), *The Recluse* (1964) and *Balls* (1964) were, in Bottoms's estimation, 'accomplished, theatrically ingenious works' that established La MaMa ETC as a place for new voices and excellent theatre. At first blush, *Balls* is a prank or a Beckett rip-off. Two ping-pong balls swing back and forth while off-stage voices, ultimately revealed as the dead in a seaside cemetery, reminisce. But it sustained a tone of quiet, meditative humour for those willing to listen. It was at this theatre that Stewart began the tradition of ringing a cowbell to call the audience to attention and welcome them to 'La MaMa, dedicated to the playwright and all aspects of the theatre'.[124]

The move to 122 Second Avenue happened on 4 November 1964, immediately following the final performance of *Balls*, the audience picking up chairs, tables, coffee pots, paintings and, presumably, ping-pong balls to help Stewart avoid a third conviction for building code violations (a felony). To minimize trouble, the theatre's address and phone number weren't included in *Village Voice* listings, there was no sign indicating it was a theatre, and Stewart would perch at the entrance during performances, keeping an eye out for meddling municipal types intent on interrupting the goings-on. The larger, flexible space attracted playwrights fatigued by the makeshift stages of most Off-Off-Broadway venues. One of those was Lanford Wilson, whose *Balm in Gilead* (1965) 'represented a striking fusion of some of the different strands of experimental work that had been developing Off-Off-Broadway'.[125] Wilson's first full-length play, it portrays the amoral existence of heroin addicts, troublemakers, sex workers and a couple attempting to claim romance in a desperate – and equally amoral – attempt to escape their situation. Ultimately, plot and situation mattered less than the 'general large pattern' created by 'breakneck fast' dialogue and actors periodically rearranging the set to emphasize its theatricality and undermine the illusion of spontaneity.[126]

The three and a half years they spent at 122 Second Avenue allowed them to set down roots and spread branches. In 1965, they and the Caffe Cino earned a special citation at the Obie Awards ceremony. They incorporated in November 1965, and received 'not for profit' status in 1967, followed by their first cheques from the Ford and Rockefeller Foundations, enabling Stewart to purchase and renovate the property that would become their permanent home. In the autumn of 1965, La MaMa sent two troupes on tour to Europe, carrying with them plays originally staged at La MaMa (among them *Hurrah for the Bridge* and *American Hurrah*), as well as others associated with Caffe Cino (*Home Free!*, *The Madness of Lady Bright* and *Thank You, Miss Victoria*) and Theatre Genesis (*Birdbath* and *Chicago*). That tour, Rosenthal explains, blazed a network of intercultural exchange routes that would mature in the 1970s and 1980s, transporting American alternative theatre to the world and 'making it possible for performers, directors, musicians, choreographers, and playwrights from Western and Eastern Europe, Latin America, the Middle East, Africa, Asia, and Southeast Asia to present their work at [La MaMa's] theatres'.[127] Among the first to travel back to La MaMa were Jerzy Grotowski and Andrei Serban, the latter arriving in the US in 1970 with a Ford Foundation grant and passport both arranged by Stewart.[128]

As always, growth and success brought challenges. Stewart had managed to shake off fire inspectors, but tangled with Actors' Equity, resulting in a shutdown in the autumn of 1966.[129] After a highly successful European tour, Tom O'Horgan's star began to rise. He formed the La MaMa Troupe and convinced Stewart to rent a rehearsal space so they could develop a workshop process like the Open Theater's. The result was a physical exuberance and consciousness of time and rhythm that contributed to what Bottoms characterizes as a 'chaotic playfulness' and a capacity for creating a '"total theatre" of multilayered sound and image – sometimes jarringly abrasive, sometimes deliriously appealing'.[130] Their 1967 production of Rochelle Owens's *Futz*, a silly, occasionally menacing yet oddly romantic story of a farmer's love for his pig was hailed by Michael Smith as a milestone, 'a dense, fierce continuity of energy, fearless physical vitality, [and] primitively expressed vocalization'.[131] But that drew the attention of Joe Papp, who hired O'Horgan to retool *Hair*, a move viewed by some members in the troupe as a betrayal of spirit and a denigration of techniques developed over months.

In 1969, Stewart wheeled her 'pushcart' to its permanent home at 74A East Fourth Street, a space that held two theatres, a rehearsal space and workshop, and an apartment for Stewart. La MaMa expanded in 1974, purchasing a property two doors down, now known as the 'Ellen Stewart Theatre', which provided an additional theatre and a dormitory for visiting artists. Over the next four decades, Stewart's energy rarely flagged, even as her health declined. She guided the production of over 100 productions a year. She continued to provide, in Richard Schechner's words, 'both beginning and world-class artists the most important kind of support – rehearsal and performance spaces, advice but not interference, administrative and box-office staff, and unlimited enthusiasm'.[132] And her 'kids' grew in number, a truly global family of performers, directors, musicians, choreographers and playwrights. Though she is no longer here to make it sound, her bell continues to ring.

Though the Off-Off-Broadway movement was essentially over by the mid-1970s, as Bottoms notes, 'Its independent, underground spirit did not die out.'[133] Its attitude and techniques endure, marking it as 'one of the most significant influences on the subsequent evolution of contemporary American theatre.'[134] And if we take full account of the crossroads paved by La MaMa, the Black Arts Movement and the Latino theatre movement, we might make the case for something much bigger.

The residential theatre movement: Acorns and oak trees

As thrilling as *Marat/Sade* or a Judson Poets' Theater musical were and as heroic as the efforts of Ralph Cook and Ellen Stewart might have been, they frankly pale in comparison to the work done far from Manhattan by artists seeking nothing more than the opportunity to create high-quality theatre for their local communities. Indeed, in terms of enabling theatre artists to find professional opportunities, playwrights to find venues for their work, and audiences to get the chance to witness live theatre, the regional residential theatre movement was the most significant theatrical development of the 1960s. According to the Theatre Communications Group, in 2015 there were 1,750 professional, not-for-profit theatres in the US.[135] In 1961, there were twenty-three.[136]

What is 'regional residential theatre'? First, it simply means anything that doesn't happen in New York City. Second, it designates a particular kind of *relationship*, a theatre not only located but rooted in a community. Third, a regional residential theatre is a professional or semi-professional company that produces its own seasons, as opposed to presenting plays by touring companies.[137]

The regional residential theatre concept wasn't invented in the 1960s. There were, as Zeigler puts it, many acorns planted, though most 'in shallow soil with no assurances that they would grow into mighty oak trees'.[138] We recall the Little Theatre movement of the 1920s and the Federal Theatre Project (FTP) of the 1930s, but these failed to move beyond the aesthetic and commercial orbit of New York City. The taproot of the 1960s regional residential theatre movement leads to theatres like the Cleveland Play House (founded 1915), Chicago's Goodman Theatre (1925), Nina Vance's Alley Theatre in Houston (1949), Nina Fichandler's Arena Stage in Washington DC, the Actor's Workshop in San Francisco (1952), Joe Papp's New York Shakespeare Festival (1954) and, especially, Margo Jones's Theatre '47 (1947).

According to Zeigler, 'The modern American regional theatre began' with Theatre '47, and Jones was 'high priestess of the movement and a measure for all others'.[139] Her book *Theatre-in-the-Round* (1951) calls for 'the creation of a permanent repertory theatre with a staff of the best young artists in America'. This would be a 'playwright's theatre' that would nourish the development of an American dramatic canon and a distinctly American acting style. It would be an accessible theatre. It would be an ambitious theatre, 'a theatre to mean even more to American than the Moscow Art meant to Russia ... or the Old Vic to England.'[140] These were the gospel principles of the regional residential theatre movement – and, by the late 1950s, those principles had found dedicated disciples.

Unfortunately, the story of acorns and oak trees told by Zeigler and other historians ignores African American owned and operated institutions like Chicago's Pekin Theatre, founded in 1905 by Robert T. Motts, and Cleveland's Karamu House. Langston Hughes considered the latter a model for a theatre located in an African American community and producing work by African Americans.[141] Histories of regional resident theatre also erase the dozens of theatres founded by black Americans during the 1960s and the role they played in fostering playwrights like August Wilson, who cut his teeth at Pittsburgh's Black Horizon Theatre years before he worked with Lloyd Richards at Minneapolis's Guthrie Theater.

Concerns noted, we turn to W. McNeil 'Mac' Lowry, the Ford Foundation and the Theatre Communications Group.[142] Lowry became the director of the Foundation's arts and humanities programmes in 1957. Among his priorities was theatre and the desire 'to offer American artists a clean slate, to encourage them to build companies devoted to process; in other words, to foster the coming together of American directors, actors, designers, and playwrights and others beyond a single production and beyond commercial sanction.'[143] After a series of field studies, Lowry convened a conference in 1959 that, in his words, laid 'the first planks in the resident theatre movement'.[144]

From 1962 to 1971, Ford provided deficit-offsetting funds to sixteen regional theatres. Nine of these were founded prior to or simultaneous with the Ford initiative: Alley Theatre, Arena Stage, Oklahoma City's Mummer's Theatre, Stratford Connecticut's American Shakespeare Festival, UCLA's Theatre Group (later the Mark Taper Forum), Cincinnati's Playhouse in the Park, San Francisco's Actor's Workshop, Milwaukee's Fred Miller Theatre (later the Milwaukee Repertory Theater) and DC's Washington Theatre Club. Seven were started with Ford grants: Pittsburgh's American Conservatory Theatre, Actors Theatre of Louisville, Providence RI's Trinity Square, Baltimore's Center Stage, Seattle Repertory Theatre, Hartford Stage Company and Minneapolis's Guthrie Theater. Ford also provided start-up money for the Theatre Communications Group (TCG), a service organization designed to assist regional theatres with production, administration and personnel management and training. As Zeigler describes it, TCG's 'emphasis ... was always on structure and stability' and did not judge theatres on quality of production, but rather on 'adher[ence] to administrative rules and manners'.[145]

The Guthrie Theater

The 'first and prototypical oak tree' of the regional residential theatre movement was the Guthrie Theater.[146] In the autumn of 1959, world-renowned director Sir Tyrone Guthrie, Oliver Rea and Peter Zeisler placed a small story in the *New York Times* inviting cities to indicate interest in a 'permanent company outside the limits of Broadway'. They emphasized that 'such a company can be fully successful and useful only if its work can be closely identified with the name of the city where it plays.'[147] Minneapolis/St Paul was especially attractive: far from New York's 'social, economic, and psychological grip'; a vibrant cultural scene; and a youthful and energetic power structure composed of the sons and daughters of the wealthy capitalists who helped put the city on the economic map – what Guthrie called the 'generation of Heirs Apparent'.[148]

The new theatre was launched with the help of hundreds of volunteers who canvased the state, raising over $2.2 million. Designed by Ralph Rapson, it included a 1,400-seat theatre with asymmetrical thrust stage designed by Tanya Moiseiwitsch. The forty-seven-member company included veteran actors Hume Cronyn, Jessica Tandy and Zoe Caldwell, and newcomers Ellen Geer, George Grizzard and Joan van Ark, all working on an Equity contract negotiated by the newly founded League of Repertory Theatres. The first season featured a rotating repertory composed of Shakespeare's *Hamlet*, Molière's *The Miser*, Chekhov's *The Three Sisters* and Miller's *Death of a Salesman*. With 22,000 season ticket holders and $300,000 in advance sales, it was, as *Life* magazine named it, 'the miracle in Minneapolis'.[149] Yes, the Guthrie was unable to completely fulfil the ideals that motivated the movement. But it was, as Zeigler puts it,

> the second major turning point of the regional theatre revolution because it further legitimatized the movement and gave it national weight. It gave hope to all regional theatres that they too could become known on a national level, that the *Times* might soon cover their opening nights, and that actors like Hume Cronyn and Jessica Tandy might soon set aside a season for them.[150]

In 1966, *Variety* reported, 'For the first time since the heyday of stock, there are more professional actors working in regional theatre than in Broadway and touring productions.' Equally important, the 'extraordinary growth of the professional resident theatre and its stability have opened up a vast new market for experienced theatre people interested in steady work.'[151] Writing in 2015, Jim O'Quinn notes that thirty-two of the last thirty-four Pulitzer Prize-winning plays premiered at regional theatres:

> Once upon a time, professional theatre in America operated centrifugally: From the creative crucible of New York City, theatre spun out, via the touring circuit or the scattered outposts of resident stages, to the nation at large. Today that dynamic is precisely reversed . . . Broadway is . . . no longer the singular, or even the primary, font of the nation's theatrical creativity.[152]

The Black Arts Movement

In his 1968 manifesto, 'The Black Arts Movement' (BAM), Larry Neal called for a Black Nationalist movement that would ignite a 'radical reordering of the Western cultural aesthetic'.[153] He did not seek to reform existing institutions, create legislation or improve the enforcement of existing laws. Neal had no faith in white people or American democracy. He sought a revolutionary transformation that would enable African American political, economic and cultural self-determination. While the BAM did not achieve those goals, it was 'arguably the most influential U.S. arts movement ever'.[154] Starting in the early 1960s and picking up momentum in 1965, 'cultural groups, writers' and artists' workshops, theatres, bookstores, study circles, dance companies, schools, journals, small presses, reading series, galleries, museums, public art spaces sprouted up wherever there was a Black community, large or small.' These reached 'a grassroots audience of millions – an amazing achievement for such a politically and aesthetically radical cultural movement'.[155]

Though the artists, critics and audiences of the BAM celebrated all forms of art, drama and theatre were held in particular esteem. In 'The Revolutionary Theatre' (1965), LeRoi Jones (later Amiri Baraka) argued that theatre was not only a tool to 'force change; it should be change'.[156] Neal agreed, viewing it as 'perfectly consistent with Black America's contemporary demands. For [it] is potentially the most social of all the arts. It is an integral part of the socializing process.'[157] For Jones and Neal, theatre was an art of collective witness and affirmation, an effective method to counter racist stereotypes and model revolutionary transformation. In a more pragmatic vein, Harold Cruse, author of the influential *The Crisis of the Negro Intellectual* (1967), viewed the theatre as a keystone community institution that would materially support the struggle for cultural, political and economic independence.[158]

The Black Arts Repertory Theatre/School

Close on the assassination of Malcolm X in February 1965, Jones, Neal, Askia Touré, the brothers Charles and William Patterson, Clarence Reed and Sonia Sanchez founded the Black Arts Repertory Theatre/School in Harlem. Though the name suggested an exclusive focus on the dramatic arts, BART/S was much more than a theatre. It sponsored poetry readings, seminars and live jazz performances on flatbed trucks. BART/S lasted barely a year, the victim of mismanagement and violent internal conflicts. As Baraka described it later, 'Even while we did our heroic work of bringing the art, the newest strongest boldest hippest most avant of the swift dark shit to the streets, you could look up at that building and swear it was in flames.'[159] It was an inspiration. Neal writes, '[T]he Black Arts group proved that the community could be served by a valid and dynamic art. It also proved that there was a definite need for cultural revolution in the black community.'[160]

Ed Bullins and the New Lafayette Theatre

After Baraka (whose story is told by Susan Stone-Lawrence in her chapter in this volume), the most significant BAM playwright was Ed Bullins. Inspired by Baraka's *Dutchman* (1964) and *The Slave* (1964), he got thoroughly drunk one night in 1965 and wrote his first play, *Clara's Ole Man*, following that two weeks later with another (*How Do You Do?*), and another a week after that (*Dialect Determinism, or, The Rally*). They evince the diversity of theme and style that would characterize the *oeuvre* of this prolific and stylistically peripatetic writer. He teamed up with Baraka, Sanchez, Marvin X and future Black Panther party leader Bobby Seale to found the cultural and political centre Black House. However, clashes concerning the role of culture in the revolution led to X and Bullins being expelled, though Bullins would remain an ally. As Minister of Culture for the Black Panthers, he composed a series of remarkable agitprop plays that simultaneously stumped for the cause of Black Power while deconstructing the theatrical experience. *The Theme Is Blackness* (1966), for example, plunges its audience into darkness for twenty minutes, pressing them to explore their preconceptions about what exactly a 'Black theatre' is.[161]

In 1967, Bullins received an invitation from Robert Macbeth to join the New Lafayette Theatre (NLT). Its mission was simple: 'To show black people who they are, where they are, and what condition they are in.'[162] Like Bullins, Macbeth had no fear of controversy. The 1967–8 season featured African American Ron Milner's *Who's Got His Own*, but also the white South African Athol Fugard's *Blood Knot*. Further, Macbeth opened the theatre with the assistance of the Ford Foundation and made no secret about it. Black nationalists considered that treasonous.

When he arrived in Harlem, Bullins hit the ground running, though his first plays for the NLT wouldn't be staged there – it had been firebombed by one of those disagreeable nationalists. *Goin' a Buffalo*; *A Son, Come Home*; and *The Electronic Nigger* were staged at the American Place Theatre, winning Bullins a Vernon Rice Drama Desk Award. That was followed in 1968 by *In the Wine Time* at the NLT's new theatre. Set on a 'small side street of a large northern American industrial city in the early 1950s', *In the Wine Time* portrays the lives of Cliff and Lou Dawson, their nephew Ray and their friends (and rivals) who gather to drink, talk, love and fight on the stoop of their apartment building.[163] It is a work of exquisite, elegiac longing – Lou for Cliff's love, Cliff for Ray's success, Ray for a beautiful young woman who 'passed the corner every evening during my last wine time'.[164] And it is a perfect example of the innovative approach Bullins took to realism. Mance Williams explains, 'Bullins' technique was to allow his characters to tell their own stories, revealing to each other and to the audience only what they want to', thus providing insight into the lives of black people, but also affirming them as creators, as artists of speech, movement and imagination.[165]

Bullins was a dynamo. While with the NLT, he wrote two dozen plays, a novel and multiple essays. He ran the NLT's playwriting workshop, mentoring Martie Charles, J.e. [sic] Franklin, Neil Harris, OyamO, Sonia Sanchez, Ben Caldwell, Marvin X, Martha Charles and Richard Wesley. He was a prolific editor, producing annual issues of the NLT's house journal, *Black Theatre* (which at its peak boasted 8,000 readers), two drama anthologies and the 'Bible of the Black Arts Movement', the 1968 Black Theatre issue of *The Drama Review*.

He and Macbeth couldn't resist courting controversy. The NLT received bomb threats for their 1968 production of *We Righteous Bombers*. The play was advertised as the work of 'Kingsley B. Bass, Jr', murdered in the 1967 Detroit uprising. Not only was Bullins the author, but he 'borrowed' plot, characters and pages-long passages from Camus's *The Just Assassins*. In 1969, the NLT staged a season of ritual drama. Because they were 'conceived as uniting black people in their common struggle with racism', Macbeth and Bullins banned white reviewers.[166] That cost the Lafayette its Ford funding. The playwriting workshop was shut down in 1970 over disagreements about whether members could stage their plays with money from the workshop budget. Bullins clashed with Jules Irving of the Lincoln Center over a 1970 production of *The Duplex: A Black Love Fable in Four Movements*, which Bullins viewed as little more than an updated minstrel show.

But controversy didn't slow Bullins down or harm the quality of his work. He won an Obie for distinguished playwriting and the Black Theatre Alliance Award for the NLT's 1971 production of *The Fabulous Miss Marie*, a ruthlessly honest, undeniably loving portrayal of the black bourgeoisie on the eve of the Civil Rights Movement – and his best play. He received his first Guggenheim Fellowship that year and two National Endowment for the Arts playwriting grants in 1972, while also coordinating the playwriting workshop at the New York Shakespeare Festival. Though the New Lafayette closed in 1973, it was by no means the end of Bullins, who continued to write plays into the new millennium.

Concept East Theatre

In August Wilson's words, 'Detroit is to the Black Theatre movement what New Orleans is to jazz, because of the contributions' of the Concept East Theatre (CET).[167] Between 1960 and 1961, Woodie

King Jr, David Rambeau and Clifford Frazier scraped together just enough money to rent and renovate an empty tavern in the heart of black Detroit. At the time, there was no capital-B Black theatre in Detroit, no theatre that could provide steady opportunity 'for aspiring Black actors, writers, directors, costume or scenic designers to work in a professional theatre environment tailored to their experience'.[168] Concept East would change that, becoming 'the only people's theatre in the heart of the black community' of Detroit.[169] In its first season, the CET produced nine plays, including a dance piece, two plays by the Reverend Malcolm Boyd, and two by Ron Milner: his first play, *Life in Agony*, and an early draft of his masterwork, *Who's Got His Own*.

Like *The Warning – A Theme for Linda* (1969) and *What the Wine-Sellers Buy* (1973), *Who's Got His Own* is a work of conventional realism. It tells the story of a family in jeopardy. The father, a violent, intolerant patriarch, has died. As they plan the funeral, his widow and children are forced to confront the lies they have told about themselves, their feelings about the father, and their relationships, often intimate, with white people. It is a scorching experience, as emotionally exhausting as *Who's Afraid of Virginia Woolf*. Unlike Albee's play, Milner's ends on a note of commitment. Tim stands alone on the stage, speaking to his father's chair: 'Gone be a whole lotta' changes here, soon. Damn soon. Yeh. You jus' keep watchin', ol' man. They gon' know we come from a long line of men – and got a long line comin'. Damn right. Damn right. Damn right . . .'[170] Milner's realism, emphasis on the nuclear family and ultimate affirmation of virtuous black manhood made his play a hit in Detroit and in 1966 when it was produced at the NLT.

When it closed in 1978, CET had provided opportunities for dozens of theatre artists, affirmed the value of black culture and consciousness, and ushered onto the national scene actors and writers like S. Epatha Merkerson, Dorothy Robinson, Aku Kadogo, Ernie Hudson, Bill Harris and Tony Brown.

Barbara Ann Teer and the National Black Theatre

In a 1968 article for the *New York Times*, Barbara Ann Teer declared the American theatre fundamentally corrupt, an institution that, 'with all its cancerous, immoral perverseness, has consistently robbed the black man of his true culture and re-dressed him to suit its own capitalistic needs'. She rallied her fellow black Americans to 'begin building cultural centers where we can enjoy being free, open, and black, where we can find out how talented we really are, where we can be what we were born to be, and not what we were brainwashed to be, where we can literally "blow our minds" with blackness.'[171] Born in 1937 to a family of educators and community leaders, Teer excelled academically and artistically. Despite finding success as a dancer and actor – she worked regularly in theatre, television and film, winning a Drama Desk Award and several Obies – she grew increasingly disgusted by the racism of white producers and directors, the stereotypical roles and the tokenism of the white theatre scene. Embracing the idea that a Black theatre should reject the white Western aesthetic, model revolutionary change and materially support the cultural, political and economic independence of African America, she founded the National Black Theatre (NBT) in 1968 on 125th Street in Harlem.

The NBT differed from BART/S, the New Lafayette Theatre and Concept East in its holistic approach to Blackness. As James Smethurst describes it, the NBT 'institutionally and ideologically resembled Sun Ra's Arkestra more closely than a traditional theatre ... in that the communal NBT addressed every aspect of the black theatre worker's life rather than simply his or her skills'.[172] Teer's theatre was 'governed by a broad, mythic vision of the spectrum of African and African American culture'.[173] It 'presented no public performances during its first two years of existence, concentrating instead on the training of actors and technical staff as well as on the development of a viable, non-mimetic, non-European dramaturgy that would appeal to a broad black audience'.[174] In the meantime, the NBT developed into a vibrant cultural centre, hosting lectures, readings, concerts and symposia that featured the leading lights of African American art and culture.

Teer's holistic approach to theatre emphasized raising consciousness, intelligence and spirit. Theatre wasn't just entertainment but 'an exaltation and celebration of the universal life force.'[175] Performers and audiences came to the NBT to transform. Actors, called 'liberators', went through a process of 'decrudin', evolving through a rigorous process of self-examination and technical training from 'Nigger' to the highest stage of consciousness and capacity, 'The Revolutionary.' For audiences, NBT developed 'ritualistic revivals', described by Mance Williams as a 'a musical experience of overpowering creative force that entertains and transforms the audience'.[176]

In 1986, President Ronald Reagan proclaimed, '[T]he National Black Theatre is a cultural treasure. It is one of the 63 most important art institutions in America.'[177] The NBT is still going strong today, despite Teer's passing in 2008. Over its forty-year history, it has produced over 300 original theatre works, won dozens of AUDELCO Black Theatre Excellence Awards, and a Kennedy Center Drama Prize for the 2013 production of *Detroit 67*. The current 64,000-square-foot complex encompasses an entire city block of Harlem. And as is evident from its three core programmes – Theatre Arts, Entrepreneurial Arts and Communication Arts – the NBT remains committed to the Black Arts Movement's vision of theatre as a living archive of African American tradition; a powerful, evolving expression of beauty, strength and spirit; and a material force for the economic, political and cultural empowerment of black America.

Theatre collectives: The power of community

Historian Timothy Miller characterizes the 1960s as a time of 'communal fever' during which 'thousands upon thousands of new communities were established throughout the land ... founded by spiritual seekers of all sorts'.[178] Though their beliefs varied, those who lived in such communities believed that they needed to separate from the mainstream and the majority, that the individual was less important than the group, and that life needed to be lived according to explicit principles.

Given the inherently collaborative and social nature of the medium, it's no surprise that theatre artists were drawn to the idea of an 'intentional community', as Miller calls it.[179] Poet and playwright Paul Goodman had long argued that the primary responsibility of art was 'the physical re-establishment of community'.[180] He felt that the possibility of living an authentic, moral life in the US had been rendered impossible by consumerism, authoritarianism, militarism, patriotism and patriarchy. The radical theatre collectives of the 1960s wanted to change how art was made and the relationship between those who made art and those with whom they shared it. As James Harding and Cindy Rosenthal put it, for these groups, '[m]aking theatre was . . . as much an experiment in the practice of radical democracy as it was an exploration of the possibilities of theatre as such'.[181]

Wherever a stage could be found or built, there was probably a troupe nearby. So, it is impossible to include in this survey even widely recognized groups like Amiri Baraka's Spirit House, the San Francisco Mime Troupe, Bread and Puppet Theatre, the Open Theater (though Timothy Youker's chapter in this volume treats it in some detail) and the Performance Group, let alone lesser-known groups like Antioch University's Otrabanda, Latino street theatre groups of the early 1960s like El Nuevo Teatro Pobre de las Américas, or the many feminist collectives founded in the early 1970s.[182] (However, see above for discussion of the National Black Theatre and below for El Teatro Campesino.) But we can delve into two theatre collectives that exemplified the desire to change the form and process of theatre in order to make the world a better place.

The Living Theatre

By the time they settled their case with the Internal Revenue Service and packed their bags for Europe in 1961, Julian Beck and Judith Malina's Living Theatre (LT) had been creating bold, against-the-grain theatre for more than a decade. They met in 1943. Beck was a painter who favoured the bold lines of abstract expressionism, Malina an actor and director training with the famed Erwin Piscator, known for his work with Brecht. They shared a passion for poetry, collaboration and people, and a deep disgust with 'patriotic, triumphalist, middle- and upper-middle-class American culture'.[183] Their first works were heartfelt, no-budget productions of poetic drama by the likes of Auden, Eliot, Lorca, Stein and Williams. Beck would later write, 'Language is the key . . . The community is love . . . [and] rises and falls with language.'[184] The Living, as they called themselves, weren't trying to change the world, but simply to 'find a space where they could live and work as they pleased, opposing American society but content to make a separate peace'.[185]

As the decade progressed and the evils of Cold War capitalism intensified, the Living's rebellion grew more overt, both personally and artistically. They were jailed in 1957 for refusing to take shelter during an air-raid drill. And while they remained faithful to poetry, they also explored Brecht and Artaud. At their 14th Street theatre, they staged Jack Gelber's *The Connection* (1959), Brecht's *In the Jungle of Cities* (1960) and *Mann is Mann* (1962), and Kenneth Brown's *The Brig* (1963). And they hosted meetings, dance concerts, poetry readings and art exhibits.

Erika Munk views this period as one in which Malina and Beck sought 'a way to close the gap between their aesthetics and their politics'.[186] They were active politically, organizing the 1961 General Strike for Peace and creating street performances. But the link between art and politics was hard to find in the theatre. *The Connection* is about the tantalizing elusiveness of wisdom and harmony. A group of heroin addicts wait for the arrival of their dealer – their 'connection'. As they wait, they chat, squabble, complain, quietening down occasionally to nod along to the jazz improvisations of the Freddie Redd Quartet, who are waiting, too. The connection arrives, they shoot up, and continue to chat, squabble, complain and nod along until one of them collapses, overdosed. The audience waited with them. There was no curtain. The performers accosted audience members during the intermission for spare change. Like the heroin high, the unity of aesthetics and politics – the possibility of an intentional community – was elusive and ephemeral. But then there was the music. Bigsby sees the Redd Quartet's performance as a potent counterpoint to the community of addictive appetite for whom they perform: 'a powerful image of the way in which spontaneous individual freedoms can be merged into a form which is generated rather than imposed.'[187] *The Brig* was an even more harrowing examination of imposed form and the ruthless ruination of community. Set in a Marine Corps jail, it tells a simple, brutal tale. A new prisoner arrives, is taught the rules, is ordered to complete meaningless tasks and, when he inevitably fails, is beaten. A prisoner is released. Another prisoner suffers an emotional collapse. As Munk describes it, the fourth wall here 'was as absolute as *The Connection*'s was permeable'.[188] A chain-link fence, crowned by barbed wire, separated the audience from the stage. *The Connection* gave its audience ephemeral hints of *communitas*. *The Brig* suggested there could be no such thing in a world ruled by violence, hierarchy and patriarchy.

While community might have been elusive on their stage, the politics of the Living were entirely certain. Rosenthal marks *The Brig* and the ensuing conflict with federal authorities concerning tax evasion as 'an early highpoint in [their] commitment to creating anarchist and pacifist art'.[189] That commitment extended to the way they lived and created. The Living's tour of Europe was a time of 'collective creation' and the systematic devolution of authority and power away from Beck and Malina. *Mysteries and Smaller Pieces* (1964), for example, not only lacked an author, but, as Beck described it, 'opened the door to a subversive technique: the courage not to be cast in a role'.[190]

Mysteries and the other works composed during their exile – *Frankenstein* (1965), *Antigone* (1967) and *Paradise Now* (1968) – closed the gap between aesthetics and politics. *Paradise Now*, for example, consisted of a series of dramatic rituals that described a movement up a spiritual and political ladder – each rung a step towards insight and utopia. Between each ritual, the audience was invited to react or participate. Munk recalls a performance she attended at Hunter College as both idealistic and infuriating. She found, as many others did, that, despite their call for a political revolution, the Living failed to promote effective dialogue and promoted irrationality.[191] Bigsby sees it otherwise: 'The achievement of *Paradise Now* . . . did not lie in the banalities paraded as crucial insights but in the use it made of physical presence of the actors, the resources of the human voice . . . the creative power of those who could no longer behave as mere observers.'[192]

Regardless of how their work was received, the Living 'had evolved into a large and unruly tribe' that lived according to a shared vision of 'peaceful, non-violent revolution'.[193] Which is not to imply that everyone in the group agreed on the how that vision could be put into practice. When the company returned to Europe in 1970, it split into four subgroups, each with a different vision of how theatre could foment a radical transformation. Beck and Malina wanted to create art outside of conventional venues – streets, strikes, factories and favelas. Others wanted to pursue a spiritual path. What the Living achieved during the next four decades is a story for another volume.[194]

The Free Southern Theater

The Free Southern Theater (FST) was founded in October 1963, deep in Jim Crow territory, at the Tougaloo College Drama Workshop in Jackson, Mississippi. It was founded by three black activists from the North: Doris Derby and John O'Neal, field directors for the Student Nonviolent Coordinating Committee (SNCC), and Gilbert Moses, a journalist for the *Mississippi Free Press*, a weekly paper founded by Medgar Evers, who had been murdered that July. The three were shortly joined by Tulane University professor and *Tulane Drama Review* editor Richard Schechner. They intended to 'establish a legitimate theatre in the deep South', 'provide opportunity for black involvement in the theatre', 'evolve social awareness into plays written for a black audience', and 'open up a new area of protest in the . . . struggle for freedom'.[195] However, they also wanted 'to develop a form that is unique to black people, like blues and jazz'.[196] This desire for a Black Aesthetic intruded a fundamental contradiction into the FST's vision and praxis. Annemarie Bean explains, 'The civil rights movement gave the Free Southern Theater its purpose, but not its aesthetic, because there was no aesthetic of integration.'[197] As with the Living Theatre, these questions didn't just concern theatre, but how decisions were made, whether white people should be involved, whether white people should attend performances.

Like everybody else involved in the struggle against white supremacy, the three white and five black members of the FST were in constant danger. This was one of the reasons they were so closely connected with the SNCC. Schechner explains, 'This was not like a conventional touring show; we needed to be immediately welcomed into the community . . . Without the movement, we wouldn't have had the physical wherewithal.'[198]

On their first tour of rural Mississippi and Louisiana in 1964, they presented Martin Duberman's *In White America* (1963) and Beckett's *Waiting for Godot* (1952), plays written by white men. Civil rights activist Fannie Lou Hamer saw clear connections between *Godot* and her community: 'Every day we see men dressed just like these, sitting around bars, pool halls, and on the street corners waiting for something!'[199] But though both plays provided emotionally resonant drama and, in the case of Duberman's play, historical consciousness, neither came 'out of the black southern experience'.[200] The shortcomings of liberal reform and non-violent action were becoming evident, as were reasons to reconsider the presence of whites in the company, which some thought hampered communication and organization. So, while their 1965 summer tour included two works developed collectively in community workshops – *The Jonesboro Story* and *The Bougalusa Story* – there were too many unresolved issues. The company suspended operations in the autumn.

The FST moved to New Orleans, hoping to gain organizational and financial stability. This angered some members. What about their mission to bring theatre and consciousness to poor rural blacks?[201] And there was the question of Blackness. Moses and actor Denise Nicholas advocated a 'non-integrationist direction' and the resignation of all white company members.[202] This didn't immediately happen, though Schechner resigned in March 1966, replaced as chairman of the board of directors by Tom Dent, a New Orleans native and veteran of New York's Umbra poetry group. Their production of Moses' *Roots* in 1966 signalled the abandonment of integration as ideology and aesthetic in favour of 'the goals of black subjecthood of the Black Arts Movement'.[203]

Roots was first presented at an abandoned supermarket in the Desire section of New Orleans, one of the poorest and blackest districts of the city. Bean explains that the play neither evokes the sympathy of spectators nor provides positive, propagandistic visions of blackness. Instead, the two characters, Dot and Ray, 'an old Negro couple, to be played by young actors', are presented in absurd fashion. One wears a gas mask, the other a bag.[204] They live a life of comic, desperate repetition. Ray picks cotton every day, even when it's out of season. But rather than undermining a sense of Black consciousness and pride, the absurdity of their situation emphasized, as Bean describes it, 'their ability to be constant, loyal, and silently present'.[205]

The year 1966 was a turning point for the FST. They presented plays by white writers during their 1966 and 1967 tours, and whites would still remain in the company. But by 1968, they were presenting material by black writers exclusively. In the 1970s, they provided support to the growing community of small theatres in New Orleans. And they continued to produce work by black Americans, including O'Neal's series of one-man shows featuring his character Junebug. However, despite Rockefeller and Ford Foundation grants and the support of Arthur Ashe, Harry Belafonte, Julian Bond and other African American celebrities, the FST was unable to thrive, closing its doors in 1980.

Gay and queer drama: Out of the closet

In the 1960s, to be anything but heterosexual in America was to be closeted or in danger. Though all agreed that the closet should be a choice rather than a necessity, there were disagreements in the LGBTQ community about what strategies best served that goal – the liberal, tie-and-jacket path of polite pickets and gradual reform or the radical path of glitter-bombed, high-kicking provocation? The drama and theatre produced by the LGBTQ community during the decade reflected those different perspectives, as did representations of non-heterosexuals by heterosexual playwrights (see Susan Stone-Lawrence's chapter on Baraka in this volume).

Though of course there were lesbian playwrights – Megan Terry and María Irene Fornés coming to mind – their sexuality was generally not a subject of conversation or art, even in friendly places like the Judson Poets' Theater. It was in the 1970s that lesbian playwrights, lesbian plays, and theatres and theatre collectives like It's Alright to be a Woman Theatre (1970) and At the Foot of the Mountain (1974) affirmed the diversity of women's sexualities.

Drama out of the closet

As we've discussed, the Caffe Cino was a seedbed for all kinds of '[p]layful experiments in theatrical form and content'.[206] The Cino was also a safe space. Playwright Robert Patrick called it '[a] home for people chewed up and spat out by a cookie-cutter culture that tries to make us all one shape ... A steamy sanctuary'.[207] It wouldn't be right to characterize the Cino community as 'out'. As elsewhere, queerness in the Cino was a matter of code and nuance rather than manifesto or march. The plays about queer people staged at the Cino – say, Doric Wilson's take on the Oscar Wilde sodomy trial, *Now She Dances!* (1961) – kept the politics of queerness at a carefully calibrated distance. But that all changed after the premieres of two plays now considered the inaugural texts of gay theatre – 'defined as being by, for, and about uncloseted gay people' – works that 'revolutionized how gay characters could be represented theatrically'.[208]

Upon its première in 1964, Lanford Wilson's *The Madness of Lady Bright* quickly became one of the most beloved plays of the Cino clientele, running for over two hundred performances. Leslie Bright was 'not only open, but boisterously defiant'.[209] This was no small step, even for Wilson. 'I believe the idea of the play shocked me,' he told an interviewer. 'I called Neil Flanagan [a Cino regular] and said, "What can we do at the Cino? I mean can we just do anything? Could we, for instance, do a play about a screaming queen?"'[210] As loquacious as she is, Leslie is a tragic figure, an ageing drag queen in an apartment 'tucked like a pressing book with mementos, post cards, letters, photographs, pictures of men from body-building magazines'.[211] As she reminisces, she can't help but compare herself to the movie stars and bodybuilders whose pictures paper the walls. And while she savages herself as an ugly freak, she affirms her power to construct herself as she deems fit and fabulous. That same bathos is evident in her desire for a home. 'No one is home', she weeps. 'All of you are never ever, ever at home.'[212] However, as Darren Blaney notes, because the Cino was such an intimate space, 'the conflict stemming from Leslie's homesickness was perhaps symbolically resolved in the minds of the viewers'. Packed shoulder to shoulder in the tiny, glittering café, the audience not only 'sympathized with Leslie, [but] drew together in a moment of collective feeling.' In that moment, Joe Cino's theatre became 'the home for which she pined'.[213]

Robert Patrick's two-hander *The Haunted Host* opened later that year. Though it too features an overwrought drama queen, it confronts homophobia and self-hatred more lustily. Jay's lover Ed has killed himself. Jay's friend has hired a handsome (though straight) hustler (and aspiring writer) named Frank to shake him out of his malaise. There's some edge in Patrick's choices: the pairing of bullying hustler and mincing queen was a cliché in gay culture.[214] But Jay stands toe to toe with Frank. Blaney points to the way that Jay controls their conversation:

Jay Tell me, Frank, how long have you been heterosexual?
Frank What do you mean? I've always been heterosexual!
Jay Started as a kid, huh? Tsk-tsk. Tell me, do you think one of your teachers, or possibly even one of your parents might have been heterosexual? Do you think that might have been the reason you—

Frank (*Interrupting*) All right, all right, just shut up, okay?
Jay Okay, Frank. Gee, I didn't think you'd be so touchy about it. Wow. *(Brief pause)* Tell me, is your play heterosexual?
Frank (*Snappy*) You mean does it sleep with plays of the opposite sex?
Jay (*Delighted to have drawn wit*) Oooo. Getting off, ain'tcha? Well, you know, you people do tend to let heterosexuality creep into all your work.[215]

Moments like these, Blaney argues, 'contributed to a nascent sense of "gay liberation" by promoting visibility, destabilizing normative social constructs, providing a template for individual self-empowerment, and exposing oppression'.[216] When Jay kicks Frank out of his apartment at the play's end, it is a sign of his renewed confidence in his art and friends. When Frank goes out of the door, so does the straight mind.

As durably popular as *The Madness of Lady Bright* and *The Haunted Host* were, they were mostly a coterie phenomenon. Mart Crowley's *The Boys in the Band* brought gay drama itself out of the closet. Opening at the Off-Broadway Theatre Four in April of 1968, it ran for more than one thousand performances and was adapted into a 1970 film by William Friedkin. It remains a controversial text. But that's to be expected of a play that has been called the *Uncle Tom's Cabin* of gay literature.[217] When Emory – one of seven gay friends, one attractive male prostitute and a straight acquaintance gathered to celebrate Harold's birthday – leans out of a window and asks, 'Who do you have to fuck to get a drink around here?' he is loud and proud, but also plays to stereotypes of the 'swishy' gay man. But what especially irked viewers then – as it can do now – is the devolution of the party into a battle royal of queens viciously attacking each other and, in the process, exposing their unrelenting hatred for themselves as gay men. Edward Albee thought it a disaster: 'I went to see *Boys in the Band* several times, and more and more I saw an audience there of straights, who were so happy to be able to see people they didn't have to respect.'[218] But Tony Kushner sees the matter differently: 'When I was writing [*Angels in America*], the freedom to write [the character of Roy Cohn] as big and theatrically as I wanted to comes in part from plays like *Boys in the Band*. *Boys* was so risky and outrageous, you feel there is this very dangerous game being played where the stakes are high, the tensions are very real.'[219] However we judge the play, there is no doubt that it is exhilarating, laugh-out-loud funny (Michael: 'There's one thing to be said about masturbation: You certainly don't have to look your best.'[220]) and moving.

The Theatre of the Ridiculous

If, in the early spring of 1966, you were seeking the most outrageous, dangerous and unrepentantly 'out' theatre, you found it at the Play-House of the Ridiculous production of *The Life of Lady Godiva*. It began with a spotlight on Mother Superviva – John Vaccaro, who also directed – 'dressed in an English *fin de siècle* type nun's habit, with brimming hood, white bib, and blue gown', holding a 'long cigarette holder', recumbent on a chaise longue under a gaudy Tiffany lamp.[221] 'Nudity', she tells us, tasting every syllable, 'is the quintessence of essence, though it is sickrilegious [*sic*] to say so.' A spotlight is cued, falling on a 'sheer curtain with peacock feather and tendril designs' through which we see a 'wooden white horse' upon which sits Peeping Tom (Charles Ludlam), in a taxi-driver's cap and jacket, coin-changer hanging lasciviously, and Lady Godiva, 'a buxom beauty ... dressed in a Gibson Girl gown with lace collar coming up to her chin'. After holding the tableau for an exquisite moment, Godiva cries, in 'an exaggerated British accent', 'Did you say *big*? Why, my dear, it was one of the pillars of civilization!'[222] What followed was, in Bottoms's words, 'a misassembled jigsaw puzzle of smutty puns, vulgar aphorisms, and random pop cultural references, in which characters frequently change accents, change costumes, and even repeat whole sequences of each other's dialogue without explanation'.[223]

Though anarchic, Tavel's play was incisively satirical, taking on both the pornographic gaze of straight culture and the salacious expectations of the audience. This acidly arch attitude towards theatre itself was a legacy of the time Tavel spent as a set assistant for Jack Smith and as writer at Warhol's Factory, where he scripted improvisatory scenarios for Warhol's 'superstars.' (One of those, Mario Montez, appeared in *Godiva*, Tavel's *Screen Test* (1966) and Ludlam's *Big Hotel* (1967).[224]) While at the Factory, Tavel began to explore a 'disturbing new twist on [the] conjunction of the blatantly fake with the apparently "real"'.[225] It was all a bit too much for 'It Girl' Edie Sedgwick, who got him kicked out for good.

That disturbing twist was evident not only in the scripts written for the Ridiculous company by Tavel, Ludlam, Jack Smith and Kenneth Bernard (who joined the group in 1968), but in the approach to rehearsals and directing taken by Vaccaro. Vaccaro had no respect for actors; they were 'cowards and egocentrics'.[226] Like Warhol, he preferred those who had mastered the art of everyday theatricality. As Penny Arcade, a performer who joined the company in 1967, puts it, 'Anybody could be in the Playhouse of the Ridiculous theatre. It was all street stars. Homosexuals, heterosexuals, lesbians – it didn't matter, nobody cared about those things. It was all outsiders.'[227] That didn't mean Vaccaro treated them kindly. Photographer and Factory habitué Leee Childers recalls 'megalomaniac fits – throwing things, screaming obscenities, and humiliating these teenage kids in his theatre company who were already on speed, sleeping on someone's floor, and didn't have money for a McDonald's hamburger. He frightened them, and it frightened him, I think that's why he'd let it go so far sometimes.'[228] He would goad the actors during performances, altering the script as mood and sensibility deemed fit. Bottoms writes, '[I]f the company's history was defined in part by ongoing creative tensions between its members, these conflicts seem – in themselves – to have been perversely fundamental in shaping what appeared on stage.'[229]

Those tensions couldn't be maintained for long. Tavel left in March 1967, tired of watching Vaccaro take liberties with his scripts, the breaking point when Vaccaro insisted Tavel cut two thirds of the script for *Gorilla Queen*. Vaccaro called it an 'insult to the people in the group'; its densely layered puns and polyphonic entendres killed improvisation. The success the play enjoyed under the direction of Lawrence Kornfeld at Judson Poets' Theater (1967) is a point in Vaccaro's favour. Its campy boisterousness was enthusiastically embraced by the downtown crowd, including *New York Times* critic Dan Sullivan.[230]

A similar criticism could be levied against Charles Ludlam. When Ludlam was introduced to Vaccaro, he had given up on acting. But Vaccaro adored his 'pasty, corny, mannered, campy' style. In *Godiva* and *Screen Test*, he was incandescent. In the latter, he entered in a wig designed by Salvador Dalí, declaring that he was 'Norma Desmond'.[231] Tavel remembers the moment as 'brilliant'.[232] For Ludlam, it was when he discovered the singular beauty of 'teetering on the edge of being a man and a woman'.[233] Ludlam's genius on stage (most notably in *Camille* (1973)) was matched by what he wrote on the page. He composed over two dozen plays before his death in 1987, including *Big Hotel* (1967), *Conquest of the Universe, or When Queens Collide* (1968), *Stage Blood* (1975) and *The Mystery of Irma Vep* (1984). Childers argues, 'Ludlam followed theatrical traditions and used a lot of drag. People felt very comfortable with Charles Ludlam . . . They never felt embarrassed. But John Vaccaro was way past that. Way, way past that. John Vaccaro was dangerous.'[234] Ludlam, on the other hand, thought Vaccaro was far too timid when it came to nudity and homosexuality – and entirely inconsistent in his focus on gay themes.[235]

The Moke-Eater (1968) was one of a pile of scripts Kenneth Bernard sent to Vaccaro just as the company was falling apart. Vaccaro was smitten. Gerald Rabkin writes, 'In contrast to Tavel's arch verbalism and Ludlam's distinctive blend of travesty and tradition, Bernard brought to the Ridiculous a nightmare imagination rooted in the grotesque.'[236] An extended riff on Tennessee Williams's *Camino Real* (1953), *The Moke-Eater* follows Jack, a strapping, straight, white American salesman, as he enters a sinister village looking for someone to repair his car. As he waits, he is forced to participate in a series of violent rituals, culminating in the entrance of the Moke-Eater, 'the amorphous manifestation of the destructive energy of the play', which proceeds to devour an elderly man. Jack manages to escape, only to have his car break down in the next town – identical to the one he just left.[237] It was a pitiless evisceration of masculinity, the American dream and actor Bruce Pecheur, who played Jack. Declaring that he had 'gone beyond Artaud', Vaccaro directed the other actors – including Pecheur's wife Sierra Bandit – to do everything they could to truly frighten him.[238] The cruelty was all too real.

Asian American theatre

Esther Kim Lee notes that the word 'Asian American' didn't exist until 1965 – nor did 'Asian American theatre'.[239] The word was coined by historian Yuji Ichioka to semantically unify Americans descended from the many regions of Asia and replace racist terms like 'Oriental'. Ichioka was part of the Asian American Movement, whose origins are generally traced to the San Francisco Bay Area of

1968, which witnessed the founding of the Asian American Political Alliance at Berkeley, the student strikes at San Francisco State University and the tenant resistance movement at the International Hotel.

The East West Players

Asian American theatre preceded all that. Lee traces it to the founding of the East West Players (EWP) in 1962 and their first production, an adaptation of Akira Kurosawa's film *Rashomon*. To understand the significance of EWP, we must take stock of the ways that 'the imagined Asianness that appeared on theatre stages' since the earliest days of the US 'had little to do with the realities of Asia or Asian immigrant communities in the United States' and often strengthened racist attitudes towards them.[240] Stereotypes abounded: the childish, pidgin-speaking 'Chinaman'; the scheming, opium-smoking villain; the innocent, tragic lotus blossom; the femme fatale dragon lady. The 1950s saw a string of Broadway hits featuring sympathetic Asian characters: *The King and I* (1951), *The Teahouse of the August Moon* (1953), *The World of Suzie Wong* (1958), *Flower Drum Song* (1958) and *A Majority of One* (1959). In all of these, the major roles went to white actors. Asian Americans were never cast in roles where ethnicity didn't matter. Yellowface was considered perfectly acceptable into the 1970s – long after blackface was relegated.

Hollywood actors James Hong and Beulah Quo were done with 'the "ching chong" Chinaman bit' and all too aware of the lack of opportunities for Asian American actors.[241] With El Huang, Mako Iwamatsu, George Takei (later of *Star Trek* fame) and others, they decided to produce *Rashomon* – a popular play and an opportunity to experiment with a 'fusion of Eastern and Western cultures'.[242] To honour that fusion, they named themselves the 'East West Players'. Despite tensions between the film and theatre actors, *Rashomon* was performed on 3 April 1965, to positive notice and, with several cast changes, ran for another six weeks at the Warner Playhouse.[243]

In 1967, EWP became a non-profit company, formed a board of directors, and began what they later called the 'church basement period', named for the space they used in exchange for doing maintenance work. As Lee tells it, the EWP used this time to develop their signature style. The fourteen productions of this period included 'five Western plays, four Japanese classic pieces in English translation, three original plays, and one collaborative piece from the acting workshops'.[244] These were presented in three styles. 'Intercultural interpretations of canonized Western plays in either Western or Eastern settings' included Carlo Goldoni's *The Servant of Two Masters* (1745), set in Chinatown. 'Japanese classics in traditional settings but performed in English' included Junji Konishita's *Twilight Crane* (1949) and *Lady Aoi* (1954) by Yukio Mishima. Original plays included Soon-Tek Oh's play about the Korean War, *Martyrs Can't Go Home* (1967), and his adaptation of the Chinese novel *Camels Were Two Legged* (1967). By 1971, the EWP had invented 'a new version of Asianness that was ... intercultural and artistic'[245] and fit for film and television.

Ford Foundation funding enabled them to sponsor an annual playwriting contest that, in its third year (1971), was won by Frank Chin's *Chickencoop Chinaman* and Momoko Iko's *Gold Watch*. This signalled an emerging wave of Asian American drama, but it was also a time of challenge for the East West Players: they lost their basement space, were unable to find an affordable replacement, and Mako was in Japan. But they made it through the crisis as a stronger group and EWP continues to this day to promote the development of Asian Pacific performance, create opportunities for Asian and Pacific Islander artists, and provide education and mentorship to all aspects of the theatrical arts.

Oriental Actors of America

Political organization complemented artistic excellence. The Oriental Actors of America was founded on 3 March 1968, to banish yellowface, promote 'greater use of Oriental talents' and protest against *Here's Where I Belong* at the Billy Rose Theatre, in which a white actor played a Chinese servant.[246] There was plenty of picketing to be done, unfortunately, including a 1968 revival of *The King and I* at New York City Center in which eight of nine Asian parts were cast with whites (and all but one understudy was white) and the Repertory Theater of Lincoln Center's 1970 productions of *Lovely Ladies, Kind Gentlemen* and *Good Woman of Setzuan* and their 1972 production of Edward Bond's *Narrow*

Road to the Deep North. While we shouldn't overstate the impact of the OAA – they were generally ignored – Lee argues that their persistence and the suit they filed in 1972 (*Sab Shimono et al vs. the Repertory Theater of Lincoln Center*) opened a place for artists like Ping Chong and Frank Chin and created an environment that made possible Stephen Sondheim's *Pacific Overtures* (1976), the first Broadway show to feature an all-Asian American cast, including the roles specified as non-Asian.[247]

The efforts of East West Players and the Oriental Actors of America bore fruit in the early 1970s with the founding of San Francisco's Asian American Theater Company, Seattle's Northwest Asian American Theatre and New York City's Pan Asian Repertory Theatre. Asian American theatre continues to evolve today as conceptions of identity, culture and theatre are explored, debated and, most importantly, staged.

Latino theatre

Latino communities in the US have a long and robust theatre history.[248] But the 1960s was an especially significant decade. It was then, Ramón H. Rivera-Servera writes, that Latino 'theatre movements consciously assumed a relationship to Latino group identity, culture, and politics that resulted in the development of an artistic and scholarly legacy that continues to influence Latino theatre practice in the present.'[249]

El Teatro Campesino

In 1965, Southern California witnessed what Nicolás Kanellos calls a 'spontaneous appearance ... of a labor theatre in the agricultural fields, under the directorship of Luis Valdez, and its creation of a full-blown theatrical movement that conquered the hearts and minds of artists and activists throughout the country'.[250] Valdez was born in 1940 to a family of Mexican American farmworkers, exposing him to the brutal labour conditions of Californian agriculture, the traditions of Catholic ritual, and traveling tent shows (i.e. *carpas*).[251] He wrote his first full-length play – *The Shrunken Head of Pancho Villa* (1964) – while a student at San Jose

State College. After graduation, he joined the San Francisco Mime Troupe, working briefly with them before travelling home to Delano to support the farmworkers' strike. With Agustín Lira, he organized a small group of workers as El Teatro Campesino (ETC) to create entertaining, propagandistic theatricals. Their early works were brief skits (*actos*) staged on flatbed trucks in the fields. They were, in Jorge Huerta's words, 'simple but not simplistic',[252] drawing upon Brecht, *commedia dell'arte* and the *carpa* tradition of improvisatory, pungently drawn, audience-engaged satirical humour. Both the shows and the company's internal social dynamics were guided by an ethos of cooperation and mutual support.[253] The company took their *actos* across the country, galvanizing support for the strike and inspiring the development of like-minded troupes in communities and college campuses across the country like Teatro de la Esperanza in Santa Barbara, La Compañía de Teatro de Alburquerque, Su Teatro in Denver, Teatro Dallas and Borderlands Theater in Tucson.[254]

Their travels exposed the ETC to broader issues affecting Latinos. They explored new subject matter and refined their aesthetic – called *rasquachismo* – an 'aesthetics of the underdog'[255] that deployed verbal tricks and 'improvisational physicality' to poke fun at the elite and valorize the creativity of the marginalized and oppressed.[256] The published *actos* only hint at their wicked, incisive mischief. *Los Vendidos* was first staged at a Brown Beret rally in East Los Angeles in 1967. Miss Jiménez has come to Honest Sancho's Used Mexican Lot and Mexican Curio Shop on the behest of Governor Reagan, who hopes to expand his appeal by adding a typical Mexican American to his administration. Passing over a farmworker, a 1950s-style gang member and a revolutionary, she settles on the tie-and-jacketed, college-educated, ambitious Eric. In a surprise twist, Eric revolts, with his fellow robots – now revealed as human beings – to join him, steals the money, chases away the woman, and leaves with the salesman, now revealed to be a robot.[257]

The ETC's work evolved as the national Latino movement gained momentum. In 1968, they developed a puppet play, *La conquista de México*. It is no less satirical than *Los Vendidos*: it retells the history of the Spanish conquest of Mexico, putting gringo Texan accents in the mouths of the conquistadors and Spanglish in the Indians'. But it also gestures towards broader historical and political ideas, suggesting that contemporary Latinos are a colonized community and that unity is required to defeat white supremacy. In 1968, the ETC met the Mexico City company Los Mascarones at the international Théâtre de Nations festival in Nancy, France. To their mutual surprise, they discovered shared techniques and concerns and recognized the need to collaborate in the future. In 1971, the ETC moved to San Juan Bautista in Northern California to initiate 'an intense collective human and aesthetic exploration' they called 'theatre of the Sphere'.[258] They worked with Peter Brook in 1973 in an eight-week experimental workshop, performed in 1974 at the Quinto Festival in Mexico, and continued to expand and evolve their style.

Valdez was also finding his own, independent path. While the ETC toured *La Carpa de los Rasquachis* (1972), he began work on a play about the infamous 1943 Sleepy Lagoon murder trial of seventeen Mexican American youths. *Zoot Suit* premiered at Los Angeles's Mark Taper Forum in 1978 and ran for almost a year. It later transferred to Broadway, the first play by a Mexican American to be staged there. The work of El Teatro Campesino continues to this day as, in its own words, 'an ensemble theatre company committed to generating social change through the arts . . . creating new works to explore the changing multicultural face of the Americas'.[259]

Latino theatre in New York

The outsized reputation of Valdez and El Teatro Campesino has tended to overshadow the work done by other Latino playwrights, poets and theatre companies, particularly in New York City. The history of Latino theatre in the city begins with the 1953 production of *La carreta* by Puerto Rican writer René Marqués. The play dramatizes the story of Puerto Rican immigrants who travel from the countryside to a San Juan slum and then to the US. It affirmed the value of 'serious dramatic material based on the history, language, and culture' of working-class Puerto Ricans.[260] The production's director, Roberto Rodríguez, and actress Miriam Colón founded El Nuevo Círculo Dramático the next year, producing work into the early 1960s. In 1964, Joe Papp's New York Shakespeare Festival started including Spanish-language productions, and in 1965, *La carreta* was revised Off-Broadway, starring Colón and a young and incandescent Raúl Juliá. Colón would go on to found the Puerto Rican Traveling Theatre (PRTT) company in 1967. Sponsored by Mayor John Lindsay's Summer Task Force Program and the Parks Department, they performed in both English and Spanish across the city, finding a permanent home in the Theatre District, where it continues to stage works both new and old.

The early 1960s witnessed an exposition of improvisational street theatre that drew upon Latin American people's theatre traditions to entertain, inform and agitate.[261] These were generally short-lived, with the exception of Teatro Cuatro. Originating on the Lower East Side on Fourth Avenue (hence the name) under the direction of the Argentinean Oscar Ciccone and Salvadorean Cecilia Vega, it allied with Valdez and the Chicano theatre movement in the late 1960s and became officially associated with Papp's Shakespeare Festival in the late 1970s, organizing biennial festivals of Latino popular theatre. Though Ciccone and Vega became managers of the Papp organization's Latino productions, Teatro Cuatro carried on, becoming a repertory company located in East Harlem.[262]

In general, Latino theatres of the 1960s understood identity in geopolitically broad terms. For example, Teatro Repertorio Español produced classical Spanish plays and works by contemporary playwrights from across Latin America. An exception to this trend was the Nuyorican movement, a cultural movement of New Yorkers of Puerto Rican descent that came out of the Lower East Side, East Harlem and the South Bronx. Like the theatre of the Black Arts Movement, which emerged out of the same urban cauldron of pride, desperation and creativity, Nuyorican theatre was diverse in form and setting, ranging from collectively composed and performed street theatre to conventional drama produced on Broadway. Colón's Puerto Rican Traveling Theater was a vital influence, for sure, but the 'Nuyorican' aesthetic found its full poetic development in the hands of the performance-poets of the Nuyorican Poets' Café, founded in 1973 by Miguel Algarín, Miguel Piñero, Bimbo Rivas and Lucky Cienfuegos. And it found its dramatic paragon in Piñero's *Short Eyes*, a prison drama that premiered at Joe Papp's Public Theater in 1974 and was awarded both an Obie and New York Drama Critics award.

Conclusion: Into the new millennium

We return again to the scene we drew at the start of this chapter, a scene in which who made and watched theatre, what counted as theatre, and where theatre was made and encountered expanded and transformed. If we wish to understand the legacies of 1960s theatre, it is in that very diversity. Should we wish – and I think we should – for a similar expansion and transformation in our own times, we would be wise to recognize that theatre depends on community, and community is at its most creative when it is committed not to art, not to politics, but to the exploration, critical appraisal and strengthening of community itself. In that respect, theatre is at one and the same time the seed and fruit of our collective longing for something beyond ourselves.

3

Edward Albee

Helen Shaw

Introduction

In a 1966 interview in *The Paris Review*, Edward Albee spoke to the composer (and Albee's former lover) William Flanagan about becoming a playwright. 'When I was six years old, I decided, not that I was *going* to be, but with my usual modesty, that I *was* a writer,' said Albee. 'So I started writing poetry when I was six and stopped when I was twenty-six because it was getting a little better, but not terribly much.' A teenaged Albee turned his hand to fiction ('an incredibly bad novel'), yet, he went on wryly in his interview with Flanagan, 'I was still determined to be a writer. And since I was a writer, and here I was twenty-nine years old and I wasn't a very good poet and I wasn't a very good novelist, I thought I would try writing a play, which seems to have worked out a little better.'[1]

The one-act play Albee wrote at twenty-nine was *The Zoo Story*, a cannonball into international waters. Those waters were already roiling: in 1958, the year of *The Zoo Story*'s three-week, headlong composition, Genet published *The Blacks*, Ionesco published *The Killer* and Beckett premiered *Krapp's Last Tape*. Eugene O'Neill's *A Touch of the Poet* represented serious literary efforts in New York that year, and it was doing a brisk business on Broadway at the Helen Hayes Theatre amid the surrounding hullaballoo of musicals like *Bells Are Ringing* and *My Fair Lady*. Meanwhile, though, Off-Broadway was thirsty for American work of appropriate heft and weight: in 1958, *The Village Voice* refrained totally from giving its Obie Award for Best American Play. Clearly, audiences associated the explosive, experimental instinct with European movements, and, indeed, Albee's one-act itself first went onstage not in the US but in Germany, in a 1959 production at Berlin's Schiller Theatre Werkstadt.

In 1960, though, New York finally saw *The Zoo Story*, a terrifying yawp that would force American theatre's attention down to the Village and into the minds of bohemian outsiders. The work wasn't a *total* break with tradition: the play appeared at the Off-Broadway Provincetown Playhouse, where the experimental work of O'Neill, Susan Glaspell, Djuna Barnes and others had been presented in the 1920s, and any more recent theatregoers who had been drinking deep from Tennessee Williams and Thornton Wilder would have recognized Albee's modernist touches. Too, *Zoo Story* appeared on a double bill with the Irish Beckett's *Krapp's Last Tape*, giving it a companion with an impeccable intellectual imprimatur. Yet it was still this – Albee's first produced play – that fired the starting pistol for a period of radical American writing. After *Zoo Story*, more and more US writers dared to stand toe-to-toe with European Absurdist and existentialist works. Through his example and his direct activism, Albee helped spur a golden age of Off-Broadway experiment, beginning the process which made him that strange (and now much-missed) hybrid: the revolutionary statesman.

Over the years, other experimental American playwrights of his stature either loosed their hold on theatre as a form (as did Sam Shepard), moved towards film (as has Tony Kushner), or were left in the ghetto of critically acclaimed, commercially ignored geniuses (see María Irene Fornés). Albee alone managed to bestride Broadway like a colossus, while *also* needling the world like an angry gadfly. In 1996, when Bill Clinton presented him with a Kennedy Center Honor, the President toasted him: 'Tonight our Nation, born in rebellion, pays tribute to you ... In your rebellion, the American theatre was reborn.'[2] Can any other US dramatist claim the same dual crown? Somehow, even in the face of success – that dangerous killer of the transgressive instinct – Albee's fractious, provocative spirit continued undaunted, infusing even his late plays. He was a shark swimming in the mainstream, and it may be that we must thank him both for the thriving experimental US playwriting scene and *also* for whatever niche still exists on Broadway for adventurous American drama.

Dawn of the 1960s

In Albee's early plays, we find an animating rage, a delight in language and disguise, and the sense that the playwright has just prepared the hangman's noose for anything the audience might hold sacred. He comes by that apostate's tone honestly: at age twenty, he had already abjured two American saints, the Nuclear Family and the Dollar. After a tumultuous childhood in Larchmont, New York – including dismissals from one academy, one military school and Trinity College – Albee permanently left his wealthy but chilly home, leaving behind adoptive parents he would dramatize in a variety of unhappy ways. Rejecting his family's astonishing resources (his father was a multimillionaire heir of the Keith-Albee vaudeville empire), Albee lived cheaply downtown in New York's Greenwich Village with his partner, the aforementioned composer William Flanagan, and worked as a telegram delivery boy for Western Union.

Despite such bohemian surroundings, artistic accomplishment had thus far eluded the twenty-nine-year-old Albee. His poetry had failed to get the mark of approval from Thornton Wilder: in an encounter at the MacDowell Colony in New Hampshire, the great playwright had read Albee's poems and then gently encouraged him to turn towards plays. The encounter had an impact; later, Albee would mythologize the conversation, adding in the delicious (and spurious) detail that Wilder had set his poems adrift, page by page, in a New Hampshire lake. We can also hear some echoes of Wilder's interest in metatheatre and parable in Albee's *oeuvre* – think of the 'instructive stories' in *Who's Afraid of Virginia Woolf* and *The Zoo Story*, and the delight in Greek tragic structure in 2002's *The Goat, or Who Is Sylvia?*

Albee's mid-1950s efforts – all unpublished – were by his account unwieldy, and in his essay 'On the Zoo Story'[3] he claims only the three-act sex farce he wrote at age twelve as a forerunner to the breakthrough one-acts of 1958–60. If he doesn't recognize the writer before 1958 as truly 'himself', perhaps he's right about those earlier efforts. Albee said, 'The thing that happened with *The Zoo Story* was that I suddenly discovered myself writing in my own voice.'[4] The shock of that new voice would galvanize a decade *mirabilis* in which Albee would alternate between Tony Award-winning hits and critic-savaged flops, contribute to the re-establishment of American playwriting and derail the narrative common among commentators of the time that the age of giants (O'Neill, Williams, Miller) had passed forever.

The Zoo Story

In *The Zoo Story*, Peter, a passive, repressed publishing executive in his forties, reads a book on a bench in New York's Central Park. Jerry, a man 'no longer handsome', who evinces 'a great weariness',[5] enters. 'I've been to the zoo,' Jerry announces, though Peter doesn't look up. 'I said, I've been to the zoo. MISTER, I'VE BEEN TO THE ZOO!' (15). From this point on, Jerry will command Peter's attention, dragging him into an exchange that will transgress all boundaries. In the duo, we see two decades crashing into each other. Peter is the 1950s husband, the always conforming 'man in the gray flannel suit'. Jerry is the post-beatnik outsider, who will do violence in the cause of truthful communication.

Jerry's assault on Peter's privacy begins normally enough, and Peter's recognizable discomfort is, at first, comic. Jerry conducts an awkward conversation; Peter responds, constrained by politeness and respect for social order:

Jerry	I bet you've got TV, huh?
Peter	Why yes, we have two; one for the children.
Jerry	You're married!
Peter	(*with pleased emphasis*) Why, certainly.
Jerry	It isn't a law, for God's sake.
Peter	No . . . no, of course not. (17)

Of course, Peter *does* rather feel that marriage, his two daughters, his two cats and his two parakeets conform to the law of the land. He is an honest citizen, and he does not question his enfranchisement. Still, his curiosity piqued by Jerry's constant references to 'what happened at the zoo' (33), Peter cannot quite pull himself away from this increasingly fraught encounter.

Soon, though, Jerry's responses begin to expand. In contrast to the tidy Noah's Ark life Peter describes, Jerry paints his own rooming house as a ring of hell guarded by his slatternly landlady and her snarling dog. All the city's unwanted live there (the 'colored queen who wears a kimono and plucks his eyebrows', a Puerto Rican family), but it is the dog ('malevolence with an erection') that tortures Jerry (29).

By this point, the play feels like a gospel (a meeting on the road to Damascus, perhaps), and the story of the dog is framed, by Jerry himself, as a parable. 'THE STORY OF JERRY AND THE DOG,' Jerry announces portentously to Peter. The dog hates Jerry, constantly tries to bite him and, at first, Jerry tries to woo him with raw hamburger. When the ploy doesn't work, he tries poison. A thrilling, hypnotic account ensues – the rat-poison leaves the dog near death's door, but after it recovers, the two have an encounter, a rare moment of understanding. Man and beast stare, rapt, into each other's faces.

> **Jerry** It's just . . . it's just that . . . (*Jerry is abnormally tense now*) . . . it's just that if you can't deal with people, you have to make a start somewhere. WITH ANIMALS! (*Much faster now, and like a conspirator*) Don't you see? A person has to have some way of dealing with SOMETHING. If not with people . . . if not with people . . . SOMETHING. With a bed, with a cockroach, with a mirror . . . no, that's too hard, that's one of the last steps. (27)

Jerry's trial with the dog foreshadows his dealings with Peter. After having extended the hand of kindness (by telling the story) and having been met with Peter's incomprehension and disgust ('I DON'T WANT TO HEAR ANYMORE'), Jerry tries cruelty.

Jerry begins pushing Peter off his park bench. Roused to a pathetic territorialism, Peter fights back. Jerry pulls a knife and tosses it at Peter's feet. Peter snatches it up. Jerry rushes forward and impales himself on the blade. Whatever has happened at the zoo will have to remain a mystery, and all we ever know is that it had to do with communication, hard-won through bars. Jerry's lunge is a deliberate act of self-sacrifice and, as the play ends, the quasi-realistic situation has become saturated with ambiguity and metaphor.

Albee, who flirted with a conventional life in advertising before his dash for the Village, said that the pair were his two selves, 'the two Edwards, the one who lived back in Larchmont, and the one who lives in New York City'.[6] Critics have seen even greater symbolism in the couple: Rose Zimbardo, in her landmark essay

'Symbolism and Naturalism in Edward Albee's *The Zoo Story*', sees the pair as Jesus (Jerry) and Saint Peter (Peter). She finds deep significance in Jerry's taking 'the subway down to the Village so I could walk all the way up Fifth Avenue to the zoo. It's one of those things a person has to do; sometimes a person has to come a very long distance out of his way to come back a short distance correctly.' This, she says, points to 'Christ's descent into Hell and Resurrection which are necessary before the Redemption can begin'.[7] Her reading has influenced later critics, though Albee gave such analyses short shrift. Certainly, salvation and the transmutation of matter – vegetable into animal – operate all through the text, and the last words of the play are Jerry's ironic imitation of the horrified Peter: 'Oh ... my ... God.'[8] In later plays, like *Tiny Alice* (1964) and *A Delicate Balance* (1966), Albee's metaphysics does contain a sort of demiurge – or, at the least, a terror that shapes man's ends. But *Zoo*'s Biblical parallels may also point to Albee's formal influence by writers like T. S. Eliot, Wilder and Genet, all of whom hung their dramatic works on sturdy religious armature.

In *The Village Voice* review of *The Zoo Story*'s double bill with *Krapp's Last Tape*, Jerry Tallmer noted the similar 'voltage' of the two plays – both, he says a 'brief tour-de-force'.[9] Yet while he calls *Krapp's Last Tape* the 'most amazing piece of incidental writing of the last decade', Tallmer seems concerned that *Zoo Story*'s electricity is random lightning: 'He knows ... how to bring you up deftly to the edge of your seat. Whether he has anything less sick than this to say remains to be seen.'[10] Famously, the first round of mainstream reviews sent Albee's producers into despair, but the bill was rescued by raves from *The New York Post* and other afternoon papers. Audiences responded enthusiastically, Albee won an Obie, and the play continued to play in New York theatres in eight different productions for the next six years. Perhaps most importantly, it crashed like a wave over the other artists of the period. John Guare talks, in rapturous tones, about seeing the Albee/Beckett evening: 'The production ended. I was in a daze. I was lost but I was home. I was at sea but not drowning. The future had finally shown up. Whatever theatrical revolution had started in England and France had finally hit America.'[11] *The Zoo Story* galvanized Guare's dreams of becoming a playwright – and we see its warm shadow also lying across other writers, like David Mamet, Sam Shepard, Amiri Baraka, Ed Bullins, Mac Wellman and Adrienne Kennedy.

The Sandbox and *The American Dream*

The dam had burst. The next year, 1960, saw three more of Albee's one-acts: *The Death of Bessie Smith*, *The Sandbox* and *FAM and YAM*. Where *The Zoo Story* used allegory and parable to critique conformity, these other short pieces levelled direct attacks on American hypocrisies. Albee's membership in the fraternity of Absurdist masters was by now assured, and his status as figurehead of the anti-establishment was cemented when, in 1961, Senator Prescott Bush (George W. Bush's grandfather) took to the Senate floor to call *The Zoo Story* 'filthy' and protested the play's upcoming tour to Argentina.

Two of the 1960 one-acts are rarely revived: *FAM and YAM* (a nasty satire about a Young American Playwright interviewing a Famous American Playwright, who is easily recognizable as the Broadway realist William Inge) and the cinematic, lacerating *The Death of Bessie Smith*. The latter communicates a sense of Dostoyevskian horror, and it may be this claustrophobic quality that has condemned it to Albee's back catalogue. It did, however, do one thing that would reverberate all through Albee's career – it was his first collaboration with Alan Schneider. Schneider had directed *Krapp's Last Tape* in the Provincetown Playhouse double bill as he was Beckett's 'chosen director' in the United States. After his partnership with Albee formed, it proved durable. Schneider directed every one of Albee's New York premieres that decade except for 1967's *Everything in the Garden*.

Albee's avowed favourite of all his plays is one of the one-acts from that year: *The Sandbox*. Self-deprecatingly, Albee once said, '*The Sandbox*, mind you, is only eleven minutes long. And you can't make too many mistakes in eleven minutes.'[12] Asked to write a one-act for a Spoleto festival and still in the middle of crafting his longer work *The American Dream*, Albee poached his *Dream* characters and put them into a Beckettian tableau, where they continued to bicker and fret. The playlet is dedicated to his maternal grandmother, who lived with the Albees in their Larchmont mansion and was a humorous, acerbic, welcome presence in young Edward's life. In fact, Albee loved his two grandmothers in a way he could not bring himself to feel about his parents. His maternal grandmother was a bright spot from a grey upbringing, and his paternal grandmother willed him a legacy of $100,000, which manifested as an allowance of $25 a week.

Mommy, Daddy, the Young Man and the Musician all gather. Mommy and Daddy soon lug Grandma onstage to plunk her into a miniature 'beach'; namely, the titular sandbox. Most of the play is spent waiting for Grandma to die. Per the stage directions,

> At the beginning of the play, it is brightest day; the Young Man is alone on stage, to the rear of the sandbox, and to one side. He is doing calisthenics; he does calisthenics until quite at the very end of the play. These calisthenics, employing the arms only, should suggest the beating and fluttering of wings. The Young Man is, after all, the Angel of Death.[13]

In the play's quick eleven minutes, Mommy and Daddy just have time to lug Grandma to the sandbox, where she behaves both like an infant banging her toy shovel and as a cynical truth-teller. Condescending Mommy and passive Daddy wait for her to die. Eventually, the Young Man, a glowing blonde hunk who hasn't been given a name yet by 'the studio' (91), is dispatched to bring her to her rest. The play is fully metatheatrical in its humour. The Musician has been brought in to pretty-up the transitions (Grandma has to ask him to quieten down so she can shout over him), and the rather dim beefcake, who bestows Death's kiss on her brow, doesn't know enough not to break character.

> **Grandma**   I . . . I can't move . . .
> **Young Man**   Uh . . . ma'am; I . . . I have a line here.
> **Grandma**   Oh, I'm sorry, sweetie; you go right ahead. (94)

The Sandbox is a case of surprising parallel construction: at almost exactly the moment that Beckett was composing *Happy Days*, in which an oblivious married couple live out their post-apocalyptic days in a mound of earth, morally vacant Mommy and Daddy were dumping Grandma in her sandbox-cum-grave. And much of Albee's later work plays in this same sandbox: the ruthless *drama à clef* is, for all its bizarre touches, based on Albee's own parents, and angelic figures recur in all his deathwatch dramas, including *All Over* (1971) and *Three Tall Women* (1991).[14]

The American Dream (1961) was Albee's second hit Off-Broadway, doing well in its premiere at the York Playhouse, then continuing to play in other downtown theatres. Looked at from a distance, Albee's deliberate homage to Ionesco can seem strained (a review of the 2008 revival called it 'laboriously symbolic'[15]), and the bitterness about the American family is less bracing in a theatre now so used to such plays. Albee's anti-sentimental attitudes have sunk so far into the theatrical water table that it's difficult to remember that they were once startling and fresh. In this play, Albee slashes out something almost primitivist by the standard of his other material, but its fauvist emotional colours provide a bright underlay for his later work. Certainly we will see the same 'mother' appear – always called Mommy by an uxorious husband, always devastatingly cold towards the child who wants her love. She stalks through *Three Tall Women* and *A Delicate Balance* (1966), but it's later that Albee develops the bitch-mother character into something both more and less monstrous.

The American Dream continues Albee's jeremiad against the moneyed American family – his own – again pitching another hypocritical Mommy and Daddy against another poor Grandma, the play's lone candid voice. (Albee's own grandmother, his ally in an unsympathetic childhood, had died in 1959, but his parents hadn't seen fit to inform him.) Albee transformed the hunky angel of *The Sandbox* into the titular character, a bland personification of American hopes, who shows up at the door only to be immediately absorbed into the hungry family. This time, though, Albee includes a shadow version of himself, Mommy and Daddy's absent 'bumble', the adopted baby who couldn't live up to expectations. Albee claws at a number of sacred American monoliths here – but the most damning indictment is his equation of Mommy's shopping trips with her long-ago visit to the adoption agency.

The 'play in one scene' begins with Mommy and Daddy waiting in their parlour, irritated, for some sort of service call. Mommy fills the time with her outraged account of trying to buy a hat to her specifications, while Daddy attends with half an ear. Earlier that day, while wearing a newly purchased 'lovely little beige hat', Mommy has run into the chairman of her women's club, who tells her that the hat in question is not beige but wheat-coloured. Mommy marches back into the store to protest.

> **Mommy** And I made an absolutely terrible scene; and they became frightened, and they said, 'Oh madam; oh, madam.' But I kept right on, and finally they admitted that they might have

made a mistake; so they took my hat into the back, and then they came out again with a hat that looked exactly like it. I took one look at it, and I said, 'This hat is wheat-colored; wheat.' Well, of course they said, 'Oh no, madam, this hat is beige; you go outside and see.' So I went outside, and lo and behold, it was beige. So I bought it.
Daddy (*Clearing his throat*) I would imagine that it was the same hat they tried to sell you before.
Mommy (*With a little laugh*) Well, of course it was!
Daddy That's the way things are today; you just can't get satisfaction; you just try.
Mommy Well, *I* got satisfaction.[16]

The elevation of 'satisfaction' over any other state seems to be at the heart of Albee's critique of consumerist smugness. 'Satisfaction' comes from the sense that service, even obeisance, has been rendered. It's a thin, meaningless thing. Mommy doesn't mind that the store's 'replacement' hat is the same hat, because, in forcing the salesman to lie, she has imposed her will on truth itself – the perquisite of the rich.

The couple's long-awaited guest is Mrs Barker, chairman of the women's club and volunteer at the Bye-Bye Adoption Agency. Despite her brusque manner, she cannot figure out why she has been summoned, and the characters themselves seem confused about her presence. They even seem confused about whether she is one or multiple. 'Speak to them, Grandma' (112) commands Mommy, but Grandma cannot see 'them' at first, though the moment of blindness passes. This sense of a person as a kind of swarm increases our understanding that we're watching symbolist satire. In one body, there will be many.

Emasculated Daddy, never entirely attentive, is aroused by the visitor. He manages to emerge from his passivity and terror only to descend further into immaturity. At Mommy's invitation, Mrs Barker removes her dress and Daddy erupts with excitement: 'I blushed and giggled and went sticky wet' (115). Still, he does perform one vital function: just as in Albee's parents' marriage, the Daddy supplies the wealth. Mommy informs Daddy, 'I have a right to live off of you because I married you, and because I used to let you get on top of me and bump your uglies; and I have a right to all your money when you die' (106).

Grandma, though, has made no such bargain, and Mommy is eager to shuttle her off, threatening her constantly with the nursing home. Just as their counterparts do in *The Sandbox*, Mommy and Daddy have plans to evict Grandma from the home, from *life* if possible. Grandma enters with a pile of boxes, a mysterious collection of 'some old letters, a couple of regrets ... Pekinese ... blind at that' (143) which will be all she'll take with her when the 'van' comes to take her away. Her last gift to the household is the explanation, to Mrs Barker, of why she has been summoned – she must answer for the botch her agency has made of Mommy and Daddy's long-ago adoption of a 'bumble; a bumble of joy' (127). We learn that the adopted son hasn't survived. The parents have cut off all the bumble's disappointing parts (a nose that went up in the air, a 'you-know-what' that it wanted to touch), and it has died. Just as with the wheat-coloured hat, Mommy wants 'satisfaction', but, with the bumble dead, she hasn't got her money's worth.

The strange answer to the family's frustration arrives when a Young Man knocks at the door, looking for work. As he says himself, he's a 'clean-cut, Midwest farm boy type' (133), and he's heralded by an ecstatic Grandma as the American Dream. As fortune would have it, he is the lost bumble's missing twin, and he has suffered strange pains in the night that correspond to the family's mutilation of their adopted son. As the play moves towards conclusion, the piece might seem to be an outlier in Albee's *oeuvre* – at first it does not seem to end with any sort of death. But then Grandma steps in front of the curtain and away from the world of the play, sending the Young Man in to greet the family, which rapturously accepts him as the bumble's replacement. Is he, like the identical beige hat, simply the same bumble again? As with the hat, it doesn't matter. Mommy and Daddy's attitude towards reality must stand, and the curtain goes down at Grandma's gentle promptings. She remains outside, forgotten, departed, but – as with so many of Albee's dying figures – somehow beatific.

In a preface, Albee calls the play an 'examination of the American Scene, an attack on the substitution of artificial for real values in our society, a condemnation of complacency, cruelty, emasculation and vacuity; it is a stand against the fiction that everything in this slipping land of ours is peachy-keen.'[17] The furious Albee was also exorcising the demons of his own childhood – the overbearing mother, near-silent father, his own tortured sense of not measuring up. Some of the most outrageous elements of *Dream*, the ones taken for satire, come directly from life: Mel Gussow's biography quotes Albee as saying, 'They bought me. They paid $133.30.'[18]

It was also in 1961 that the first edition of Martin Esslin's influential book *The Theatre of the Absurd* came out, a powerful piece of critical cataloguing that detailed the perceived project of writers like Albee, Beckett, Vian, Genet, Ionesco and Pinter. Esslin took the term from Camus's *The Myth of Sisyphus*: 'The divorce between man and his life, the actor and his setting, truly constitutes the feeling of Absurdity.'[19] Esslin selects for his taxonomic group those playwrights who 'express the senselessness of the human condition and the inadequacy of the rational approach by the open abandonment of rational devices and discursive thought'. Where the Existentialists laid out their complaints as carefully as court briefs, the Absurdists would meld matter and form, unhinging language and using 'a pattern of poetic images',[20] like Beckett's ashcans or Ionesco's rhinoceros heads, to strike through an audience's complacency.

Esslin included Albee on the strength of *The Zoo Story*, and by the third edition (1980), Esslin was able to expand on Albee's position in this overwhelmingly European tradition. He writes:

> The convention of the Absurd springs from a feeling of deep disillusionment, the draining away of the sense of meaning and purpose in life, which has been characteristic of countries like France and Britain in the years after the Second World War. In the United States, there has been no corresponding loss of meaning and purpose. The American dream of the good life is still very strong.

In discussing *The American Dream*, Esslin points to the way that Albee attacks American optimism via the 'oily glibness and sentimentality of the American cliché', and formally, certainly, this is the crux of the play's linguistic charms. It may also be that it took a writer born into the American 'dream of the good life' to communicate its emptiness – and that it was not formal concerns but personal ones that ushered America's theatre into a new Absurdist ferocity.

Albee himself addressed his inclusion in Esslin's catalogue in his customarily tart way, writing an essay for the *New York Times*

Magazine in February of 1962 called 'Which Theater is the Absurd One?' In this, Albee distinguished between the book ('excellent') and the grouping action, because, as he complains, labels 'can be facile and can lead to nonthink on the part of the public'. Some of this is his native contrarianism, since he goes on to discuss the genre and the author with real warmth and admiration. He cites Esslin's summation of the Absurdist project: 'For the dignity of man lies in his ability to face reality in all its senselessness; to accept it freely, without fear, without illusions – and to laugh at it.' And Albee responds: 'Amen.'[21]

Here we come, though, to Albee's real critical point – that, in 1962, Broadway 'panders to the public need for self-congratulation and reassurance and presents a false picture of ourselves to ourselves'. This coddling pseudo-art, he notes, is the *real* absurdity. He isn't specific about which plays are the boulevardier 'Broadway realism' he decries; surely hits like *A Thousand Clowns* and *A Shot in the Dark* were not to his taste. But he ends on an optimistic note, calling for a new theatre that includes the courage of the avant-garde, while allowing for the post-Chekhovian realism that he considers appropriate for American tastes. If we can put aside the 'standard responses' that ask for entertainment rather than challenge, he promises, 'You may no longer be content with plays you can't remember halfway down the block.' These are the words of someone ready to storm the barricades. Albee wasn't planning to stay safely downtown, and in October of that same year he was on Broadway himself.

Who's Afraid of Virginia Woolf?

Who's Afraid of Virginia Woolf? (1962) enjoyed the sort of success that has had only the rare subsequent American parallel. This intimate, eviscerating quartet looms over all Albee's *oeuvre*, indeed over the American theatre. When *Woolf* arrived on Broadway in 1962, critics were divided. Audiences, on the other hand, were near-unanimous. It won the Tony, the New York Critics Drama Circle Award, and it nearly won its playwright a Pulitzer, though the nominating committee's recommendation was ignored by a frightened supervisory board that deemed the play outrageously vulgar. Albee himself bemoaned a theatre in which Broadway success overshadows all other types – in another *New York Times* piece published before the show's opening, Albee asked why, 'if this play is a success, it will be a more important success'[22] than any other project. And yet Albee's own accounts of his career wax and wane with his presence uptown. He wasn't content to have a European and Off-Broadway career, and in the 1960s he opened fully seven plays on Broadway.

In more ways too, *Woolf* stands apart from all of Albee's other work. *Woolf* totally veils its Absurdist core with its realistic elements. 'It gives an illusion', said Albee, 'of being a completely naturalistic play, observing all the proper time barriers and everything.'[23] Despite a rigorously structured series of dualities, an enacted rite (George says a Latin mass) and a nearly Maeterlinckian journey from night into dawn, the play willingly lets us read all its symbols as realistic, and the most aesthetically conservative theatregoer can find himself at home in Martha's living room. In New Carthage, visitors are unwelcome, but not otherworldly (as they are in *The Lady from Dubuque*). The pulsating dread emerges from lives lived incompletely, rather than some mysterious outer dark (as it does in *A Delicate Balance*). This surface realism so wooed audiences that they would take a long time to forgive later journeys away from the conventional. Those who kept expecting another red-blooded *Woolf*ian slugfest would sulk at Albee's constant experimentation, some until *The Goat*, forty years later.

All but its most vicious detractors allow that *Woolf*'s humour makes it delicious. Richard Schechner, in his infamously homophobic critique, 'Who's Afraid of Edward Albee?' calls the play full of 'morbidity and sexual perversity which are there only to titillate an impotent and homosexual theatre and audience', but even *he* admits the comedy crackles.[24] *Woolf* is long for Broadway, running over three hours, but its constant battles create a sense of headlong velocity. In his essay 'Which Theater is the Absurd One?' Albee may have specifically asked that audiences put 'aside your standard responses'[25] to enjoy difficult work, but here, by making the thing deliriously consumable, he does most of the work for us. Critics have been divided on *Woolf*'s genre, so that some, like Elizabeth Phillips, catalogue it as Absurd, while others, like Marvin Plotinsky, think of it as realistic psychological drama, and Albee's dramaturgical coyness lets both camps have a case. Matthew Roudané sees it as unique in yet another way, as Albee's most 'affirmative play,' finding in it a spirit of resolution and a language that 'privileges a grammar of new beginnings, however uncertain such new beginnings may prove to be'.[26]

The night we spend with history professor George (forty-six, 'thin; hair going gray') and his wife Martha ('a large, boisterous woman, fifty-two, looking somewhat younger') does not seem, at first, as though it could possibly end in any such 'new beginning'. The play's first act, 'Fun and Games', starts as one event is ostensibly ending: the couple stumble in, soused from a faculty party, and George, for one, is ready for bed. But Martha, daughter of the president of the college and filled with boozy *noblesse oblige*, has invited over a younger couple – Nick and Honey, the new biology professor and his meek little wife.

When their guests arrive, Martha and George's customary sparring becomes more dangerous than usual: Martha mentions their son (offstage, to Honey), which infuriates George. Martha also reveals that George, groomed to take over his department, and then the college, by her father, simply didn't have the stuff. Martha needles him for his 'bog'-like inertia:

Martha You see, George didn't have much . . . push . . . he wasn't particularly . . . aggressive. In fact he was sort of a . . . (*Spits the word at George's back*) . . . a FLOP! A great . . . big . . . fat . . . FLOP!
(*CRASH! Immediately after FLOP! George breaks a bottle against the portable bar and stands there, still with his back to them all, holding the remains of the bottle by the neck. There is a silence, with everyone frozen. Then . . .*)
George (*Almost crying*) I said stop, Martha.
Martha (*After considering what course to take*) I hope that was an empty bottle, George. You don't want to waste good liquor . . . not on your salary.[27]

The second act, 'Walpurgisnight', accelerates still further – the act is named for a witches' sabbath, so there's drinking, music, seduction, chaos – with Honey spinning woozily before she goes dashing for the bathroom. George attacks Martha about her body, her age ('Martha had her daguerreotype in the paper once') and her sexual appetites, claiming, 'helpfully', that she makes him sick. It closes with Martha's departure to bed with the ambitious Nick, who has confessed his disinterest in his own wife (whom he married during a false pregnancy) and his lust for advancement.

In the constant jockeying for power, George seems defeated, but the third act, 'The Exorcism', brings him back for a pyrrhic victory. Nick's impotence ('Him too fulla booze,' says Martha) has rendered the attempted infidelity ridiculous, and George – fed up with the illusions of his festering marriage – announces that his and Martha's 'sunny-Jim' is dead. George intones a Latin mass for the dead as Martha furiously struggles against the news. Nick and the audience realize, almost in the same moment, that the child so rapturously described has been a fiction, dreamt up years ago as a shared weapon in the couple's combative love. Once George has ripped away his marriage's compensatory mechanism, Nick and the bewildered Honey leave quietly, their own illusion-filled marriage shaken. The evening's long, long series of games, evasions, transgressions, confessions and near-runs with alcohol poisoning culminates in rapprochement. 'It will be better,' offers George. 'It will be ... maybe' (128). Though the plot has been described as the breakdown of a marriage, it actually seems to be the portrait of its mending. Roudané is right: the final lines of the play are exquisitely gentle:

> **George** Are you all right?
> **Martha** Yes. No.
> **George** (*Puts his hand gently on her shoulder; she puts her head back and he sings to her, very softly*)
> Who's afraid of Virginia Woolf,
> Virginia Woolf,
> Virginia Woolf.
> **Martha** I ... am ... George ...
> **George** Who's afraid of Virginia Woolf ...
> **Martha** I ... am ... George ... I ... am ... (128)

The play feels indebted to Ibsen and Strindberg – as in *Ghosts*, as in *A Doll's House*, what is *known* about a marriage and what is *true* about a marriage are put into violent conflict, and the biting and tearing quality of George and Martha's interactions seem like a swingin' 1960s version of Strindberg's *Dance of Death*. Because of these modernist echoes, we might find ourselves hunting through *Woolf* for a moral in a way we do not in Albee's other works. Of course, his other work is not amoral. Every part of it is formed from righteous outrage, and in general, Albee's work chops away at lazy or conventional attitudes. But here, Albee actually issues a prescriptive lesson. Even beyond his usual contempt for abstract ideals (marriage, America), he seems almost to have written an 'issue play' in which he proposes right action in a relationship. In an interview, Albee described finding the title for the play (it was a pun scrawled on a mirror in a downtown bar), and what it meant to him: 'And of course, who's afraid of Virginia Woolf means who's afraid of the big *bad* wolf ... who's afraid of living life without false illusions.'[28] Sacrifice your idols, he tells us, give up your private fictions and deal with one another honestly.

Woolf is, on its realistic surface, a family play, but symbolically (and as with most American family dramas) it can also be read as an indictment of the American project. New Carthage refers to the African city so hated by the Romans that, after its defeat, its fields were apocryphally 'sown with salt' so no crop could grow there. The name evokes defeat, sterility and greatness brought low. In 1962, the Cuban missile crisis was terrifying the nation – could a nuclear winter have been the modern equivalent of those ancient, blasted fields? Some see the characters George and Martha as a deliberate evocation of George and Martha Washington, and certainly the characters are parents to an imaginary boychild, who shares certain blond characteristics with Albee's vision of the American Dream. (Albee himself said the characters are based on friends of his named Willard Maas and Marie Menken who also drank and raged in the wee hours, though, as always, he wouldn't disavow metaphors found by others.)

Much is made of the two men's specialities: history for George and biology for Nick. George prods Nick into talking about chromosomes, then hyperbolizes:

Martha, this young man is working on a system whereby chromosomes can be altered ... well not all by himself – he probably has one or two conspirators – the genetic makeup of a sperm cell changed, reordered ... to order, actually ... for hair and eye color, stature, potency ... I imagine ... hairiness, features, health ... and *mind*. Most important ... Mind. All imbalances will be corrected, sifted out ... propensity for various diseases will be gone, longevity assured. We will have a race of men ... test-tube-bred ... incubator-born ... superb and sublime. (34)

In 1962, emerging from the Eisenhower 1950s and not yet anticipating the radical 1960s, America did seem to be poised between two options – the slick, Kennedy-approved tomorrowland or a blinkered nostalgia. Albee's affection stands with George. Albee, after all, is a gay man whose mother totally rejected his homosexuality. For him, as for all 'othered' by a fearful world, a future of biological 'correction' that biologist Nick seems to offer would be dystopia. Yet while Albee gives George the great lines and the intellectual upper hand, he also makes it clear that George must figuratively (and literally in the action of the play) throw away his book, to engage, to rescue his own present.

Religious connotations also bubble away beneath the surface. C. W. E. Bigsby – one of Albee's most devoted champions – called *Woolf* 'in essence a modern secular morality play. The gospel which it teaches ... is the primacy of human contact based on an acceptance of reality. To Albee, this is essentially a Christian objective ... a son is sacrificed for redemption.'[29] We associate George with his dragon, but is it Martha who breathes fire? Or falsehood? The name 'Martha' also refers to a Christian saint, though a rather less-than-saintly one: when the Biblical Martha met Christ, she was obstreperous and impatient, 'cumbered about with many things' and in need of admonishment to listen to the Word. The play's metaphysical gravity can sometimes be difficult to sense. The precision of the banter and the naturalism are so persuasive that psychologists and marriage counsellors pore over it as a purely transparent document – 'It is mind-boggling what Edward Albee knows about the heterosexual relationship,' Elaine Stritch once said.[30] Yet, especially on repeat viewings and readings, *Woolf* roils with a concentrated sense of death, of existential seriousness, of heroic acts, of man's inherent loneliness, of triumph over worldly weakness.

All through his work, Albee tends to exaggerate this sense of a 'teaching play' by interrupting his ping-pong dialogue with stories – almost stand-alone short stories – that are deliberately told as parables. Jerry's dog story in *The Zoo Story* encapsulated that play's theme, as later, Tobias's story about the cat does in *A Delicate Balance*. In *Who's Afraid of Virginia Woolf?*, the parable is George's famous 'bergin' set piece – a story so powerful the play itself does not seem to know if it happened to George, to a friend of his, or to no one. In a masterful piece of storytelling, George tells Nick the tale of the boy he knew in his adolescence who mistakenly ordered 'bergin' rather than bourbon ('Give me some bergin please ... bergin and water') – and the resulting hilarity marked George's 'grandest day of my ... youth.' The boy, George tells Nick, had earlier been responsible for his mother's death, in an accident with a shotgun, then:

> **George** The following summer, on a country road, with his learner's permit in his pocket and his father on the front seat to his right, he swerved the car, to avoid a porcupine, and drove straight into a large tree.
> **Nick** (*Faintly pleading*) No.
> **George** He was not killed, of course. And in the hospital, when he was conscious and out of danger, and when they told him that his father *was* dead, he began to laugh, I have been told, and his laughter grew and he would not stop, and it was not until after they jammed a needle in his arm, not until after that, until his consciousness slipped away from him, that his laughter subsided ... stopped. And when he was removed from his injuries enough so that he could be moved without damage should he struggle, he was put in an asylum. That was thirty years ago.
> **Nick** Is he ... still there?
> **George** Oh, yes. And I'm told that for these thirty years he has ... not ... uttered ... one ... sound. (51)

The bergin boy's demoniacal laughter seems to echo through the play, but is the story 'true'? The play's obsession with truth and illusion makes the question urgent. The bergin story's perfect structure makes us distrust it: it ends in campfire tale cliché, and Nick's very enthralment makes it obvious that George is manipulating him. But we are *later* led to believe that the story is all too true, that the boy is George himself and (or?) a character in a novel George wasn't permitted to publish. The knot of what is true about the bergin boy is never unsnarled, and it forms a hard pith for the play around it – the bergin enigma could be the play in miniature. First, most obviously, it is a funny story that turns into a sorrowful one, just as the play is. Second, bitter laughter is the bricks-and-mortar of *Woolf*, the laughter of devastating guilt and loss, laughter that recalls an earlier joy but is now a reaction of existential shock. Third, Nick's growing sense that the bergin tale may be autobiographical foreshadows the way he (and we) will be invited to penetrate the swarm of George and Martha's fictions. And finally, Albee sets the story up as a counterweight that will swing the plot to its inevitable conclusion. The bergin boy represents one tragically asymmetrical family – one son, no parents. The work of the three-hour evening inverts that asymmetry, neatly and devastatingly, to its exact opposite.

Tiny Alice

A certain air of hysteria hangs around *Tiny Alice* (1964), Albee's psychosexual mystery play, not least because the play tends to agitate the senses. The *manner* of the play is Jesuitical, intellectual, dry; the *matter* of it all fevered delirium. At the time, critical reception was confused and even bitter, but that didn't stop its weirdness from entering the bloodstream of American theatre: watching plays in the mid-2010s, one is struck at how influential *Alice*'s gothic sensibility has proven to be.

Tiny Alice begins with a visual pun. Two men, the Cardinal and the Lawyer, bicker in a walled garden that holds a cage for two red birds. According to Albee, these pets 'need not be real'[31] – in fact, the birds' toy-like stillness foreshadows the play's many images of confinement and simulation. The wordplay (there are cardinals and Cardinals) also hints at the deep structure of *Tiny Alice*, a thriller that both depends on the slipperiness of language and savages our tendency to confuse 'the representative of a ... thing with the thing itself' (449).

The Lawyer has come to announce a staggering financial gift to the Church, given by his mysterious employer Miss Alice. Her only demand is that the Cardinal send his secretary, the sweet-tempered Brother Julian, to be the Church's agent – a position that will eventually entail his living at Miss Alice's manor. Julian is a purist naïf, a lay brother whose religious fundamentalism has made him fragile: he hasn't been at Miss Alice's mansion long before he tells the Butler that he once checked himself into an asylum, traumatized at the realization that most men shape 'a false God in their own image' (452). Miss Alice's home, though, is a bad place for such absolutism. It's a labyrinth of images, and Julian is baffled like a rat in a mirrored maze.

In the library, there is a gigantic doll's house, a scale replica of Miss Alice's palace. Everything in and out of this model seems to be a strange game: there is abusive sexual play between Miss Alice and the Lawyer, and eerie correspondences manifest between the estate and its doll-sized miniature. (When a fire breaks out in one, it breaks out in the other too.) The billionaire Miss Alice, we learn, is herself an image – a priestess and avatar for the *real* Alice, a supernatural power that inhabits the model. Julian, unknowing, is seduced into marrying the human version, but the cabal soon informs him that, in taking 'Alice', he has been wedded to their god instead. Julian rejects his new priesthood and is shot. He then dies alone in an ecstasy of martyrdom, his arms flung into the shape of crucifixion, as the shadow of the true Alice moves over him.

Critics and audiences found *Tiny Alice*'s events so confounding that, several months into the run, Albee staged a press conference at the Billy Rose Theatre to explain it. Some had called it genius; others called it baffling, obscurantist, self-indulgent. Harold Clurman, writing in *The Nation*, was withering: 'The surface or fabric of *Tiny Alice* is specious ... Its artistic method is too generalized to wound or even to touch us. Its pathos is weak, its scorn jejune.'[32] Philip Roth's attack in *The New York Review of Books* was launched along sexual-political lines, averring that Julian was a masked gay character. Roth asked when a play would be produced on Broadway in which 'the homosexual hero is presented as a homosexual and not disguised?'[33] Albee's reputation was knocked off its previously unassailable plinth. From a distance of fifty years, the rejection of Albee's *soi-disant* 'opera'[34] seems excessive. Certainly, it ends with an overwritten monologue-aria (which Albee would later cut from eleven minutes to two), but the play does have occasional majesty, moral seriousness and an indelibly brilliant *mise en scène*. Even on the page, the sequence in which lights move through the miniature mansion creates a real sense of terror.

Gussow sums up the reactions: 'Depending on one's point of view, it is either a tantalizing intellectual exercise, a deeply probing study of religious martyrdom, a work with a severely schizoid personality, or simply a flagrant act of hubris.'[35] It occupies a strange place in Albee's catalogue. It treats subjects that Albee more or less abandoned subsequently. 'I've developed elaborate theories about it,' Albee told Gussow, 'about molecular structure and everything being part of something infinitely larger and infinitely smaller than itself. And the one thing that I do think is important ... was the relationship between martyrdom and sexual hysteria.'[36] But Albee admits that he isn't sure if it 'holds together intellectually', though – typically for Albee – in later interviews he disagrees with even this characterization. Whatever the case, Albee does not return to this sort of ecstatic liturgical language in his later work, nor will he ever again seem so directly under the sway of Genet and Sartre. He develops his other approaches forward through the decades; the overtly religious one ends here.

A Delicate Balance

In 1966, Richard Burton and Elizabeth Taylor played George and Martha in Mike Nichols's film adaptation of *Who's Afraid of Virginia Woolf?*, and Albee stepped again onto the wire suspended between blockbuster commercial success and aesthetic adventure. Albee could only walk such a narrow ledge because of his astonishing pace – in January of that same year, his adaptation of James Purdy's allegory *Malcolm* came to Broadway and *A Delicate Balance* arrived in September. The film let the critical community re-evaluate *Woolf* and, of course, Albee himself. Stanley Kauffman called the drama 'the best American play of the last decade',[37] an assessment that soothed the wounds of *Tiny Alice* and launched Albee into the stratosphere shared by the celebrity super couple Dick and Liz.

A Delicate Balance won acclaim, as well as the 1967 Pulitzer Prize (the first of Albee's three), though it has also been attacked as derivative of *Woolf*. Certainly, *Balance* and *Woolf* share a great deal: we are back in a living room cum battleground, and a pair of unwelcome visitors have once again shown up on the doorstep. Yet in *Balance*, Albee's comic voice is far bleaker, reviving his lacerating attitude towards his parents to paint a portrait of a wealthy couple in the end stages of surrender and hypocrisy. Also very *un*like George and Martha, *Balance*'s Agnes and Tobias do not seem to likely find a 'deeper truth', nor do their brittle exchanges run with the kind of blood we find between that other pair. Tellingly, Albee's project in the later play seems more despairing about what age and compromise hold. In 1965, Albee and his mother had achieved détente – or, at least, she and Albee were willing to see each other, which they had not done in seventeen years. (His father had died earlier in the decade.) The contact seemed to give Albee even more fodder for his acid-etched portraits. *A Delicate Balance*'s house, its high ceilings and its drunken sister sleeping off a binge upstairs recall Albee's unhappy youth, and when Albee wanted to explain his source material to the original Tobias and Agnes – married actors Hume Cronyn and Jessica Tandy – he took them to meet his mother.[38]

The play takes place in Agnes and Tobias's sumptuous 'library-livingroom',[39] though no one in the family reads, and few really live. As is frequently the case with Albee, there's value in paying attention to the play's time signature. *A Delicate Balance* stretches from Friday night until Sunday morning – what will be, for Tobias, a long, dark weekend of the soul. The idea, though, of a 'weekend' presupposes work. Tobias and his wealthy family have shaken loose of such concerns and this idleness has unshaped their lives. Indeed, the 'nest of gentry' environment helps give *Balance* its languorous, Chekhovian air. The play is a wistful, grey work: Albee frequently uses the dialogue direction 'triste' to establish the 'watercolour' mood.

At first, Tobias and Agnes seem to be a fully functional, if complacent, ageing couple. Despite needling from Agnes's alcoholic sister Claire, they sail along imperturbably. Where *Woolf* begins with the couple bursting into their own home, a prediction of the way George and Martha will crash into a new phase of marriage, *this* couple is discovered in tableau: Agnes seated, Tobias standing, looking at the cordial bottles. In stasis, Agnes dominates. She toys with the idea of destabilization, wondering coolly, if 'I might very easily – as they say – lose my mind one day' (13), while Tobias, busying himself with cognacs and anisettes, is the picture of self-effacement and courtly propriety. 'We will all go mad before you' (13), he reassures her. Agnes fondly describes her calm existence as 'a suntan rather than a scalding' (17), yet her poise conceals cruelty and self-aggrandizing pretension. She is most revealed when she berates the weaker, funnier Claire, who lives with them, a kind of 'clear-seeing' Cassandra in their midst.

Agnes, affronted by Claire's drunkenness, stands on her own dignity in gorgeous, vicious reams of prose:

> *If* you come to the dinner table unsteady, *if* when you try to say good evening and weren't the autumn colors lovely today

you are nothing but vowels, and *if* one smells the vodka on you from across the room – and don't tell me again, *either* of you! that vodka leaves nothing on the breath: if you are expecting it, if you are sadly and wearily expecting it, it *does* – *if* these conditions exist ... *persist* ... then the reaction of one who is burdened by her love is not brutality – though it would be excused, believe me! – not brutality at all, but the souring side of love. (20)

While Agnes is issuing bravura speeches ('I have never known whether to applaud or cry,' Claire admits), the family's long-held balance is shifting. Daughter Julia comes home, fleeing her fourth failed marriage; then Agnes and Tobias's 'oldest friends' Harry and Edna arrive unannounced, suitcases in hand. For Julia, it is a homecoming, and, indeed, there are overtones of Pinter's *The Homecoming* (which enjoyed its first Broadway run at the same time) throughout. But for Harry and Edna it is a desperate flight to an unfamiliar refuge. They report that, sitting quietly at home earlier that day, they were gripped by a terrible fear. Says Harry, 'There was nothing ... but we were very scared' (43). What frightened them? There isn't an answer, just a reference to a bottomless terror, something Agnes will later call a disease and even a plague. 'It was like being lost: very young again, with the dark, and lost' (44), whispers Harry, shaking.

The decision about whether or not to let them stay rests with Tobias. Julia is shrill – she wants to talk about her latest 'marital disaster', though Agnes quells her, and she's furious at the idea of Harry and Edna taking over 'her' room. Claire knows what is happening, that Harry and Edna want succour, comfort, warmth.

> **Claire**   A special room with a night light or the door ajar so you can look down the hall from the bed and see that Mommy's door is open.
> **Julia**   (*No anger; loss*) But that's my room.
> **Claire**   It's ... *the room*. Happens you were in it. You're a visitor as much as anyone now. (75)

The more that the interlopers assert their position, the more manic Julia grows. After a hysterical, regressive episode, she brandishes Tobias's pistol, then collapses again in tears.

Even before Harry and Edna arrive, the house had been full of refugees. Julia has fled her husband, Claire has fled life and Tobias has fled the marital bed. *A Delicate Balance* asks what rights our relationships grant us – and it does so by correlating those rights (conjugal, parental, filial, proprietary) with physical rooms. Because of the guests, Tobias and Agnes must sleep in the same room as they have not done in ages, and the change unearths a trove of old pain. Even the kitchen seems unfamiliar once the servants, its rightful inhabitants, are asleep. Julia, ostentatiously playing the 'at-home' daughter to her family, can't find the coffee beans: 'Those folk must lock them up before they go to bed,' (108) she complains. Who actually belongs in the house? Whose is it really? Tobias reminisces about the comforts of childhood, only to hear, from Agnes, 'Well, my darling, you are not young now, and you do not live at home' (99).

It wouldn't be an Albee play without a dead or missing son, so there is Julia's brother Teddy, whose early death has sent Tobias into a lifelong withdrawal from first his vows (Claire refers to his long-ago infidelity), then his wife's body (fearing another pregnancy), then his wife's bedroom, and finally from almost every meaningful contact. He is, his daughter says, a 'cipher', a code that hasn't any interest in being read. Yet just as *Zoo Story*'s Jerry and *Woolf*'s George did before him, Tobias relates a story about himself that suggests the opposite. In the tale, told just before Harry and Edna arrive, Tobias tells Claire and Agnes about a cat of his that suddenly – without reason – stopped liking him. 'I hated her, well, I suppose because I was being accused of something, of failing,' (39) he says, baffled at her suddenly withdrawn affection. He shakes the cat, strikes it and then takes it to the vet to have it killed. Tobias's story about the cat exerts the same threat Albee's other two parable-stories do: it reveals the teller as someone capable of snuffing out life. In *The Zoo Story*, Jerry sees the dog in himself, and through the action of the play he becomes able to kill himself. George has, in a work of fiction, killed his parents, and we see him become able to kill his fictional son. But what or who will Tobias kill?

In its allusive way, the parable predicts Tobias's true 'choice' about Harry and Edna, though he loudly claims otherwise. Preoccupied with ideas about duty in the absence of love, Tobias tries to 'wear the hair shirt' (as he feels he should have done for the cat), and he aggressively *demands* Harry and Edna stay. At the end of his long night's meditation, he delivers an anguished aria: 'I DON'T WANT YOU HERE! YOU ASKED?! NO! I DON'T (*Loud*) BUT BY CHRIST YOU'RE GOING TO STAY HERE! YOU'VE GOT THE RIGHT!' (122) he shouts. But Harry and Edna are evicted anyway. They do not stay in the face of such horrible anti-welcome; Tobias's hesitation has functioned as his choice. So, as he once did with the cat, Tobias will have a distant, anaesthetizing force do away with an unwanted friend.

Edna is rueful: 'It's sad to come to the end of it, isn't it, nearly the end; so much more of it gone by . . . than left, and still not know – still not have learned . . . the boundaries, what we may not do . . . not ask, for fear of looking in a mirror' (123). Albee continued asking about the nature of these 'boundaries' and the dutiful side of love throughout his work, just as he would return to questions about marriage, a foolishly idealistic mechanism for fighting off the 'dark sadness'. For all his sympathy with the nihilists, there's a vivid warning here against anything (liquor, self-satisfaction, gender roles, cowardice) that allows us to retreat from life. Albee himself called the play 'a cautionary tale' written, as he said all serious plays are, 'in the hope they will become unnecessary'.[40] *A Delicate Balance* has been revived again and again. As of this writing, that hope hasn't born fruit.

Other works

Astonishingly, Albee had still *other* plays produced in the 1960s, and though they are generally considered minor pieces, they shed some light – dim, reflected – on the more thrilling works. In 1963, Albee began his career of literary adaptations with a Broadway production of *The Ballad of the Sad Café*, a treatment of Carson McCullers's achingly sad novella about a love triangle among a mining town's misfits. In the heated *Ballad*, we see the ease with which Albee moves into lyric, not to mention his interest in the grotesque and the conflation of violent and erotic impulse. In fact, if we revisit any of his works after we read *Ballad*, our ear is newly attuned to the way Albee had, all along, been using sex as a dramatic engine. The awkward, wrong-footed banter between Peter and Jerry, for example, will seem more like courtship, and even the morganatic marriages – all those poor domineering Mommies and vacant rich Daddies – will seem covertly physical.

The other adaptations of this decade were far less successful: a tin-eared reworking of James Purdy's innocence-to-experience allegory *Malcolm* (1966) and the 'Americanized' version of Giles Cooper's English play *Everything in the Garden* (1967). Both were notorious flops, and when a 1970s attempt at *Lolita* also went sour, Albee gave up on the adaptation game. There was another crucial activity in this period, however. In 1961, Albee and his producers Richard Barr and Clinton Wilder (the pair to whom *Woolf* is dedicated) banded together to create the Playwrights Unit, an Off- and Off-Off- Broadway arrangement that produced young American writers on the playwright-first paradigm that had worked so well for Albee. The Playwrights Unit only lasted a decade, closing in 1971, but its voracious appetite for new work gave the world LeRoi Jones's *The Dutchman*, as well as early work by playwrights like Sam Shepard, Megan Terry, Leonard Melfi and Jean-Claude van Itallie.

At the end of the 1960s, Albee returned to the avant-garde with a pair of intertwining one-acts, performed on Broadway in a 1968 repertory of short works. These plays were the Beckettian *Box* and the 'cut-up' work *Quotations from Chairman Mao Tse-Tung*, which twines his own writing around figures speaking found texts from Mao and Will Carleton's poem 'Over the Hill to the Poor-House'. In his introduction, Albee insists that

> [a] playwright ... has two obligations: first, to make some statement about the condition of 'man' (as it is put) and, second, to make some statement about the nature of the art form with which he is working. In both instances he must attempt change.[41]

The audience (not to mention most critics other than Harold Clurman) was not willing to listen to Albee's 'obligations'. After their first run on Broadway, *Box* and *Mao* have not been revived often, perhaps because the pieces are built both on abstractions and the playwright's wishful fantasy of an erudite public. Yet reading them delivers a sense of a restlessly inventive writer with catholic tastes. They demonstrate the development of Albee's relationship to symbolism, politics, family, theatricality and dramatic composition. They show too that Albee's greatest tool was his musical ear for language, particularly the self-deluded patter of the self-important. Even in a text heavily reliant on other sources, one of the pleasures is ferreting out that sound, listening for it even as Mao and Carleton constantly interrupt ... the marvellous 'Albee dialogue' winning out over all.

Conclusion

From the first, crucial success of *The Zoo Story*, Albee was central to a revitalization of new American playwriting, one that married two seemingly incompatible impulses. As New York emerged from the 1950s, commercial success Off-Broadway had come at a cost – *The Iceman Cometh* (a touchstone production for Albee) and Williams's *Summer and Smoke* made enough money that it was becoming as difficult for a playwright to be produced Off-Broadway as it was on. On the other hand, the uncommercial Off-Off-margins were full of experiment: Julian Beck and Judith Malina's Living Theatre, Theatre Genesis, La MaMa, the Judson Church movement and dozens more. But even those experimenters writing dramatic plays like van Itallie and Shepard had turned their backs on an 'uptown' (read: capitalized) theatre that featured few new names and seemed, to them, to be totally out of touch.

In the 1960s, Albee rejected this division – he dedicated his energies to Off-Broadway but he *also* believed his work belonged *on* Broadway; he (and his producers) didn't doubt it could speak directly to mainstream audiences. He offered his contemporaries a model of a successful transgressor, an experimenter raking in Pulitzers and box office. The fanfare that attended him – a *New Yorker* cartoon, a *Time* cover – wedged open a door between downtown and uptown that many thought had swung shut behind O'Neill.

The decades following Albee's great successes witnessed an avalanche of new American writing – and all of it would debut in a theatrical scene made welcoming in part by Albee. Is that scene *still* welcoming? As we look out at an American theatre that is again divided between the largely commercial Broadway and the adventurous scenes elsewhere, there is cause to worry. It may be that we have simply stopped looking to Broadway for a certain kind of excellence: experimental literary offerings there are few and far between (Will Eno's 2014 *The Realistic Joneses*, a few Ionesco revivals, some Shepard), and of US playwrights, only Albee, August

Wilson and David Mamet have the kind of name recognition that can open a non-musical on Broadway without a movie star. Yet Off-Broadway and in the thriving regional theatres, two generations after *The Zoo Story*'s Athena-like debut, the Albee sensibility is alive and well. Albee's greatest plays start in clarity and then move into abstraction, and we can see the heirs to that technique all around us. It was exemplifying this stepwise, hybrid approach – the true bridging of uptown craft and downtown radical disorientation – that has proved to be Albee's most influential contribution to the form. We can trace a straight line from Albee to the latest crop of innovators like Eno, Annie Baker, Stephen Karam, Taylor Mac, Young Jean Lee and Suzan-Lori Parks. They're all of them his children – a functional Albee family after all.

4

Amiri Baraka

Susan Stone-Lawrence

Introduction

When he spoke at the Provincetown Tennessee Williams Festival in 2007, honoree Amiri Baraka said,

> Certainly, if you are black, or a woman, or gay, or poor, it should be obvious that you have to struggle to simply be *who you are*. The civil rights movement or the gay rights movement and the struggle against women's oppression or the anti-imperialist struggles give open voice and paradigm to that.[1]

The focus on intersectionality may surprise readers. The controversial poet-playwright speaking these words had a well-earned reputation for angry rhetoric as well as volatility, profanity and blasphemy. Statements from his cultural nationalist period, beginning in the middle of the 1960s, garnered accusations of sexism, homophobia and reverse racism. After shifting to a more inclusive, Marxist–Leninist stance a decade later, he looked back at his late-1960s to early 1970s output as 'Hate Whitey' material.[2] Heterosexist male chauvinism also featured significantly in his poetry and plays of that period. White women and gay men were demeaned in the process of building up an idealized form of black masculinity and Black Power. The problem of identifying Baraka's politics – both the positive, empowering politics and the oppressive, demeaning politics – speaks to his mercuriality. Throughout his life and work, he evolved, reflecting his constant search for inner truth and his unflagging commitment to challenging injustice, especially when he found it within himself.

Ironically, at the beginning of the 1960s, Baraka did not privilege the category of blackness that would provide his most often recognized thematic content and political cause. When asked in 1960 why his work did not focus on ethnic identity, the then LeRoi Jones replied,

> [I]t's just that that's not the way I write poetry ... I would deal with it when it has to do directly with the poem, and not as a kind of broad generalization that doesn't have much to do with a lot of young writers today who are Negroes (although I don't know that many). It's always been a separate section of writing that wasn't quite up to the level of the other writing. There were certain definite sociological reasons for it before the Civil War or in the early part of the twentieth century, or even in the thirties, but it's a new generation now, and people are beset by other kinds of ideas that don't have much to do with sociology, per se ... it doesn't have anything to do with what I'm writing at the time.[3]

This declaration shockingly contrasts with almost everything he wrote afterward. Baraka would soon perform an ideological about-face and traverse his share of changes over the following years. Those turbulent times would awaken in him the necessity for social and political change.

He had been politically active prior to 1965, traveling to Cuba in 1960 as part of a delegation sponsored by the Fair Play for Cuba Committee and picketing the United Nations in 1961 after the assassination of Patrice Lumumba. But among the most often recounted of his radical moves occurred when Jones reacted to the assassination of Malcolm X by leaving his white wife and biracial daughters in Greenwich Village.[4] The poet-playwright relocated to Harlem, where he co-founded the short-lived but seminal Black Arts Repertory Theater/School with the assistance of federal anti-poverty funds. Two years later, he married an African American woman, Sylvia Robinson, in a Yoruba ceremony.[5] In 1967, he received a new Sunni Muslim name, Ameer Barakat (meaning 'blessed prince'), which he later transformed to its Swahili form –

Amiri Baraka. Sylvia became Amina ('faithful'). At that time, he also embraced the strict – and strictly sexist – vision of Black Power of Maulana Karenga's Kawaida philosophy.

But much as Malcolm X did after his Hajj to Mecca, Baraka later qualified his separatism to emphasize multicultural unity among economically oppressed brothers and sisters of all races. In the 1970s, Baraka's plays and essays embraced an integrated international effort to fight the forces of capitalist imperialism while continuing to provoke and demand confrontation of racist tendencies and blatant oppression in contemporary US society. Be that as it may, the mid-1960s manifestation of his cultural nationalist ideology marks the quintessential line between what are often considered the first two of the three major phases of his life's work. Arguably, it was during these mid-1960s years that he produced his most important essays, poems and plays.

Baraka's contemporary, poet and critic A. B. Spellman, uses the term 'history of fairly radical breaks' to designate the kinds of sharply contrasting shifts that we see in the careers of African Americans during the 1960s, when so much was changing socially, economically, politically and culturally.[6] However, one could argue that the tensions that caused these breaks built gradually, their impulses simmering below the surface before gushing forth. That appears to be the case with Baraka. As he explains, 'The typology that lists my ideological changes and so forth ... doesn't show the complexity of real life ... We go from step 1 to step 2 ... But there is real life between 1 and 2.'[7] Baraka preferred the following timeline for his works:

- The Beat Period (1957–62)
- The Transitional Period (1963–65)
- The Black Nationalist Period (1965–74)
- The Third World Marxist Period (1974–2014)

Although he primarily produced poetry and essays during the Beat Period, Baraka also wrote his first plays during this time. These anti-establishment works challenge conventional morals and contain sexually provocative (and, perhaps surprisingly, gay) themes, but race does not appear as explicitly in these plays as in later periods. The Transitional Period includes *Dutchman*, the most well-known and acclaimed play of Baraka's career, and other dramas in which the playwright's growing ambivalence about interracial relationships is apparent. The Black Nationalist Period is when he ceased writing under the name LeRoi Jones in favour of Amiri Baraka. The plays written during this period are typically short in length and explode with intense revolutionary force. Then, after a decade of militant indictments of racism and wicked satire of its representatives, Baraka shifted to a Third World-focused Marxism, attacking imperialist and capitalist oppressors of the proletariat masses of all ethnic identities. The plays he created during the last forty years of his career are consistently the longest he wrote. Their epic plots involve dozens of characters (sometimes more than a hundred) and span extended periods of time.

Beginnings

Everett Leroy Jones was born on 7 October 1934 into a Newark, New Jersey, family with a history of defying racism. One of his namesakes, his maternal grandfather Thomas Everett Russ, 'lost a business to arson in Alabama before coming to Newark'.[8] Another, his father, Coyette Leroy Jones, fled South Carolina to live with his married sister in Newark after hitting a white movie theatre manager who ejected him from the cinema for eating peanuts.[9] The young Leroy grew up in a multicultural, middle-class neighbourhood, but Italian Americans bullied him at his integrated high school, and participation in cotillion taught him about the troubling preference for 'yellow' skin over brown within the African American community. Nevertheless, his experiences with racism didn't dampen his enthusiasm for Western art. Symbolic of that enthusiasm, while attending Howard University, he changed his name to its French spelling, though he was also inspired by African American journalist Roi Ottley.[10]

After failing out of college at nineteen, Jones joined the Air Force, where he found comfort in books and the independent thought and self-expression they inspired. However the incompatibility of mid-twentieth-century United States military service with Marxist ideology, particularly the ideology expressed in the periodical publications to which he subscribed and submitted his writing, led to his 1957 undesirable discharge.[11]

The Beat Period: *The Eighth Ditch* and *The Baptism*

After his discharge, Baraka immersed himself in New York's bohemian Greenwich Village community, where he met a white, Jewish woman named Hettie Roberta Cohen and married her in a Buddhist ceremony in 1958. The couple co-edited *Yugen*, a quarterly poetry magazine that published Beat writers. LeRoi became close with Allen Ginsberg, Frank O'Hara and Diane DiPrima, among others. Under the name Totem Press, the Jones's started publishing books, including 1961's *Preface to a Twenty Volume Suicide Note*, which LeRoi dedicated to Hettie. In this, his first published collection of verse, Jones makes a point of identifying himself as not African,[12] and neither of the two poems that include Hettie's name in their title mentions whiteness.[13] In his autobiography, Baraka reflects that he 'was "open" to all schools within the circle of white poets of all faiths and flags', but had lost his connection to blackness.[14] As evidence of how his 'social focus had gotten much whiter',[15] Baraka notes that the first issue of *Yugen* included an equal number of black and white contributors, but the third issue did not include a single black writer.[16] Yet, at the time, he 'could see the young white boys and girls in their pronouncement of disillusion with and "removal" from society as being related to the black experience', qualifying them as 'colleagues of the spirit'.[17]

Baraka later felt these associations had prolonged his adolescence, but he was a hub for the bohemian scene. He and Hettie hosted weekend-long parties that Ginsberg described as 'the one place in New York where everybody met'.[18] It was a free-wheeling time for him. In addition to other extramarital affairs, Jones had an extended relationship with DiPrima, mother of Dominique, his daughter born of that relationship. They also created *The Floating Bear*, a key publication of the late Beat movement. In 1961, they published *The Eighth Ditch*, one of Baraka's first plays. Later included in *The System of Dante's Hell*, the script tells the story of two soldiers, one educating the other, a compliant protégé, on various subjects ranging from philosophy to politics to cultural identity while introducing him to anal sex. When the other soldiers who share the barracks become jealous, a gang rape occurs. At the time, any representations of gay sex were illegal. Authorities intercepted the issue of *The Floating Bear* containing the play. The US Postal Service and FBI arrested Jones for 'sending obscene materials through the mail', though he successfully defended himself against the charges.[19] The New York Poets Theatre, which Baraka co-founded with DiPrima and several other fellow artists, produced *The Eighth Ditch* at the New Bowery Theatre on St Mark's Place in 1964, but the police closed it after a few performances.[20]

This play and other writings by Baraka during the early 1960s are what José Esteban Muñoz describes as 'homoerotic or queerly valenced works'.[21] Of these, *The Baptism* offers one of the more favourable portrayals of a gay man in the period. Performed by Present Stages at the Writers' Stage Theatre, New York City, the play opened on 23 March 1964. In this satire, the character called Homosexual defends an adolescent boy – Jesus in disguise – against the sanctimonious judgments of a 'generally ridiculous' Minister and Old Woman.[22] The latter try to take sexual advantage of the Boy, who masturbates while praying because contemplating God 'always gives [him] a hard-on'.[23] Stereotypically flamboyant, often joking about being gay, Homosexual is straightforward about his attraction, unlike the self-righteous hypocrites condemning the boy's natural desires while they plot his violation. Homosexual's self-sacrificing bravery earns Jesus's appreciation, the opposite of the retributive ire the son of God visits upon the rest of the church full of sinners lacking charity.[24]

This is daring material, for sure, but it and other writings of the period felt increasingly hollow to Jones. In a 1979 interview with Debra L. Edwards, Baraka explained how he had 'thought of the whole Beat thing as a publicity gimmick' but esteemed the movement for the way it transformed literature through its rebellion against an American establishment exemplified by Eisenhower and McCarthy.[25] *The Baptism* clearly reflects such an anti-establishment defiance of traditional norms, especially the pervasive and legal homophobia of the period. While written during his Beat Period, *The Toilet* is, in Muñoz's words, 'the most homerotic' of Baraka's writings and demonstrates the ambivalence he endured between 1963 and 1965.

The Transitional Period

The Toilet

The Toilet received a 1962 student-directed Actors Studio staging, and Lee Strasberg advised pursuit of an Off-Broadway run.[27] The production opened on 16 December 1964 at the St Mark's Playhouse. Set in the private, all-male space of a high school boys' bathroom, the drama depicts the tragedy of secret interracial gay lovers called out and forced to fight by their peers in order to save face and uphold their manhood. It ends with the black boy, Foots, kneeling beside the body of the white boy, Karolis, 'weeping and cradling the head in his arms'.[28] In a 1978 interview for *Theatre Quarterly*, Baraka called the ending of the play 'tacked on'.[29] He originally intended to end the play with the fight, but his integrationist ideology inspired him to depict the 'kind of friendship that existed across traditional social lines'.[30]

At the time, Baraka primarily aligned himself with Beat writers and artists because of their opposition to traditional norms rather than any particular aesthetic or focused political commitment. However, during this time he met a number of African American writers dedicated to dealing with specifically political subject matter. In 1960, Baraka joined Julian Mayfield, John Clarke, Harold Cruse and other members of the Free Play for Cuba Committee for a meeting with Fidel Castro in Cuba at the first anniversary celebration of the Cuban revolution.[31] The trip introduced the 25-year-old Jones to civil rights activist Robert F. Williams, who utilized armed self-defence in his Monroe, North Carolina, chapter of the National Association for the Advancement of Colored People – a tactic more closely aligned with Malcolm X's philosophy of self-determination than with the NAACP, which generally supported non-violent struggle. These interactions with politically engaged African Americans, his direct experience of the hypocrisy and lies of the American establishment, his growing awareness of anti-colonial struggle and the increasingly violent actions against the civil rights movement heightened the poet-playwright's awareness of and public commitment to being African American, to being 'Black'. Many of his associates in the Village did not understand or sympathize.

That lack of understanding and sympathy convinced him that Greenwich Village was not his proper place. As Baraka writes in his 1964 manifesto, 'The Revolutionary Theatre', 'Most white Western artists do not need to be "political", since usually, whether they know it or not, they are in complete sympathy with the most repressive social forces in the world today.'[32] Because centuries of white supremacy had promoted Eurocentric preferences and biases as unmarked standards of supposedly universal knowledge and aesthetics, European ideas had dominated Baraka's thoughts throughout most of his education and creative development. '[T]hough altered somewhat by [his] Eastern Buddhist reading', his conception of intellectualism was basically apolitical until he became conscious of blackness.[33] At times, the process of extricating himself from the status quo his awakened self could no longer accept was unpleasant to those around him.

For example, Baraka denounced *The Toilet* set designer Larry Rivers at a 1964 Village Vanguard symposium. He accused his friend of being 'all over in these galleries, turning out work for these rich faggots' and attacked him as 'part of the dying shit just like them!'[34] Such 'viciousness' dispelled the notion of 'some intellectual and emotional connection' between the friends.[35] The rift created that day lasted twenty years.[36] But something else besides concerns about bourgeois co-optation may have been involved. When originally produced in 1964, *The Toilet* appeared 'on a double bill with a play by Frank O'Hara', whose room-mate Joe LeSueur outed Baraka in 2003.[37] LeSueur suggests Baraka had an affair with O'Hara, also reported to have had a relationship with Rivers.[38]

There's no conclusive proof of homosexual relationships, but Jones definitely valued his friendships with openly gay peers. In 1979, he applauded his Beat friends, especially Allen Ginsberg, for their honesty in declaring their sexuality years before the LGBTQ Rights movement took off.[39] In a 1964 interview with Judy Stone, Baraka praised Ginsberg as the 'one white man in New York I really trust . . . I trust him and love him completely.'[40] And though he had begun criticizing homosexuality as a form of cultural subjugation and burning his bridges with the liberal white arts community, when Baraka became a victim of near-deadly police brutality during the 1967 Newark uprising, the supporters who united to mount his legal defence included Ginsberg and James Baldwin.[41]

A Recent Killing

Amidst the personal turmoil of the summer of 1964, Baraka wrote his first full-length script, *A Recent Killing*, not staged until 1971. Although he later identified the work as primarily about the 'hidden and open horrors' of the military, 'specifically the use made of people by forces that they cannot comprehend',[42] the play also reveals its author's growing ambivalence towards homosexuality. Complementing a storyline involving the murder of a white lieutenant by his adulterous lover – the African American wife of another military man – the drama focuses on the inner conflict of the main character, Len. This '22-year-old northern Negro with a few years of college' described as '[s]ensitive, energetic, [and] "newly" intellectual', experiences simultaneously homosexual desires and the oppressive power of homophobia.[43] Like Baraka, Len spends most of his time on the base reading, keeps books in his footlocker, and is disciplined for reading while on guard duty.[44] Additionally, Len struggles to survive the conformist brutality of the military. When told he cannot be a poet because he is not a 'fairy' or a 'faggot',[45] Len defends himself in terms of compulsion. His writing is what he thinks 'about doing all the time . . . to find out' his true identity.[46]

The appearance in Len's fantasies of a famous gay literary character draws together his desires for men and writing. Evelyn Waugh's Sebastian Flyte (from *Brideshead Revisited*), who Baraka 'thought . . . was marvelous!',[47] appears to Len in visions strikingly similar to the fantasies of his ex-girlfriend that animate earlier scenes of the play. Flyte taunts Len, clutching at his shoulders and neck, whispering to him in seductive purrs, kissing him behind the ear and on the cheek, and enticing him to admit that he is a poet.[48] Even if Flyte's visits to Len exist solely to signify the importance of thinking for oneself and embracing the life of mind and culture, Baraka eroticizes the scenes and does not frame them negatively in any way. However, he does the reverse with Fag and Black Fag, whom Len encounters sitting on the toilet in the stockade after his arrest for desertion. They appear vain, effeminate, crude and proudly promiscuous while they harass Len and vie for attention from the other enlisted men. These stereotypes present an unflattering portrait and inject obscene comic relief, though they also comment on the haphazard standards of military discipline.

Baraka later dismissed *A Recent Killing* as 'lyrical, searching, confused ... essentially petty bourgeois radicalism, even rebellion, but not clear and firm enough as to revolution'.[49] In much the same way as he promoted insurgency over contemplation in 'The Revolutionary Theatre', Baraka exclaimed that 'the act is more legitimate, it is principal!'[50] This parallels what Baraka described in 1970 as the black community's association of homosexuality with 'a sort of avoidance of reality – a refusal to deal with reality'.[51] We know that Baraka's militant comrades questioned his commitment to Black Revolution because of his Greenwich Village associations. In keeping with the macho emphasis predominant in the Black Power era and the related expectations of unequivocal heterosexuality, Baraka denied both his gay friends and rumours suggesting a 'homosexual past'.[52] Decades later, Baraka rejected his cultural nationalist chauvinism as typical of the 'Homophobic Ignorant Negro' mindset he saw as contributing to the 1984 murder of his sister and the 2003 murders of his youngest child and her lover – all three of whom were lesbians.[53] In the aftermath of the latter tragedy, the Barakas expanded the scope of their political activism and became 'ardent antiviolence activists speaking out directly on LGBTQ issues'.[54]

Dutchman

The Playwrights Unit, established by Edward Albee, showcased *Dutchman* in January 1964.[55] On 24 March that year, the play opened an extended run Off-Broadway at the Cherry Lane Theatre and went on to win the *Village Voice* Obie Award for Best American Play of 1963–4. It has since attained canonical status. Judged by Mike Sell as 'rightfully considered the opening salvo of the [Black Arts Movement] as dramatic movement',[56] *Dutchman* communicates its author's disenchantment with the status of African Americans in White America and presages Baraka's impending cultural nationalist period.

This most famous and critically acclaimed play by Baraka presents a deadly interaction between an archetypal white She-Devil temptress and a seemingly assimilated young African American. Lula relentlessly provokes Clay to break out of his bourgeois pretence and unleash the angry blues within him, which he does in a climactic three-page diatribe. After the black man reveals the intensity of righteous indignation and authentic racial feeling surging through 'the pure heart, the pumping black heart' beating beneath his three-button suit and Harvard tie,[57] Lula murders Clay by stabbing him in the chest. Her fellow subway passengers (a mix of black and white people) remove the body at her command. Mission accomplished, Lula writes something in her notebook then turns her attention to a fresh 'young Negro' who has just boarded the train. The action concludes with 'an old Negro conductor' greeting his junior 'brother' and tipping his hat to Lula as he moves down the aisle and out of the car.[58] Integrated citizens from both sides of the black–white binary perpetuate an unending cycle of systemic racism against black people.

Susan Sontag criticized the murder in *Dutchman* as 'simply not credible in terms of the more or less realistic action that has gone before' and 'found the spasmic sexual contortions and raucousness in Jennifer West's performance as Lula almost unbearable'.[59] She seems to have missed the layers of metaphor embellishing the drama. Baraka cited three women from his life, including his ex-wife, as inspiration for Lula, but he also acknowledged that he drew from the legend of the Flying Dutchman.[60] In addition to the obvious connotations of Lula's habitual eating of apples and sharing them with Clay, many critical readings suggest mythical origins for Lula.

Charles D. Peavy notes that Lula 'embodies certain characteristics of Lilith, the demon woman of the Talmudic tradition'.[61] Anna Maria Chupa writes about Lula as a Destructive Bitch and Death Goddess.[62] Werner Sollors explains Lula's calling herself 'Lena the Hyena',[63] 'the ugliest woman in a L'il Abner contest' as incorporating 'the connotation of the animal that preys on carcasses'.[64] He cites other allusions, such as 'the West African goddess Erzulie', whose lover – Damballah, the serpent god – appears in certain poems by Baraka, and 'the white witch in Black America, of whom James Weldon Johnson warned his brothers' in his poem 'The White Witch', which is also the name of a ghost ship like *The Flying Dutchman*.[65] Hettie Jones remembers that her ex-husband's poetry 'once referred to [her] as the biblical witch of Endor'.[66] Baraka's autobiography names a 'Dolly Weinberg', an older white woman (mid-to-late thirties to his twenty-three), a Communist, working-class bohemian who spent half her weekly check on a psychiatrist, who was the first white woman with whom he ever slept.[67] However, he explains that 'the bitter, evil quality that surfaces in Lula' does not equate to any living human being but exemplifies 'the seductive nature of America', which uses the white woman 'to advertise just about everything ... furniture, detergents, atomic bombs' and the deadly cost of succumbing to its wiles.[68]

Following the success of *Dutchman*, Jones spent a term in limbo, torn between worlds. He was increasingly committed to a group of black cultural nationalists, most with white wives and lovers, who found themselves conflicted about how to free themselves from what they perceived as social and sexual hypocrisy. They disapproved of the involvement of white people in their agenda even while they 'were all hooked up to white women'.[69] Baraka recalls, 'We talked a black militance and took the stance that most of the shit happening downtown was white bullshit and most of the people were too. The fact that we, ourselves, were down there was a contradiction we were not quite ready to act upon, though we discussed it endlessly.'[70] A distance 'that had never existed before' grew between LeRoi and Hettie, and he found himself, as he put it, subconsciously choosing black women for his liaisons.[71] And whereas he used to associate with the Black Mountain crowd, now he primarily socialized with black friends.[72] Even after the assassination of Malcolm X provided the definitive compulsion to move, he fluctuated for a time, making mournfully guilty return visits to his wife and their two daughters.

The Slave

Gradually, concern for his identity as a black man, his growing commitment to black liberation, and doubts about whether he could remain a revolutionary while married to the 'enemy' won. *The Slave* was written during this awkward transition. First presented at St Mark's Playhouse in December 1964, the drama focuses on 'a black would-be revolutionary who splits from his white wife on the eve of a race war'.[73] In her autobiography, Hettie Jones calls it 'Roi's nightmare', recalling that the director, Leo Garen, used photos of the Jones children – Kellie and Lisa – on the set, and the character of Grace delivered a line she herself had actually uttered in an argument with her husband.[74]

The plot describes a home invasion, during which Walker, a black nationalist revolutionary, holds his ex-wife, Grace, and her new husband, a white college professor named Easley, hostage. The three characters confront each other about a range of issues and simmering resentments. Walker, in particular, expresses both hostility and wounded vulnerability concerning his relationship with Grace. His dialogue ranges from the outright rage of the shouted lines, 'You're mighty right I want to kill you. You're mighty goddamn right. Believe me, self-righteous little bitch, I want to kill you', to his sorrowful disbelief that she did not understand that his 'crying out against three hundred years of oppression' was not directed at her.[75] Walker suspects even his most trusted white friends and family when he questions Grace about her use of the word 'nigger'. Like his character, Baraka had become cynical about the apparent inclusivity of his bohemian environs and started to discern that that kind of countercultural scene was for privileged youths not ready to take their place in the establishment.

That growing mistrust directly impacted how gender and sexuality were treated in his work during this period. *The Baptism*, *The Toilet* and *A Recent Killing* present gay characters nobly opposed to heteronormative institutions – and even suggest that homosexuality is essentially rebellious. But Walker's disrespect of Easley as 'Faggy' presages a psychosexual break with Greenwich Village bohemia and the 'HalfWhite Negro' attitudes of Howard University.[76] Walker calls Easley 'faggot professor', 'a faggoty intellectual', 'Professor No-Dick' and 'that closet queen, respected, weak-as-water intellectual'.[77] *The Slave* was the last play produced before his break with his Village associations, and before Eurocentric intellectualism was added to the playwright's list of targets for disparagement, a symptom of his interest in defining a more robust, action-oriented form of thought and expression.

The Slave climaxes with Walker killing Easley and Grace dying in an explosion. Before she dies, Walker suggests to Grace that he has killed their two daughters, presumed asleep upstairs. The audience never sees the girls to know for sure what happens to them, but a child screams as Walker leaves the house. For Walker, letting the girls live may have represented a greater cruelty than if he had smothered them in bed like the 'second-rate Othello' he considers himself to have played to his wife's Desdemona and Easley's Iago.[78] Ironically, Baraka dedicated the anthology *Selected Plays and Prose of Amiri Baraka/LeRoi Jones* – which contains *The Slave* – to his biracial daughters, Dominique DiPrima and Kellie and Lisa Jones.[79] These girls might have found themselves upstairs during the anticipated race war.

In light of the inflammatory content of *The Slave*, a friend asked the play's white producer 'if he didn't feel somewhat threatened by the play's implications', and received the response, 'Oh he's not serious. It's only a play.'[80] However, in the context of the civil unrest and assassinations surrounding them in the 1960s and their focused determination to act upon heightened awareness of historic injustices, many adherents of Black Power, including Baraka, believed the revolution was at hand and the need for violence a certainty. They 'were trying to create an art that would be a weapon in the Black Liberation Movement'.[81]

The Black Nationalist Period

Baraka wanted to show African Americans their beauty in such a way that they would no longer see their traits and features as ugliness, and he hoped they could unite for social change by confronting their shared experience of victimhood.[82] Baraka believed theatre should 'force change', in contrast to his earlier belief in the white liberal artists' aesthetic demanding separation of art from politics.[83] Seeking to reverse the victimhood of the black men he had represented in *Dutchman*, *The Toilet* and *The Slave*, Baraka's new work called for 'new kinds of heroes – not the weak Hamlets debating whether or not they are ready to die for what's on their minds, but men and women (and minds) digging out from under a thousand years of "high art" and weak-faced dalliance'.[84] To start practising his theory, he co-founded the Black Arts Repertory Theater/School with, among others, Sonia Sanchez and Larry Neal.

After Baraka left Greenwich Village abruptly on 21 February 1965, 'hurling denunciations at the place of [his] intellectual birth',[85] he moved to Harlem and established the groundbreaking institution in an old brownstone near Lenox on 130th Street with the help of federal anti-poverty funds.[86] Beginning with an inaugural parade along 125th Street with a newly designed Black Arts flag, sponsoring street-corner theatre and jazz shows featuring the elite of the Manhattan cultural scene, and later performing guerrilla theatre in which a black actor with a gun chased someone who looked white,

BART/S created quite a stir, while promoting cultural empowerment and community education.[87] It was a volatile mix of programme and people. BART/S imploded by the end of the year,[88] but the impression it made upon like-minded individuals inspired the growth of a broader Black Arts Movement across the nation. Among the prominent figures associated with BART/S during its brief existence were jazz musicians Sun Ra and Albert Ayler, whom Baraka asked to compose soundtracks for his plays, and the notorious African American gangster Bumpy Johnson, who encouraged the organization's self-determination instead of reliance upon governmental agencies.[89] That combination of Black Nationalism and gangster attitude caused offence. When Sargent Shriver – brother-in-law of the late President Kennedy and architect of the Johnson administration's War on Poverty programme – came to BART/S on a tour of Harlem Youth Opportunities Unlimited programmes, Baraka said, 'Fuck Shriver', and refused to admit him.[90] Actions such as this and the choice to produce cultural nationalist plays in whiteface generated negative publicity and accusations of reverse racism at BART/S. Another of the street shows – the same script that won the Obie for its downtown production – *Dutchman* received negative criticism (as 'anti-white'). That and the slight against Shriver cost BART/S its funding.[91] As Sell notes, 'The most corrosively ironic aspect of this revocation was that it was called by foundation administrators who had given Baraka the money precisely because of the acclaim the play had received at the Cherry Lane Theatre. Having gone home, Baraka's play became too black for comfort.'[92]

As he wrote in 'The Revolutionary Theatre', 'White men will cower before this theatre because it hates them. Because they themselves have been trained to hate.'[93] The introduction to his 1969 anthology *Four Black Revolutionary Plays: All Praises to the Black Man* escalates this discourse to an extreme level of militancy with the proclamation: 'Unless you killing white people, killing the shit they've built, dont read this shit, you wont like it, and it sure wont like you' [sic].[94] In his 1994 essay on the movement, Baraka would characterize such bold declarations as 'cloaked ... in the starkest terms of cultural nationalism and Hate Whitey language'.[95] His plays written between 1965 and 1974 suggest the playwright heeded Clay's speech in *Dutchman* about murdering white people as the antidote to neurosis.

Experimental Death Unit #1

Among the four black revolutionary plays collected in the anthology, *Experimental Death Unit #1* provides one of the most unforgettable images of the Artaudian 'theatre of assault' Baraka envisioned with 'actual explosions and actual brutality'.[96] The play first appeared as part of a benefit performance at St Mark's Playhouse on 1 March 1965 to raise money for the rent and renovation of the BART/S brownstone. Its plot follows a group of black militants who discover two pretentious white male beatniks, one of whom has clobbered the other unconscious during a fight over the attentions of a drunken African American prostitute. The militants shoot the woman and decapitate the two whites to augment a dripping collection of white heads on pikes, which they hold as standards at the front of their marching ranks.[97] As director of the production downtown and at BART/S, Baraka asked a white painter friend, Dominique Capobianco, to create papier mâché face masks to replicate the actors' features exactly, resulting in a shocking degree of verisimilitude.[98]

The startlingly graphic depiction of the deaths is symptomatic of the way Baraka perceived relations between whites and blacks at the time as well as the emotional surgery required to extricate himself (and black revolutionary culture more generally) from the bohemian decadence in which he had been immersed. Despite their initial, high-minded conversation about philosophy, the beatniks in the play become slaves to their urges and brutally compete for the right to the forty-year-old streetwalker's flesh. Duff wants to debase her as a beast of burden, and Loco regresses to infancy (perhaps mammy nostalgia) as he expresses his desire to consume her hairy, smelly body. The woman, similarly, seems to have degenerated from what 'could probably have been an attractive woman, in another life'.[99] Her dishevelled appearance suggests the relinquished self-worth her behaviour evidences when she sells her carnal favours to individuals she clearly despises. When she tells them they descend from people who 'eat meat with their hands' like in 'them old Robin Hood pictures', her dialogue indicates a consciousness of Black Power values that she has chosen not to uphold.[100] Therefore, her careless attempts to ingratiate herself to her 'soulbrother', the Leader of the soldiers, fail to save the life she has already spiritually relinquished.[101]

As Cornel West writes in *Race Matters*, cultural changes in the 1960s made 'black bodies more accessible to white bodies *on an equal basis*', increasing opportunities for consensual interracial sex although dehumanizing racist myths persisted.[102] According to Frantz Fanon, whose writings Baraka read, 'The civilized white man retains an irrational longing for unusual eras of sexual license, of orgiastic scenes, of unpunished rapes, of unrepressed incest', and ascribes to black people 'his own desires' for such abandonment of his purported morality.[103] Many of Baraka's dramatic works respond to this racist longing by enacting a role-reversal of racist stereotypes, presenting whites as crude, bestial, lecherous and unintelligent. By exploring the hidden urges whites outwardly denied but projected blacks, Baraka undermined the typically unquestioned demonstrations of white decency in mid-twentieth-century media, particularly among white progressives. He portrayed whites as psychologically damaged, hysterical, utterly foolish and ravenous, humiliating themselves in their efforts to devour the black objects of their attraction. In Leslie Catherine Sanders' assessment, relationships with whites in Baraka's plays 'signify a lack of self-knowledge and self-acceptance, stymied or misappropriated creative energy, narcissism, and self-degradation' for black characters.[104]

A Black Mass

A Black Mass reworks Elijah Muhammad's myth of the creation of the white race by an ancient black scientist named Jacoub. Baraka wrote the script in his BART/S office in 1965 and engaged Sun Ra and his Myth Science Arkestra to provide the score. The play received its first production in May 1966 at Proctor's Theatre (a former movie house) in Newark with a cast including Baraka's second wife and a woman who indulged his brief experiment with Afrocentric polygamy: Olabumi Osafemi. The play's plot focuses on a wilful mishap generating a feral, id-controlled, soulless, white male beast. This loincloth-clad, lizard-like creature gurgles, vomits, chews, spits, wheezes, scratches, laughs, snarls and repeatedly exclaims the word 'White!'[105] The Beast lunges towards three African women, 'grabbing throats or trying to throw open their robes and stick his head in'.[106] Tiila – played by Sylvia Jones before she changed her name to Amina Baraka – becomes infected as a result of the attack. Her skin turns white, her words degrade into grunts, 'and she moves like an animal robot' while compulsively shouting, 'White! White! White!'[107]

The other women bemoan Tiila's fate, and the magicians Tanzil and Nasafi admonish Jacoub for his error. Jacoub insists he can teach his creation to feel and to love, citing its recognition of the woman, but Tanzil counters that the unholy brute only perceived 'pure female spoor and meat' instead of 'the black beautiful lady of our universe'.[108] Jacoub maintains that he can teach the beast and save Tiila despite the others' argument for banishing the unfortunate beings to 'the cold north' as the only viable option. The women sing then shriek to Sun Ra's magical soundtrack, but Jacoub breaks their spell and releases the beasts from the invisible bonds containing them. Tiila joins her partner monster to kill the rest of the characters in the play 'with fangs and claws'.[109] The two white abominations then turn on the audience, 'drooling and making obscene gestures', before leaping off the stage to kiss and lick the theatregoers while continuing to invoke whiteness.[110] After the creatures exit, a Narrator warns the audience of the ongoing presence of 'beasts in our world', who require killing or imprisonment 'in their caves' and necessitate a 'Holy War', a 'Jihad'.[111] Again, a Black Nationalist Period play concludes with an unambiguous message about the urgency of separating from whiteness.

Great Goodness of Life: A Coon Show

As Baraka observed two decades later in his eulogy to his sister, Kimako, 'Fanon says that some of the oppressed are made sick by oppression, and instead of killing our enemies, too often we want to be them. Being close to them makes the pathological feel more human, less oppressed.'[112] When Baraka returned home to Newark at the end of 1965, he felt disappointed by his parents' expressions of loyalty to his white ex-wife and their grandchildren as well as their disapproval of his new relationship with an African American woman. He doubted their support of his evolving personal and ideological commitments.

In 1966, Baraka wrote *Great Goodness of Life: A Coon Show* while angry with his father for not understanding that he did not legally have to respond to questions from the FBI.[113] As he told Theodore R. Hudson in a 1970 interview, '[W]hat [he] did was take that situation and draw it to an extreme.'[114] Although the script appears in the *Four Black Revolutionary Plays* anthology with the reverential dedication, 'For my father with love and respect',[115] Baraka admitted to Hudson that he based his main character, an archetypal Uncle Tom, on Coyette Leroy Jones. Court Royal, an avowedly law-abiding yet persecuted figure, works for the Post Office as did the senior Jones. Ultimately, he succumbs to brainwashing by the white supremacist establishment, betrays his race, and murders a son whom the drama conflates with multiple saintly Black martyrs (Malcolm X, Patrice Lumumba, Medgar Evers etc.). Baraka added insult to injury by his choice of actress to portray the Young Woman, whom Court fails to defend or protect from accusations and sexual harassment at the hands of 'KKK-like figures'.[116] When Baraka directed the first production at Spirit House, in November 1967, he cast his sister, Elaine Jones (later Kimako Baraka), in the role.

Amidst his disconcerting trial for 'harboring a murderer' – a charge which he fails to reconcile with the routine order of his previously conventional existence – Court witnesses Hoods 1 and 2 push the Young Woman across the stage in front of him, tormenting her by 'pulling her hair, and feeling her ass'.[117] Hood 1 explains that she is drunk and asks Court if he wants to 'smell her breath'. The paternal black man responds by joining the slander with prudish condescension, declaring, 'I smell it from here. She drinks and stinks and brings our whole race down.'[118] He makes no attempt to prevent the Young Woman's doom decreed by the disembodied Voice of judgment, who will later order him to execute his own son.

Seemingly without recourse against the accumulating atrocities disrupting the bucolic setting of his 'old log cabin',[119] Court becomes increasingly agitated and physically registers his shock by shivering, bulging his eyes and losing control of his limbs in jerking dance moves as if he were a marionette. He approaches the degradation and diminished agency of his attorney, John Breck, a clockwork Negro wound up by a 'huge key in the side of his head', who grins and slobbers as he crawls across the stage.[120] However, Court sustains enough integrity to reject Breck's advice that he plead guilty.

Even so, the words of Young Victim indicate that the father, whom the son terms a 'half-white coward', has consistently refused to heed warnings about systemic injustice.[121] Just as he seems sufficiently moved by the plight of his convicted son to request sentencing in solidarity with the 'murderer', Court receives absolution due to his graceful acceptance of fate and 'infinite understanding of the compassionate God Of The Cross'.[122] Unfortunately, the conditions of release dictate that Court use a gold and diamond gun to put a silver bullet into his son. The Voice promises Court he can keep the gun, and his soul will be 'washed (*pause*) white as snow'.[123] Longing to be 'fulfilled', 'happy' and 'relaxed', Court shoots Young Victim in the face, resulting in the dying utterance of 'Papa' from his ankh-wearing sacrifice.[124] Having unequivocally resolved his ambivalence in favour of acquiescence to the establishment, Court plans to celebrate his purification, freedom and epiphany that 'life is a beautiful thing' by going bowling.[125] Clinging to such comforting emblems of bourgeois decency (television, car, home, club, thirty-five years on the job) has reaped rewards of security and consumerist contentment.

Madheart

In a 2002 interview with Joyce A. Joyce, Baraka discussed how the play *Madheart* symbolized his divorce from his white first wife and his separation from his white associates.[126] Henry C. Lacey describes *Madheart* specifically as 'an exorcistic work',[127] and Charles D. Peavy analyses how multiple Baraka plays include a white woman as demon and 'the chief impediment to the black male's realization of his identity'.[128] I have written extensively elsewhere claiming that the process of writing this play 'helped Baraka resolve his conflicted conscience sufficiently to support his decisive break from his formerly bohemian lifestyle and consequent adoption of the militant separatism he would sustain until the 1974 inauguration of the Marxist-Leninist phase of his career'.[129]

Baraka wrote *Madheart: A Morality Play* in 1966 in response to then San Francisco State College Black Student Union President Jimmy Garrett's invitation to come to California and serve as a faculty member in the first Black Studies programme, though that programme wouldn't be instituted until after a violent student strike.[130] The play first appeared in print in 1968's *Black Fire: An Anthology of Afro-American Writing*, co-edited by Baraka and his Black Arts Movement colleague Larry Neal. Produced under Baraka's direction by the Black Arts Alliance in May 1967, the play had sets and props designed by Emory Douglas, who would become Minister of Culture for the Black Panther Party, armed members of which flanked the stage to provide security.[131] The Panthers could not have predicted that the playwright's growing attachment to Maulana Karenga's Kawaida doctrine of cultural nationalism – evidenced by references within the script for *Madheart* – would soon become a source of tension. Indeed, Baraka would side with the Africana studies professor and Kwanzaa creator in an acrimonious and deadly rift between Karenga's US organization and the BPP.

The plot of *Madheart* revolves around Black Man killing Devil Lady and marrying Black Woman, much to the distress of his assimilationist Mother and Sister. Several scholars view it as a sequel to *Dutchman*. Sanders considers Devil Lady 'a grotesque, magical version' of Lula, emblematic of 'the racial struggle for domination that white society imposes on blacks'.[132] Kimberly Benston names Clay's killer the 'forerunner' of Devil Lady.[133] Werner Sollors calls Devil Lady 'a Black nationalist extension of Lula'.[134] Peavy interprets Devil Lady as a 'reincarnated' Lula.[135] And Beth McCoy astutely connects the title *Madheart* to Clay's invocation of 'the pure heart, the pumping black heart' incomprehensible to Lula.[136] But despite his initial enthrallment, Black Man quickly extricates himself from the orbit of Devil Lady's 'pussy [that] rules the world'.[137]

Already, on the second of the text's nineteen pages, Black Man proclaims his intention to kill Devil Lady, and he proceeds to attempt her murder at least five times. His methods include skewering her through the heart to the stage floor. He also stabs her in the abdomen and genitals. But a pronouncement from Black Woman, '[B]e still in the grave where you have fun', appears to deliver the ultimate death blow to Devil Lady, who moans her final utterance, screams and 'writhes and stiffens in death'.[138]

After eliminating Devil Lady, Black Woman parallels Lula's taunting of Clay by provoking Black Man to claim her as his own.[139] In an example of what Baraka later judged 'some really kind of backward statements in terms of Black women–Black men relationships',[140] Black Man slaps Black Woman four times and compels her to 'submit' to him rather than remain prey for white men.[141] Black Woman, whose fecundity eclipses Devil Lady's frigidity, accepts Black Man's 'seed' and joins him on his mission to deliver Mother and Sister from their pernicious obsession with Devil Lady and the hegemonic culture she represents.[142]

Spewing a vitriolic philippic comparable to Clay's Bessie Smith speech at the conclusion of *Dutchman*, Black Man attacks the dead woman one final time. He demands of Devil Lady, 'Die, you bitch, and drag your mozarts into your nasty hole. Your mozarts stravinskys stupid white sculpture corny paintings deathfiddles, all your crawling jive, drag it in and down with you, your officebuildings blow up in your pussy' before stomping her in the face and throwing her off the stage into an explosion of smoke and light.[143] Black Man achieves the fulfilment of the impulse Baraka acknowledged led to his second marriage: 'a yearning to be completely whole. To be able to struggle with my whole heart and soul, with my whole being, for what was deepest in me, which I took, then, as Blackness'.[144]

Much as the Black Nationalist Baraka felt his second marriage to an African American woman confirmed his commitment to racial authenticity compromised by his interracial marriage, his separatist ideology of the nationalist period presumed an adamant rejection of homosexuality as a degrading weakness and symptom of Western corruption. As Cheryl Clarke explains, Black Power ideologies tended to adopt the 'popular conception of male homosexuality as passivity, the willingness to be fucked', which contradicted movement ideals by being 'antithetical to the concept of black macho, the object of which is to do the fucking'.[145] Hence, the assimilated Sister in *Madheart* declares, 'If I have to have a niggerman, give me a faggot anyday',[146] implying that such a lover would most closely approximate her preference for whites.

Celebrity satires: *J-E-L-L-O*, *The Sidney Poet Heroical* and *Rockgroup*

Originally written in 1965 and first performed as part of the BART/S street repertory before appearing on a double bill with *A Black Mass* at the Proctors in Newark in May 1966,[147] *J-E-L-L-O* presents a parodic representation of the radio and television fixtures 'Jack Benny and Rochester, and what happens when Rochester digs hisself'.[148] This 'long hair, postuncletom' Rochester emancipates himself by robbing the entire cast of *The Jack Benny Show* –

including the announcer selling the eponymous name brand gelatin.[149] Rochester also thwarts Benny's wife when he snatches a moneybag from beneath her skirt instead of grabbing her the way she anticipates. And Dennis Day is portrayed as a 'highvoiced fag', helpless to resist Rochester's larceny before fainting with a comically protracted moan.[150]

Two other plays Baraka wrote in the 1960s parody celebrities while casting aspersions on decadent sexuality as symptomatic of racial inauthenticity and cultural appropriation: *The Sidney Poet Heroical* and *Rockgroup*. Baraka wrote the former during his 1967 trial.[151] The script satirizes Sidney Poitier and Harry Belafonte and was excluded from the 1978 anthology, *The Motion of History and Other Plays* because publishers feared a lawsuit.[152] The play, which received a limited production at Woodie King's New Federal Theatre during the mid-1970s, traces the career trajectory of the title character losing his connection to his roots until he realizes he must reclaim and champion his blackness. A critical turning point occurs when a life-size, talking Academy Award awakens Sidney from the bed he shares with a naked white woman and shows him in the mirror that his skin has turned white.

Rockgroup shows a comparable degeneration associated with maniacal fandom, this time without a happy ending. Dealing with musical appropriation, this play was published by Baraka and his Black Arts Movement cohorts – Larry Neal and A. B. Spellman – in the December 1969 issue of their magazine *The Cricket*. It presents a group of four young men in 'Beetle [sic] suits and wigs', played by actors in 'whiteface'.[153] Introduced as 'The Crackers', these 'White boys' play 'Geetahs' and sing inane lyrics of 'white shit white shit white shit', casting a spell of 'hocuspocus in the clouds allright'.[154] Throughout their performance, something moves and moans beneath a black cloth on the stage. They gather their money and go home to their cave, where what was hidden under the black cloth, the secret of their genius, is revealed: a 'chained nigger (in falling down konk and raggidy sequined stage evening clothes)'.[155]

Slave Ship

Baraka wrote *Slave Ship: A Historical Pageant* 'just before the Newark rebellion'. He states in his Introduction to *The Motion of History and Other Plays* that the 'impending explosion is the heat you feel' from the 'flatly nationalist and anti-white' script.[156] Jihad Press published the play in 1967, and the playwright directed the original Spirit House production in March of the same year, four months before his hometown hosted The National Conference on Black Power.

The play depicts the agonies of the Middle Passage through a fourth-wall-breaching, multi-sensory onslaught designed to immerse the audience in the experience of transatlantic slave-trade captivity. The stage directions describe an opening in darkness and indicate that lights do not come on fully until midway through the action. In the meantime, only a dim light appears at the top of the set to indicate the location of the voices speaking on deck above the blackened cargo hold that constitutes the *mise en scène*. At intervals, blindingly bright lights illuminate the white sailors as they brandish their whips and make fun of the misery permeating the world below. Like the shocks of the sudden flashing lights, sounds and smells assault the audience more intensely in the darkness. The slave ship rocks and groans, Yoruba drums play songs of worship, chains rattle, whips crack, babies cry and bells ring. People scream, moan, sing, chant and attempt to comfort one another through their sufferings. Incense burns to thicken the air as the aroma of the splashing sea collides with the funk of the amassed bodily excretions unavoidable in confinement. Limited verbal dialogue tells the horrors of rape, desperate searching for separated loved ones and the tragedy of Dademi, who chokes her child before strangling herself with her chain.

When the lights abruptly come fully up halfway through the play, they do so to reveal an obsequious, shuffling 'Negro' with his hat in hand, 'agreeing with massa' and 'scratching his head and butt' as he advances towards the audience.[157] Continued light changes off and on suggest the progression of time until the sailors appear as plantation owners, and the recently introduced 'Tomish slave' reports to the white man about a planned "volt ... uhhhh ... revolt'.[158] Race traitor Tom next hides from the fracas that ensues, while scarfing down pork chops he received as his thirty pieces of silver.[159] The scenes proceed further through history, presenting slaves who now all have English names and sing Christian songs. New Tom/Preacher attempts to look dignified despite communicating in his 'pseudo-intelligent patter' for 'the boss'.[160] During his sermon about non-violence, he tries to hide the burned corpse of a baby killed in a 'blown-up church'.[161]

Against the preacher, the music of saxophones and drums (provided by an Archie Shepp score for the 1969 productions) rises to accompany a chorus singing 'When We Gonna Rise', an anthem of empowerment transcending the centuries. Far from subtle in communicating its stance, *Slave Ship* climaxes with the killing of New Tom by a Temptations-style line of African dancers emerging from the titular vessel to vindicate the ancestors. They embody a kind of temporal crossroads by performing 'a new-old dance' Baraka names the 'Boogalooyoruba', invoking simultaneously the newest dance craze and a truly old-time religion.[162] Despite Preacher's calls for help from 'white Jesus boss', the insurgents make him 'daid' before turning on the Voice of God, whose 'long blond blow-hair' fails to save even his immortal divinity from their resolve.[163] The lights fade while sounds from the beginning of the play return and half-light fixes the actors in their motion of executing the disembodied presence of the Eurocentric deity. A blackout punctuates the deed before lights come up again to welcome the audience to a dance party, ratcheted to heights of jubilation by throwing the preacher's head into the centre of the celebration.

When Baraka looked back upon *Slave Ship*, he affirmed the historical pageant's 'hot note of rage'.[164] Regardless of its failure to indict capitalism as the true enemy of people of all colours, the play 'killed no one who did not need killing'.[165] That point was emphasized in the 1969 Free Southern Theater (FST) tour, where audiences would greet the performances they witnessed with ferocious enthusiasm and approval of the play's violent conclusion. The FST co-founder Gilbert Moses, who directed the production, 'intended to arouse his audience's militancy and direct them to take action in their own lives'.[166] The tactic seems to have worked because Black participation in voter registration drives drastically rose in some of the cities visited by performances of *Slave Ship*.[167] Audiences also responded to performances in light of the urban uprisings that occurred in dozens of cities during the decade. Val Ferdinand (later Kalamu ya Salaam) wrote in the April 1970 *Negro Digest* about a fist-waving audience standing and singing, 'When we gonna rise up!' in response to a West Point, Mississippi, performance.[168] A member of that same audience confronted the actor playing a whip-wielding slave driver, threatening, 'I want to see you after the show.'[169] In Greenville, Mississippi, the blacks 'were ready to revolt after the performance was over and ... were only reluctantly persuaded to go home'.[170] Harry J. Elam, Jr. also describes a Baton Rouge crowd prevented from rioting by bolting the auditorium doors.[171]

Following the stir created by the FST tour, *Slave Ship* continued to incite strong reactions when shows ran in New York. For the staging at the Brooklyn Academy of Music, Moses sought to amplify the claustrophobic experience of confinement in a ship's cargo hold, a desire captured effectively by set designer Eugene Lee placing the audience within the ship.[172] They sat on uncomfortable benches that forced them to lean forward, losing all semblance of aesthetic distance and absorbing the disturbing spectacle of screaming, childbirth, rape and vomit as part of the ordeal. For a special highlight, these performances featured a slave auction which, on one night, allowed *New Yorker* drama critic Edith Oliver to purchase a ten-year-old black boy.[173] Such conditions encouraged 'disorientation and even hysteria' so hypnotic that 'many whites attempted to stand up and join the singing chanting blacks ... even though it was their own destruction', a phenomenon Elam considers proof of 'the infectious power' of the performance event.[174] Clive Barnes, a white critic for the *New York Times*, ended his review with a blessing of the work: 'Peace, "Slave Ship" – do your thing.' The honour of this commendation carries greater emphasis coming as it does after Barnes spends paragraphs judging the play 'racist' and a 'get whitey' piece of 'propaganda', which had him frightened because of his identity as 'whitey' sitting among others of his race in the 'deliberately segregated audience'.[175]

Conclusion

Baraka's other late-decade plays continued to respond to the political situation faced by black Americans. Published in 1967, *Arm Yrself or Harm Yrself* explores the diminished effectiveness of armed self-defence against homicidal cops when African Americans allow arguments among themselves to disrupt their vigilance.[176] *Home on the Range* was read in 1967 as part of the Black Communications Project, which supported the student strike at San

Francisco State College.[177] When produced at Amiri and Amina's Spirit House performance space and artists' residence in spring 1968, the play was enhanced by an Albert Ayler jazz improvisation. Again, Baraka subverts racialized presumptions of intelligence and decency through his depiction of Black Criminal's encounter with a comically incomprehensible, Germanic gibberish-speaking white family, obsessed with television, status symbols and a longing to consume black bodies. *Police* (1968) shows a Black Cop objectified by his white peers, who consider him a 'savage' and proceed to cannibalize him after they orgasm over his suicide by 'penis-pistol' when he can no longer cope with the suffering he has routinely caused in the line of duty.[178] *Black Power Chant* (1968) offers a choreography of unison stomps and turns to accompany shouts that 'White people are killing US', juxtaposed with a list of instructions for achieving proper militancy through training to shoot, fight and survive tests of physical endurance.[179] Designed as 'An agitation to be done' in the location of its namesake, *Board of Education* (1968) demands that seat holders should 'step down' if they will not teach black history.[180]

The 1970 NewArk-produced play *Junkies Are Full of (Shh . . .)* demonstrates an aggressive level of self-determination through its portrayal of Afrocentric Newark citizens killing an African American drug dealer and the Italian gangsters and Jewish accountants profiting from the spread of heroin in the community.[181] This drama also displays a markedly more didactic dramaturgy than the ritualistic form that dominated Baraka's Black Nationalist period. Indeed, epic dramaturgy began to dominate his playwriting by the time of his shift in 1974 to Third World Marxist ideology, a shift that endured to the end of his life on 9 January 2014. Although he exchanged a Black nationalist agenda for a socialist one that included white people among the oppressed, Baraka continued to emphasize the primacy of black liberation.

Baraka's political and artistic legacies were evident within two years after his passing. In May of 2014, the people of Newark – the city Baraka dedicated years of his life to improving – elected his son Ras as mayor, and the new mayor appointed his brother Amiri, Jr to chief of staff. The next year, Woodie King, Jr's New Federal Theatre dedicated its forty-sixth season to Baraka. The company's 2015 theatrical year began with a revival of *Dutchman* and closed with the world premiere of Baraka's last play, *Most Dangerous*

Man in America (W. E. B. Du Bois). Kimberly W. Benston assessed his legacy well: 'The salvation of his own soul and that of his people are inextricable.'[182] Who those 'people' were may have changed through his shifting career progression, but Baraka remained constant in his devotion to their cause.

5

Adrienne Kennedy

Lenora Inez Brown

Introduction

When Adrienne Kennedy (pronounced *Add*-rienne) burst onto the downtown, Off-Broadway theatre scene in 1964 with her first play, *Funnyhouse of a Negro*, the shy and retiring 34-year-old Cleveland native, wife and mother of two, quickly established herself as a lyrical playwright who captures an emotional fervency with nightmarish images that paint a rarely seen picture of the African American experience. Kennedy became known for intense one-act dramatic adventures, eschewing the then-traditional theatrical and dramatic rules of realism in favour of a unique expressionistic style that mixes theatrical and literary genres and styles (classic Greek icons, African images, Victorian-era motifs or scenarios from classic Hollywood films). What truly sets Kennedy apart, however, is the rarely discussed fact that she was one of the first African American playwrights to engage the African diaspora and themes of internationalism in her work. This is likely due to the fact that Kennedy often travelled and lived abroad from 1960 to 1969. These experiences set her apart from most Americans at the time – African American or white – and firmly placed Kennedy among the vanguard of creative thinkers and theatrical writers both then and now. Also, unlike many African American writers of the time, Kennedy did not grapple head-on with civil rights struggles in the United States. She did not ignore those struggles, however, but instead placed them within the context of the individual's struggle for freedom from colonialist rule, which accounts for the references to leaders such as Patrice Lumumba, Frantz Fanon and Malcolm X in her plays. But Kennedy also broke the mould by referring to her experiences living internationally and including physical references to cities and political structures outside the African continent such as Victorian royalty and British literary figures.

All of Kennedy's works confront the complications racial difference plays in terms of acceptance, expectation and the perception of self and other, particularly when viewed through the lens of the dominant white culture. Her writing clearly demonstrates that African Americans are shaped by multiple groups, beliefs and movements (artistic and political), and yet are often forced to declare an allegiance to a single identity despite those many forces. Kennedy's work illustrates that, as a result of these opposing perspectives, psychological and political struggles divide the African American's self, especially the female self. Quite simply, Kennedy's writing makes it clear that African Americans, especially African American females, are outsiders because they are not allowed to claim allegiance or affinity to those who shape them, regardless of their origin.

Early life and career

Kennedy was born Adrienne Lita Hawkins on 13 September 1931, in Pittsburgh, Pennsylvania, the only daughter of Etta and Cornell Wallace Hawkins. Her father, a Morehouse College graduate, was an executive for the YMCA and later worked for the City of Cleveland in the Civil Rights Office. Kennedy reaped the benefits of a privileged upbringing in a well-off, integrated Cleveland neighbourhood. Kennedy's sole sibling, Cornell Hawkins, served in the Army and attended Ohio State University for a brief time. She graduated from Ohio State in 1953 with a major in education. As ethnically and religiously diverse as her childhood neighbourhood was, Kennedy experienced segregation and racism during summer trips to visit family in the South and at Ohio State University, where she remembers that many white female classmates, '[o]ften from southern Ohio towns . . . were determined to subjugate the Negro girls. They were determined to make you feel that it was a great inequity that they had to live in the same dorm with you . . . [T]he often open racial hatred of the girls in the dorm continued to demoralize me.'[1]

Kennedy married Joseph C. Kennedy in 1953. Following his military service in Korea, she travelled with him to Liberia, Nigeria and Ghana in the autumn of 1960 while he was a doctoral candidate studying at Columbia University and working for the African Research Foundation. During this time abroad, the couple's second son, Adam, was born (their first son, Joseph Jr, was born in the United States). Kennedy's travels also included visits to London, Paris, Casablanca and Rome, all cities she features in her plays.

Kennedy defied many expectations and stereotypes regarding writers – and especially female writers – at the time. As a wife, mother and a trained educator with a desire to write plays, she had difficulty fitting in with the Columbia graduate students and their wives. The Columbia crowd expected Kennedy to talk about motherhood and the downtown crowd, where she was often the only African American writer in the group writing. Her memoir suggests that she thought she failed to fit in because she was not from the East Coast. To her, ethnicity seemed to have little bearing on her assessment of success.

Almost immediately upon entering Ghana, Kennedy experienced her first professional success as a writer with the publication, under a pseudonym, of her short story 'Because of the King of France' in the journal *Black Orpheus*. Even after seven years of unsuccessfully submitting work, this achievement did not allow her to feel a total success. 'I was twenty-nine years old and a failure in my eyes,' she recalled, but she did feel that 'Africa had ignited a fire inside me.'[2] That fire was one of artistic and political connection to a line of great African writers such as Chinua Achebe, Wole Soyinka and Eufua Sutherland.

First-hand exposure to African cultures – their art, strong royal lineages, great thinkers, and grand accomplishments of people, intellectuals, royalty and change-agents – altered Kennedy's consciousness regarding the possibilities for those of African descent. She later wrote, 'A Black man living in a palace catapulted my consciousness onto a new level. A black living in a palace and the president of a country . . . the idea of it made my blood rush.'[3] This confirmed the beliefs she had acquired raised in a family that embraced the thinking of W. E. B. Du Bois and others who had achieved great success and stature among the established, influential and well-educated African American community. But something was different for her in Ghana.

As the civil rights movement gained momentum in the United States, African countries were similarly engaged in a pursuit for independence from colonialist rule. The struggle for independence in Africa was, at the time, more violent than in the United States, punctuated with the assassination in early 1961 of Patrice Lumumba, the prime minister of Congo. Kennedy writes, 'Just when I had discovered the place of my ancestors, just when I had discovered this African hero, he had been murdered... Even though I had known of him so briefly, I felt I had been struck a blow. He became a character in my play ... a man with a shattered head.'[4] The impact of living abroad, Lumumba's assassination and the growing power of anti-colonial and civil rights movements permeates Kennedy's writing. Violence and history regularly coincide in drama, but rarely does theatrical writing so willingly acknowledge the psychological and emotional impact of these moments on individual characters by showing how the self becomes fractured. Usually, writers chart the cause and effect rather than attempt to physically illustrate the emotional devastation violence ignites. Kennedy writes about the moment at hand even when it is shaped by past aggressions, whether personal or political.

Although a tradition of African American female playwrights from Angelina Weld Grimké to Zora Neale Hurston to Alice Childress to Lorraine Hansberry existed, these were not the writers Kennedy studied as she cultivated her writing. She did read Lorraine Hansberry and acknowledged her influence opening doors for African American writers and women in theatre, but the writers she sought out in bookstores when she lived in Cleveland and was eager to meet once she moved to New York and began studying at Circle in the Square were Samuel Beckett, Eugène Ionesco, Tennessee Williams and Arthur Miller. When Kennedy met director Michael Kahn, he commented on her writing, 'Gosh, you're a lot like Lorca and a little like Tennessee,' and she said, 'Those are my idols.'[5]

Kennedy's attraction to Williams began when she saw a touring production of *The Glass Menagerie* at Karamu House, Cleveland's socially progressive and interracial theatre. She was particularly taken by the fact that the play was built around memories, with little distinction made between the past and present. Action didn't flow through flashbacks; it simply flowed to different moments in the story and the character's evolution. Most importantly, Williams wrote about outsiders, men and women who didn't fit and would never fit in. Similarly, Miller's most memorable characters were also outsiders who were often able to blend in even as they felt horribly out of step with the expectations and demands of society. Thin veneers and facades were what made Miller and Williams's characters vulnerable and memorable. Their characters rarely let their emotional angst run free. Finally, Lorca's work focused on charting his characters' emotional traumas and the imagery associated with that psychological journey. This is where Kennedy broached new territory for African American playwriting specifically (and American playwriting in general): her main characters only shared their emotional angst through the story, making the world both terrifying and exciting. As Gaby Rodgers notes, 'The language is often repetitive and circular. This repetition gives the text a traumatized and haunted air'[6] as they navigate the old worlds of personal isolation and exclusion anew. This likely reflected the pressures of her family's social prominence:

> I came from a family that was very social, very prominent, but inside our house we had these seemingly endless conflicts, these arguments. And I really wanted to get that down. I couldn't understand that as a young person. How could we be a certain way on the outside and another inside our house?[7]

While most consider the outsider quality to be present in all of Kennedy's work, critical discussion often considers the nature of this alienation solely in terms of her autobiography. Yes, Kennedy is quoted as stating that autobiography is important to playwriting, but too many assume that her plays are autobiographical. Kennedy readily acknowledges how her life informs the genesis of character names and dramatic scenarios, but these characters and dramatic worlds are largely imagined. Sadly, her collaborators and readers so connect Kennedy with her characters that acceptance of her work has sometimes suffered. As Michael Kahn notes in a 1990 interview, 'I felt that Sarah [from *Funnyhouse*] was Adrienne and I knew that Clara [*Owl Answers*] was her aunt.'[8]

Margaret B. Wilkerson comments on this tendency to glean too much autobiographical influence in Kennedy's work:

> While Kennedy drew on close relatives and family stories in shaping this play [*Funnyhouse*], she does not treat them literally

but uses them as metaphors for particular forces at work in Sarah's life. Thus while Sarah's conflict is intensely personal and emanates from Kennedy's own explorations of her consciousness, it is also metaphorical and symptomatic of the ambiguous state of a people who were created out of the clash of African and European cultures.[9]

In truth, Kennedy did nothing different from most playwrights: she incorporated elements from her life into an entirely fictional world. Where Kennedy differs is that she willingly acknowledges which moments inspired her plays and does little to mask these moments. The other great difference: she is an African American woman. With so few plays by African American women providing vivid insight into the harrowing reality of navigating both a white world and the realities of the African American experience, critics and theatregoers alike – then and now – can be overwhelmed by the level of challenge and honesty her plays contain. Often, playwrights mask their autobiography, as Williams did when he included the Blue Moon Casino and described it as he remembered it, as he encountered it as a child. Or, when Arthur Miller wrote lines like 'Attention must be paid', a particularly Brooklyn Jewish expression that Elia Kazan actively worked to sound less so in order that the play would resonate universally. Because Kennedy creates worlds where an African American woman/girl confronts what it is to be black in a white world with few attempts to temper or explain the harrowing reality for whites (or to explain or excuse the pain so it is easier for whites to accept and begin to understand the root of the pain, prejudice, exclusion and problem), many find it easier to push her painful work aside by framing it as simply autobiographical. Unfortunately, this was also true of the black community. Kahn offered the following assessment in an interview with Howard Stein: 'I think Adrienne was severely ostracized. Her plays were considered neurotic and . . . not supportive of the black movement.'[10] In essence, if the play articulates just one African American woman's problem, many would choose to assume that the problem doesn't really exist. But truths too unimaginable to exist do exist, do occur. When a society or group can't bring itself to meet the challenge and its culpability in creating that situation, the problem is ignored and so can be the author.

What also takes Kennedy's work into more dangerous and personally revealing territory is that she chose to discuss intimate issues rarely discussed in polite circles or on the stage, then or now, such as menstruation or the incredibly demoralizing journey associated with female hair loss. Many cultures regard hair as an extension of a woman's sexuality and femininity – long hair especially so. Even more so for African American women, identity struggles are often tied to hair given the various textures and its descriptors – nappy, kinky, good, straight, Indian – and the fact that those descriptors were often seen as extensions of the African American's personality, class or behaviour. Nappy or kinky hair was equated with poor hair and suggested a host of negative personality traits. Good or straight or Indian hair was seen as similar to 'most white women's hair', and those who had such hair were often seen as more like good people, or whiter. To achieve straighter hair, better hair, more 'like white' hair, many African American women used straighteners with harsh chemicals and lost their hair. Once bald, they also lost the trait most associated with femininity. So, what is an African American woman with little or no hair? All of this history Kennedy captures in a single image of an African American woman with thinning hair in her first play, *Funnyhouse of a Negro*.

Kennedy confronts a similar, uniquely African American concern more often in her plays than many other African American writers, especially in the 1960s: the intra-racial controversy of prejudice toward those with different skin tones. During the 1960s, such discussions were unusual and in some circles considered unseemly to discuss outside the community. Historically, if such discussion of, say, colour differentiation occurred during a play, a writer would address it as Alice Childress did in *Wedding Band*, where a clearly realistic world exists and characters offer comments about the issue to other characters, or their jobs are defined (and obstacles created) by skin colour. Kennedy's plays do something rather different, something reminiscent of Williams or Lorca, presenting the psychological reality the characters experience rather than the social or political reality. This is especially true of *Funnyhouse*. As a result, Kennedy doesn't provide a safety net for audiences. Her plays immerse the audience in the characters' emotional trauma regarding their skin tone. In later plays, her characters present that struggle of seeing or imagining themselves as white, a strategy that we also find in many of Kirsten Greenidge's plays.

Because her work was not obviously connected to the civil rights movement, it dealt with matters considered by many African

Americans to be inappropriate or demoralizing to discuss publicly, and because she showed the internal struggle racial oppression and spiritual paralysis caused within the individual, rather than using the emotional upset to fuel action or protest or confrontation of the 'other', she was not received well by the African American community. Theatre historian and critic Paul Carter Harrison places the negative response to Kennedy's work from certain black writers in context:

> During the 1960s, many black radicals rejected her work as being not black, but more European. The ritualistic elements of her work, deliberately or otherwise, seemed more of a response to Afro-centric aesthetics than all the black protests and agit-prop plays being written at the time ... And she employed a language that was magical.[11]

It is no wonder that her first producer, Edward Albee, was drawn to Kennedy's work. Both writers tackle timeless and universal human struggles that society prefers to ignore and they do so in unflinching, unflattering ways. These plays are not plays to sit back and watch, but frightening worlds to become immersed in and in which to struggle to achieve calm or balance. The emotional journey Kennedy's plays evoke may be the reason she has had so few productions. What remains the most interesting and ironic truth regarding Kennedy's work and its power is that, although she may be one of America's least produced major playwrights, she is among the most widely studied African American playwrights, and her work has, arguably, influenced the greatest number of contemporary American writers of any ethnicity.

Kennedy and the Black Arts Movement

As an African American playwright, Kennedy is now sometimes grouped with the Black Arts Movement (BAM) and its male writers: Amiri Baraka, Ed Bullins, Richard Wesley. During the 1960s, however, Kennedy was not actively embraced by the movement. Kennedy's work embraces African influences in a more holistic and culturally self-reflective way, advocating for action in a different way, one committed to understanding where the subtle and not so subtle injustices live in image, word and historical absence without calling for a publicly faced set of actions.

The Black Arts Movement is best described by Olga Barrios as 'concerned with the effort to define a black aesthetic that could, in turn, help define African American artistic production and ... help achieve self-determination and a restoration of the community's history. But gender issues were not often included within this agenda.'[12] On the one hand, how could an African American artist writing about the challenge of existing in a white and black world not be embraced by BAM, even if the protagonists were female? On the other hand, failure to embrace Kennedy suggests a vision of what drama should look and sound like, making exclusion expected and easy to execute. Many BAM plays adhered to the rules of realism and one-act structures. Those that didn't might include poetic language, but certainly placed the male character to the fore.

The BAM strove to provide a more balanced depiction of black men (and black male writers) and to highlight the racist tendency to paint black men as highly sexual, violent, unambitious and anti-intellectual. With lines that cast black men as rapists (as in *Funnyhouse*) or perpetrators of incest (as in *A Beast Story* or *Rat's Mass*), Kennedy was often seen as perpetuating negative images associated with black males, furthering her ostracization by the movement. Although the negative depiction of African American men was not her intent, she nevertheless encountered resistance from the African American community for these depictions. As a result, few African American male scholars discuss Kennedy's men with as much consideration as Ishmael Reed offered in 2012 upon learning that she would not receive a Pulitzer Prize.

> Another roadblock ... is that her male characters don't fit the 'black boogeyman' cast. Her portraits of black men ... are talented and intellectual. Throughout her plays, Kennedy insists on showing black men who are devoted to uplifting the community. Good Citizens ... Her black men are not uniformly positive. They are balanced. They can be brutes as well as professors and directors of *Hamlet*.
>
> Kennedy points out that the men of her family are aristocrats, not the incest perpetrator of *Precious*, a black-skinned beast with two or three lines.[13]

Kennedy remains one of the few black writers from this era – male or female – who embraced an avant-garde style of imagery, emotional tenor and format. In addition to eschewing a conventional act structure, she composes plays out of fragmented visions or movements. Her plays are replete with short sentences and visual moments. The spare, condensed language embraces a level of anxious emotion and psychological discord. Her work not only places the black American within a variety of cultures, including West African cultures, but makes way for a uniquely female voice and perspective in theatre. This innovative form and willingness to peel away the historic layers to the self (as seen personally and defined by the large society) make her writing viscerally engaging, thought-provoking and so exceptional that all writers who claim the title of 'avant-garde' such as Ntozake Shange, Aisha Rahman, Robbie McCauley and Kirsten Greenidge were influenced by Kennedy, whether they realize it or not.

Kennedy's numerous non-black supporters and collaborators further separated her from the Black Arts Movement, which emphasized political, economic and social separation from whites. Regardless, her work never avoided bringing African American perspectives to the stage. As she put it, 'I took up being a writer because I wanted to break through barriers ... One thing is important to know: If you don't write for a total audience, you are not going to survive as a playwright. I wanted to communicate with people.'[14] Even so, theatre scholars do consider her work to have an activist bent. Robert Brustein writes, 'I liked Adrienne's unflinching honesty, her simple poetic style and her capacity to contemplate injustice without whining about it. She manages to combine issues of social justice and personal relationships in a most unique way.'[15] Finally, Kennedy was committed to integrated casts and crews. Many of her directors and supporters were white or Jewish, such as Michael Kahn, Gerald Freedman and Edward Albee. This connection with many directors rather than just one, during a time when the playwright–director collaboration was considered critical to ensuring continued production and theatrical life, may have contributed to Kennedy's inconsistent production history. Howard Stein offers, 'The most painful thing of all is to find the writers who have no director. No director discovers them. They don't discover a director and it goes on and on and on.'[16] Kahn certainly believed 'she wasn't served well by more realistic directors than me'.[17]

The tendency is for theatres to produce work that reflects a world that is either all black or all white or all Asian or all Native American, when in reality the world is decidedly more mixed. Kennedy knew that depicting America as one ethnic group fails to reflect reality. One group may predominate, but rarely does one group exist in a vacuum. Such a point of view was radical during a time when the Black Arts Movement advocated separatism, and non-culturally specific theatres regularly claimed they did not know of non-white actors, designers or directors, especially those outside Manhattan.

In addition to subject, casting, and political statement (or lack thereof), Kennedy's work proved both challenging and innovative in its length and use of language. All of Kennedy's work is brief. All of her plays are one-acts with running times no longer than ninety minutes; many are sixty minutes or less. Even so, her one-acts can stand alone as an evening of theatre. Her language both frames the action as narration and inserts the main character(s) in the centre of the psychological storm. Kennedy's language and imagery often repeat. Less like a poetic refrain, language and image return to underscore the event or memory's emotional impact. In fact, the constant intrusion of repeated images paints the picture of a living nightmare. Events don't occur once and then leave an individual alone to recount them in organized monologues when the moment seems right. No. Kennedy shows that harrowing memories intrude upon wakeful moments and push an individual to relive the moment not necessarily as it was but how it has been recorded in mind and spirit. The repetitious language and imagery illustrate the insidious hold frightful memories have. It isn't that individuals do not move on – they do. Time won't allow anyone to simply stand still – but the memories continue to swirl, harass and harangue, making it appear as if the individual hasn't moved on. The repetitious language shows that scarred individuals move forward with pain, and sometimes in spite of it. The existence may not be calm, peaceful or healthy – and for some characters the struggle for peace proves too great – but the journey is always forward.

Funnyhouse of a Negro

Kennedy began writing what would become *Funnyhouse of a Negro* during her time in Rome (she moved from Ghana to Rome during the final months of her pregnancy) and on the two-week ocean journey back to the US. The voyage provided Kennedy with the necessary solitude needed to write what mattered to her. She also began *The Owl Answers* at this time, for the two works were originally conceived as one piece, but through the writing process she began to see the plays as separate.

Funnyhouse of a Negro follows Negro Sarah as she struggles to understand and separate herself from her reality and her nightmarish imaginings of severed heads with thinning hair, African masks and sounds from her past. Throughout the play, Sarah sees herself as Queen Victoria and the Duchess of Hapsburg. Together, these women examine Sarah's life, especially her memory of her black father exacting violence upon her white mother. Worried that Sarah is up to no good, the white Landlady occasionally interrupts the narrative with her own assessment. After discovering Sarah's dead body hanging, it is Raymond, Sarah's Jewish boyfriend, who has the last word and claims that much of what Negro Sarah said was a lie, leaving the audience to wonder who to trust: a black woman or the white people left behind to tell the story.

The play chronicles the final moments before Sarah's death and the harrowing memories and images that plague her as she tries to assert, unsuccessfully, a place for herself in this world. Kennedy completed the final version of the play after a semester of development at Circle in the Square's Writer's Workshop in 1962. Edward Albee ran the workshop at what was one of the most influential Off-Broadway theatres of the time. Kennedy writes, 'January 1962. I studied with Albee for one semester. That was a huge breakthrough for me. I had been in New York all those years and everybody kept saying how promising I was. Everybody was promising me out of my life!'[18] Actors, playwrights and directors came to Circle in the Square to develop talents and identify new ways of telling stories. Among Circle's illustrious alumni are Yaphet Kotto, Richard Brooks and Diana Sands (who was to premiere the role of Sarah, but a previous commitment prevented her from doing so).

Kennedy's decision to join Albee's writing class in 1962 was easy, but finding the courage to remain in the class of thirteen as the only African American and one of two women proved more challenging:

> There were about thirteen people in the seminar. Your play was done in workshop ... They did my play, and it was very

controversial. In many ways had it not been for Edward Albee, I would have thought maybe my play was a total flop ... Yes, because so many people in the workshop didn't like it. I was the only Black person in the group, I was already self-conscious, there were only two women. People sort of had a hostility to it.[19]

When asked what she thought attracted Albee to *Funnyhouse*, which he produced in 1964, Kennedy offered, 'There is something about that play that he truly loved, he loved the language, he loved the rhythms in the monologues, and he liked the form. He took a strong stand for the play.'[20] According to Albee, what attracted him was less specific but insightful: 'I read her work, was startled and thrilled and put her in my class immediately.'[21]

During the 1960s, Circle in the Square was comprised of Off-Broadway performers, playwrights and other theatre artists, many of whom went on to become giants in the American theatre. Circle's stable of writers embraced new forms, story lengths and unflinching depictions of dysfunctional lives. What it did differently from other performance collectives like Mabou Mines or Richard Schechner's The Performance Group was to focus on new work and the writer's story, whereas those other collectives most often took classic texts and re-imagined them through cultural appropriation or created new pieces by combining texts from other works. Kennedy's work represents the evolution from a searing look into societal landscapes to personal and emotional landscapes with bold visuals to punctuate the journey. She preceded artists like Sam Shepard, who also used image-laden work to highlight societal or emotional questions.

While in the workshop, Kennedy found it difficult to change her words once they were committed to paper, but Albee fought to rein in the text and strengthen the story. It wasn't just basic narrative Kennedy sought to change, but the use of the word 'nigger'. In fact, she rewrote the script without the offensive term, but director Michael Kahn and Albee encouraged her to remain true to her first draft:

I had a script, an original script of *Funnyhouse*. And then when I went into the workshop at the Circle, I (literally) took out the word 'niggers'. And I gave it to Michael. Then as it got closer to the production, he said, 'Albee says you have another script, and that's the one we should do. You know, the script you handed in to get in the class.' So I did the first one. After that the script remained exactly the same.[22]

In addition to encouraging her to hold fast to challenging language and imagery, Albee also had to convince her to remain in the class:

> Shortly after classes began, she took me aside and told me she wished to withdraw from the class and withdraw her play, *Funnyhouse of a Negro*, from consideration. I asked her why, and she said I've decided this play hurts too much, it's too private and I don't want to share it. I told her that the play was far too good to be abandoned or destroyed and that I wouldn't let it happen.[23]

The play's first reading at Circle in the Square proved controversial, and the next reading, a week later at the Actors Studio, also divided the audience: '[A]gain the play was extremely controversial. But a lot of people said it was just wonderful, they loved it. It was about split down the middle... people started talking about *Funnyhouse*.'[24]

Audiences, especially white audiences, were unsure how to engage with the story of a young Negro woman who is convinced that her white mother was raped by her black father or with a set that featured African masks and Victorian images floating in the air around her as the character loses her hair and her Jewish boyfriend desperately seeks to enter her apartment while she hangs herself. Throughout the play, the markers that help establish theatrical reality shift, so that the audience, like Negro Sarah herself, finds it impossible to separate reality from fiction and fact from imagination.

However, the black actors 'just loved that play', especially Billie Allen, the first to portray Negro Sarah on stage because Diana Sands had committed to perform in James Baldwin's *Blues for Mr Charlie*.[25] But it wasn't until the play was produced two years later that black playwrights began to know the work and respond. During that two-year period, Albee sought financing for an Off-Broadway production with his partners Richard Barr and Clinton Wilder, and Kahn and Kennedy discussed the play and its imagery to prepare for the production. Kahn describes the scene:

> When I first met Adrienne, instead of explaining the play to me, she brought me loads and loads of photographs and reproductions

of paintings. From that, I really understood what the power of the images was for her. And for some reason, even though I was a white boy from Brooklyn, I shared a lot of those understandings of the same images. But that was how she explained the play, and we never really did discuss much of the psychology.[26]

Funnyhouse of a Negro premiered at the East End Theatre on 14 January 1964 and, though it was a hit with theatre people, it closed after thirty-four performances. The play's brief length, an hour, gave Albee some pause, but in the end he decided to showcase *Funnyhouse* alone rather than on a double bill:

> It seemed to me the play was too powerful to diminish its effectiveness by an accompanying piece. Even though I believe our ticket prices were two or three dollars at the time, we lowered our prices and did Adrienne's play twice an evening. Even with that, alas, some people complained that they were getting too short an evening.[27]

As Kennedy recalled, 'Theatre people and the famous had come out in the snow ... but larger audiences stayed away.'[28] Still, *Funnyhouse* became the 'cult play of the season until *Dutchman* came along'.[29] And because of this play's success, theatre leaders such as Jerome Robbins wanted to see the play and commission her. *Funnyhouse* received the 1964 Obie award for Distinguished Play, and Kennedy secured a number of prestigious national grants, such as the Guggenheim and the Rockefeller, which allowed her to focus full time on writing.

Cities in Bezique

A year later, in 1965, Kennedy completed her next play, *The Owl Answers*. She says of it,

> [I]t is my favorite play. I captured a lot of things I had been trying to do for fifteen years, for example in the monologues. The lady in the play is an older version of Sarah. All the people in this play are based on me, my mother and my aunt ... In fact, Joe Papp said to my son last year that of all the plays that he has ever produced it was the best written.[30]

But Papp's beloved 1969 production at the Public Theater almost never happened.

Because of *Funnyhouse* and her work with Albee, Kennedy began receiving commissions from many theatres, including the Public Theater, where she submitted a work titled *Cities in Bezique*. When Gerald Freedman, the Public Theater's Artistic Director, read the play, he found it 'totally incomprehensible ... [I]t could not be produced as presented. But I loved the title. I was captivated by Adrienne's daring and originality. It had mystery, poetic imagery and glamour ... Instead of the commissioned play, I suggested we produce two other one-acts ... under the umbrella of this title.'[31] Freedman had also read *The Owl Answers*, which had premiered that year at the White Barn Theatre in Westport, Connecticut, as a benefit for the Free Southern Theater, and found that play beautiful and full of the lyricism for which the Public was searching. He thought to pair it with another short work to make a full evening and obtained *A Beast Story*, originally commissioned by Herbert Blau and Jules Irving for the Lincoln Center Theater.

Like *Funnyhouse*, *The Owl Answers* follows a female protagonist, though this one has one of the longest names in Western theatre: She Who Is Clara Passmore Who Is the Virgin Mary Who Is the Bastard Who Is the Owl. Reflecting that name, She Who Is has multiple selves and struggles to be acknowledged by a male father figure who also has multiple names and personas, first Dead White Father and then The Negro Man. She Who Is travels through time and space via a subway car to London to see her father, but is denied entry by the guards because she is not descended from a white person. During her voyage, Clara encounters historical figures – Shakespeare, Chaucer and William the Conqueror. Like Sarah from *Funnyhouse*, Clara's travels through time and space reflect a struggle to sustain a relationship with her father and connect romantically with a man, here the Negro Man. The play ends with the Negro and Clara confronting one another. Clara attacks the Negro Man with a butcher's knife. The Negro Man 'backs out further through the gate' and Clara falls on the side of the burning altar and then is transformed into an owl.[32] The play's last line is Clara saying, 'ow ... oww' as an owl and the play's last action is the father rising from the dead and blowing out the candles on the bed.[33]

The many names and perspectives of each character allow Kennedy to focus less on the psyche of one individual and more on the truth that every person plays multiple roles and each role brings a way of behaving, a way of interacting in the world, that is not always in sync with the others. That is also true of the characters history. Kennedy's characters in *The Owl Answers* carry their past with them, and that past is both a historical lineage and also a pattern of behaviour or treatment, as is the case with the Bastard's Black Mother Who Is the Reverend's Wife Who Is Anne Boleyn (BBM). It was BBM who gave birth to Clara Passmore following an assignation with the character Goddam Father Who Is the Richest White Man in the Town Who Is the Dead White Father Who Is Reverend Passmore (GF). We see here a paradox: for Clara to be a bastard, she must be a fatherless child conceived out of wedlock, yet she has BBM's last name and one of her mother's names is Who Is the Reverend's Wife. The names alone tell us how Clara came to be in the world and that the union between BBM and GF may be more common law than sanctioned by the church. And isn't that what happened between Henry VIII and Anne Boleyn: A union that was sanctioned by one, newly formed church and shunned by another?

Throughout the play, Kennedy uses the imagery of white birds turning clockwise, swooping down and screeching, alternating with Haydn's Trumpet Concerto and human characters uttering owl sounds. In these stage directions, we see what drew Robbins and other directors to her work: a strong sense of theatrical space and effect. Her stage directions do considerably more than paint the scene and define a character's physical movements. The directions infuse the world with passion and prepare the director to create a world where nothing in it sits still except the characters. The rapid shifting of imagery in *The Owl Answers* relates to the train's rapid movement between stops. Some images flit by in a blur, while others pull the eye and slow the train.

Throughout the narrative, characters travel to sites in London and elsewhere, the protagonist recounting as she ponders her version of her existence – how she came to be related to whom and what her ancestry enables her to do and impels her to be. The obstacles she faces are those who refuse to accept that American and world history or global lineage present complications to ideas of cultural purity. Her very existence steps outside such conventional thinking, challenging the idea that a person, especially an African American, can be African, Native American, British, Welsh, Scottish,

Irish, Asian – a multitude of ethnicities regardless of how they look. The resistance She Who Is faces comes from those who are unable to accept the historical truth concerning race in America and the colonial system. She Who Is reminds us in her name and in her actions that Africans and those of African descent are everywhere throughout history, even at the royal palaces of England. But the guards refuse She Who Is entry to the Tower, forcefully reminding audiences that she and her various selves cannot exist in this world. Like so many, the guards do not think it is possible for one being to contain many selves or multiple cultural ancestors: 'If you are his ancestor why are you a Negro? . . . Keep her locked there.'[34]

But her existence is the answer to that question. Whereas many playwrights might go on at length to explore the intricacies of a thematic point or question, Kennedy captures the entirety in a single character's name. Through the very existence of her characters, with their complicated genetic ancestry and globally influenced worldview, Kennedy confronts the tired arguments and feeble rationales concerning the socially crippling belief that African Americans are all the same and express a single point of view. At least that's the case when reading the work. When experiencing the performance, the character names rarely fill the air, but when they do their impact is great.

What audiences hear in place of those fecund names are descriptions of how those mixed heritages came to be, how the African mixed with other cultures is a part of yet apart from society. Unfortunately, the frantic search She Who Is undergoes as she travels via the subway through her familial memories to both foreign lands and somewhat welcoming places like the Columbia's Teachers College may distract the audience from the greater investigation of cultural and ethnic fusions throughout time. But even the religious references to Mary the Virgin Mother of God, St Paul's and St Peter's Cathedral ask audiences to recall the land where these individuals are from. These are identified as being not from Africa, but from the Middle East, a place of many cultures – non-white cultures – and yet these figures are also bathed in white, very much like She Who Is, who is dressed in a white dress, with white wedge sandals, and is described as having 'pallid skin'.

Amid these images and sounds is violence – toward oneself or others. In *Funnyhouse*, the violence that arises from society's inability to see each aspect of the character's self is purely psychological until the final hanging. In *The Owl Answers*, each self must choose and fight for the right/space to either remain invisible or stand up for every ancestral influence – especially those bloodlines white society would prefer to ignore; Kennedy depicts this internal battle as a literal fight among the selves. Because society refuses to accept a diversity of being (its ancestry and intellectual influences) and forces an individual into the choice of killing off one self in favour of another, Kennedy presents the terrible repercussions She Who Is will encounter if she remains poised to not only deny parts of herself but exact violence upon those who would force her to do so. She Who Is holds a bloody butcher's knife at the play's end while she and the Negro Man struggle to escape the burning altar. As the scene concludes, the BBM stabs herself while the Dead White Father looks on, bemused, as if to suggest that he enjoys knowing that he created the intra-racial self-hatred exhibited by the Passmore women and that he was the cause of their destruction. The Negro Man escapes the violent scene, disappearing into the night.

It is scenes like this that have earned Kennedy a reputation for being unsympathetic to African American men. This reading of her work led her to find little support from the Black Arts Movement. But Kennedy was not anti-African American. Her work did, however, present the struggle of living in a society as a representative of the thing its great literature and laws and culture hold up as undesirable.

Like Freedman, Joseph Papp thought *The Owl Answers* was more powerful and poignant than *Funnyhouse* and so he gave it a lavish production. Kennedy says of the production:

> *The Village Voice* . . . the reviewer said it was just like *Funnyhouse*, so he sort of dismissed it. But Joe Papp liked it . . . he gave it a very beautiful and expensive, a big production. And it ran for three months with his Rep Company. That was the second year of the Public Theater at its new location on Lafayette. To me, *The Owl Answers* is much better than the other play that goes with it, *A Beast's Story*.[35]

Sadly, most viewers failed to understand the levels of social commentary, artistic critique, exploration of human struggle and timeless classic tales laden with incest, rape and murder, all under the guise of religious practice. But Papp's production led people – and especially grantors – to believe again in Kennedy and she was funded, thus enabling her to spend three years in London writing.

The second play in *Cities in Bezique* is *A Beast Story* (sometimes titled *A Beast's Story*). Quite simply, *A Beast Story*, written in 1961, chronicles a family of beasts – mother, father and daughter – as they endure acts of violence, including murder, infanticide and suicide. The script calls for one actor to portray the Beast Daughter, but Gerald Freedman cast three women in the role, thereby transforming the character into a chorus, as well as echoing Kennedy's fascination with divided selves. The change physically manifests the Beast Daughter's struggle with herself and society's expectations, and provides insight into the emotional unrest such struggles cause.

Freedman approached the play as if it were a one-act about a family – a brother and sister – whose story is told not through linear narrative, but the repetition of words and images. 'I sensed the images came from a fractured consciousness,' Freedman remembered. 'I sensed the story was a fractured episode of abuse as seen through a child's consciousness. I could not substantiate that literally, but that is what seeped through the images and language.'[36] And here is where Kennedy's reputation for writing autobiographical dramas truly overwhelms the creative imagination that she exhibits as a writer and playwright. Critics and directors have erroneously claimed that each of the families and characters depicted is a creative depiction of Kennedy's family because of this influence of the 'fractured consciousness'. People from her past do influence her characters, as Wilkerson notes, by providing a name such as a childhood friend named Sarah Clara or a literary or historical figure. But Kennedy's characters exist as reflections of remembered or imagined moments rather than the documentation of reality. Kennedy writes plays that respond to events she or those she loves have experienced, but she seeks to transform such an experience into a broader work.

Unfortunately, neither critics nor audiences appreciated the play, and it is the only play Kennedy has gone on record saying that she did not get right, and that it is not one of her favourites. *A Beast Story* is not only the least produced of her plays, but the only play she does not allow to be anthologized. It was originally published with *The Owl Answers* under the title *Cities in Bezique* and in another anthology, *Kuntu Drama: Plays of the African Continuum*.

Since then, she has refrained from releasing the publication rights. As a result, the play proves challenging to find, study and produce.

The use of animals in *The Owl Answers* and *A Beast Story* reflects a momentary fascination in Kennedy's dramaturgy, one that she maintains in two additional plays of the period: *A Rat's Mass* and *A Lesson in Dead Language*. Again, the fractured human selves tie Kennedy's work to the African diaspora's legacy of colonization and slavery and African cultures.[37] Anthropomorphic representation of animals plays a central role in West African rituals, masks and mythology. Yes, the Greeks also emphasized animal–human combinations with the sexually rapacious satyr, for example, and some of Kennedy's animal-humans behave similarly, but they also exist as tormentors who live outside the bounds of preferred familial behaviour.

A Rat's Mass

Kennedy's foray into animal-centric playwriting continued with *A Rat's Mass*, which was begun in 1963 and premiered in 1966. At the heart of this play is the often-ignored reality Kennedy presents on stage in most of her plays: that the African American is influenced and shaped by a number of cultural and historical forces that are at once at war with each other yet integral to shaping the African American identity. These difficult situations featured in Kennedy's work may not always drive a person to suicide, but are almost always ignored or undermined by the play's white characters. Take, for example, Raymond in *Funnyhouse*, who ends the play with a line that tells us that Sarah lied to us and that he, Raymond, someone who recently came to observe and know her life, can reveal the truth:

> Her father never hung himself in a Harlem hotel when Patrice Lumumba was murdered. I know the man. He is a doctor, married to a white whore. He lives in the city in rooms with European antiques, photographs of Roman ruins, walls of books and oriental carpets. Her father is a nigger who eats his meals on a white glass table.[38]

Similarly, *The Owl Answers* concludes with Clara's transformation into an owl, thereby allowing her to escape the horrors of this human coil but retain a presence with a haunting (if not terrifying) voice. If her voice wasn't heard in the light of day while she was a human, no one can ignore her screeching during the night. And the same can be said of Rosemary in *A Rat's Mass*, the white girl/woman whose actions end the play about an African American brother and sister who remember (and misremember) childhood events that took place at the playground.

In *A Rat's Mass*, a black brother and sister, depicted as rats, engage in childhood games with their neighbourhood friend, Rosemary. However, the games they play are decidedly more adult, with a violation of childhood crushes between friends depicted as the play's central, distorted memory. Throughout the piece, the Catholic Mass and its symbolism reign as Rosemary, a white Italian, shapes much of what Sister Rat recalls. Rosemary wears a white communion dress, illustrating her purity, while the two light-skinned black children are depicted as dirty, filthy rodents. Jesus, Joseph, Mary, Two Wise Men and a Shepherd also figure in the play, progressing silently throughout the space in a designed order.

A rarely discussed fact about *A Rat's Mass* is how it might appear to an audience as a response to Baraka's *Dutchman*, with colourful accents from both Frantz Fanon and the Catholic Mass. *Dutchman*, a celebrated play of the Black Arts Movement, takes place on a subway car and features two characters: a white woman and an African American man. Although *A Rat's Mass* was written in 1963, its premier production followed the stage and film versions of Baraka's play and the audience would likely have made connections Kennedy hadn't initially intended. *A Rat's Mass* features a soundscape redolent with the chugging and screeching of the New York subway circa 1965. Kennedy's play also features an African American male and a white female, but here the implication is that an innocent childhood friendship gave way to a violent and unholy assignation, the same emotional tenor that runs beneath Baraka's sexually charged two-hander.

Because Kennedy often explores characterization across various plays – *The Owl Answers* features an older version of Sarah, for example – critics sometimes place these characters within the world of Negro Sarah from *Funnyhouse*. This leads some to think *A Rat's Mass* merely repeats the ideas in *Funnyhouse*, casting Kennedy as a one-hit wonder: 'Reviewers noted the similarities to *Funnyhouse*: both plays explored a "light-skinned Negro woman's mental anguish and search for a sense of identity".'[39] However, in this play, Kennedy also takes Fanon's discussion regarding whites who discussed African languages 'as animal sounds' and casts her brother and sister as human rats who make rat-like sounds at intervals. Of course, rats also live in the New York subway tunnels and are the lowest, most reviled rodent. Rats are an object of hatred and disgust; so too were many blacks as they fought for equal rights, as they pursued housing and education, and were denied equal access in spite of the 1964 Civil Rights Act.

Kennedy never embraced political causes as an activist as vocally as those in the BAM, but she did write about the pain of racial injustice, and *A Rat's Mass* demonstrates this fully. This play further underscores her dedication to crafting works that articulate the terrific struggle African Americans face – locating a personal identity and unique culture while acknowledging the influence of all cultures and political figures. Many in the Black Arts Movement eschewed this truth and would go so far as to scorn such an observation as assimilationist.

The greater challenge Kennedy faced in the theatre world is that she is female. In spite of Lorraine Hansberry and Alice Childress's successes, such a truth was difficult for the world and theatre to embrace: a female writer who longs to do nothing other than write, just as her female characters long for nothing more than to be seen for who they are – individuals who defy the then-traditional definitions of femininity and African American culture.

London plays: *The Lennon Play, A Lesson in Dead Language, Sun*

Following the New York success of *Funnyhouse*, Kennedy's groundbreaking play was produced in France, Denmark and Italy, leading her to take up residence in London for a period. Prior to departing for London, Kennedy began adapting John Lennon's nonsense stories into a play after reading them to her young sons. 'My son Joe had Lennon's nonsense books, and the children constantly sang Beatles songs. Often I sat among their toys reading the nonsense books, *A Spaniard in the Works* and *In His Own Write*.'[40]

The Lennon Play: In His Own Write was presented in London in 1967 to an invited audience with Victor Spinetti, an actor and friend of Lennon, directing. Kennedy used her Rockefeller grant to fund her time in London. The play seemed to do well enough to pique Spinetti's interest and that of others; however, Kennedy was removed from the project and, because she did not belong to a British writers' union, she was not protected. After meeting with Laurence Olivier and Kenneth Tynan of the National Theatre, Kennedy hoped they would support her work on the play. They did not. She wrote to Lennon, who worked to have her immediately reinstated as a collaborator. Lennon called Tynan and said, 'I don't want Adrienne Kennedy put out of the play.'[41] When the play premiered at London's National Theatre in June of 1968, the writing credits were listed as Lennon in collaboration with Kennedy.

In 1964, prior to the presentation of *The Lennon Play*, Kennedy completed *A Lesson in Dead Language*, a play about seven schoolgirls who are on the brink of womanhood, studying Latin and taught to fear their bodies by their teacher, the White Dog. More than any other Kennedy play, the repetition in language is clear and profound, for the teacher regularly tells her students to recite or write phrases on the board as they speak them. This traditional form of learning takes on a harrowing quality as the girls must walk the stage in white dresses with red spots (signifying menstrual blood), ignoring their accidents rather than given the chance to clean their dresses and make themselves presentable. Of course, the act of reminding audiences that young women bleed prevents audiences from hiding and acknowledging how much young girls are like women and need to know what challenges lie ahead because of their femininity.

Both *The Lennon Play* and *A Lesson in Dead Language* were presented in April 1968 by the English Stage Society at the Royal Court Theatre and neither received positive reviews. *A Lesson in Dead Language* was admonished for being brief and incomprehensible. Following the London premieres of *Funnyhouse* and *A Lesson in Dead Language* at the Royal Court, Michael Billington wrote, 'Unfortunately the phantasmagoric nature of the action ... only serves to confuse ... Miss Kennedy's language has a controlled, deliberate rhythm to it, but even this suffers from the belief that anything said three times is poetry.'[42] The treatment she received in London – the removal from a project she pitched to the famous Beatle and developed on her own in the States, as well as the poor reviews from leading London critics – was difficult. Her writings in *Deadly Triplets* allude to the difficulty and anger she felt. In spite of this reception, the Royal Court Theatre commissioned a new work from Kennedy, *Sun: A Poem for Malcolm X Inspired by His Murder*, which the Royal Court produced in 1969.

As with other Kennedy plays, the writing of this piece began long before the commission. In this case, 'she had been commissioned by Jerome Robbins to write something for the Theatre Lab and had begun to write about Malcolm but did not finish it.'[43] While in London, she worked on something about Leonardo da Vinci and combined Malcolm and Da Vinci's Vitruvian Man together. As in *A Glass Menagerie*, written by one of her earliest playwriting heroes, Kennedy's play *Sun* calls for projections, music and movement and the imagery reflected da Vinci's sketches. The play itself reads more like a poem than any of Kennedy's earlier plays, all of which are praised for their poetic nature due to her exacting prose and striking imagery.

Beyond poetry, Kennedy's work captures a particular artistic sensibility, one seen most readily in downtown New York City theatres, Off-Broadway and in plays produced for the adventurous theatre-going audience. Even though many in Manhattan found her work challenging and divisive, regardless of its adventuresome and innovative nature, many leading artists supported her work. One would have hoped for an audience in London, but Kennedy steeps her work in American references and African American imagery not readily understood by the English literati, critics or film producers such as Joseph Losey, who wrote, 'Dear Mrs Kennedy, I read these plays only because Diana Sands suggested it, but I'm not attracted to this material at all. Joe Losey.'[44]

The British critics Billington and Irving Wardle were even less enthusiastic about Kennedy's style. They expressed an inability to embrace a new form or examine and praise its innovations, many of which are commonplace in today's theatre – visual projections, poetic form and a melding of psychological and physical realities so that the audience and the characters experience the same events with a similar level of discomfort and inability to find emotional resting places. Many of Kennedy's contemporaries composed works with clear endings that may not have tied up all loose ends neatly, but at least did not pose new questions by having a character cast doubt on what just occurred. Kennedy's work mines the mysteries of her characters' lives and extends that level of uncertainly beyond the play's end because her plays, as in real life, rarely end neatly or stop without immediately leading to another new adventure, however small.

General response to her work

In a 1992 discussion of Anglophilia in *The Owl Answers*, Michael Kahn offered his insight into the challenge Kennedy faced finding wider acceptance:

> I thought it was very honest to present that England being such a colonial power. It was a very honest response to power and glamour and whiteness. It was very honest about all those things which made her get undiscovered in the seventies.
>
> I went to the revival of *The Owl Answers* that Joe Papp put on ... and talked to a lot of the actors who were very angry about being in the play because they felt it was not presenting a positive image of blackness. I think Adrienne was severely ostracized. Her plays were considered neurotic and ... not supportive of the black movement.[45]

Billie Allen, who originated the role of Sarah in 1964, discussed this reaction to Kennedy's work in 2007 when she directed a revival of *Funnyhouse*:

> Black people were very upset about putting our business and tightly held secrets in the streets. There we were, out there, with our knotty locks, pulling them out from the scalp, and tossing them into the air. Also, the play used the N-word, 'nigger', which greatly offended the African American community [sic], and many others, too. They were angry with me for accepting this role. Why would you want to put that on the stage? But by 2006 more people had read the play and experienced it, and the audience was more ready to receive *Funnyhouse*, because we had become more accepting of our selves.[46]

Even so, Kennedy's words struck a raw nerve, especially speeches that conveyed a dislike for black hands touching white or fair

African American women. According to Allen, 'They thought *Funnyhouse* was another play putting African American men down. But it's not meant literally, and I tried to impart that to audiences. My feelings are that these words are those of an unhappy bride, unhappy in her marriage.' These lines were at times quite radical for an African American woman to write down. Says Allen,

> [The lines] too real. And on a certain level derogatory, and too insensitive to a certain [audience] . . . when it comes out [the discussion of colour] it is very different. You know nobody had owned up to it [when *Funnyhouse* premiered], and nobody had come out and said it in public. The Anglo aesthetic and standard of beauty – we don't really know how deep, deep and damaging it is.[47]

Another concern among theatregoers, especially African Americans, was the depiction of the black experience. By the mid-1970s, it began to be common to see black women (or women of colour, more generally) expressing their most personal struggles and intimate experiences in order to connect with audiences and realize the feminist dictum: the personal is political. But in the 1960s, this mantra hadn't yet taken hold, especially among female playwrights. To have female characters discuss female baldness, menstruation, rape and incest (imagined or real) without the veneer of metaphor or implied horror (as with Blanche DuBois and others) simply wasn't done. Couple this bold subject matter with characters who express open anger if not disdain toward family members, and the play's subject matter and presentation make it difficult to process.

Clive Barnes of the *New York Times* responded more favourably to Kennedy's work. In 1969, Barnes wrote, '[Kennedy's] plays read like nonsense and yet, when acted, their phrases float accusingly in the mind.'[48] Even Walter Kerr expressed appreciation for Kennedy's imagery that the London critics could not when reviewing *Cities in Bezique*: 'All roles blur, blend, divide and recombine . . . Sounds, sights, gestures recur as in a dream that won't move forward.'[49] Barnes went on to write, 'Of all our black writers, Miss Kennedy is most concerned with white, with white relationship, with white blood.'[50] Add to that a compressed running time of far less than two hours, the common run time for most non-musical theatrical productions, and Kennedy's work squarely placed itself outside the mainstream.

As the 1960s progressed and the 1970s blossomed, a national conversation connecting the African American to the countries of Africa and the nations of the African diaspora arose. Kennedy did not actively participate in these political conversations as Amiri Baraka did, and there is little to suggest that she sought to have her work seen as just a political narrative. By the late 1960s, she did write the Malcolm X play, *Sun*, and a play for the Yale School of Drama, *An Evening With Dead Essex* (1973), about the African American veteran Mark Essex, following his racially motivated rampage killing. Most of her work during the 1960s, however, avoids any overt connections to and discussions of politics, racial injustice or violence in the United States. Until *Dead Essex*, Kennedy's references to major black thinkers and politicians were done to reflect on her own experiences, which in turn conveyed how American blacks engage in a similar struggle to those of blacks in other countries.

As ready and willing as the Off-Broadway community was to push boundaries and explore new forms, the larger theatrical community was less so. The regional theatre movement was beginning to take root and grow in major cities across the United States, but the season selections were Broadway hits, plays by local writers, or Shakespearean classics. Challenging voices like Kennedy's rarely found a place on the regional theatre stage. In fact, most of her productions have been on college and university campuses. Even culturally specific theatres known to produce plays by African American, Asian American or Latina/o writers shied away from producing Kennedy's plays.

Conclusion

Throughout *Funnyhouse*, *A Rat's Mass* and other Kennedy plays from the 1960s, dialogue and images recur, forcing the audience to sit up and take notice, to enter the character's experience as well as experience the play's cyclical nature. Perhaps it is the simple fact that Kennedy explored experience and dramatic form that set her apart from her colleagues. Her works unfolded in a short, one-act format, and a time period with ritualistic elements and repetitions was used throughout to connect the moments and the intense emotional journey. Repetition and religious procession (characters/icons) coalesce in her work to provide a rhythm but also hearken to the most traditional and ancient ways of telling stories. No matter the culture – African American, Greek, Japanese – physical or linguistic (sometimes both) patterns repeat in order to emphasize.

Central to Kennedy's work is the use of memory – her characters' and her own. Many of her plays present meditations on particular incidents in a single, usually female, character's life. Through the use of language redolent with imagery and dramatic action that rarely marks time as it chronicles its passage, Kennedy captures the essence of memory where everything happens seemingly all at once and yet separately. Few writers before or since have managed to create such a dramatic world. Given the depth of imagery and emotion and the similarity some dramatic events have to her own life, a rich world of criticism forging her personal life to her plays has emerged. In truth, the characters are wholly fictional, imagined by the playwright and given the opportunity to reappear in separate works in an attempt to know them more deeply and completely. That these characters, especially the lead female characters, like the same movies Kennedy likes, attend the same college, live in the same cities, enjoy the same poetry, casts something of a pall over her work early on. Personal memoir must be somehow reductive and simpler than generating a fully imagined work. Of course this says nothing of from where so-called fully imagined works emanate.

To some, the height of Kennedy's career occurred during those first five years: *Funnyhouse of a Negro*, *The Owl Answers*, *A Beast Story* and *A Rat's Mass*. In an email, Kennedy remarked how difficult it has been and how hard she has worked to be seen as a writer with a life beyond the 1960s. Some may claim that her later works stand out, but most know her for this early work and its emotional style replete with harrowing imagery and repetitive language. Because of this, even Kennedy had difficulty seeing her future as a writer:

> I came to feel that my following for the plays was quite stabilized and I am grateful for that. But then nothing happened to those plays. It was quite a crisis for me to know where I would go from there, how I could move on, what was realistic. Because I am not grant supported now. The biggest crisis I have had to face was what to do now with my writing talent, now that that phase is over.[51]

But she did and does continue to write impactful works that address the challenges confronting African Americans and she teaches writing, continuing to change the landscape of the dramatic form. In January 2018, at the age of eighty-five, Kennedy will have her first new production since 2008, *He Brought Her Heart Back in a Box*, premiere at New York's Theatre for a New Audience. The play, set in Montezuma, Georgia and New York City, continues her exploration of seemingly disparate topics of Jim Crow and Nazism and weaves them together with the ideas of sexual hypocrisy and references to the other Elizabethan playwright, Christopher Marlowe. The fugue-like writing of her early work is as present in this new play further demonstrating that her work was ahead of its time. Similarly, the emotionally unsettling nature of her work remains. During the sixties, her work provide difficult for many theatregoers and critics. At the time, those waiting for a dramatic story to unfold in a linear form despite the use of remembered moments that interrupt the play's present action. Kennedy's remembered moments ebb and flow, rather than injecting themselves into the present action as flashbacks do, because her characters' memories rarely rely on a moment in the present to catapult the play's action to a past moment, or the past to leave the flashback and return to the present. For Kennedy's characters, the past lives with the present and comes to the fore when the present fails to suppress it.

6

Jean-Claude van Itallie

Timothy Youker

Introduction

Jean-Claude van Itallie's sudden vault to fame in the mid-1960s, effected by the critically lauded 634-show run of his dramatic triptych *America Hurrah*, marked the point at which the artists and aesthetics of Off-Off-Broadway theatre began to become visible to mainstream audiences and critics. John Lahr, writing in 1970, declared, 'Since Jean-Claude van Itallie's *America Hurrah*, off-Broadway and off-off-Broadway have become American theater. International attention has made it hard for even the *New York Times* to ignore them.'[1] For a period of about two to three years, van Itallie was practically the poster boy for Off-Off-Broadway in the eyes of mainstream America, appearing in the *New York Times* and major magazines. Van Itallie's highly visible role in this larger development might partly be a simple case of being in the right place at the right time, but it undoubtedly helped that his work was at once highly characteristic of the countercultural scene from which he emerged and yet distinguished from it by an approach that pleased highbrow critics. Van Itallie also benefited immensely from his close collaboration with the Open Theater, the experimental acting group led by Joseph Chaikin. The productive tension that arose between van Itallie, a rigorously formalistic writer who stated that '[if] you want to be innovative, you have a particular responsibility to be clear', and Chaikin, who was almost pathologically resistant to allowing his work to become settled, closed or institutionalized, created a body of work that balanced disciplined approaches to process with underground theatre's political anarchism and linguistic scepticism.[2] Examining van Itallie's work with the Open, with a focus on *Almost Like Being* and *I'm Really Here* (also known as the 'Doris' Plays, both 1964), *America Hurrah* (1966) and *The Serpent* (1968), reveals a playwriting process that mingled the different agencies of playwright, actor and director; that made what playwright and avant-garde chronicler Arthur Sainer has described as 'the attitude of performer offering self rather than character' integral to its meaning; and that, despite its caustic critiques of mass media and popular culture, earned numerous plaudits from the mainstream press.[3]

Van Itallie's own account of his background seems to connect his origins and upbringing to his main concerns as a writer: 'In 1940, at the start of the holocaust, I emigrated from Belgium, at the age of four, with my parents. I was raised in Great Neck, a prosperous Long Island suburb, where antiseptically pretty streets and houses seemed devoid of signs of work, old age, disease or death.'[4] The van Itallies were fortunate enough to be among the wave of middle-class Jewish families to find safety from the Nazis in the US, but van Itallie saw Great Neck's serenity as disquietingly bland. His attitudes about suburban homogeneity were probably informed in part by his experiences as a young gay man coming of age in the 1950s, which gave him first-hand experience of how cultural uniformity was achieved by suppressing vital truths about people's inner lives. After graduating from Harvard and moving to New York in 1958, he became exposed to a burgeoning underground theatre scene that often concerned itself with how the placid surface of middle-class American culture conceals ugly realities.

Van Itallie's early play *War* was produced in 1963 by the Playwrights Unit, an entity created by Edward Albee and producers Richard Barr and Clinton Wilder as a 'ladder' to Broadway production for promising new writers.[5] *War* depicts two men – the Elder Actor and Younger Actor – engaged in a series of improvisation assignments for an acting class, using the old costumes and props cluttering the Elder Actor's apartment. As the two of them rapidly switch identities – sailors, children, a strolling couple, soldiers on the march – their games became fraught with a mixture of Oedipal rivalry and sexual tension. Whenever the 'war' between the two actors becomes too tense, the Lady, a maternal dream figure in an apricot-coloured Edwardian dress, swans into the room to calm them down with baby talk, pantomime stories and French pleasantries. The men's 'improvisations' and transformations resemble the transformation work that would make the Open Theater famous, but in *War* the games and exercises remain bounded within an autonomous dramatic world. Because of the play's fictional frame, it is the characters rather than the actors themselves who transform before the audience's eyes. Van Itallie notes that *War* 'works best on a proscenium stage' and decorates the back wall of the Elder Actor's apartment with 'an old and frayed backdrop, representing a stylized European park scene'.[6] Thus, van Itallie was still writing work with a 'fourth wall' (albeit a perturbed one), which, to recall Sainer's distinction, instructed actors to offer characters rather than themselves.

War shows how, even before he met Chaikin, van Itallie shared the linguistic scepticism that characterized so much Off-Off-Broadway and avant-garde work of the period. Language in his plays tends to impose itself between people instead of helping them to connect. A dialogue is a game or a battle in which words are mere ammunition; pleasantries and clichés are shields that characters hold up to mask their motives. Language in his plays indexes truth mainly when it flags the effects of or relationships between bodies, as in the 'war' between the two actors in *War*. This linguistic scepticism reflects a confluence of sociopolitical, biographical and personal influences. American experimental playwrights, spurred in part by the translation of Artaud's *The Theatre and Its Double* into English in 1958 and, later, by the political rhetoric surrounding the war in Vietnam, began truly to embrace linguistic scepticism in the 1960s. As van Itallie himself recounted: 'There was an ambivalence about language that we all had ... because we had been lied to. We were discovering in the sixties that we had been lied to by the establishment in every way.'[7] Van Itallie elaborates on this issue in a letter published along with the text of *The Serpent*:

> Words, as you're aware, have become terribly misused ... Contemporaneously, a long speech is suspect because speeches are the vehicle by which politicians and other power people deliver us their hypocrisy. General conversation most often conforms to the modes and intent of a repressive middle-class

atmosphere, and often words curdle in our mouths as we speak them – words feel like traps set by the powers that be, physical and metaphysical and often like a betrayal of where you sense the reality is actually at.[8]

The biographical factor was van Itallie's own bilingual upbringing. Growing up in America with Belgian parents, he spoke English at school but, when at home with his mother, spoke both English and French. 'I believe in knowing as many literal and figurative languages as possible,' he would later say in interview. 'If you're raised in more than one language, you're lucky because then you realize that reality is not contained in a single language.'[9] The professional factor was his work in the television industry.

From 1962 to 1967, van Itallie worked for the CBS Network, first as a researcher and then as a writer, mostly for the religious programme *Look Up and Live*, which addressed a variety of political, philosophical and cultural topics that were typically (though sometimes loosely) related to questions about Christian morality or faith. The programme was a good fit for van Itallie, who has been interested in topics related to faith and spirituality throughout his career. And because of its Sunday-morning time slot, *Look Up and Live* was able to run material that would have been too controversial for primetime audiences (regular hosts included the radical theologian Dr William Hamilton, who was highly critical of organized religion). Van Itallie's TV work included adaptations of work by famous playwrights (Tennessee Williams' *Camino Real*, James Baldwin's *Blues for Mister Charlie*, selections from *Hamlet*), documentary segments drawing on interviews and archival research, and dramatized excerpts from non-fiction books on religious and philosophical topics, ranging from civil rights activist Sarah Patton Boyle's memoir *The Desegregated Heart* to Friedrich Nietzsche's 'The Madman'. Van Itallie also researched and wrote documentary programmes for NBC's *New York Illustrated* series, as well as a few original scripts for CBS, such as *Hobbies: Or Things are Fine with the Forbushers* (1967), in which a man who supposedly won thirty minutes of free TV airtime in a contest expresses his opinions about American culture and speaks out against the war in Vietnam. Producing adaptations and documentaries required him to handle various formal and stylistic problems: how to convert a book excerpt into a voiceover illustrated by photos or mimed reenactments, how to condense tape-recorded interview responses into monologues, how to make a dramatic scene designed to unfold in a three-dimensional environment work within the two-dimensional frame of the television screen.[10] At the same time, projects such as *Hobbies* gave him the opportunity to consider how the forms of intimacy evoked by televisual images differed from those offered by the theatre. All of this work would inform his plays both directly and indirectly.

Van Itallie quickly became disillusioned with the Playwrights Unit, because the treatment that he received from them felt patronizing (van Itallie characterized their attitude as 'These are baby plays by baby playwrights, and we're going to offer a kind of nursery school').[11] He also saw some of his short works performed at the minuscule but vibrant Caffe Cino, from which impresario Joe Cino helped launch the careers of Lanford Wilson, Sam Shepard and Tom O'Horgan, but he decided that he disliked what he referred to as the 'generally swishy loudness' of that venue.[12] Despite being openly gay himself, van Itallie never seemed to feel a strong sense of allegiance with the downtown venues most associated with queer culture, such as the Caffe Cino and John Vaccaro's Play-House of the Ridiculous. Their campy, zero-budget approach, which framed mess and excess as forms of cultural rebellion, didn't synch with his interest in formal clarity. He was more satisfied by the relationships that he developed in the mid-1960s with Ellen Stewart's La MaMa Experimental Theater Club (where early versions of *Motel* and *Interview* – then called *Pavane* – were performed in 1966) and, especially, with Chaikin and the Open Theater.

The most significant effect that van Itallie's work with the Open had on his writing was a shift in how he understood and treated the relationship among performer, spectator and space, a shift that was typical of experimental theatre in the 1960s. This was particularly true in New York. 'Once you look for it', Scott Proudfitt writes, 'the idea of "space", and how to share it, is everywhere in the mid- to late 1960s downtown New York arts scene.'[13] Off-Off-Broadway, like the Off-Broadway movement of the preceding generation, began as a space for playwrights who were excluded from or uninterested in the mainstream theatre scene in New York. Centred in Greenwich Village and adjacent neighbourhoods, it was an archipelago of cafes, basements, lofts, garages, churches, converted storefronts and the occasional purpose-built theatre. Companies typically worked in close quarters, in spaces that they shared with multiple artists and that sometimes doubled as those artists' living spaces. It was also a somewhat crowded, jumbled cultural space, accommodating clashing influences including Pop Art, camp, rock music, postmodern dance, New Age psychology, existentialism, the Beats, the European Theatre of the Absurd and the theories of Bertolt Brecht and Antonin Artaud. Proudfitt, however, attributes this preoccupation with space not only to material factors, but also to the influence of acting teacher Viola Spolin and her 1963 book *Improvisation for the Theatre*, which connects the social and political energy of theatre to performers' and spectators' capacity for spontaneous interaction in a shared space.[14] *Motel*, *The Serpent* and the workshop shorts make the co-presence of actor, spectator and space essential to the play's form and meaning (though the level of actual audience involvement in each piece varies). The Canadian media theorist Marshall McLuhan, whom van Itallie has cited repeatedly in discussions of his own work and of American culture more generally, wrote in his 1964 book *Understanding Media* that 'the medium is the message', by which he meant that the meaning of any artwork made in a given medium is always connected somehow to the specific ways in which that medium affects human perception and relationships. In the van Itallie/Open collaborations, the medium of theatre becomes part of the play's message.[15]

'Playwright of the Workshop'

By 1963, Chaikin had achieved some notoriety as a member of Judith Malina and Julian Beck's Living Theatre, but he had chosen not to follow Malina and Beck when they went into self-imposed exile in Europe. Instead, he agreed to help run what began as an informal acting workshop consisting mainly of former students of acting teacher Nola Chilton, who had also emigrated that year, relocating to Israel. Chaikin eventually decided to call this workshop the Open Theater. The name reflected a spirit of inclusion (anyone who was interested was free to attend) and openness to exploring diverse methods and styles. Critic and director Gordon Rogoff brought van Itallie to his first meeting of the Open Theater 'two or three or four months' after its inception, and van Itallie became a regular attendee.[16] Several other playwrights were involved with the group (most notably Megan Terry), but when the first public showcase of the Open's work, entitled 'Aspects', premiered at the Sheridan Square Playhouse in April 1964, the programmes credited van Itallie with the special title 'Playwright of the Workshop'.[17] Further showcases followed, including a programme that ran from February to May 1965 at Sheridan Square, which included several van Itallie playlets, and Open actors also appeared in the productions of the 'Doris' Plays at the Vandam, under the direction of Chaikin (*I'm Really Here*) and Open member Sidney Walter (*Almost Like Being*). After Walter and other Open members relocated to Minneapolis to co-found the Firehouse Theater, they premiered van Itallie's short play *Where is de Queen?* (a dream play centred on the figure of Queen Victoria) in 1966.

In workshop and other collective creation settings, van Itallie had to negotiate the tension between his own impulse to create finished work and the group's desire to subordinate his work to process-oriented research. Regardless, Chaikin saw van Itallie's scenes, exercises and short plays as instrumental in the Open Theater's development in the mid-to-late 1960s: 'His role in the early stages, and our collaboration from that point ... had a great to do with all that followed.'[18] At the same time, working with the Open forced van Itallie to adopt a new approach to writing. Robert Pasolli insists that writing for workshops and collective creations produces a fundamentally different relationship toward the actors and the material:

> The writer is defined not by the fact that he had written a script on which the work is based, as in the case of traditional production, but on the fact that he *will* write a script related to the work which the troupe is improvising. When the work is done and ready to be shown publicly, one can look back and say that the writer structured the workshop investigation to make it understandable to outsiders.[19]

Rhea Gaisner, who was involved in the Open's early sessions, puts it somewhat differently, stressing that '[t]he playwright who is creatively functioning with a group is not simply its secretary'; he or she also helps guide the actors' improvisations, provides material that structures their work, and incorporates elements of that work into texts that further his or her own creative agenda.[20]

One early example of this symbiosis was the 'Odets Kitchen', an exercise scripted by van Itallie as a way for actors to refine two of the Open's signature techniques, informally called 'inside-outside' (essentially, using improvisation to create a dynamic contrast between a scene's banal 'outside' reality and its normally invisible psychic 'inside') and 'sound-and-movement' (the employment of the whole body and the full range of the voice to communicate feelings or concepts nonverbally). Pasolli explains:

> The 'Odets Kitchen' was an investigation into the reality behind surface behaviour ... To begin with, three actors simply performed the script, which was labeled the 'outside' ... Then, using the vocabulary of sound-and-movement, the same three actors improvised what they imagined to have been going on *behind* the external behavior of the three characters, but which the naturalistic mode had not made visible.[21]

Open Theater scholar Eileen Blumenthal elaborates: 'Van Itallie devised what he described as "realistic scene of the boring variety, such as might have been written by Clifford Odets." The characters were a couple and their daughter. The wife was "bitter, romantic ..."; the husband was "self-indulgent, affectionate, proud, stupid"; and their child was "precocious" and restless.'[22] Once the three actors performed the outside followed by the inside, they re-established the outside, repeating the original scene a second time. While this scenario is an acting exercise, it also critiques, on a dramaturgical level, the conventions of American Realism that the Open's methods rejected, showing the zones of psychic experience that 'kitchen-sink' realism leaves out.

Van Itallie wrote several other workshop shorts during this period, each with clear relationships to practical exercises that Chaikin and the Open were developing at the time. The unpublished workshop playlet *Picnic in Spring* was built around Chaikin's 'illusion and reality exercise', in which an actor's emotional state and attitude toward the content of a scene are determined by her spatial position in relation to a set of concentric circles drawn on the floor. In the case of *Picnic in Spring*, a scenario involving pairs of lovers in a forest that was gradually, ominously expanding, the different attitudes were illusory love, banal indifference and the feeling of dread when one passes from the former to the latter.[23] *An*

Airplane: Its Passengers and Portents allowed for work on the Open's version of 'parts of a whole', an exercise inherited from Viola Spolin in which actors join together to embody the various pieces of a single multipart entity – in this case an aeroplane and its passengers and crew as it takes off, flies and crashes. In both of these cases, van Itallie took an exercise devised to teach actors to perform spontaneously and made it the basis for a fixed text that demonstrated and utilized what the Open actors had learned from that exercise.

Chaikin and the Open actors imagined and performed moods, atmospheres or ideas, which van Itallie picked up and fleshed out and clarified, or they invented and played with game structures that van Itallie adapted into dramaturgical structures. For example, his one-act plays *The First Fool* and *The Hunter and the Bird* (both 1964) feature characters inspired by the Open's experiments with trying to react to environments and situations as a total innocent might. In the latter case, the innocent is a bird conversing with a hunter who has just wounded it, observing and learning from his behaviour until it finally shoots him with his own gun. *The Girl and the Soldier* (1965) takes its inspiration from the same illusion-and-reality exercise that inspired *Picnic in Spring*. The titular Girl stands stationary at centre stage, inhabiting an illusory world of romance, while the Soldier moves between her world and an external reality of endless birth and death, which he describes in a violent stream-of-consciousness monologue punctuated by drumbeats. *Thoughts on the Instant of Greeting a Friend in the Street* (1965, co-written with Sharon Thie), builds on the 'inside-outside' concept that the Open developed with the Odets exercise. As two friends exchange banal greetings on the sidewalk, both deliver inner monologues about the possibility of sudden death in a world where people randomly perish in traffic accidents, and atomic bombs could fall on New York at any given moment.

Though they were directly inspired by workshop exercises, van Itallie's one-acts were not just tidied-up transcripts. 'I don't listen to the actors talk and then write down their words,' he explained to an audience at the University of Connecticut in 1969.

> I have watched the direction which the actors go, or I have suggested direction, or I have watched the direction which has been suggested like Chaikin and I have seen what possibilities

there are, what kind of other dimensions it was possible to go into but not to use the verbal thing because they [the actors] are not verbally trained [nor] do they express themselves that way.[24]

In the same talk, he expressed doubt that a suitable dramatic text could be created directly through actors' improvisations: 'I may be proven wrong yet. [But] I think it's a myth that's been pushed by the actors themselves and encouraged by the directors ... in order to get [the actors'] commitment to a whole piece.'[25] While the above remark was made in reference to experimental actors and directors in general rather than to the Open Theater specifically, van Itallie's frustration with this 'myth' became a recurrent theme in his accounts of his work with the Open.

The 'Doris' Plays

The 'Doris' Plays – *Almost Like Being* and *I'm Really Here* – emphasize another key concept from the Open's experiments: 'perfect people'. Pasolli explains: 'Perfect people are the sanitized, regularized and glamourized types which the image-makers have us all secretly believing we ought to be.'[26] Popular culture, for Chaikin, perpetuated a 'big set-up', in which entertainment and advertising encouraged consumers to identify themselves with specific, reified identity categories, while celebrities recommended standardized ways of embodying those categories.[27] Consumers internalized the 'perfect' models of characters in popular entertainment and then tried (inevitably without success) to duplicate those models in their own imperfect everyday lives. Chaikin gives an example: 'These two people are standing together, holding hands, with Shelley Winters and Gary Cooper right between them, and the experience they are having doesn't resemble the thing that happened when Shelley Winters said it to Gary Cooper at all ... It is frustrating because they can't really do it, and they can't keep from trying to do it.'[28] 'Perfect people' exercises underscored the slippage between fantasy and reality, either by placing stereotyped 'perfect people' into situations in which their behaviour becomes obviously irrational, or having them suddenly engage in taboo behaviour while maintaining their smiling facades.

The 'Doris' Plays estrange and send up Hollywood's manufacture of 'perfect people' by presenting manically compressed pastiches of romantic musical comedy films of the sort that might feature Doris Day. *Almost Like Being* charts a love triangle involving musical star Doris, the handsome but inarticulate studio sound engineer Rock, and the wealthy Knockefeller. The triangle resolves with Doris choosing Rock and Knockefeller abruptly falling for Doris's 'negro maid' Billy (written like a Butterfly McQueen stereotype). The play ends with all four leads joining in a closing musical number.[29] *I'm Really Here* starts out by giving a similar treatment to travel romances, with vacationing Doris falling for Rossano (a parody of Italian leading man Rossano Brassi), the suave guide on a Parisian tour bus, but the play takes a dark turn when Doris invites Rossano up to her hotel room, where he stabs her to death.

Van Itallie wrote *Almost Like Being* and *I'm Really Here* during a ten-day trip to the Berkshires with other members of the company, and it incorporates elements inspired by their exercises. But, as with most of van Itallie's plays with the Open, the words on the page were his. Nonetheless, *Almost Like Being* and *I'm Really Here* arguably would not have existed, at least not in precisely the same form, without the Open's experiments with the 'perfect people' and 'inside-outside' exercises. The Open helped him generate forms to contain his words and physical analogues to complement them.

Both plays are 'staged films' in which the actors behave as if filmed by invisible cameras, as explained by this extended stage direction from the beginning of *Almost Like Being*:

> This play is to be done as if it were a movie being shot by several cameras. When the individual actors are not, for a moment or two, on camera, their expression is deadpan and bored. They are 'turned on' for their 'bits'. Often Doris will make a facial expression especially for the camera, or she will address it instead of another actor. The actors will always know exactly where the camera is at a given moment – sometimes a closeup, sometimes a two-shot, panning, etc. This technical device should serve as a comment on the action.[30]

As someone who wrote for television regularly, van Itallie had put a substantial amount of thought into how a camera crops our view of its subject and directs our gaze and attention in ways that live theatre typically does not. In a talk on adapting dramatic plays for other media that he gave in 1966, van Itallie noted that in film 'the eye is the eye of the camera, totally controlled by the director', meaning that while theatre is a communal activity, 'watching the movie we are alone', individually experiencing the story as communicated by the director/camera.[31] The action of the 'Doris' Plays appears to unfold in a fictional 'world', just as the action of *War* does; however, the continued visibility of the actors when they are not 'turned on' by the camera makes the interplay between cropped cinematic flatness and the actors' three-dimensional presence essential to the plays' meaning. Van Itallie's characters represent collective fantasies, and as such should not be able to bleed, fart, panic or die. Yet, as embodied figures in the theatre, they can do all of these things. At the same time, the play uses its own liveness to draw the audience's attention to what the medium of theatre offers that film does not (a shared experience in a shared space), and in doing so underscores the comparative loneliness of film-going.

By the standards of 1960s Hollywood, van Itallie's Doris is the 'perfect' woman – pert, gracious, intellectually vapid, and at once virginal and subtly sexualized (she performs a nightclub act in a Virgin Mary costume in *Almost Like Being*). However, she faces periodic eruptions of violence, dread and other embodied experiences that would never find their way into an actual Hollywood romance, eruptions with which Doris is too psychically vacant to cope. Midway through *Almost Like Being*, Doris and Rock share a long elevator ride. As the ride progresses, van Itallie reveals the psychic 'inside' of the scene, which includes Doris's nauseous claustrophobia and Rock's fear that the cable will snap. In *I'm Really Here*, before the stabbing starts, Doris interrupts her still innocent-seeming assignation with Rossano and, as the stage directions describe it: '*She turns her ass to him and the audience, tilts it coyly and farts a long thin fart.*'[32] The trauma of being murdered triggers a meandering swansong in which she strings together her thoughts with song lyrics by Rodgers and Hammerstein, Lerner and Loewe, and Cole Porter:

> **Rossano** (*Leaving*)   Au revoir, Miss Prettyasabutton. This time, c'est la vie.
> **Doris** (*On the floor, in increasing fear*)   But the other man, the nice one, is coming to save me. I'm always saved. Someone will

come. I'll be all right. Everything's coming up roses, Doris. Doris. Doris, take hold of yourself. I'm going to wash that man right out of my hair. I'm going to—I'm alone. Doris. Some enchanted evening you will see? meet? see? a stranger. But I'm Doris. I love Paris in the springtime when it drizzles. Doris. I'm alone. Help me. Forgive me. I'm alone. I can't die. Doris can't die. Die? Die? *I'm* dying. *I* am dying. Really dying. I'm *really*— (*She screams very loudly in fear*)[33]

Incredulous at the thought that she is even capable of dying, Doris cannot accept the cruel truth that, as a woman, no matter how much she tries to be a 'perfect' fantasy icon, she is ultimately just another female body being served up for male consumption. Moreover, Doris's horror seems to be not only at being an *I* that can be killed, but also at the fact that she is an embodied *I* at all, that there is an individual buried underneath the mass of pop culture clichés, with no means of articulating itself.

America Hurrah

While van Itallie's writing as 'Playwright of the Workshop' was embedded in the process-oriented practical experiments, he also wanted to produce dramatic texts that would reach wider audiences than those that the Open's showcases attracted.[34] Although he was ambivalent about commercial theatre, he saw his peers' tendency to play for their own cliques as bad for their work. 'It can be very frustrating', he wrote, 'to put in months of effort on a production that you know beforehand will be seen only three or four times. We need larger audiences. This is necessary because the work itself – if it continues to be done mostly in Greenwich Village – runs the risk of becoming done for and by a closed group, a coterie.'[35] Producer Stephanie Sills initially had the idea of packaging the previously written one-act plays *Motel* and *Pavane* (to be retitled *Interview*) and the new play *TV* into a single evening of theatre, and convinced an initially sceptical van Itallie of the concept's promise.[36] *America Hurrah* opened at the Pocket Theater at Sheridan Square on 7 November 1966. Chaikin directed *Interview*, and Open member Jacques Levy directed *TV* and *Motel*, but the Open Theater's name was not attached to the production.

Chaikin did not see *America Hurrah* as an Open work: 'Jean-Claude van Itallie wrote the plays and brought them in, but, unlike *The Serpent*, he did not work them out improvisationally with the actors, but addressed himself to whatever caught his interest in the exercises and themes we were working on (except for *Motel*, which he had written independently).'[37] In reality, Chaikin's remark undersells the group's influence on *Interview* and *TV*, which read like suites of virtuoso technical demonstrations for actors trained in Chaikin's experimental methods. It is fair to say that *America Hurrah* is not a true collective creation. Like the 'Doris' Plays, it represents a waypoint between van Itallie's more conventionally autonomous dramatic works such as *War* and the group's later work on *The Serpent*, in which the act of collectively creating the event would become essential to the play's received meaning. The text of *America Hurrah* consists of van Itallie's words, but the meaning of *America Hurrah* is inseparable from the formal and stylistic elements that van Itallie pulled out of his work with Chaikin.

Interview: A Fugue for Eight Actors breaks apart into three distinct movements of its own, structured around several types of song, dance or game and using text partly based on workshop improvisations. The play began as an attempt to write a text for eight voices that structured a set of banal interactions – four interviews for four different jobs, conducted simultaneously – within a tight musical form including simultaneous speech, refrains and counterpoint. Its inspiration was an Open exercise called 'Breathing and Talking Together', which focused on training actors to start and stop speaking simultaneously and to speak multiple texts at once such that all of the words were intelligible.[38] Van Itallie, a self-confessed 'musical ignoramus', chose the title *Pavane* because he was vaguely aware that a pavane was a form of dance, but composer Marianne de Pury rightly pointed out to van Itallie that the piece more closely resembled a fugue, with its contrapuntal structure and its emphasis on multiples of four.[39] 'You could practically map it out', van Itallie later wrote. 'AB, ABC, ABCD, AABBCD, AABBCCD, etc.'[40] After writing a first draft of the piece, van Itallie added additional sequences that riffed on the same themes as the original interview fugue, many of which seemed designed to make use of exercises and techniques that Chaikin and his actors were exploring. The Open's input into the play was not direct, but its indirect influence is clear.

Interview begins with the First Interviewer onstage. The First Applicant enters to apply for a house-painting job, and the First Interviewer asks him a series of banal questions. Soon, the Second Interviewer and Second Applicant enter and begin their own exchange regarding a floor-washing job, starting with the same initial questions, and their dialogue overlaps in counterpoint with the first pair's. This pattern continues with two more pairs, until there are eight people onstage speaking an interview fugue. The questions are all standardized queries about the applicants' names, experience, skills and reasons for leaving their last places of employment. The Applicants' answers, on the other hand, contain periodic micro-eruptions of frustration, desperation and wounded pride. After a while, the Interviewers begin speaking as a corporate entity, finishing each other's sentences. The characters physicalize their repressed aggression by playing leapfrog and riding on each other's backs. In addition to making use of the Open actors' work on simultaneous speech, the sequence builds on the Open's existing 'inside-outside' approach, with the actions of the interviewers and interviewees physicalizing the 'inside' emotions that the banal 'outside' of the interview questions and answers conceal.

From there, *Interview* shifts into a series of monologues, presented as the cast rapidly switches among implied settings and characterizations. A woman on the street tries and fails to get a passer-by to stop and direct her to Fourteenth Street. A Gym Instructor promises to teach his students to 'look like the guys in the movies' while expressing his overpowering craving for a smoke.[41] A telephone operator struggles to do her job while nursing a painful stomach ailment, only to keel over and be rushed into surgery. Two men seek guidance, from a reticent priest and a greedy psychiatrist respectively. A young woman arrives at a party and starts apologizing to the seemingly uncaring party guests: she was unable to attend because she just died in a traffic accident.

This middle segment is clearly inspired by the Open's method of 'transformations', an approach to characterization that they derived from Spolin's exercises and developed in part through their earlier work on Megan Terry's plays.[42] While the psychological realist approach of Stanislavsky equates truthful acting with the ability to plot out a performance as a linear chain of actions motivated by a character's fixed objectives, transformation work requires actors to switch personas, objectives and given circumstances mid-scene. The middle part of *Interview* requires the cast to portray a kaleidoscope of urban characters, repeatedly changing roles as the scene goes on: 'The actors walk straight forward toward the audience, and then walk backwards toward the rear of the stage. Each time they approach the audience, they do so as a different character. The actor will need to find the essential vocal and physical mannerisms of each character, play them and drop them immediately to assume another character.'[43] The staging also makes use of 'Parts of the Whole', both in a concrete sense (when actors embody the circuits manipulated by the Telephone Operator, for example) and in a more abstracted sense, as explained by Pasolli: 'Imagining society to be a machine, the actors searched for the mechanical part in it which a doctor would play, a street cleaner, an intellectual, a congressman.'[44] The resulting action denies any sense of 'character' as a continuous and immanent property that can be represented through simple labels or social exchanges.

In the play's final segment, the actors hold a square dance in which a politician shakes hands and chews the fat with constituents. The constituents, who include returning characters from the play's middle segment, non-verbally communicate their concerns; the Politician responds with a past-tense narration of his canned response. For example, when the Telephone Operator reappears, 'making the same noise she made when her stomach hurt her', the Politician's response is: 'Nobody knows more about red tape than I do, I said knowingly and I wish you luck, I said, turning my smile to the next one.'[45] Despite his physical proximity to them, the Politician does not truly see these people as people, and he has already consigned their interaction into the past before it has even finished happening.

A handful of themes link the sections of *Interview*: feelings of nausea and malaise, unfulfilled desires for help or guidance, speech being used not as a means of genuine interpersonal contact but as a gesture, part of a social code used to hold other people at a distance. The Third Applicant describes how he went to see a psychiatrist after he suddenly found that television commercials and the odour of beer inexplicably began to nauseate him ('The television was one thing and I was a person, and I was going to be sick').[46] The Psychiatrist responds by chanting:

Blah, blah blah blah blah blah HOSTILE.
Blah, blah blah blah blah blah PENIS.

Blah, blah blah blah blah blah MOTHER.
(*holding out his hand*)
Blah, blah blah blah blah blah MONEY.[47]

Here, as in the square dance with the Politician, the professionalization of 'help' enables an empty, ritualized transaction to stand in for actual acknowledgment and healing.

The middle play, *TV*, takes place in two worlds simultaneously: the realistically portrayed world of television network employees Susan, Hal and George, and a chameleonic TV world, initially confined upstage left, in which scenes from various programmes play out. The text leaves the exact nature of Hal and Susan's jobs ambiguous. They sit in a viewing room, watching television and making 'check marks' in order to fill a quota as part of an unexplained rating system.[48] Hal and Susan are also engaged in a secret workplace romance and seem unable to articulate their ambivalent feelings about the relationship. George, their older, married supervisor, is also infatuated with Susan. As the play goes on, the figures in the TV world gradually invade the 'real' characters' space, until the two worlds completely overlap.

The TV figures, five actors dressed in grey with black horizontal lines painted across their faces, present pastiches of popular 1960s television programmes, including one about a superhero called *Wonderboy*, the Western melodrama *The Endless Frontier*, a variety show hosted by 'Lily Heaven' (originally performed as 'a loudmouthed pop singer with a Pepsodent smile', according to Robert Brustein), and a sitcom called *My Favorite Teenage Daughter*.[49] These programmes alternate with commercials and faux news segments about the war in Vietnam. In total, the same five rapidly transforming actors portray about fifty characters.

When asked to speak at a UNESCO meeting about the differences among theatre, film and TV, van Itallie stated: 'TV is to film as a cartoon is to a picture. Television is a series of cartoon, or iconic, images.'[50] When reading these remarks, it is helpful to remember that televisions, in the 1960s, produced much lower-fidelity images than what one might see on a movie screen during the same period. The same can be said of their sound. This inability to broadcast crisp, detailed images and high-quality sound led television producers to favour loud colours and bold, straight lines in scenery and costumes for live broadcast, and that tendency toward broadness also often characterized TV acting. Van Itallie's cartoon analogy explains why the TV figures in *TV* are more like archetypes or stereotypes than rounded characters.

The portrayal of the TV figures draws upon the Open's work on transformations and especially 'perfect people' to show how television's panoply of cartoonish images recommend certain idealized identities to viewers. For all of their superficial differences, this multitude of characters all find themselves in scenarios involving the acting out of conventionalized gender roles – men playing the hero and demanding women's attention, while women joyfully labour to meet others' emotional needs. These varied depictions of gender relations in the TV world often either resonate with or provide counterpoint to the relationships among the three studio characters. Susan fixes coffee, fetches food and helplessly tolerates Hal and George's harassment and petty mistreatment of her. The men dismiss her opinions and deride her intelligence, and at one point George slaps her in the face for laughing too hard at a joke. At the same time, TV figures including Lily Heaven, Luci Baines Johnson and a string of other female figures enact the Doris-like 'perfect person' model of nurturing, submissive femininity that has interposed itself in the place of Susan's own interiority.[51] Susan describes herself as 'a hysteric', and it's no wonder given that the TV world provides her with so few models for active resistance to sexism.[52] Meanwhile, the TV world models a masculinity that is alternately heroic and needy. Wonderboy rescues a helpless housewife from her scientist husband, whose experiment transforms him into a monster. The nature of the experiment is unclear, but the husband asserts that, if he succeeds, 'no one will be hungry for love. Ever again.'[53] In the final programme, *My Favorite Teenage Daughter*, the titular daughter has no date for the prom, and her father mortifies her by offering to be her date himself. Simultaneously, George tries to butt into Susan and Hal's plans to go on a movie date. The sitcom characters move into the 'real' characters' space, the dialogue in both worlds starts to overlap, and the 'laugh' track provided by the TV People starts responding to Susan, Hal and George. When Susan declares, 'I'M going to go home and fix my apartment and you two can have dinner toGETHER [*sic*]', the hysterical laugh track, and the fact that all three remain onstage, 'their faces frozen into laughing masks', undercut any impression that Susan might finally be asserting herself.[54] Susan remains as impotent as Beckett's tramps are when they resolve to leave the stage; the 'perfect' social world of TV depends on laughing off resistance to patriarchy as a mere gag.

The text of *TV* begins with an epigraph from McLuhan's *Understanding Media*: 'The youth Narcissus mistook his own reflection in the water for another person . . . He was numb. He had adapted to his extension of himself and had become a closed system.'[55] *TV* stages such a 'closed system' in action. It can be thought of as an 'inside-outside' scene in which the characters' own 'insides' have been displaced and overwritten by television.

In contrast, the last play in the triptych, *Motel: A Masque for Three Dolls*, enacts a violent response to the cultural malaise that leaves the characters of *Interview* and *TV* paralysed. *Motel* takes place in a generic motel room, 'anonymously modern, except for certain "homey" touches', on the fictional Route 666.[56] In place of regular human figures, stage directions call for three larger-than-life-sized dolls with disproportionately large heads, operated by actors in platform shoes. The Motel-Keeper resembles an older woman, with square breasts and hair curlers that 'suggest electronic receivers'.[57] Her voice comes from a loudspeaker, and she wears mirrored glasses that exist primarily to irritate and distract the audience with reflected light or images of themselves. The Man and Woman represent a generic travelling couple, with removable clothes that come off as the action proceeds. The Motel-Keeper's monologue, a rambling advertisement for her motel and its features, makes up the play's entire spoken text. As the Motel-Keeper drones on, the couple engage in escalating acts of vandalism within the room, first stripping and jumping on the bed, then tearing out bathroom fixtures and ripping pages from the Gideon Bible, then writing obscenities and drawing genitalia on the walls in lipstick, and finally, in their only direct interaction with their host, beheading the Motel-Keeper.

Motel, which was conceived before van Itallie joined the Open, constitutes his effort at realizing some of Antonin Artaud's propositions for the Theatre of Cruelty. Like so many American playwrights and directors, van Itallie read Artaud in the early 1960s and became interested in adapting some of his theories to the American stage.[58] In Artaud's Theatre of Cruelty, performers enact humanity's darkest collective fantasies in productions that assault and overwhelm the spectator's nervous system. Artaud intended this combination of imaginative anarchy and sensory overload to restore enervated moderns to the condition of 'Total Man' – beings understood not merely in psychological or economic terms but in terms of humanity's shared metaphysical condition (which, for, Artaud, was a rather bleak one).[59] *Motel* is a study in anarchy and overload. Van Itallie writes in his initial stage directions that in this play, 'The sensory nerves of the audience are not to be spared.'[60] The room's colour scheme consists of 'violent combinations of oranges, pinks and reds against a reflective plastic background', meaning that, like the Motel-Keeper's reflective glasses, the scenery itself has the potential to glare irritatingly at the audience. This sensory assault intensifies as the play proceeds, climaxing with a mixture of loud rock music, a civil defence siren, bright headlights shining directly into the audience area, and fans designed to blow onstage debris at the spectators.

Van Itallie's text also connects *Motel*'s style to that of French belle-époque avant-garde author Alfred Jarry (himself a key influence on Artaud). *Motel*'s epigraph comes from William Butler Yeats' famed description of the storied, riot-inducing 1896 premiere of Jarry's play *Ubu Roi* at the Théâtre de l'Oeuvre: 'after all our subtle colour and nervous rhythm, after the faint mixed tints of Conder, what more is possible? After us the Savage God.'[61] While 'Savage God' may have had multiple meanings for Yeats, the phrase must have referred at least in part to Jarry's Père Ubu, an amoral, scatological, buffoonish anti-hero who usurps the throne of Poland, plunders the national treasury, stuffs anyone who protests into a de-braining machine, and abuses standard political phraseology to the point that its essential vacancy becomes blatant. Jarry originally conceived *Ubu Roi* as a puppet play, and it was staged at the Théâtre de l'Oeuvre with actors in bulky costumes that made them look like gigantic puppets. Jarry's backdrop, painted by some of his artist friends, mashed up indoor, outdoor, tropical and polar features, evoking an irrational non-place in the same way that Jarry did when he famously declared that his play was set in 'Poland, which is to say nowhere.'[62] Van Itallie's motel room is also nowhere, though its status as a non-place is nauseating rather than fanciful. The room's furniture and modern conveniences mostly come from a catalogue, and even the handmade 'homey' touches, such as the antimacassar and the hooked rug, sound like generic products imbued with a commodified cosiness. It is, in the Motel-Keeper's words, 'the perfect 1966 room'.⁶³ The room's alienating homogeneity, clearly framed as a product of late capitalist mass production, also extends to its guests. The Woman doll, in particular, looks like a human commodity, a grotesque of a large-breasted pin-up model, with shoulders 'thrown way back, like a girl posing for a calendar'.⁶⁴ When the Man and Woman smash the room and kill its keeper, they are similar to Jarry's Ubu in that they consume and destroy indiscriminately in an orgiastic outburst that is at once horrific and liberating.

The Motel-Keeper presents herself as the personification of the 'old idea' of enclosure, of creating place and enabling action by demarcating space: 'I am the room, a Roman theatre where cheers break loose the lion; a railroad carriage in the forest of Compiègne, in 1918 and again in 1941.'⁶⁵ Her references to the Treaty of Versailles and the French surrender to Nazi Germany only throw her motel room's placelessness into relief. Once, van Itallie suggests, we closed off spaces in order to create events within them, in order to set a place apart from the everyday flow of time. Now we create mass-produced spaces that are so indistinct they could be anywhere. Implicitly, van Itallie is connecting the motel room's bland neutrality to the way in which a commercial theatre serves as a neutral non-place filled with inoffensive, mass-produced products. While *Motel* does not involve the audience in the action as directly as *The Serpent* later would, part of its cumulative effect is to remind the audience of its own physical presence within the theatre space, and to make that space anything but homey or comforting.

Motel may seem to give *America Hurrah* a nihilistic conclusion, suggesting that the only way to end the intolerable conditions suffered by *Interview*'s job applicants and *TV*'s numb corporate lackeys is to smash everything. But in his short essay 'Should the Artist Be Political in His Art?', printed in the *New York Times* in September 1966, he suggests that he wants to help his spectators achieve metaphysical wholeness, arguing that the alienation of our dream lives from our everyday material surroundings is the principle cause of modern malaise and escalating military violence. In a passage using very similar imagery to his description of his childhood in Great Neck, he writes: 'The more our outside reality is full of American summer sunshine, suburban lawnmowing, bright skies and blooming rhododendron, the more often our dreams include the boom of the final thunderclap, and the ultimate bright white dissolving light.'⁶⁶ In the face of this disjunction between our violent dreams and our anodyne everyday lives, artists are not free to concern themselves solely with aesthetic questions. He writes:

> This would be fair if things were as compartmentalized as the various sections of *The Sunday Times*. But the fact is they aren't anymore. If a bomb from the political section is dropped, the roses in the gardening section are going to suffer. The classifications are there for the convenience of the editors. Unfortunately, they perpetuate separations in our minds too.⁶⁷

Van Itallie sees contemporary American culture's chief problem as an artificial compartmentalization of art from politics, of dream life from waking life, of our darker impulses from our daily performance in the social role of 'Good Person'. By identifying solely with sanitized fantasies, we psychically maim ourselves and, consequently, we find ourselves impotent and dumbfounded when our darker, disavowed dreams, 'the monolithic insurance building and the metal birds of total destruction', come to life in front of us.⁶⁸ In order to heal this separation, the dramatist's purpose is to produce 'a private dream reshaped and publicly revealed to be everyone's'. He concludes, 'Any metaphor that an artist can construct for the theater which will cause public recognition of lost limbs . . . will be a political one.' This search for poignant metaphors and restored wholeness would become an essential part of van Itallie's next collaboration with the Open, *The Serpent,* as well as many of his subsequent works.

America Hurrah received glowing reviews from most of the major newspaper critics in New York. Brustein's paean to *America Hurrah* in *The New Republic,* later reprinted as an introduction to the Grove Press edition of the play, declared that van Itallie 'has . . . discovered the deepest poetic function of the theatre which is not, like most American dramatists, to absorb the audience into the author's own personal problems under the pretext of that they are universal, but rather to invent metaphors which can poignantly suggest a nation's nightmares and afflictions'.⁶⁹ Lahr gave the play a similarly complimentary review. Ross Wetzsteon of *The Village Voice* was less enthusiastic, claiming that *America Hurrah* wasted talented actors on texts that merely succeeded in replicating the blandness that van Itallie sought to satirize: 'Modern life is mechanical and unfeeling; television is banal and irrelevant; motels are sick and lifeless ... All this applies, by and large, to the scripts as well.'[70] However, the most significant response was that of Walter Kerr, drama critic for the *New York Times*. Kerr wielded substantial influence over the theatre-going public in New York, and he was not always kind to avant-garde productions. His review of *America Hurrah*, entitled 'A Whisper in the Wind', began: 'I think you'll be neglecting a whisper in the wind if you don't look in on *America Hurrah*, three views of the USA.' Kerr saw the play as an important 'first try' at finding original means of generating poetic effects in the theatre, and praised both the acting and Chaikin and Levy's direction.[71] Thanks to the critics and to word of mouth, the play's two-year run was sustained not only by members of the downtown scene and other regular attendees of experimental theatre but also by theatregoers with more mainstream or conventionally highbrow tastes, who flocked to the Pocket Theater to catch the 'whisper in the wind' to which Kerr had referred.

Starting in the summer of 1967, theatres outside New York began to mount their own productions of *America Hurrah*, leading to major censorship controversies that turned the play into an international cause célèbre. In London, the Royal Court Theatre had to register itself as a private club in order to perform the play, because the Lord Chamberlain's Office refused to license it for public performance. In Sydney, the audience formed a barricade to stop vice officers from arresting the actors. In Chicago, authorities threatened to revoke the liquor license of a cabaret that tried to produce *America Hurrah*. In Mobile, Alabama, the mayor forced the University of South Alabama to end a production of *America Hurrah* that was playing to packed houses.[72]

Judging from the most significant favourable reviews of *America Hurrah*, the professionalization that Chaikin and other Off-Off-Broadway artists feared was precisely what allowed van Itallie to become a crossover hit. In an article published two weeks after his initial review, Kerr wrote about *America Hurrah* alongside Terry's *Viet Rock*, using them as positive and negative examples, respectively, of how to incorporate the techniques of experimental acting collectives such as the Open into 'legitimate' drama and theatre. Kerr contrasted van Itallie's 'control of his devices' with Terry's 'loose method' and 'unrefined attitudinizing', suggesting that van Itallie had successfully 'tamed' the rough, anarchic energies of the

American avant-garde theatre, whereas Terry's work remained too self-indulgent to count as proper drama.[73] Brustein asserted that with *America Hurrah* 'the concept of theatrical unity finally becomes meaningful in this country, and the American theatre takes three giant steps toward maturity.'[74] The implication, again, is that *America Hurrah* was a more 'grown-up' play than the downtown theatres had produced up to that point.

As Brustein's remarks suggest, the play's premiere came to be seen as a significant cultural event. Once it was clear that *America Hurrah* had become a bona fide hit, van Itallie was interviewed and photographed by major magazines; he wasn't being treated like a 'baby playwright'. In 1967, the play won the Outer Critics Circle Award and the Drama Desk's Vernon Rice Award. The media attention turned van Itallie into a kind of unofficial spokesperson for Off-Off-Broadway during the late 1960s. One illustration of *America Hurrah*'s historical importance is the fact that in 2012, Matthew Weiner's multi-award-winning television drama *Mad Men*, a show set in 1960s New York, included a scene in which Weiner's cynical adman protagonist, Don Draper, attends a performance of *America Hurrah*. Weiner's choice to include *America Hurrah* reflects the production's status as a cultural touchstone of the period.

The Serpent

Chaikin was, in his own words, 'disgusted' by how the cast of *America Hurrah* embraced their new-found fame and he worried that *America Hurrah*'s success might tempt the Open Theater to compromise its process-over-product principles. Consequently, while veteran Open members such as Joyce Aaron continued to offer regular workshops that were open to any interested parties, Chaikin chose to focus his own attention on a hand-picked group of actors who were willing to commit to a highly intensive schedule, and to work without a playwright during the initial phases of his next project.[75] He originally planned to devise a piece about the 'lost years' in Jesus's biography, the years not covered by the narratives provided in the Gospels.[76] Work on *Genesis* began as preparation for the Jesus project, but the group soon became more interested in the Garden of Eden and the Fall. Drawing on a pool of grant money that he had received from the National Endowment for the Arts, the National Endowment for the Humanities, the New York State Council on the Arts and the Ford Foundation, Chaikin brought in a series of teachers to give the company practical, historical and philosophical instruction, including voice teacher Kristen Linklater, singing coach Richard Peaslee, dance therapy specialist Joseph Schlichter, religious scholars Joseph Campbell and Paul Goodman and critic and theorist Susan Sontag. By the time Megan Terry (who would later drop out) and van Itallie joined the project, the actors had already produced a substantial amount of material through improvisation, and Chaikin restricted the writers' agency with two rules: any new material 'must be concerned with exile, alienation and man's aloneness – the principal themes of the workshop's version of the story of Adam', and 'the workshop dynamic of the exploration and discovery should somehow be built into the eventual piece.'[77] It was only at the very end of the process, after months of work, that van Itallie, Chaikin and dramaturg Roberta Sklar set about making a finished text out of the mass of available material. Van Itallie recounts that when the company was on a boat crossing the Atlantic, en route to the project's premiere in Rome, 'I sat down with Joe and Roberta Sklar, and I wrote down all the scenes that we had on three-by-five cards, and we went through them and we decided rather quickly which pieces to keep and which pieces to throw out. And then I said "Okay, give me an hour or two."'[78] The resulting piece premiered at Rome's Teatro delle Arti on 2 May 1968 and then toured across Europe.

Chaikin aptly encapsulates *The Serpent*'s aims and structure in a statement from his introduction to the text: 'The text follows the narrative of Genesis, and is at the same time a repudiation of its assumptions, thus forming a dialectic.'[79] The play centres on van Itallie and the company's interpretation of the events recounted in Chapters 3, 4 and 5 of Genesis: Eve's temptation, the expulsion from Eden, Cain's murder of Abel and the recounting of the generations of Adam's descendants (the last of these being supplemented by the 'begats' from the Gospel of Matthew). A chorus of four kneeling women narrates much of the action, rocking and chanting in imitation of orthodox Jewish davening, and also share a collection of musings and confessions based on interviews that van Itallie conducted with actresses in the company. In performance, the play included multiple occasions for directly acknowledging and even physically interacting with the audience, permitting them to participate in certain parts of the event.

The main body of the play is preceded by an extended prologue depicting events that post-date the primal events of Genesis. This prologue gives the play a backwards, burrowing structure, reflecting how Chaikin (in Blumenthal's words) 'wanted to explore connections over "vertical time", links with mythic roots, rather than horizontal, linear history'.[80] First, the actors warm up in front of the audience as themselves, using the full performance space, indicating to the audience that the performance will surround and involve everyone in the room. Then the actors join a procession accompanied by a bongo drum during which they periodically freeze to demonstrate physical motifs that will recur throughout the performance. In the next scene, a physician chants a matter-of-fact description of autopsy procedures and the brains of gunshot victims while engaging in a ritualized mime of an autopsy. Gunshots periodically interrupt the action. The following scene, 'Kennedy-King Assassination', had its germ in a series of twelve stills from Abraham Zapruder's film recording of John F. Kennedy's assassination. The company translated these twelve stills into twelve tableaux, and devised a movement *étude* in which they moved from tableau to tableau, first in order, then in reverse order and then in a shuffled sequence. As they were working on the scene, Martin Luther King and Robert Kennedy were assassinated, and brief representations of their shootings were added. In a striking reversal of linear chronology, the autopsy precedes the assassinations, and this depiction of modern-day violence prefigures the play's later depiction of the mythic first murder.

The construction of *The Serpent*'s central episodes, 'The Garden' and 'The Curses', exemplifies how the final text of *The Serpent* weaves together contributions from the actors, van Itallie and the expert consultants who spoke to them. 'The Garden' began with improvisation work, described by Chaikin in his book *The Presence of the Actor*:

> While working on the garden sequence of *The Serpent*, the premise was that everyone had his garden-in-the-mind, this place that the world isn't, this utopia – where creatures are themselves ... An authentic image came; somebody got on the stage and introduced it ... One actor will get up and do his garden and if

another actor is sensitive to it, he will join him so that they make a little world. A third actor may or may not join, depending on whether this garden does or does not signal anybody else ... Soon somebody will start a world with its own logic, its own rules and its own sense. Then we have a garden.[81]

In the final text of *The Serpent*, van Itallie writes that the animals of the Garden are 'personal, previously selected by each actor as expressing an otherwise inexpressible part of himself'.[82] The animals all breathe in unison, a representation of the unity of prelapsarian Creation.

As the company worked on Eve's temptation by the serpent, the decision to represent the serpent as a chorus of five male actors moving as a single body – an entity that Lahr aptly describes as 'a writhing thicket of knees and elbows, producing apples in large and seductive arcs of the arm' – came from actor Roy London. The company worked on it, and then van Itallie wrote the serpent's lines.[83] The idea that the chorus of women narrating the apple-eating would imitate davening worshippers in a synagogue came from van Itallie. 'The Curses', in which God's voice speaks through the bodies of his creatures to condemn humanity for eating from the tree, began with a lengthy group discussion about 'what the "irreversibles" (Chaikin's word) were in the human condition'.[84] They asked each other what it meant to be cursed, to experience something as 'locked, fixed, unchangeable', and from those conversations van Itallie distilled the curses that appear in the text.[85] The idea that God's voice would come from his own creations – from Adam and the animals in the Garden – was originally sparked by a remark by Sontag.[86] Working off the original idea led to the method described in the text: each time God speaks, one actor pulls up another by the armpits, and the actor who has been pulled up speaks, as if possessed, in a deep, resonant God-voice.[87] The content of the curses, like the speeches of the davening women's chorus, reflect van Itallie and Chaikin's interests in Jewish theology and mysticism, but they also draw upon what the company learned from Goodman and Sontag. The above summary suggests rough divisions of labour, but group members frequently crossed those divisions – actors suggesting content for the text, the playwright suggesting an approach to movement and so on.

The first side of the play's dialectical argument essentially reiterates the central concerns expressed in van Itallie's earlier plays. In the cursing scene, God proclaims:

> Now shall come a separation
> Between the dreams in your head
> And those things which you believe
> To be outside your head
> And the two shall war within you.
>
> Accursed, you shall be alone.
> For whatever you think,
> And whatever you see or hear,
> You shall think it and see it and hear it, alone.[88]

This curse essentially describes the rationalist separation of dreaming and waking experience that van Itallie criticized in his essay 'Should the Artist Be Political in His Art?' Remembering how that essay links psychic compartmentalization to our ability to disavow our responsibility for the modern world's escalating violence, one can see how God's curse connects to the chant recited during the assassination scenes:

> I mind my own affairs.
> I am a little man.
> I lead a private life.
> I stay alive.
>
> I'm no assassin
> I'm no president.
> I don't know who did the killing.
> I stay alive.
>
> I keep out of big affairs.
> I am not a violent man.
> I am very sorry, still
> I stay alive.[89]

The curses and the choral chant during the assassination scene present the Fall as akin to the ruinous psychic dismemberment that van Itallie describes in 'Should the Artist Be Political in His Art?' and depicts in *America Hurrah*. The characterless little people populating the fallen world of *The Serpent* recall the interchangeable interviewees in *Interview*, and they are as incapable of processing America's dream life as Doris in the 'Doris' Plays. Van Itallie frames Cain's murder of Abel as a collective dream, disowned as a myth, only to return to confront us in the person of Lee Harvey Oswald.

The play's unhinged chronology also resonates with its themes of alienation and strandedness, as suggested by the women's chorus:

First Woman of the Chorus	In the beginning everything is possible.
Second Woman of the Chorus	I've lost the beginning.
Third Woman of the Chorus	I'm the middle.
Fourth Woman of the Chorus	Knowing neither the end nor the beginning.[90]

The chorus, who are 'descendants of Eve, vessels containing her experience and inheritors of God's curses', describe the same kinds of petty cruelty and quiet desperation that fill *America Hurrah*: unhappy marriages, empty friendships, the feeling of being trapped in one's own skull, a mother's secret wish that her child would go off to school and 'never come home', a dinner guest's repressed desire to 'throw the food / Ax the table, / Scratch the women's faces, / And grab the men's balls.'[91] The women describe a horde of lemmings all thoughtlessly running together to a watery grave.[92] The rush of lemmings recalls the imagery from 'Should the Artist Be Political in His Art', in which van Itallie described a modern civilization sleepwalking its way to annihilation because it refuses to own up to its violent fantasies. When one of the women asks, 'Would my dreams recognize me? / Would they come to me and say / "She's the one who imagined us"?' her question echoes van Itallie's stated concern that by 'refusing to recognize our paternity' of our dreams, by denying, sanitizing, compartmentalizing ourselves, we give our fantasies their own uncontrollable agency.[93]

The other side of the play's dialectic emerges through the manner in which the actors inhabit the stage and interact with the audience. As Lahr puts it, 'The energy of the event becomes its theme.'[94] The 'theme' to which Lahr refers is the capacity for theatre itself to create an Edenic space, shared by performer and spectator, in which every choice becomes possible and our maimed psyches become whole again. In his introduction to the play, van Itallie notes that theatre's 'original religious function' is 'bringing people together in a community ceremony, where the actors are in some sense priests or celebrants'.[95] *The Serpent* underscores that point by having the players begin and end the play among the audience, sharing space with the spectators as themselves. They also hand out apples to spectators during the apple-eating scene, inviting the audience to share in Adam and Eve's ecstasy of discovery. As Proudfitt points out, the simple act of sharing food is inherently a community-building gesture.[96] During the apple-eating sequence, performers mingled with the audience while acting out the ecstasy of gaining knowledge of good and evil. Chaikin and van Itallie allowed the cast to improvise freely in this scene, so what exactly took place varied from performance to performance. Often it involved cast members touching or kissing spectators.[97]

In the climactic (in more than one sense) 'Begatting' sequence, the company enacts the mythic original discovery of sex, and the sensual contact among the actors' bodies provides a more consoling and more energetic form of connection than anything that the play's characters (or any of *America Hurrah*'s characters) had achieved through dialogue. In the end, the performers walk out of the performance space through the audience, as themselves, singing an old popular song (the original production used 'On Moonlight Bay', a love song written by Edward Madden and Percy Wenrich in 1912, but the text itself does not call for a specific song). While Genesis, as read by van Itallie, argues that our curiosity and self-awareness doomed us to an alienated existence in which it is impossible to begin anew, Chaikin's performers counter-argue, through their actions, that the actors' total self-awareness and ritual presence potentiate new beginnings, that curiosity is not the Original Sin that spoils creation but is, in fact, that which makes creation possible.

The Serpent's initial European tour took the company to a variety of venues, including universities, theatre festivals and middle-class playhouses; audience responses to the performance were equally varied. Plunka notes that while festival and student audiences enjoyed it, older and more middle-class audiences became cold, nervous or even hostile. These latter audiences were, in Plunka's words, 'a bit unnerved by the actor–spectator interaction', and their response 'upset several Open Theater members'.[98] Positive audience response aids the presentation of any theatre piece, but the strain that poor reception had on the cast of *The Serpent* indicates how inordinately the piece depended on having audiences committed to maintaining the kind of shared space that the Open's ritual was designed to produce.

While the performance of *The Serpent* was supposed to create a kind of utopian space, the creation process itself was not always harmonious, especially not where control and ownership of the final text were concerned. Sometimes, van Itallie's ability to process and revise the actors' own thoughts met with their approval, as one of the actresses from the women's chorus recounts:

> Jean-Claude asked us to come to his house, which we did, and he asked us questions about ourselves, and we talked about ourselves and our lives. I think he was fabulous to come up with the speeches he had the four women do. My own, for instance, were things I said to him, but he put them in a brilliant way. I could never have done it, but they were from me. They're wonderful.[99]

Both Chaikin and Pasolli, however, suggest that not everyone was pleased with how van Itallie fulfilled his role in the process. Chaikin notes that in the final days before the premiere, 'everything was difficult: people with each other, the actors in relation to the work, in relation to me, in relation to van Itallie . . . There was a sense of betrayal, that each of us had somehow betrayed the other.'[100] Actors who had seen *The Serpent* as the communal property of the company disliked the amount of agency that van Itallie suddenly seemed to have. As Pasolli puts it, 'What had once belonged to the troupe in common looked at the time of the opening very like van Itallie's property; to many of the actors, it seemed that Chaikin had given the piece away.'[101] The ill feelings of some company members worsened when van Itallie received exclusive rights to the text of *The Serpent* (the Open Theater only retained the right to perform it without paying a royalty).[102]

Van Itallie also believed that he had given up a significant amount of control during the process: 'A large part in the creation of the ceremony was "letting go". For my part, I let go of a great many words, characters and scenes.'[103] But he nonetheless insisted on the authority of the text that he created for the Open. Writing for the benefit of companies considering their own productions of *The Serpent*, van Itallie calls the subtitle 'A Ceremony' an accidental trap, in that it promotes misinterpretation of the text as something other than a fully scripted drama. In van Itallie's opinion, 'to perform it, even as a ceremony, it is a play in the very usual sense in that if you vary the text you do so at your own peril'.[104] These disputes about who truly created and owns *The Serpent* undercut, somewhat, the sharing ethos that the Open Theater's work tried to enact.

When the Open returned to the US, they presented *The Serpent* at universities, including Harvard and in their loft in Manhattan. The overall critical response was positive, and *The Serpent* won the Vernon Rice Award and became one of the first Off-Off-Broadway performances to win an Obie Award from the *Village Voice*. Some critics praised *The Serpent* specifically for lacking the vices that they attributed to other well-known experimental groups. Kerr wrote: 'There is nothing of the sloppiness here that defined Tom O'Horgan's work and that will apparently dog to the death the living theater [*sic*]. Nor does the evening try to subsist merely on the merely coarse enthusiasm Richard Schechner brings to so much of the business of letting go.'[105] Martin Duberman, in *Partisan Review*, noted that, unlike the Living Theatre and Performance Group, the Open 'know the difference between attacking an audience and challenging it'.[106] These reviews echo somewhat van Itallie's own assessments; he admired the Living Theatre, but he also observed that in negotiating the tension between what he called 'honesty' and 'professionalism', the Open, despite Chaikin's fear of becoming an institution, erred more toward 'professionalism' than the Living did.[107]

As *The Serpent* gained notoriety, the audiences changed in ways that disappointed van Itallie. 'Most audiences go [to the theatre] as critics,' he stated in 1969. '[That] is to say ... expecting to come out with a certain intellectual conclusion. In this sense, to be critical is to be armed. To be creative, on the other hand, is to be unarmed.'[108] The reviews of *The Serpent* produced audiences who came armed with expectations, 'looking forward to things they had read about', which to van Itallie meant that they were less receptive to being changed by what they saw.[109] While van Itallie ended the 1960s with a much broader audience than he had had when he first began working with the Open Theater, and had helped to expand public awareness of America's experimental theatre scene, he was also finding that, at least in this one respect, the greater visibility that he had once hoped for was working against his creative aims.

Conclusion

Along with the blockbuster success of the 1968 musical *Hair* (co-written by former Open Theater member Gerome Ragni) and Edward Albee's transformation into a Pulitzer-anointed Broadway playwright, the success of *America Hurrah* and *The Serpent* helped usher in a period in which Off-Off-Broadway was increasingly seen as a professional stepping stone for Broadway-bound writers and actors and as a mine of bankable material for Broadway producers. By the end of the 1960s, Actors Equity had modified its rules to make it easier for professional actors to perform in small experimental productions, and the Obie and Drama Desk Awards had made work in Off-Off-Broadway venues eligible for consideration. Van Itallie himself, however, did not become a Broadway playwright, continuing instead to work with Chaikin on productions such as *Mystery Play* (1973) and *Struck Dumb* (1988) and seeing his plays produced at La MaMa, Theater for the New City and various regional theatres. While *The Serpent* was on tour in Europe, he met the Tibetan Buddhist teacher Chögyam Trungpa, and from the 1970s onward he has been a practising Buddhist, hosting workshops at Shantigar, a spiritual retreat in rural Massachusetts. As indicated by later works such as *The Tibetan Book of the Dead: or How Not to Do It Again* (1983), Buddhism provided a new basis for his commitment to using theatre as a means of awakening his audiences to a more holistic sense of self. True to the recurring cultural critique within his 1960s works, he has avoided following the 'perfect' career trajectory prescribed by commercial theatre and the fantasies of success that it recommends to artists.

Documents

Compiled and edited by Bradley Allen Markle

Awards

Obie

The 'Obie' (short for 'Off-Broadway') Awards were created in 1955 by Jerry Tallmer, founder, associate editor and film and drama critic for the Village Voice *newspaper. They were first awarded at the conclusion of the 1955–6 season. Starting in 1965, Off-Off-Broadway productions were recognized. Award categories vary and not every category is awarded annually. In 1969, categories were eliminated in favour of 'outstanding achievement.' Categories returned the next year.*

1960 Obie Awards

Award for Best Actor	Warren Finnerty, *The Connection*
Award for Best Actress	Eileen Brennan, *Little Mary Sunshine*
Award for Best All-Around Production	Julian Beck, Judith Malina, *The Connection*
Award for Best Director	Gene Frankel, *Machinal*
Award for Best Foreign Play	Jean Genet, *The Balcony*

Award for Best New Play	Jack Gelber, *The Connection*
Award for Distinguished Performance by an Actor or Actress	William Daniels, *The Zoo Story* Patricia Falkenheim, *Peer Gynt*, *Henry IV, Part I* Donald Davis, *Krapp's Last Tape* Vincent Gardenia, *Machinal* Elisa Loti, *Come Share My House* John Heffernan, *Henry IV, Part 2* Nancy Marchand, *The Balcony* Jock Livingston, *The Balcony*
Award for Distinguished Plays	Samuel Beckett, *Krapp's Last Tape* Jack Richardson, *The Prodigal* Edward Albee, *The Zoo Story*
Award for Set Design	David Hays, *The Balcony*
Award for Special Citations	Brooks Atkinson

1961 Obie Awards

Award for Best Actor	Khigh Dhiegh, *In the Jungle of Cities*
Award for Best Actress	Anne Meacham, *Hedda Gabler*
Award for Best Director	Gerald Freedman, *The Taming of the Shrew*
Award for Best New Play	Jean Genet, *The Blacks*
Award for Best Music	Teiji Ito, *King Ubu*, *In the Jungle of Cities*, *Sotoba Komachi*, *The Damask Drum*, *Han's Crime*
Award for Best Off-Off-Broadway Production	Theodore J. Flicker, *The Premise*
Award for Best Overall Production	David Ross, *Hedda Gabler*
Award for Distinguished Performance by an Actor or Actress	Godfrey Cambridge, *The Blacks: A Clown Show* James Coco, *The Moon in the Yellow River* Lester Rawlins, *Hedda Gabler* Joan Hackett, *Call Me By My Rightful Name* Gerry Jedd, *She Stoops to Conquer* Surya Kumari, *The King of the Dark Chamber*
Award for Special Citations	Bernard Frechtman, *The Blacks*

1962 Obie Awards

Award for Best Actor	James Earl Jones, *Clandestine on the Morning Line*, *The Apple*, *Moon on a Rainbow Shawl*
Award for Best Actress	Barbara Harris, *Oh, Dad, Poor Dad, Mamma's Hung You in the Closet and I'm Feelin' So Sad*
Award for Best Foreign Play	Samuel Beckett, *Happy Days*
Award for Best Musical	C. Bernard Jackson, Jerome Eskow, James Hatch, *Fly Blackbird*
Award for Set Design	Norris Houghton, *Who'll Save the Plowboy?*
Award for Best New American Play	Frank D. Gilroy, *Who'll Save the Plowboy?*
Award for Distinguished Performance by an Actor or Actress	Clayton Corzatte, APA Repertory Geoff Garland, *The Hostage* Gerald S. O'Loughlin, *Who'll Save the Plowboy?* Paul Roebling, *This Side of Paradise* Sudie Bond, *Theatre of the Absurd* Vinnette Justine Carroll, *Moon on a Rainbow Shawl* Rosemary Harris, APA Repertory Ruth White, *Happy Days*
Award for Special Citations	Ellis Rabb, *The Hostage*

1963 Obie Awards

Award for Best Actor	George C. Scott, *Desire Under the Elms*
Award for Best Actress	Colleen Dewhurst, *Desire Under the Elms*
Award for Best Director	Alan Schneider, *The Pinter Plays*
Award for Best Production (Musical)	*The Boys from Syracuse*
Award for Best Production (Play)	Luigi Pirandello, directed by William Ball, *Six Characters in Search of an Author*

Award for Performance	Jacqueline Brookes, *Six Characters in Search of an Author*
	Joseph Chaikin, *Man is Man*
	James Patterson, 'The Collection' in *The Pinter Plays*
	Olympia Dukakis, *A Man's a Man*
	Madeleine Sherwood, *Hey You Light Man!*
	Eli Wallach, *The Typists*, *The Tiger*
	Michael O'Sullivan, *Six Characters in Search of an Author*
	Anne Jackson, *The Typists*, *The Tiger*
Award for Special Citations	*The Second City*
	Jean Erdman, *The Coach With Six Insides*

1964 Obie Awards

Award for Best American Play	LeRoi Jones, *Dutchman*
Award for Design	Julian Beck, *The Brig*
Award for Best Director	Judith Malina, *The Brig*
Award for Best Performance	Gloria Foster, *In White America*
Award for Best Play	Samuel Beckett, *Play*
Award for Best Production (Musical)	Judson Poets Theatre, *What Happened*
Award for Best Production (Play)	Living Theatre, *The Brig*
Award for Direction	Lawrence Kornfeld, *What Happened*
Award for Distinguished Performance	Taylor Mead, *The General Returns from One Place to Another*
	Ronald Weyand, *The Lesson*
	Philip Bruns, *Mr. Simian*
	Marian Seldes, *The Ginger Man*
	Lee Grant, *The Maids*
	Joyce Ebert, *The Trojan Women*
	Jack Warden, *Epiphany*
	Estelle Parsons, *Next Time I'll Sing to You* and *In the Summer House*
	Diana Sands, *The Living Premise*
	David Hurst, *A Month in the Country*

Award for Best Music	Al Carmines, *Home Movies*, *What Happened*
Award for Special Citations	Judson Memorial Church

1965 Obie Awards

Award for Best American Play	Robert Lowell, *The Old Glory*
Award for Best Musical Production	*The Cradle Will Rock*
Award for Best Direction	Ulu Grosbard, *A View from the Bridge*
Award for Best Costumes	Willa Kim, *The Old Glory*
Award for Distinguished Plays	María Irene Fornés, *Promenade* and *The Successful Life of 3*
Award for Distinguished Performances	Sada Thompson, *Tartuffe* Rosemary Harris, APA Repertory Roberts Blossom, *Do Not Pass Go* Robert Duvall, *A View from the Bridge* Margaret De Priest, *The Place for Chance* Joseph Chaikin, *Victims of Duty* and *The Exception and the Rule* James Earl Jones, *Baal* Frances Sternhagen, *The Room* and *A Slight Ache* Dean Dittmann, *The Cradle Will Rock* Brian Bedford, *The Knack*
Award for Special Citations	The Paper Bag Players Caffe Cino and Cafe La Mama

1966 Obie Awards

Award for Best Actor	Dustin Hoffman, *The Exhaustion of Our Son's Love*
Award for Best Actress	Jane White, *Coriolanus* and *Love's Labour's Lost*
Award for Set Design	Ed Wittstein, *Serjeant Musgrave's Dance* Lindsey Decker, *Red Cross*

Award for Best American Play	Ronald Ribman, *The Journey of the Fifth Horse*
Award for Distinguished Plays	Emanuel Peluso, *Good Day* Sam Shepard, *Chicago*, *Icarus's Mother* and *Red Cross*
Award for Distinguished Performances	Sharon Gans, *Soon Jack November* Michael Lipton, *The Trial* Mari-Claire Charba, *Birdbath* Kevin O'Connor, *Chicago* Jess Osuna, *Bugs* and *Veronica* Gloria Foster, *Medea* Frank Langella, *Good Day* and *The White Devil* Florence Tarlow, *Istanbul*, *Red Cross* and *A Beautiful Day* Douglas Turner Ward, *Day of Absence* Clarice Blackburn, *The Exhaustion of Our Son's Love*
Award for Special Citations	Theatre for Ideas Theater in the Street Peter Schumann Joseph H. Dunn H.M. Koutoukas

1967 Obie Awards

Award for Best Actor	Seth Allen, *Futz*
Award for Best Director	Tom O'Horgan, *Futz*
Award for Best Lightning	Johnny Dodd, *The White Whore*, *The Madness of Lady Bright*, *Chas. Dickens' Christmas Carol*
Award for Distinguished Plays	Sam Shepard, *La Turista* Rochelle Owens, *Futz* Henry Livings, *Eh?*
Award for Distinguished Performances	Tom Aldredge, *Measure for Measure*, *Stock Up on Pepper Cause Turkey's Going to War* Terry Kiser, *Fortune* and *Men's Eyes* Stacy Keach, *MacBird!* Robert Salvio, *Hamp*

	Robert Bonnard, *The Chairs* Rip Torn, *The Deer Park* Neil Flanagan, *The Madness of Lady Bright* Eddie McCarty, *Kitchenette* Bette Henritze, *Measure for Measure*, *The Wilder Plays*, *The Distinguished Person*, *The Rimers of Eldrich* Alvin Epstein, *Dynamite Tonite*
Award for Special Citations	Tom Sankey The Second Story Players The Open Theatre La Mama Troupe Jeff Weiss Joseph

1968 Obie Awards

Award for Best Actor	Al Pacino, *The Indian Wants the Bronx*
Award for Best Actress	Billie Dixon, *The Beard*
Award for Best Musical	Gertrude Stein and Al Carmines, *In Circles*
Award for Best Director	Michael A. Schultz, *Song of the Lusitanian Bogey*
Award for Best Foreign Play	Vaclav Havel, *The Memorandum*
Award for Best Design	Robert LaVigne, *A Midsummer Night's Dream* and *Endecott and the Red Cross*
Award for Distinguished Plays	Sam Shepard, *Forensic and the Navigator* and *Melodrama Play* John Guare, *Muzzeka* Israel Horovitz, *The Indian Wants the Bronx*
Award for Distinguished Direction	Rip Torn, *The Beard* John Hancock, *A Midsummer Night's Dream*
Award for Distinguished Performances	Roy Scheider, *Stephen D.* Peggy Pope, *Mama* Moses Gunn, The Negro Ensemble Company repertory Mari Gorman, *The Memorandum* and *Walking to Waldheim*

	John Cazale, *Line* and *The Indian Wants the Bronx*
	Jean David, *Istanboul*
	James Coco, *Fragments*
	Cliff Gorman, *The Boys in the Band*
Award for Special Citations	The Negro Ensemble Company
	The Fortune Society
	San Francisco Mime Troupe
	El Teatro Campesino

1969 Obie Awards

Note: In 1969, categories were eliminated.

| The Living Theatre, *Frankenstein* |
| Jeff Weiss, *The International Wrestling Match* |
| Julie Bovasso, *Gloria & Esperanza* |
| Judith Malina, *Antigone* |
| Julian Beck, *Antigone* |
| Israel Horovitz, *The Honest-to-God Schnozzola* |
| Jules Feiffer, *Little Murders* |
| Ronald Tavel, *The Boy on the Straight Back Chair* |
| Nathan George and Ron O'Neal, *No Place to be Somebody* |
| Arlene Rothlein, *The Poor Little Match Girl* |
| Theatre Genesis, for Sustained Excellence |
| Open Theatre, *The Serpent* |
| Om Theatre, *Riot* |
| Performance Group, *Dionysus in '69* |

1970 Obie Awards

Award for Best American Play	Paul Zindel, *The Effect of Gamma Rays on Man-in-the-Moon Marigolds* Megan Terry, *Approaching Simone*
Award for Best Foreign Play	Joe Orton, *What the Butler Saw*
Award for Best Musical	Gretchen Cryer, Nancy Ford, *The Last Sweet Days of Isaac* Robert Livingston, Gary William Friedman, Will Holt, *The Me Nobody Knows*

Award for Best Performance	Sada Thompson, *The Effect of Gamma Rays on Man-in-the-Moon Marigolds*
Award for Distinguished Direction	Alan Arkin, *The White House Murder Case* Melvin Bernhardt, *The Effect of Gamma Rays on Man-in-the-Moon Marigolds* Maxine Klein, *Approaching Simone* Gilbert Moses, *Slave Ship*
Award for Distinguished Performances	Beeson Carroll, *The Unseen Hand* Vincent Gardenia, *Passing Through Exotic Places* Harold Gould, *The Increased Difficulty of Concentration* Anthony Holland, *The White House Murder Case* Lee Kissman, *The Unseen Hand* Ron Leibman, *Transfers* Rue McClanahan, *Who's Happy Now?* Roberta Maxwell, *Whistle in the Dark* Austin Pendleton, *The Last Sweet Days of Isaac* Fredericka Weber, *The Last Sweet Days of Isaac* Pamela Payton-Wright, *The Effect of Gamma Rays on Man-in-the-Moon Marigolds*
Award for Distinguished Plays	Murray Mednick, *The Deer Kill* Vaclav Havel, *The Increased Difficulty of Concentration*
Award for Distinguished Production	Chelsea Theatre Center Andre Gregory, *Alice in Wonderland*
Award for Special Citations	Charles Ludlam, The Ridiculous Theatrical Company John Vaccaro, Theatre of the Ridiculous Richard Foreman Stanley Silverman Gardner Compton Emile Ardolino Andre Gregory

Drama Desk–Vernon Rice

The Drama Desk–Vernon Rice Awards are awarded by the Drama Desk organization, founded in 1949 by New York theatre critics, editors, writers and publishers. From 1955 to 1963, the award was named in honour of New York Post *critic Vernon Rice, among the first to treat Off-Broadway theatre seriously. In 1965, the name was changed to the Drama Desk–Vernon Rice Awards.*

1960 Vernon Rice Awards

Edward Albee, *The Zoo Story*
Rick Besoyan, *Little Mary Sunshine*

1961 Vernon Rice Awards

Joan Hackett, *Call Me by My Rightful Name* (Performance)
Tom Jones and Harvey Schmidt, *The Fantasticks*
Richard Barr and Clinton Wilder for Theater '61 productions of new playwrights, especially Edward Albee and Jack Richardson
Boris Tumarin, *Montserrat* and *The Idiot* (Direction)
Theodore J. Flicker, *The Premise*

1962 Vernon Rice Awards

Arthur Kopit, *Oh, Dad, Poor Dad, Mamma's Hung You in the Closet and I'm Feelin' So Sad*
Barbara Harris, *Oh, Dad, Poor Dad, Mamma's Hung You in the Closet and I'm Feelin' So Sad* (Performance)
Cicely Tyson, *Moon on a Rainbow Shawl* (Performance)
Geoff Garland, *The Hostage* (Performance)
Association of Producing Artists for its entire repertory season

1963 Vernon Rice Awards

Oliver Hailey, *Hey You, Light Man!*
William Hanley, *Whisper into My Good Ear* and *Mrs. Dally Has a Lover*

Murray Schisgal, *The Typists* and *The Tiger*
The Boys from Syracuse, for best overall production
The Coach with the Six Insiders, for best overall production

1964 Drama Desk–Vernon Rice Awards

Gloria Foster, *In White America* (Performance)
Imelda de Martin, *The Amorous Flea* (Performance)
Lewis John Carlino, *Cages, Telemachus Clay*, and *Double Talk*
In White America, for best overall production
The Streets of New York, for best overall production

1965 Drama Desk–Vernon Rice Awards

Robert Lowell, *The Old Glory*
Harold Willis, *A Sound of Silence*
Ulu Grosbard, for his staging of *A View from the Bridge* by Arthur Miller
James Earl Jones, *Othello* (Performance)
Barbara Ann Teer, *Home Movies* (Performance)
Susan Towers, *Shout from the Rooftops* (Performance)

1966 Drama Desk–Vernon Rice Awards

Douglas Turner Ward, *Day of Absence* and *Happy Ending*
William Alfred, *Hogan's Goat*
John Arden, *Serjeant Musgrave's Dance*
Kevin O' Connor, *Six From La Mama* (Performance)
Irene Dailey, *Rooms* (Performance)
The Living Theatre, for its work abroad

1967 Drama Desk–Vernon Rice Awards

Jean-Claude van Itallie, *America Hurrah*
Lanford Wilson, *The Rimers of Eldritch*
Dustin Hoffman, *Eh?* (Performance)

Stacey Keach, *MacBird!* (Performance)
Joseph Hardy, *You're a Good Man, Charlie Brown* (Direction)
Bill Hinnant, *You're a Good Man, Charlie Brown* (Performance)
Will Lee, *The Deer Park* (Performance)

1968 Drama Desk–Vernon Rice Awards

Helen Hayes, best performance by an actor or actress in a repertory company, *The Show Off*
Ron Cowen, *Summertree*
Israel Horovitz, *The Indian Wants the Bronx*
Ed Bullins, *The Electronic Nigger and Others* (also known as *The Ed Bullins Plays*)
Donald Driver, for his adaptation of *Your Own Thing*
Joseph Papp's Public Theater
The Negro Ensemble Company
Al Carmines, *In Circles* (Music)
Tom O' Horgan, *Tom Paine* (Direction)
Galt MacDermot, *Hair* (Music)
Robert Moore, *The Boys in the Band* (Direction)

1969 Drama Desk Awards

Note: In 1969 the awards were considerably broadened, opening up to all Manhattan theatre, including Broadway performances. Additionally, voters were restricted to critics, editors and reporters who had attended the majority of the season's productions. A weighted percentage system was used to tabulate the votes and the candidates are listed here in order of the percentage of votes they received.

Performance	James Earl Jones, *The Great White Hope* Jane Alexander, *The Great White Hope* Al Pacino, *Does a Tiger Wear a Necktie?* James Coco, *Next* Alex McCowen, *Hadrian VII* Donald Pleasence, *The Man in the Glass Booth*

	Nicol Williamson, *Hamlet* Ron O'Neal, *No Place to Be Somebody* Joseph Wiseman, *In the Matter of J. Robert Oppenheimer* Marian Mercer, *Promises, Promises* Bernadette Peters, *Dames at Sea* Dustin Hoffman, *Jimmy Shine* Dorothy London, *The Fig Leaves are Falling* Nathan Georg, *No Place to Be Somebody* Linda Lavin, *Little Murders* Ron Leibman, *We Bombed in New Haven* Douglas Turner Ward, *Ceremonies in Dark Old Men* Jerry Orbach, *Promises, Promises* Brian Bedford, *The Misanthrope* Frank Langella, *A Cry of Players*
Best Direction	Edwin Sherin, *The Great White Hope* Gordon Davidson, *In the Matter of J. Robert Oppenhemier* Tom O'Horgan, *Futz!* Neal Kenyon, *Dames at Sea* Alan Arkin, *Little Murders* Michael A. Schultz, *Does a Tiger Wear a Necktie?*
Best Scene Designers	Ming Cho Lee, *Invitation to a Beheading* and *Bully* Boris Aronson, *Zorba*
Best Costume Designers	Tanya Moiseiwitsch, *The House of Atreus* Patricia Zipprodt, *1776* and *Zorba*
Best Composers	Al Carmines, *Peace* Burt Bacharach, *Promises, Promises*
Best Lyricists	George Haimsohn and Robin Miller, *Dames at Sea* Fred Ebb, *Zorba*
Best Choreographer	Grover Dale, *Billy*
Best Musical Book Writer	Peter Stone, *1776*

The Most Promising Playwrights	Charles Gordone, *No Place to Be Somebody*
	Lonne Elder III, *Ceremonies in Dark Old Men*
	Elaine May, *Adaptation*
The Vernon Rice Award	Joseph Chaikin

1970 Drama Desk Awards

Outstanding Performance	Zoe Caldwell, *Colette*
	Sada Thompson, *The Effect of Gamma Rays on Man-in-the-Moon Marigolds*
	Fritz Weaver, *Child's Play*
	Frank Grimes, *Borstal Boy*
	Lauren Bacall, *Applause*
	Melba Moore, *Purlie*
	Ryszard Cieślak, *The Constant Prince*
	Lewis J. Stadlen, *Minnie's Boys*
	Stacy Keach, *Indiana*
	Cleavon Little, *Purlie*
	Tammy Grimes, *Private Lives*
	Colleen Dewhurst, *Hello and Goodbye*
	Stephen Elliott, *A Whistle in the Dark*
	Niall Toibin, *Borstal Boy*
	Ron Leibman, *Transfers*
	Christopher Walken, *Lemon Sky*
	Austin Pendleton, *The Last Sweet Days of Isaac*
	Brian Bedford, *Private Lives*
	Sandy Duncan, *The Boy Friend*
	James Stewart, *Harvey*
	Ethel Merman, *Hello, Dolly!*
Outstanding Director	Harold Prince, *Company*
	Jerzy Grotowski, *The Apocalypse*
	Alan Arkin, *The White House Murder Case*
	Joseph Hardy, *Child's Play*
	Ron Field, *Applause*
Outstanding Scene Design	Boris Aronson, *Company*
	Jo Mielziner, *Child's Play*
	Fred Voelpel, *The Memory Book*

Outstanding Costume Design	Freddy Wittop, *A Patriot for Me* Willa Kim, *Promenade* and *Operation Sidewinder* Theoni V. Aldredge, *Peer Gynt*
Outstanding Choreographer	Ron Field, *Applause*
Outstanding Composer	Stephen Sondheim, *Company* Kurt Weill, *Rise and Fall of the City of Mahagonny*
Outstanding Lyricist	Stephen Sondheim, *Company* Bertolt Brecht, *Rise and Fall of the City of Mahagonny*
Outstanding Book Writer for a Musical	George Furth, *Company*
Most Promising Playwrights	Paul Zindel, *The Effect of Gamma Rays on Man-in-the-Moon Marigolds* Stanley Eveling, *Dear Janet Rosenberg, Dear Mr. Kooning* Susan Yankowitz, *Terminal*
Most Promising Musical Writers	C. C. Courtney and Peter Link, *Salvation* Nancy Ford and Gretchen Cryer, *The Last Sweet Days of Isaac* Gary William Friedman and Will Holt, *The Me Nobody Knows*
The Vernon Rice Award	Not awarded

Antoinette Perry Award ('Tony')

The Antoinette Perry Award for Excellence in Broadway Theatre (or 'Tony' for short) is presented by the American Theatre Wing (which founded the award in 1947) and the Broadway League (a trade association for the Broadway theatre industry). It honours Broadway productions and performances, as well as regional theatre. The nominating committee is a rotating group of several dozen theatre professionals. Eligible voters include members of the various professional organizations, theatre owners and operators, producers, general managers and others invested in Broadway drama, musicals and other theatricals.

1960 Tony nominees and winners

Best Play	**Winner** *The Miracle Worker* – William Gibson **Nominees** *A Raisin in the Sun* – Lorraine Hansberry *The Best Man* – Gore Vidal *The Tenth Man* – Paddy Chayefsky *Toys in the Attic* – Lillian Hellman
Best Musical	**Winners** *The Sound of Music* *Fiorello!* **Nominees** *Gypsy* *Once Upon a Mattress* *Take Me Along*
Best Performance by a Leading Actor in a Play	Melvyn Douglas – *The Best Man* as William Russell
Best Performance by a Leading Actress in a Play	Anne Bancroft – *The Miracle Worker* as Annie Sullivan
Best Performance by a Leading Actor in a Musical	Jackie Gleason – *Take Me Along* as Sid Davis
Best Performance by a Leading Actress in a Musical	Mary Martin – *The Sound of Music* as Maria Von Trapp
Best Performance by a Featured Actor in a Play	Roddy McDowell – *The Fighting Cock* as Tarquin Edward Mendigales
Best Performance by a Featured Actress in a Play	Anne Revere – *Toys in the Attic* as Anna Berniers
Best Performance by a Featured Actor in a Musical	Tom Bosley – *Fiorello!* as Fiorello La Guardia
Best Performance by a Featured Actress in a Musical	Patricia Neway – *The Sound of Music* as Mother Abbess
Best Direction of a Play	Arthur Penn – *The Miracle Worker*
Best Direction of a Musical	George Abbott – *Fiorello!*
Best Choreography	Michael Kidd – *Destry Rides Again*
Best Conductor and Musical Director	Frederick Dvonch – *The Sound of Music*

Best Scenic Design (Dramatic)	Howard Bay – *Toys in the Attic*
Best Scenic Design (Musical)	Oliver Smith – *The Sound of Music*
Best Costume Design	Cecil Beaton – *Saratoga*
Best Stage Technician	John Walters – *The Miracle Worker*

1961 Tony nominees and winners

Best Play	**Winner** *Becket* – Jean Anouilh **Nominees** *All the Way Home* – Tad Mosel *The Devil's Advocate* – Dore Schary *The Hostage* – Brendan Behan
Best Musical	**Winners** *Bye Bye Birdie* **Nominees** *Do Re Mi* *Irma La Douce*
Best Performance by a Leading Actor in a Play	Zero Mostel – *Rhinocéros* as John
Best Performance by a Leading Actress in a Play	Joan Plowright – *A Taste of Honey* as Josephine
Best Performance by a Leading Actor in a Musical	Richard Burton – *Camelot* as Arthur
Best Performance by a Leading Actress in a Musical	Elizabeth Seal – *Irma La Douce* as Irma La Douce
Best Performance by a Featured Actor in a Play	Martin Gabel – *Big Fish, Little Fish* as Basil Smythe
Best Performance by a Featured Actress in a Play	Colleen Dewhurst – *All the Way Home* as Mary Follet
Best Performance by a Featured Actor in a Musical	Dick Van Dyke – *Bye Bye Birdie* as Albert Peterson
Best Performance by a Featured Actress in a Musical	Tammy Grimes – *The Unsinkable Molly Brown* as Molly Tobin
Best Direction of a Play	John Gielgud – *Big Fish, Little Fish*
Best Direction of a Musical	Gower Champion – *Bye Bye Birdie*

Best Choreography	Gower Champion – *Bye Bye Birdie*
Best Conductor and Musical Director	Franz Allers – *Camelot*
Best Scenic Design in a Play	Oliver Smith – *Becket*
Best Scenic Design in a Musical	Oliver Smith – *Camelot*
Best Costume Design in a Play	Motley (a multi-person organization) – *Becket*
Best Costume Design in a Musical	Adrian and Tony Duquette – *Camelot*
Best Stage Technician	Teddy Van Bemmel – *Becket*

1962 Tony nominees and winners

Best Play	**Winner** *A Man for All Seasons* – Robert Bolt **Nominees** *Gideon* – Paddy Chayefsky *The Caretaker* – Harold Pinter *The Night of the Iguana* – Tennessee Williams
Best Musical	**Winner** *How to Succeed in Business Without Really Trying* **Nominees** *Carnival!* *Milk and Honey* *No Strings*
Best Producer (Dramatic)	Robert Whitehead and Roger L. Stevens – *A Man for All Seasons*
Best Producer (Musical)	Cy Feuer and Ernest H. Martin – *How to Succeed in Business Without Really Trying*
Best Author (Musical)	Abe Burrows, Jack Weinstock and Willie Gilbert – *How to Succeed in Business Without Really Trying*
Best Original Score (Music and/or Lyrics) Written for the Theatre	*No Strings* – Richard Rodgers (music and lyrics)

Best Performance by a Leading Actor in a Play	Paul Scofield – *A Man for All Seasons* as Sir Thomas More
Best Performance by a Leading Actress in a Play	Margaret Leighton – *The Night of the Iguana* as Hannah Jelkes
Best Performance by a Leading Actor in a Musical	Robert Morse – *How to Succeed in Business Without Really Trying* as J. Pierrepont Finch
Best Performance by a Leading Actress in a Musical	Anna Maria Alberghetti – *Carnival!* as Lili Daurier Diahann Carroll – *No Strings* as Barbara Woodruff
Best Performance by a Featured Actor in a Play	Walter Matthau – *A Shot in the Dark* as Benjamin Beaurevers
Best Performance by a Featured Actress in a Play	Elizabeth Ashley – *Take Her, She's Mine* as Mollie Michaelson
Best Performance by a Featured Actor in a Musical	Charles Nelson Reilly – *How to Succeed in Business Without Really Trying* as Bud Frump
Best Performance by a Featured Actress in a Musical	Phyllis Newman – *Subways Are For Sleeping* as Martha Vail
Best Direction of a Play	Noel Willman – *A Man for All Seasons*
Best Direction of a Musical	Abe Burrows – *How to Succeed in Business Without Really Trying*
Best Choreography	Joe Layton – *No Strings*
Best Conductor and Musical Director	Elliot Lawrence – *How to Succeed in Business Without Really Trying*
Best Scenic Design	Will Steven Armstrong – *Carnival!*
Best Costume Design	Lucinda Ballard – *The Gay Life*

1963 Tony nominees and winners

Best Play	**Winner** *Who's Afraid of Virginia Woolf?* – Edward Albee **Nominees** *A Thousand Clowns* – Herb Gardner *Mother Courage and Her Children* – Bertolt Brecht *Tchin-Tchin* – Sidney Michaels

Best Musical	**Winner** *A Funny Thing Happened on the Way to the Forum* **Nominees** *Little Me* *Oliver!* *Stop the World – I Want to Get Off*
Best Producer (Dramatic)	Richard Barr and Clinton Wilder – *Who's Afraid of Virginia Woolf?*
Best Producer (Musical)	Harold Prince – *A Funny Thing Happened on the Way to the Forum*
Best Author (Musical)	Burt Shevelove and Larry Gelbart – *A Funny Thing Happened on the Way to the Forum*
Best Original Score (Music and/or Lyrics) Written for the Theatre	*Oliver!* – Lionel Bart (music and lyrics)
Best Performance by a Leading Actor in a Play	Arthur Hill – *Who's Afraid of Virginia Woolf?* as George
Best Performance by a Leading Actress in a Play	Uta Hagen – *Who's Afraid of Virginia Woolf?* as Martha
Best Performance by a Leading Actor in a Musical	Zero Mostel – *A Funny Thing Happened on the Way to the Forum* as Pseudolus
Best Performance by a Leading Actress in a Musical	Vivien Leigh – *Tovarich* as Tatiana
Best Performance by a Featured Actor in a Play	Alan Arkin – *Enter Laughing* as David Kolowitz
Best Performance by a Featured Actress in a Play	Sandy Dennis – *A Thousand Clowns* as Sandra Markowitz
Best Performance by a Featured Actor in a Musical	David Burns – *A Funny Thing Happened on the Way to the Forum* as Senex
Best Performance by a Featured Actress in a Musical	Anna Quayle – *Stop the World – I Want to Get Off* as Various Characters
Best Direction of a Play	Alan Schneider – *Who's Afraid of Virginia Woolf?*
Best Direction of a Musical	George Abbott – *A Funny Thing Happened on the Way to the Forum*

Best Choreography	Bob Fosse – *Little Me*
Best Conductor and Musical Director	Donald Pippin – *Oliver!*
Best Scenic Design	Sean Kenny – *Oliver!*
Best Costume Design	Anthony Powell – *The School for Scandal*
Best Stage Technician	Solly Pernick – *Mr. President*

1964 Tony nominees and winners

Best Play	**Winner** *Luther* – John Osborne **Nominees** *The Ballad of the Sad Cafe* – Edward Albee *Barefoot in the Park* – Neil Simon *Dylan* – Sidney Michaels
Best Musical	**Winner** *Hello, Dolly!* **Nominees** *Funny Girl* *High Spirits* *She Loves Me*
Best Producer (Dramatic)	Herman Shumlin – *The Deputy*
Best Producer (Musical)	David Merrick – *Hello, Dolly!*
Best Book (Musical)	Michael Stewart – *Hello, Dolly!*
Best Original Score (Music and/or Lyrics) Written for the Theatre	*Hello, Dolly!* – Jerry Herman (music and lyrics)
Best Performance by a Leading Actor in a Play	Alec Guinness – *Dylan* as Dylan Thomas
Best Performance by a Leading Actress in a Play	Sandy Dennis – *Any Wednesday* as Ellen Gordon
Best Performance by a Leading Actor in a Musical	Bert Lahr – *Foxy* as Foxy
Best Performance by a Leading Actress in a Musical	Carol Channing – *Hello, Dolly!* as Dolly Gallagher Levi
Best Performance by a Featured Actor in a Play	Hume Cronyn – *Hamlet* as Polonius

Best Performance by a Featured Actress in a Play	Barbara Loden – *After the Fall* as Maggie
Best Performance by a Featured Actor in a Musical	Jack Cassidy – *She Loves Me* as Stephen Kodaly
Best Performance by a Featured Actress in a Musical	Tessie O'Shea – *The Girl Who Came to Supper* as Ada Cockle
Best Direction of a Play	Mike Nichols – *Barefoot in the Park*
Best Direction of a Musical	Gower Champion – *Hello, Dolly!*
Best Choreography	Gower Champion – *Hello, Dolly!*
Best Conductor and Musical Director	Shepard Coleman – *Hello, Dolly!*
Best Scenic Design	Oliver Smith – *Hello, Dolly!*
Best Costume Design	Freddy Wittop – *Hello, Dolly!*

1965 Tony nominees and winners

Best Play	**Winner** *The Subject Was Roses* – Frank Gilroy **Nominees** *Luv* – Murray Schisgal *The Odd Couple* – Neil Simon *Tiny Alice* – Edward Albee
Best Musical	**Winner** *Fiddler on the Roof* **Nominees** *Golden Boy* *Half a Sixpence* *Oh, What a Lovely War!*
Best Producer (Dramatic)	Claire Nichtern – *Luv*
Best Producer (Musical)	Harold Prince – *Fiddler on the Roof*
Best Author (Dramatic)	Neil Simon – *The Odd Couple*
Best Original Score (Music and/or Lyrics) Written for the Theatre	*Fiddler on the Roof* – Jerry Bock (music) and Sheldon Harnick (lyrics)
Best Performance by a Leading Actor in a Play	Walter Matthau – *The Odd Couple* as Oscar Madison
Best Performance by a Leading Actress in a Play	Irene Worth – *Tiny Alice* as Miss Alice

Best Performance by a Leading Actor in a Musical	Zero Mostel – *Fiddler on the Roof* as Tevye
Best Performance by a Leading Actress in a Musical	Liza Minnelli – *Flora the Red Menace* as Flora Mezaros
Best Performance by a Featured Actor in a Play	Jack Albertson – *The Subject Was Roses* as John Cleary
Best Performance by a Featured Actress in a Play	Alice Ghostley – *The Sign in Sidney Brustein's Window* as Mavis Parodus Bryson
Best Performance by a Featured Actor in a Musical	Victor Spinetti – *Oh, What a Lovely War!* as Various Characters
Best Performance by a Featured Actress in a Musical	Maria Karnilova – *Fiddler on the Roof* as Golde
Best Direction of a Play	Mike Nichols – *Luv* and *The Odd Couple*
Best Direction of a Musical	Jerome Robbins – *Fiddler on the Roof*
Best Choreography	Jerome Robbins – *Fiddler on the Roof*
Best Scenic Design	Oliver Smith – *Baker Street*, *Luv* and *The Odd Couple*
Best Costume Design	Patricia Zipprodt – *Fiddler on the Roof*

1966 Tony nominees and winners

Best Play	**Winner** *Marat/Sade* – Peter Weiss **Nominees** *Inadmissible Evidence* – John Osborne *Philadelphia, Here I Come!* – Brian Friel *The Right Honourable Gentleman* – Michael Dyne
Best Musical	**Winner** *Man of La Mancha* **Nominees** *Mame* *Skyscraper* *Sweet Charity*
Best Original Score (Music and/or Lyrics) Written for the Theatre	*Man of La Mancha* – Mitch Leigh (music) and Joe Darion (lyrics)

Best Performance by a Leading Actor in a Play	Hal Holbrook – *Mark Twain Tonight* as Mark Twain
Best Performance by a Leading Actress in a Play	Rosemary Harris – *The Lion in Winter* as Eleanor of Aquitaine
Best Performance by a Leading Actor in a Musical	Richard Kiley – *Man of La Mancha* as Don Quixote/Cervantes
Best Performance by a Leading Actress in a Musical	Angela Lansbury – *Mame* as Mame Dennis
Best Performance by a Featured Actor in a Play	Patrick Magee – *Marat/Sade* as Marquis de Sade
Best Performance by a Featured Actress in a Play	Zoe Caldwell – *Slapstick Tragedy* as Polly
Best Performance by a Featured Actor in a Musical	Frankie Michaels – *Mame* as Patrick Dennis
Best Performance by a Featured Actress in a Musical	Beatrice Arthur – *Mame* as Vera Charles
Best Direction of a Play	Peter Brook – *Marat/Sade*
Best Direction of a Musical	Albert Marre – *Man of La Mancha*
Best Choreography	Bob Fosse – *Sweet Charity*
Best Scenic Design	Howard Bay – *Man of La Mancha*
Best Costume Design	Gunilla Palmstierna-Weiss – *Marat/Sade*

1967 Tony nominees and winners

Best Play	**Winner** *The Homecoming* – Harold Pinter
	Nominees *A Delicate Balance* – Edward Albee *Black Comedy* – Peter Shaffer *The Killing of Sister George* – Frank Marcus
Best Musical	**Winner** *Cabaret*
	Nominees *I Do! I Do!* *The Apple Tree* *Walking Happy*

DOCUMENTS 239

Best Original Score (Music and/or Lyrics) Written for the Theatre	*Cabaret* – John Kander (music) and Fred Ebb (lyrics)
Best Performance by a Leading Actor in a Play	Paul Rogers – *The Homecoming* as Max
Best Performance by a Leading Actress in a Play	Beryl Reid – *The Killing of Sister George* as Sister George/June Buckridge
Best Performance by a Leading Actor in a Musical	Robert Preston – *I Do! I Do!* as Michael
Best Performance by a Leading Actress in a Musical	Barbara Harris – *The Apple Tree* as Various Characters
Best Performance by a Featured Actor in a Play	Ian Holm – *The Homecoming* as Lenny
Best Performance by a Featured Actress in a Play	Marian Seldes – *A Delicate Balance* as Julia
Best Performance by a Featured Actor in a Musical	Joel Grey – *Cabaret* as the Master of Ceremonies
Best Performance by a Featured Actress in a Musical	Peg Murray – *Cabaret* as Fraulein Kost
Best Direction of a Play	Peter Hall – *The Homecoming*
Best Direction of a Musical	Harold Prince – *Cabaret*
Best Choreography	Ron Field – *Cabaret*
Best Scenic Design	Boris Aronson – *Cabaret*
Best Costume Design	Patricia Zipprodt – *Cabaret*

1968 Tony nominees and winners

Best Play	**Winner** *Rosencrantz and Guildenstern Are Dead* – Tom Stoppard
	Nominees *A Day in the Death of Joe Egg* – Peter Nichols *Plaza Suite* – Neil Simon *The Price* – Arthur Miller
Best Musical	**Winner** *Hallelujah, Baby!*

	Nominees *The Happy Time* *How Now, Dow Jones* *Illya Darling*
Best Original Score (Music and/or Lyrics) Written for the Theatre	*Hallelujah, Baby!* – Jule Styne (music) and Betty Comden and Adolph Green (lyrics)
Best Performance by a Leading Actor in a Play	Martin Balsam – *You Know I Can't Hear You When the Water's Running* as Various Characters
Best Performance by a Leading Actress in a Play	Zoe Caldwell – *The Prime of Miss Jean Brodie* as Jean Brodie
Best Performance by a Leading Actor in a Musical	Robert Goulet – *The Happy Time* as Jacques Bonnard
Best Performance by a Leading Actress in a Musical	Patricia Routledge – *Darling of the Day* as Alice Challice Leslie Uggams – *Hallelujah, Baby!* as Georgina
Best Performance by a Featured Actor in a Play	James Patterson – *The Birthday Party* as Stanley
Best Performance by a Featured Actress in a Play	Zena Walker – *A Day in the Death of Joe Egg* as Sheila
Best Performance by a Featured Actor in a Musical	Hiram Sherman – *How Now, Dow Jones* as Wingate
Best Performance by a Featured Actress in a Musical	Lillian Hayman – *Hallelujah, Baby!* as Momma
Best Direction of a Play	Mike Nichols – *Plaza Suite*
Best Direction of a Musical	Gower Champion – *The Happy Time*
Best Producer (Dramatic)	David Merrick Arts Foundation – *Rosencrantz and Guildenstern Are Dead*
Best Producer (Musical)	Albert Selden, Hal James, Jane C. Nusbaum and Harry Rigby – *Hallelujah, Baby!*
Best Choreography	Gower Champion – *The Happy Time*
Best Scenic Design	Desmond Heeley – *Rosencrantz and Guildenstern Are Dead*
Best Costume Design	Desmond Heeley – *Rosencrantz and Guildenstern Are Dead*

1969 Tony nominees and winners

Best Play	**Winner** *The Great White Hope* – Howard Sackler
	Nominees *Hadrian the Seventh* – Peter Luke *Lovers* – Brian Friel *The Man in the Glass Booth* – Robert Shaw
Best Musical	**Winner** *1776*
	Nominees *Hair* *Promises, Promises* *Zorba*
Best Performance by a Leading Actor in a Play	James Earl Jones – *The Great White Hope* as Jack Jefferson
Best Performance by a Leading Actress in a Play	Julie Harris – *Forty Carats* as Ann Stanley
Best Performance by a Leading Actor in a Musical	Jerry Orbach – *Promises, Promises* as Chuck Baxter
Best Performance by a Leading Actress in a Musical	Angela Lansbury – *Dear World* as Countess Aurelia
Best Performance by a Featured Actor in a Play	Al Pacino – *Does a Tiger Wear a Necktie?* as Bickham
Best Performance by a Featured Actress in a Play	Jane Alexander – *The Great White Hope* as Eleanor Bachman
Best Performance by a Featured Actor in a Musical	Ronald Holgate – *1776* as Richard Henry Lee
Best Performance by a Featured Actress in a Musical	Marian Mercer – *Promises, Promises* as Marge MacDougall
Best Direction of a Play	Peter Dews – *Hadrian the Seventh*
Best Direction of a Musical	Peter Hunt – *1776*
Best Choreography	Joe Layton – *George M!*
Best Scenic Design	Boris Aronson – *Zorba*
Best Costume Design	Loudon Sainthill – *Canterbury Tales*

1970 Tony nominees and winners

Best Play	**Winner** *Borstal Boy* – Frank McMahon **Nominees** *Child's Play* – Robert Marasco *Indians* – Arthur Kopit *Last of the Red Hot Lovers* – Neil Simon
Best Musical	**Winner** *Applause* **Nominees** *Coco* *Purlie*
Best Performance by a Leading Actor in a Play	Fritz Weaver – *Child's Play* as Jerome Malley
Best Performance by a Leading Actress in a Play	Tammy Grimes – *Private Lives* as Amanda Prynne
Best Performance by a Leading Actor in a Musical	Cleavon Little – *Purlie* as Purlie
Best Performance by a Leading Actress in a Musical	Lauren Bacall – *Applause* as Margo Channing
Best Performance by a Featured Actor in a Play	Ken Howard – *Child's Play* as Paul Reese
Best Performance by a Featured Actress in a Play	Blythe Danner – *Butterflies Are Free* as Jill Tanner
Best Performance by a Featured Actor in a Musical	René Auberjonois – *Coco* as Sebastian Baye
Best Performance by a Featured Actress in a Musical	Melba Moore – *Purlie* as Lutiebell Gussie Mae Jenkins
Best Direction of a Play	Joseph Hardy – *Child's Play*
Best Direction of a Musical	Ron Field – *Applause*
Best Choreography	Ron Field – *Applause*
Best Scenic Design	Jo Mielziner – *Child's Play*
Best Costume Design	Cecil Beaton – *Coco*
Best Lighting Design	Jo Mielziner – *Child's Play*

Primary voices

Historical and cultural context

Herbert Blau
Director, co-founder of The Actors Workshop

This will not be a palace revolution because in this country there are no palaces in the theater, no center of authority except the merchandise marts. I should like to say it will be one of the aims of the revolution to drive the moneylenders from the temple, but the moneylenders have never been in the temple. And where they are they remain, for the time being, impregnable. This is not to say they shouldn't be assailed anyhow, for it is the nature of the rebellion, born of distress and aspiration, to proceed against hope.

If, as I believe, it is the nature of the theater to court peril, then it's a risk one may have to take if he wants to work in it honorably. There is a lot of desire and thinking incipient in our theater that is quickly cowed by the cocksure realism of established mediocrity. It may be true that thought collects in pools, but still water stinks if not deep. And we must talk up if we're not to be talked down to.[1]

Ed Bullins
Playwright, editor, writer-in-residence at The New Lafayette Theatre

It would seem that in America there is no way to break away from the historical (in the Western sense) definitions of drama, though never-ending revolutions occur in theater which are usually inappropriately named 'avant-garde'. These 'avant-garde' movements are not attempts, in most cases, to break or separate from Western theater's history, conventions, and traditions, but are efforts to extend Western dramatic art, to perpetuate and adapt the white man's theater, to extend Western reality, and finally to *rescue* his culture and have it benefit *his* needs.

Avant-garde theater is difficult to recognize, for it may not be truly indicative of the future and may have little other effect upon the current drama other than to be pretentious. Its characteristics may only be bizarre, e.g., penis worship, masturbation, incestuous narcissism, and ego projection. And often, avant-garde mannerisms are a collection of rediscovered conventions of a forgotten era, newly foisted upon the new generation to become clichés in themselves.

There may be nothing which can really be properly regarded as avant-garde in Western theater. (Surely, Black Drama doesn't wish to exploit this pretentious, effete, white, bourgeois term.) And this pale label (avant-garde) must not be confused with 'experimental'. 'Experimental' is generally the refuge of the inept. Experiments, especially in theater, must be designed to go somewhere, to have a positive direction and goal, even if that place is predetermined to be 'nowhere', e.g., (and only in rare cases) a *happening*.

To paraphrase Brother LeRoi Jones: it is a post-American form of Black theater we as Black Artists should be seeking. It is Black Art that is like a dagger pointed the vitals of America, and through the rips 'we' (US) can enter the new epoch.[2]

Amiri Baraka
Poet, playwright and activist, on the 1967 Newark Riots

Well, the fires; seeing US Army military weapons in a city that was supposed to be in America. I mean, you look up and see tanks, and soldiers fully armed; then you want to know where you are . . . this must not be America, because this is what they did in Vietnam or Korea. But then people, the police checking people's ID . . . I was arrested the first night of the thing, and was locked up through the period of the worst kind of burning and fighting. But the police came up into my house, which is the Spirit House on Stirling Street. My wife and child, young child was in there . . . oldest son . . . were in there, and they were on the third floor, I think, and then the National Guard and the cops came in on the first floor, destroying stuff, turning stuff over, breaking up things . . .

Well, we were driving around, looking at it, what was going on, a couple of friends and I were riding around the Central Ward – you know, I lived over there at the time – looking at what was happening, picked up a couple of people, took them to the hospital; a guy got shot in the leg, picked him up, took him to the hospital, things like that, and then we stayed out too late afterward; people had cleared off the streets and we were coming down the street and we were stopped by about twenty cops, I don't know. They pulled us out of the car and they started beating us. They split my head open, knocked my teeth out, I mean I couldn't see; I mean my face was so covered with blood I thought I was going to die, you know; there just was blood everywhere, I couldn't even see. But the people up in the window were screaming; there were black people up there who kept screaming, kept screaming – that's what cooled it out. Otherwise, I was finished. When you feel the blood in your face, you can feel it warm in your face and you can't even see for the blood; it's in your mouth, your eyes . . .[3]

W. McNeil Lowry
Head of the Ford Foundation's Program of the Arts

At its most basic levels [art] is not about money, or facilities, or public acceptance; it is about the surge of artistic drive and moral determination . . . not about buildings, or labels, or numbers, but about the artist and the standards by which he pursues his art, alone or in ensemble with others who respect the craft . . . somehow in our country businessmen or municipal and state officials appear to think art begins with real estate.[4]

Robert Patrick
Playwright

The 1960s in New York were the greatest time and place in history to be young. Jobs were abundant, rents were cheap, we all had our minds broadened by paperbacks, and most of us had had some time in college where, even if the curricula were narrow, the libraries offered self-education galore.

The Beats had paved the way, what I call 'The Other Brick Road', and tens of thousands of us came tripping down it, determined to live freely, and express ourselves unstintingly. We were not very political by today's or the 1930s' standards. Our main crusade was emotional, intellectual, and sexual self-liberation.[5]

R. G. Davis
Founder of The San Francisco Mime Troupe

I was breaking eggs without mixing them to make scrambled. We were doing everything we could to move around . . . They'd say,

'You can't do this.' I would say, 'What do you mean? You can't do what?' 'Well, you can't get up on stage and do that kind of stuff.' I'd say, 'Why not?' and we'd do it. And anybody who would say you couldn't do it, I'd say, 'Well that's a good topic. Let's do that.' So it was radical, avant-garde stuff we did . . . There were a whole bunch of people breaking rules. The hippie movement was film makers who had been painters and then painters turned into rock and roll performers and theater people were moving outside of the theater like I was . . . and women were moving out of their roles and the civil rights movement was. So we're talking about a social situation, and there was a war going on – the Vietnam War was going on – so we're trying to oppose the war in Vietnam at the same time as doing this radical stuff. Out of the fifties into the sixties you're saying, 'You can't smoke dope.' So what? Smoke it. Get arrested? No, don't get arrested. I'm not trying to break all the laws, but we're young enough to say we gotta do something here that makes some sense. And there's political sense, and social and cultural sense, and there were all kinds of inventions and innovations happening.[6]

Charles Ludlam
Actor, director, playwright

Gay people have always found a refuge in the arts, and the Ridiculous Theatre is notable for admitting it. The people in it – and it is a very sophisticated theatre, culturally – never dream of hiding anything about themselves that they feel is honest and true and the best part of themselves. NOTHING is concealed in the Ridiculous.[7]

Larry Neal
Poet, playwright, critic, activist

The Black Arts Movement is radically opposed to any concept of the artist that alienates him from his community. This movement is the aesthetic and spiritual sister of the Black Power concept. As such, it envisions an art that speaks directly to the needs and aspirations of Black America. In order to perform this task, the Black Arts Movement proposes a radical reordering of the western cultural aesthetic. It proposes a separate symbolism, mythology, critique, and iconology. The Black Arts and the Black Power concept both relate broadly to the Afro-American's desire for self-determination and nationhood. Both concepts are nationalistic.'

[T]heater is potentially the most social of all the arts. It is an integral part of the socializing process. It exists in direct relationship to the audience it claims to serve ... The theater of white America is escapist, refusing to confront concrete reality. Into this cultural emptiness come the musicals, an up-tempo version of the same stale lives. And the use of Negroes in such plays as *Hello, Dolly!* and *Hallelujah Baby* does not alter their nature; it compounds the problem. These plays are simply hipper versions of the minstrel show. They present Negroes acting out the hang-ups of middle-class white America. Consequently, the American theater is a palliative prescribed to bourgeois patients who refuse to see the world as it is. Or, more crucially, as the world sees them ...

The Black Arts Theater ... is a radical alternative to the sterility of the American theater. It is primarily a theater of the spirit, confronting the black man in his interaction with the brothers and with the white thing.[8]

Amiri Baraka

[Cultural nationalism] is ahistorical in that it tries to make African culture a static, unchanging artifact. It praises African culture in its feudalistic and slave forms, as if those were the highest pinnacles of black society. We have not evolved from some static paradise. Life then was like life today: continual and progressive struggle.[9]

Herbert Blau

Little of what goes on in the American theater, for all the occasional attention to Vital Issues, seems in touch with anything that really counts, and I don't mean didactically in touch, but rhythmically, viscerally, in the bone structure, where anxiety eats like Strontium 90. The sense of urgency of which I speak has many sources in philosophical and social history, but it has its American locus now at the launching pad at Cape Kennedy, where those great phallic capsules of a nation's energy, looking like Moby Dick, are sent deterrently into the wild blue.

What do you do about the Bomb? All questions coagulate in that.

Forget it? Leave it to the politicians? Not by a long shot – in art, at the last desperate limit, it becomes a technical matter again.[10]

Charles Ludlam

Yeah, but *Camille* is a profoundly feminist work. Drag is something people today are prejudiced against, because women are considered inferior beings. A woman putting on pants, on the other hand, has moved up. So to defiantly do that and say women are worthwhile creatures, and that I'll put my whole soul and being into creating this woman and give her everything I have, including my emotions (and the most taboo thing is to experience feminine emotions), and to take myself seriously in the face of ridicule, that's it. That is the highest turn of the statement. It's different than wanting to make women more like men. It allows audiences to experience the universality of emotion, rather than believe that women are one species and men another, and what one feels the other never does. Even the women's movement is based on conflict and anger; my *Camille* is synthesis, an altogether different tactic. So you see, we do deal with contemporary phenomenon. The historical thing is a pretext.[11]

Ed Bullins

It would be a medium for communication to raise the consciousness throughout the nation for Black artistic, political, and cultural consciousness. It would keep a hell of a lot of people working – Black theatre people – and doing what they have to do. And it would be an institution for the Black people in America who are a nation within a nation. It would be an institutional base to lay the foundations of our society and our culture and our nation. It would be an institutional form like Black schools, which are becoming more prominent.

The Black theatre would be power in a sense, power in pure terms of capitalist facilities – buildings, things, places – and power, in another sense, to control people's minds, to educate them, and to persuade them. It would be power in the sense of welding together Black artists of many disciplines, because the theatre is a collective effort of many arts which come together to get the spirit going. And we would get some unity that way When you have a Black theatre and you have a Black audience and a Black artist, then the idea of getting people back together will be passé.

The people will be together and all you will have to do while they are together will be to tell them things which are beneficial and progressive and revolutionary. Those are some of the aspects of a National Black Theatre. I believe a National Black Theatre is possible at this very moment. It just takes people to get together and to commit themselves and to realize that, like LeRoi says, they need only the heart to do it.[12]

Herbert Blau

No, I do not accept the excuse that America is still coming of age. Pleading youth and paying the damages may have been all right up through the nineteenth century, even up through World War I – after which our art had available all the enlightening benefits of disenchantment and exile; but we are now almost two thirds of the way through the twentieth century, and the least we should have learned from the catastrophes behind us is that there is nothing automatic about progress.[13]

Changes to the theatre

Ellen Stewart

Founder, director, La MaMa Experimental Theatre Club

Yes, all theatre is magic! Look, you have to understand that there are all different mentalities in this world. And we mustn't narrow ourselves to only what we like. We have to understand that if some people like what they see on Broadway, that these tastes are very meaningful and relevant to them. They like what they see on Broadway, they don't feel uncomfortable, they don't have to try to understand what they see. If we didn't have Broadway, a large part of the populace would have nowhere to go, no place to see theatre. For myself, I could never feel comfortable there, but it doesn't mean I don't respect the other's feelings. I don't want to tax myself trying to enjoy something like Broadway, which I'm never going to enjoy. I much prefer a gut connection in theatre: my gut to your gut, rather than my head to your head. But the truth is, the key to art in the theatre is universality. There may be opposite styles of working, but each has the possibility of universality: how you express and explore is your individual art form.

But you see, American culture is really closed – stultified in many ways – we have a kind of complacency. We don't even know what we're missing and so we don't care. You know, if you take North America (and even include South America!), well, that is the smallest part of the world! ... So when you speak of Broadway, you're addressing a part of American culture that is sufficient to our needs now. As to whether or not we will become more mature in that respect, I don't know.[14]

Charles Ludlam

I have been gradually trying to bring the artistic policies closer to the physicalities of Artaud's theatre as well as the verbal values. Costumes are becoming more and more environmental. The costumes alone create the whole scene-value. The fans are gigantic. I went to college at Hofstra where they put on big epics, so I learned how to put one on. My Catholic background has influenced my theatre: we burn incense during the plays; there are many ritualistic things.[15]

Judith Malina
Director, performer, co-founder of the Living Theatre

FREE THEATRE

This is Free Theatre. Free Theatre is invented by the actors as they play it. Free Theatre has never been rehearsed. We have tried Free Theatre. Sometimes it fails. Nothing is ever the same.[16]

R. G. Davis

I left at the point when the Actors Workshop got a grant from Rockefeller [*sic*], and Rockefeller lifted this company and dropped it right in New York and said, 'This is American National Theater.' Of course, that's impossible, because the Actors Workshop was a homegrown little operation and within a year they were lambasted by New York critics because the assumption was 'You're going to be a San Francisco theater company and you're going to show us what to do?' In addition, they were not that good. I mean, they were not that great to convince the New York people that Broadway – that there's something else besides Broadway or off Broadway. Very difficult.[17]

Judith Malina

[T]he theater ... is thoroughly corrupted by the inbreeding of a tradition that has begun to destroy its worthy roots.

There is a need for spontaneity. Everything else has been replaced by the film or other mechanical media.

Theater work is now so specialized that no one is permitted knowledge of another's activity. The stagehands paint the flats; the actors stand in front of them.

The only ones involved in all the aspects are the omnipotent and power-corrupted director and the nonartist producer.

There can be a *living* theater only in the work of small groups of people interested neither in effect nor success – except for the successful action.

Plays should be short enough to be easily rehearsed so that they do not deaden in the process. The plots simple. The style pure, direct; not too much scenery; music, but not too much; poetry, but not too many words; perfect tempo.

Attain perfection of production through the perfection of immediacy.[18]

Margo Jones
Stage director, producer, founder of Theatre '47

The dream of all serious theatre people in the United States in the middle of our twentieth century is the establishment of a national theatre, in which playwrights, actors, directors, designers, technicians and business managers can find an expression for their art and craft as well as earn a livelihood, and which will provide audiences with beautiful plays. If this dream has not yet become a reality, it is mainly because of the economic problems involved, but a solution is imperative lest all the wonderful ideals remain in a misty realm.

We must create the theatre of tomorrow today. We cannot postpone our dreams and ideals any longer. Our potential audiences all over America are waiting for the theatre we have been promising them. They are eager and ready to see good plays well produced, and we must not disappoint them. Let us stir up the practical realization of a potential, of a dream, of an ideal![19]

Herbert Blau

Yet before we hack at the proscenium like the cherry orchard, we ought to have pounded it with our fists, exhausting ourselves in the task of knowing its limits, so that when it crumbles, we know what we've knocked down and whether we have anything genuine to erect in its place. When I say this, I have no particular stake in the proscenium arch – though I have no doubt that when we've come full circle through the trapezoids and turtleback and clam shapes, the turntables and treadmills, ogives, ovoids, the wombs of modern theater design, the proscenium – deferring both to the Peeping Tom and the rationalist mind in us – will assert its square prerogatives.

What one does have to understand is that the stage is by nature existential, since it entertains the art of crisis. And for anything essential to take place on a stage, there must be between it and a play some mortal exchange, each testing the other's limits. Whatever its shape, the stage is a worthy antagonist, like the action painter's canvas. To fight it does not mean to abuse it; one respects his enemies. The theater even, religious in source and however secularized, is an affair of honor. From which no participant – including the spectator – is exempt.[20]

Charles Ludlam

Another fact is that all modernism was born in the theatre. Every painting technique, everything we associate with modernism – for instance, Jackson Pollock's 'scene-painting' techniques; and Salvador Dalí's dreamscapes – is like looking at a cyclorama, a barren landscape. Everything about naturalism is, in a sense, a distortion, because they (Zola, et al.) were reacting against the theatre of Sarah Bernhardt and others, and it made a mass movement. But finally it became too selective: it set out to prove a point, and proving a point is working from a preconception, and that is academic. Concept and execution is academic; going crazy and committing an atrocity is more modern. In the case of the Ridiculous, it is the only avant-garde movement that is not academic. It is not creating an academy out of former gestures and looks. If you look at today's avant-garde, it has an unmistakable look, and it moves more and more towards a vocabulary. It makes the art respectable, but it doesn't give us anywhere to go.[21]

Edward Albee
Playwright

I was suggesting that if a man writes a brilliant enough play in praise of something that is universally loathed, that the play, if it is good and well enough written, should not be knocked down because of its approach to its subject. If the work of art is good enough, it must not be criticized for its theme ... The work of art must be judged by how well it succeeds in its intention.[22]

Arthur Sainer
Critic, historian

Artaud wanted a theatre which would generate the kind of electricity that is generated when a mob rushes into the street. But there is no substitute for the passion of the street. The street is urgent, it is capable of fear and cowardice; but even in its moments of hypocrisy, the street is incapable of essential falsehood.[23]

Charles Ludlam

It has to do with humor and unhinging the pretensions of serious art. It comes out of the dichotomy between academic and expressive art, and the idea of a theatre that re-values things. It takes what is considered worthless and transforms it into high art. The Ridiculous Theatre was always a concept of high art that came out of an aesthetic which was so advanced it really couldn't be appreciated. It draws its authority from popular art, an art that doesn't need any justification beyond its power to provide pleasure. Sympathetic response is part of its audience. Basically for me, and for twentieth-century art, it's always been a problem of uncovering sources;

it proceeds by discoveries. In my case it was based on a rigorous re-evaluation of everything. Like yesterday, I was working on a sculpture, and Bill Vehr [an actor in Ludlam's company] stood over me and corrected me every time I did something that was in good taste. It's really an exercise to try to go beyond limitations and taste, which is a very aural, subjective and not a very profound concept for art. And to admit the world in a way that hasn't been pre-censored. For instance, a handy definition for avant-garde art is that it's in beige-black-white-and-gray. Ridiculous theatre is in color; it's hedonistic. Different artists define it their own way, but basically it's alchemy, it's the transformation of what is in low esteem into the highest form of expression.[24]

Luis Valdez
Playwright, co-founder of El Teatro Campesino

I think humor is our major asset and weapon, not only from a satirical point of view, but from the fact that humor can stand up on its own and is a much more healthy child of the theatre than let's say tragedy or realism. You can't do that on the flatbed of a truck. If you want to get realistic about the problems, you have to do it in indirect fashion, through dramatic images . . .

We use comedy because it stems from a necessary situation – the necessity of lifting the morale of our strikers, who have been on strike for seventeen months. When they go to a meeting it's long and drawn out; so we do comedy, with the intention of making them laugh – but with a purpose. We try to make social points, not in spite of the comedy, but through it.

There's a dramatic theory – we used to talk about it in the Mime Troupe. I think we've put a different use to it in the Teatro just out of necessity, but it is that your dramatic situation, the thing you're trying to portray on the stage, must be very close to the reality that is on the stage. You take the figure of Digiorgio standing on the backs of two farm workers. The response of the audience is to the very real situation of one human being standing on two others. That type of fakery is not imitation. It's a theatrical reality that will hold up on the flatbed of a truck. You don't need fancy lights or a curtain. This is what we're working toward – this type of reality.[25]

Julian Beck
Director, performer, co-founder of the Living Theatre

I do not like the Broadway theatre because it does not know how to say hello. The tone of voice is false, the mannerisms are false, the sex is false, ideal, the Hollywood world of perfection, the clean image, the well-pressed clothes, the well-scrubbed anus, odorless, inhuman, of the Hollywood actor, the Broadway star. And the terrible false dirt of Broadway, the lower depths in which the dirt is imitated, inaccurate.

The acting at the Living Theatre has been despised for many years, particularly by other actors. Judith [Malina] and I have worked to build a company without the mannerisms, the voices, the good speech, the protective coloring of the actors who imitate the world of the White House and who enact the trifles and suffering of the bourgeoisie. The world of conscious experience is not enough.

The actors at the Living Theatre are awkward, untutored, unconsciously defiant of the conventions which portray the people who live in democracies, who are rational, good, well balanced, and who speak museum verse. The actors at the Living Theatre want to be concerned with life and death.[26]

Arthur Sainer

Is the spectator thus more responsible in the new theatre? He is differently responsible. He is less the voyeur, less the spectator reaching into his own heart. He has been given the chance to physically test out the illusory figures performing for him and to discover that these figures may be no more illusory than he himself is, may be realer than he, may be part of a trick being played on him, may in fact be fraudulent, may be neither illusory nor symbolic at all but nervous, vibrating, questioning creatures who, like himself ... are trying to find their way in the play.[27]

Margo Jones

There is no doubt that a change has been occurring in the state of our theatre. The diminishing number of Broadway playhouses is terrifying at first glance, but rather than a sign of death I interpret it as a sign of change. A theatre is not decaying if, within five short years, it presents to the public two great playwriting talents like Tennessee Williams and Arthur Miller – to mention only the most outstanding – and new actors, directors, designers and musicians. Perhaps because of the severe financial demands on a Broadway production, the standards are very high. A certain unevenness is inevitable in any theatre, but basically I believe Broadway is at a height of development in its standards of play selection and production. Too little has been said in favor of the Broadway scene. At the moment it still stands as the center of our theatre, contains its best plays, the best actors and the best stage sets and lighting to be found in America. And it is also an experimental theatre in the sense that it will risk its all on new plays and unknown playwrights. For this alone Broadway deserves the respect and admiration of every theatre person in the country.

This theatrical center of ours, nevertheless, is frighteningly small. There are only twenty-eight legitimate playhouses in the Broadway area today, and rumors are persistent about one which is to be torn down and another which is to be taken over by a television studio. Whatever the reasons may be – and the real estate situation in New York theatre is extremely difficult – it means that the center of our activities is narrowing down. It does not mean that the American theatre is dying, for, even in New York there are areas besides Broadway where the theatre can flourish, and we have hundreds of cities where potential audiences are starved for good theatre.[28]

Artistic influence and criticism

Charles Ludlam

I don't see why art that has a history and a tradition is regressive. The danger is not so much regression, the danger is the morbid effect of repeating yourself, and that's where modernism – our contemporaries are Johnny-one-notes; each has a look (as in advertising) that he or she works for – comes in. Paintings begin to look alike in most galleries. They cater to people's need for the mass-produced, the reassurance you have when you go to a grocery store, and you see a brand name. All of a painter's works today are supposed to look alike. This to me is insane tyranny, it is absolutely sterile, and that is more of a crisis to me than the problem of diversity, or what a friend of mine calls 'virtuoso maximalism', the antidote that will supplant minimalism. Also, I don't want the savor of the art taken away, the actual enjoyment and appetite one has for creating something from something else, from something varied.[29]

Julian Beck

why do you go to the theatre

is it important to go to the theatre

is it important to read

do people who go to the theatre differ from people who don't go to the theatre

what happens to you if you go to the theatre

when you leave the theatre have you changed that is of course you are changed by each moment of experience so three hours later you are naturally different but i mean have you changed actively[30]

Lorraine Hansberry
Playwright

Might I remark on the tradition now grown up amongst us concerning what *you* call 'Domestic realism'. I think myself that American intellectual thought has been pretty much fractured by the Great Retreat. From everything. From everything, that is, that smacks of passionate partisanship. A host of labels have been created which are supposed to insulate our mentalities from 'Clichés' and 'Dogmas'. The marvel is that all the suspect clichés and dogmas under attack have a way of always turning out to be those which have been used (and, heaven knows, mis-used) in an effort to say that things are still pretty rotten in Denmark.

The more swiftly that American drama comes to believe that my dramatic experience will be larger when I know *why* the pathetic chap has turned to alcohol and not merely that he has; why to heroin; why to prostitution, despair, decadent preoccupations – the more swiftly, I insist, our drama will gain more meaningful stature. The fact of the matter is that we are all surrounded by the elements of profound tragedy in contemporary life, no less than were Shakespeare and the Greeks, but that thus far we (the dramatists, all of us, I think) are still confounded by its elusive properties and colossal dimensions. In certain peculiar ways we have been conditioned to think not small – but tiny. And the thing, I think, which has strangled us most is the tendency to turn away from the world in the search for the universe. That is chaos in science; can it be anything else in art?[31]

María Irene Fornés
Playwright, director

The beginning of the avant-garde theatre came from Europe: Samuel Beckett, Eugene Ionesco, Jean Genet. It was as if those European writers were inviting us. But even when these writers became known here, it took a few years before we actually started doing their work.

You can go to the school without walls, which is Off-Off-Broadway. There's more freedom there. There's more variety. But there, nobody's paid, so you can't demand too much.

I owe my life in the theatre to the *Village Voice*. If the *Village Voice* did not exist, I don't know if I would be writing now.[32]

Judith Malina

He has no idea of how ambitious we are.[33]

Edward Albee

Indeed it is true that a number of the movie critics of *Who's Afraid of Virginia Woolf?* have repeated the speculation that the play was written about four homosexuals disguised as heterosexual men and women. This comment first appeared around the time the play was produced. I was fascinated by it. I suppose what disturbed me about it was twofold: first, nobody has ever bothered to ask me whether it was true; second, the critics and columnists made no attempt to document the assertion from the text of the play. The facts are simple: *Who's Afraid of Virginia Woolf?* was written about two heterosexual couples. If I had wanted to write a play about four homosexuals, I would have done so . . .

I think it is the responsibility of critics to rely less strenuously on, to use a Hollywood phrase, 'what they can live with', and more on an examination of the works of art from an aesthetic and clinical point of view. I would be fascinated to read an intelligent paper documenting from the text that *Who's Afraid of Virginia Woolf?* is a play written about four homosexuals. It might instruct me about the deep slag pits of my subconscious.³⁴

Village Voice *review of Edward Albee's* The Zoo Story

He knows how to handle a situation and dialogue and bring you up deftly to the edge of your seat. Whether he has anything less sick than this to say remains to be seen.³⁵

Charles Ludlam

There is this theory in our century that any particular art form comes more and more into its own, as itself, its true nature. That paint is paint, paint is not a tree. The same is true of theatre, and the more the theatre comes to this self-realization of itself, the higher it becomes and the freer the subject matter.³⁶

LeRoi Jones (Amiri Baraka)

New talk of Black Art re-emerged in America around 1964. It was the Nationalist consciousness reawakened in Black people. The sense of identity, and with that opening, a real sense of purpose and direction. The sense of who and what we were and what we had to do.

We began to understand with the most precise consciousness that we were beings of a particular race and culture, whatever our experience. And that finally, if we were to be saved, we must be saved totally, as a race, because the deathbattle raging around and through us was an actual death struggle between two cultures.³⁷

Adrienne Kennedy
Playwright

We sailed back to New York on the *United States*. I had a completed play in my suitcase. How could I know it would establish me as a playwright and change my life? After years of writing, I had finally written of myself and my family and it would be on stage and in a book too, and I would be on the pages of *Vogue* and in Leonard Lyons' column.

And in a few months I would climb the steps to the Circle in the Square theater where I would see this play inside my suitcase performed, become a member of the Actors Studio (where Brando had been) and become a part of the Off-Broadway theater movement ... a movement that in itself would come to occupy a powerful place in American theater history.[38]

NOTES

1 Introduction: Living in the 1960s

1. Landon Y. Jones, *Great Expectations: America and the Baby Boom Generation* (New York: Ballantine Books, 1986), 10.
2. History.com, 'Baby Boomers – Facts & Summary', A+E Networks, http://www.history.com/topics/baby-boomers (accessed 30 April 2017).
3. Steve Gillon, *Boomer Nation: The Largest and Richest Generation Ever, and How It Changed America* (New York, NY: Free Press, 2014), 'Introduction'.
4. Rebecca E. Klatch, *A Generation Divided: The New Left, the New Right, and the 1960s* (Berkeley: University of California Press, 1999), 1.
5. Jerry D. Marx, 'American social policy in the 1960's and 1970's', *Social Welfare History Project*, last modified 2011, http://socialwelfare.library.vcu.edu/war-on-poverty/american-social-policy-in-the-60s-and-70s/ (accessed 10 July 2017).
6. Bureau of Labor Statistics, '1960–61', https://www.bls.gov/opub/uscs/1960-61.pdf, 28 (accessed 14 July 2017).
7. Ibid.
8. Ibid.
9. Sharon Smith, 'The Workers' Rebellion of the 1960s', *Socialist Worker*, December 1990.
10. Ibid.
11. Michael Harrington, *The Other America: Poverty in the United States*, with an introduction by Maurice Isserman (New York: Scribner, 2012).
12. Peter Dreier, 'The Invisible Poverty of "The Other America" of the 1960s is Far More Visible Today', *Truthout*, 22 March 2012, http://www.truth-out.org/news/item/8040-michael-harrington-and-deprivation-in-an-affluent-society (accessed 10 July 2017).

13 Ibid.
14 'Civilian labor force participation rates by sex, 1950 to 2005 and projected 2010 to 2050', U.S. Bureau of Labor Statistics, last modified 2005, https://www.bls.gov/opub/ted/2007/jan/wk2/art03.txt.
15 Women in the Workforce (United States Census Bureau, 2007), https://www.census.gov/newsroom/pdf/women_workforce_slides.pdf, slide 4 (accessed 10 July 2017).
16 Ibid., slide 11.
17 Patricia A. Daly, 'Agricultural Employment: Has the Decline Ended?', U.S. Bureau of Labor Statistics, https://stats.bls.gov/opub/mlr/1981/11/art2full.pdf, 30 (accessed 30 April 2017).
18 Ibid., 14.
19 Ian D. Wyatt and Daniel E. Hecker, 'Occupational Changes During the 20th Century', U.S. Bureau of Labor Statistics, March 2006, https://www.bls.gov/mlr/2006/03/art3full.pdf, 38 (accessed 10 July 2017).
20 Ibid., 42.
21 Ibid., 39.
22 James Baldwin et al., 'The Negro in American Culture', *CrossCurrents* 11 (3) (Summer 1961): 205.
23 Dan Baum, 'Legalize It All', *Harper's Magazine*, April 2016, http://harpers.org/archive/2016/04/legalize-it-all/ (accessed 10 July 2017).
24 Lauren Carroll, 'How the War on Drugs Affected Incarceration Rates', Politifact, 10 July 2016, http://www.politifact.com/truth-o-meter/statements/2016/jul/10/cory-booker/how-war-drugs-affected-incarceration-rates/ (accessed 10 July 2017).
25 'Criminal Justice Fact Sheet', NAACP, http://www.naacp.org/criminal-justice-fact-sheet/ (accessed 30 April 2017).
26 David M. Heer and Amyra Grossbard-Shechtman, 'The Impact of the Female Marriage Squeeze and the Contraceptive Revolution on Sex Roles and the Women's Liberation Movement in the United States, 1960 to 1975', *Journal of Marriage and the Family* 43 (1) (1981): 49–65, doi: 10.2307/351416.
27 David Allyn, *Make Love, Not War: The Sexual Revolution, an Unfettered History* (Abingdon: Routledge, 2016), Chapter 3.
28 Trysh Travis, 'Freaky Friday: Documents: Chester Anderson's "Uncle Tim'$ Children"', *Points Library*, 9 December 2011, https://pointsadhsblog.wordpress.com/2011/12/09/freaky-friday-documents-chester-andersons-uncle-tim-children/ (accessed 14 July 2017).

29 Gail Collins and Christina Moore, *When Everything Changed: The Amazing Journey of American Women from 1960 to the Present* (New York: Recorded Books, 2009), 38.
30 Betty Friedan, *The Feminine Mystique* (New York: W.W. Norton, 2013), xi–xx.
31 Carol Hanisch, 'The Personal is Political', February 1969, http://www.carolhanisch.org/CHwritings/PIP.html (accessed 10 July 2017).
32 National Organization for Women, 'N.O.W. Statement of Purpose, 1966', 29 October 1966, http://now.org/about/history/statement-of-purpose (accessed 14 July 2017).
33 Ellen Willis, 'Radical Feminism and Feminist Radicalism', *Social Text* 9/10 (1984): 91–118, doi:10.2307/466537, 118.
34 Adrienne Cecile Rich, 'Compulsory Heterosexuality and the Lesbian Existence' in *Blood, Bread, and Poetry: Selected Prose, 1979–1985* (New York: Norton, 1994).
35 Gail Bederman, 'Compulsory Discrimination Against "Homosexuals and Sex Perverts", 1935–1969', *The Observer*, 21 April 2010, http://ndsmcobserver.com/2010/04/compulsory-discrimination-against-homosexuals-and-sex-perverts-1935–1969/ (accessed 10 July 2017).
36 Susan Stryker, 'Transgender History, Homonormativity, and Disciplinarity', *Radical History Review* 100 (2008): 145–57, doi: 10.1215/01636545-2007-026.
37 Nicole Pasulka, 'Ladies in the Streets: Before Stonewall, Transgender Uprising Changed Lives', NPR, 5 May 2015, http://www.npr.org/sections/codeswitch/2015/05/05/404459634/ladies-in-the-streets-before-stonewall-transgender-uprising-changed-lives (accessed 10 July 2017).
38 Stryker, 'Transgender History'.
39 Hailer Branson-Potts, 'Fifty Years Later, Silver Lake Tavern Stands as a Monument to L.A.'s Gay Rights Movement', *Los Angeles Times*, 12 February 2017, http://www.latimes.com/local/lanow/la-me-ln-black-cat-anniversary-20170210-story.html (accessed 10 July 2017).
40 'L.A.'s Black Cat, Where the Fight for Gay Rights Got Its Start', WEHOville, last modified June 5, 2014, http://www.wehoville.com/2014/06/05/l-s-black-cat-fight-gay-rights-got-start/.
41 Donn Teal, *The Gay Militants* (New York: St. Martin's Press, 1995), 7.
42 Lillian Faderman, *Odd Girls and Twilight Lovers: A History of Lesbian Life in Twentieth-Century America* (New York: Columbia University Press, 2012), 195.

43 History.com, 'Baby Boomers – Facts & Summary', http://www.history.com/topics/baby-boomers (accessed 30 April 2017).
44 Ibid.
45 Melvin L. Oliver and Thomas M. Shapiro, quoted in Ta-Nehisi Coates, 'The Case for Reparations', *The Atlantic*, June 2014, https://www.theatlantic.com/magazine/archive/2014/06/the-case-for-reparations/361631/ (accessed 10 July 2017).
46 Coates, 'The Case for Reparations'.
47 Jane Jacobs, *The Death and Life of Great American Cities* (New York: Vintage Books, 1961), 50.
48 Jacques Pépin, 'A Force in America's Food Revolution', *New York Times*, 8 May 2012. D5.
49 Bill Ganzel, 'Frozen Foods During the 1950s and 60s', Wessels Living History Farm, Inc, 2007, http://www.livinghistoryfarm.org/farminginthe50s/life_15.html (accessed 10 July 2017).
50 Wikipedia, 'History of McDonald's', https://en.wikipedia.org/wiki/History_of_McDonald's#1960s_and_1970s (accessed 30 April 2017).
51 Regina Schrambling, 'Julia Child, the French Chef for a Jell-O Nation, Dies at 91', *New York Times*, 13 August 2004, http://www.nytimes.com/2004/08/13/dining/julia-child-the-french-chef-for-a-jello-nation-dies-at-91.html (accessed 10 July 2017).
52 Warren James Belasco, *Appetite for Change: How the Counterculture Took on the Food Industry* (Ithaca, NY: Cornell University Press, 2007), 10.
53 Wikipedia 'Hunger in the United States', https://en.wikipedia.org/wiki/Hunger_in_the_United_States#20th_century (accessed 30 April 2017).
54 TV History, 'Number of TV Households in America', TV History.com, n.d., http://www.tvhistory.tv/Annual_TV_Households_50-78.JPG (accessed 10 July 2017).
55 'The Season', *Time*, 31 March 1961.
56 Paul Phipps, 'TV Shows in the 1960s', *RetroWaste*, 7 April 2013, http://www.retrowaste.com/1960s/tv-shows-in-the-1960s/ (accessed 10 July 2017).
57 Aniko Badroghkozy, *Equal Time: Television and the Civil Rights Movement* (University of Illinois Press, 2013), 2.
58 Ibid., 4.
59 William L. Van Deburg, *New Day in Babylon: The Black Power Movement and American Culture, 1965–1975* (Chicago: University of Chicago Press, 1993), 249.

60 J. F. MacDonald, 'The Golden Age of Blacks in Television: The Late 1960s', *Blacks and White TV*, 2009, http://jfredmacdonald.com/bawtv/bawtv10.htm (accessed 10 July 2017).
61 Alec M. Gallup and Frank Newport, *The Gallup Poll: Public Opinion 2005* (Lanham, MD: Rowman & Littlefield, 2007), 315–18.
62 Ibid.
63 Eric Hodgins, 'Amid Ruins of an Empire a New Hollywood Arises', *Life*, 10 June 1957, 146.
64 S. Hitchman and A. McNett, 'New Hollywood: American New Wave Cinema (1967–69)', *New Wave Film.com*, 2015, http://www.newwavefilm.com/international/new-hollywood.shtml (accessed 10 July 2017).
65 Ibid.
66 Ibid.
67 Ibid.
68 Stan Brakhage, *Metaphors on Vision* (New York: Film Culture Inc., 1963), n.p.
69 '1968', *The Sixties* [TV miniseries], CNN (Playtone), 2014.
70 William Westmoreland, quoted in Tariq Ali and Susan Alice Watkins, *1968: Marching in the Streets* (New York: The Free Press, 1998), 18.
71 Wikipedia, 'Opposition to United States Involvement in the Vietnam War', https://en.wikipedia.org/wiki/Opposition_to_United_States_involvement_in_the_Vietnam_War#Public_opinion (accessed 30 April 2017).
72 Todd Gitlin, *The Sixties: Years of Hope, Days of Rage* (New York: Bantam Books, 1993), 331.
73 '1968', *The Sixties*.
74 Molefi Kete Asante and Ama Mazama, *Encyclopedia of Black Studies* (Thousand Oaks, CA: SAGE Publications, 2005), 135–7.
75 Dean Lucas, 'Black Power', *Famous Pictures Collection*, 22 May 2013, http://www.famouspictures.org/black-power/ (accessed 10 July 2017).

2 American Theatre in the 1960s

1 Jim O'Quinn, 'Going National: How America's Regional Theatre Movement Changed the Game', in Nancy Roche and Jaan Whithead (eds), *The Art of Governance: Boards in the Performing Arts* (New

York: Theatre Communications Group, 2005), available online: http://www.americantheatre.org/2015/06/16/going-national-how-americas-regional-theatre-movement-changed-the-game/ (accessed 11 July 2017).

2 Brooks Atkinson, *Broadway*, rev. edn (New York: Macmillan, 1974), 431.

3 Jack Poggi, *Theater in America: The Impact of Economic Forces, 1870–1967* (Ithaca, NY: Cornell University Press, 1968), 277–8.

4 John Kenrick, 'History of the Musical Stage: Stage 1960s I: "Soon It's Gonna Rain"', *Musicals101.com*, last revised 2014, https://www.musicals101.com/1960bway.htm (accessed 11 July 2017).

5 Mark N. Grant, *The Rise and Fall of the Broadway Musical* (Boston: Northeastern Press, 2004), 1.

6 John Kenrick, 'History of the Musical Stage: Stage 1960s II: Long Running Hits', *Musicals101.com*, 1996–2003, https://www.musicals101.com/1960bway2.htm (accessed 11 July 2017).

7 Michael Dale, 'The Rise and Fall of the Broadway Musical: Is the Fabulous Invalid Beyond Recovery?' *Broadway World*, 13 January 2005, http://www.broadwayworld.com/article/The-Rise-and-Fall-of-the-Broadway-Musical-Is-The-Fabulous-Invalid-Beyond-Recovery–20050113 (accessed 11 July 2017).

8 Howard Taubman, 'Theater: "Funny Girl"', *New York Times*, 27 March 1964, http://www.nytimes.com/1964/03/27/theaterfunny-girl.html (accessed 11 July 2017).

9 Stephen Mo Hannon, quoted in *Broadway: The American Musical* [TV series], PBS, 2004, available online: https://youtu.be/OPwMyq5_eTM?list=PLrSnQDiagrLaHwNa4CytgWNewAO71HmiJ (accessed 11 July 2017).

10 Grant, *Rise and Fall*, 295.

11 Gerald Mast, quoted in Larry Stempel, *Showtime: A History of the Broadway Musical Theater* (New York: W.W. Norton and Company, Inc., 2010), 522.

12 Alisa Solomon, 'Boris Aronson, The Jewish Avant-Garde, and the Transition to Broadway', in James M. Harding and Cynthia Rosenthal (eds), *The Sixties, Center Stage: Mainstream and Popular Performances in a Turbulent Decade* (Ann Arbor: University of Michigan Press, 2017), 97.

13 Harry Haun, 'Age of Aquarius', *Playbill*, April 2009, from *Hair* at the Al Hirschfeld Theatre, p. 7. For more on the influence of Off-Off-Broadway on *Hair*, see Stephen Bottoms, 'Selling the Ensemble: *Hair*,

Oh! Calcutta! and Commercial Theater in the Late 1960s', in Harding and Rosenthal, *The Sixties, Center Stage*.
14 Clive Barnes, '"Hair" – It's Fresh and Frank', *New York Times*, 30 April 1968, 40.
15 John Kenrick, 'History of the Musical Stage: 1960s III: The World Turned Upside Down', *Musicals101.com*, 1996–2003, https://www.musicals101.com/1960bway3.htm#Rock (accessed 11 July 2017).
16 Grant, *Rise and Fall*, 295.
17 Harding and Rosenthal, *The Sixties, Center Stage*.
18 Atkinson, *Broadway*, 442.
19 C. W. E. Bigsby, *A Critical Introduction to Twentieth-Century American Drama, Vol. 3. Beyond Broadway* (Cambridge: Cambridge University Press, 1985), ix.
20 Arthur Miller, *After the Fall*, in *The Portable Arthur Miller*, ed. Christopher Bigsby (New York: Penguin Books, 1995), 260.
21 Robert Brustein, 'Arthur Miller's *Mea Culpa*', *The New Republic*, 150, 8 February 1964, 26.
22 Howard Taubman, 'Miller Drama is Given by Repertory Group', *New York Times*, 4 December 1964, http://www.nytimes.com/1964/12/04/miller-drama-is-given-by-repertory-group.html (accessed 11 July 2017).
23 Clive Barnes, 'Theater: Arthur Miller's "The Price"', *New York Times*, 8 February 1968, https://partners.nytimes.com/books/00/11/12/specials/miller-price.html (accessed 11 July 2017).
24 Harvey Young, 'The Long Shadow of *A Raisin in the Sun*', in Harding and Rosenthal, *The Sixties, Center Stage*.
25 Ibid., 53.
26 Ibid., 62.
27 Ibid.
28 James V. Hatch, 'From Hansberry to Shange', in Errol G. Hill and James V. Hatch, *A History of African American Theatre* (Cambridge, MA: Cambridge University Press, 2003), 401–2.
29 Susan Koprince, *Understanding Neil Simon* (Columbia: University of South Carolina Press, 2002), xi.
30 Ibid, 5.
31 John Lahr, quoted in ibid.
32 Clive Barnes, quoted in Harold Bloom (ed.), *Neil Simon* (Broomall, PA: Chelsea House Publishers, 2002), 35–7.

33 Koprince, *Understanding Neil Simon*, 29.
34 'Rosencrantz and Guildenstern are Dead, Edinburgh 1966', *The Guardian*, 6 August 2003, https://www.theguardian.com/stage/2003/aug/06/theatre (accessed 12 May 2017).
35 John Hohenberg, *The Pulitzer Prize Story: News Stories, Editorials, Cartoons, and Pictures from the Pulitzer Price Collection at Columbia University* (New York: Columbia University Press, 1971), 266–9.
36 Paul Gardner, '"Tiny Alice" Mystifies Albee, Too', *New York Times*, 21 January 1965, http://www.nytimes.com/books/99/08/15/specials/albee-tiny.html (accessed 11 May 2017).
37 Marvin Carlson, 'Theater of the Sixties: The German Connection', in Harding and Rosenthal, *The Sixties, Center Stage*, 168.
38 Herbert Blau, *The Impossible Theater: A Manifesto* (New York: Collier Books, 1967), 127.
39 Herb Blau, quoted in Joseph Wesley Zeigler, *Regional Theatre: The Revolutionary Stage* (Minneapolis: University of Minnesota Press, 1973), 148.
40 Zeigler, *Regional Theatre*, 57.
41 Herb Blau and Jules Irving, quoted in Zeigler, *Regional Theatre*, 152.
42 Howard Taubman, quoted in Zeigler, *Regional Theatre*, 159.
43 Taubman, quoted in Carlson, 'Theater of the Sixties', 170.
44 Zeigler, *Regional Theatre*, 167.
45 Jules Irving, quoted in ibid., 168.
46 Carlson, 'Theater of the Sixties', 172.
47 Stuart W. Little, *Off-Broadway: The Prophetic Theatre* (New York: Coward, McCann, and Geoghegan, 1972), 13–14.
48 Ibid., 100–1.
49 Ibid.
50 Walter Kerr, quoted in ibid., 108.
51 Little, *Off-Broadway*, 226.
52 Ibid., 125.
53 Hatch, 'From Hansberry to Shange', 395.
54 Mance Williams, *Black Theatre in the 1960s and 1970s: A Historical-Critical Analysis of the Movement* (Westport, CN: Greenwood Press, 1985), 69.
55 Ibid., 70.

56 Ibid.
57 Little, *Off-Broadway*, 15.
58 Ibid., 73.
59 Brooks Atkinson, 'Work by Genet Opens at Circle in Square', *New York Times*, 4 March 1960, 21.
60 Little, *Off-Broadway*, 119.
61 Wikipedia, 'Phoenix Theatre (New York)', https://en.wikipedia.org/wiki/Phoenix_Theatre_(New_York) (accessed 27 March 2017).
62 Zeigler, *Regional Theatre*, 131.
63 Little, *Off-Broadway*, 54.
64 Ibid., 155.
65 Walter Kerr quoted in Zeigler, *Regional Theatre*, 132.
66 Zeigler, *Regional Theatre*, 3.
67 Atkinson, *Broadway*, 487.
68 Ibid.
69 Little, *Off-Broadway*, 59.
70 Michael Smith, quoted in Sally Banes, *Greenwich Village 1963: Avant-garde Performance and the Effervescent Body* (Durham, NC: Duke University Press, 1993), 51.
71 Stephen J. Bottoms, *Playing Underground: A Critical History of the 1960s Off-Off-Broadway Movement* (Ann Arbor: University of Michigan Press, 2004), 3.
72 Ibid.
73 Ibid., 4.
74 Ibid.
75 Arthur Sainer, *The New Radical Theatre Notebook* (New York: Applause, 1975), 9, 11; Bottoms, *Playing Underground*, 5.
76 Bottoms, *Playing Underground*, 5.
77 Daniel Belgrad, *The Culture of Spontaneity: Improvisation and the Arts in Postwar America* (Chicago: University of Chicago Press, 1998), 1.
78 Wendell C. Stone, *Caffe Cino: The Birthplace of Off-Off-Broadway* (Carbondale, IL: Southern Illinois Press, 2005), 1.
79 Ibid.
80 Ibid., 4.
81 Ibid., 5.

82 Bottoms, *Playing Underground*, 43.
83 Stone, *Caffe Cino*, 25–6.
84 Bottoms, *Playing Underground*, 44.
85 Ibid., 45.
86 Ibid., 53.
87 Albert Poland and Bruce Mailman, quoted in ibid., 59.
88 Michael Smith, quoted in Stone, *Caffe Cino*, 86–7.
89 Bottoms, *Playing Underground*, 281.
90 Wikipedia, 'Joe Cino'. https://en.wikipedia.org/wiki/Joe_Cino (accessed 2 May 2017).
91 Ralph Cook, quoted in Bottoms, *Playing Underground*, 106.
92 Bottoms, *Playing Underground*, 110.
93 Ibid., 108.
94 Ralph Cook quoted in ibid., 119.
95 Bottoms, *Playing Underground*, 112–13.
96 Ibid., 113–15.
97 Ibid., 115.
98 Ibid., 116.
99 Michael Smith quoted in ibid., 248.
100 Michael Smith quoted in ibid., 306.
101 Bottoms, *Playing Underground*, 306.
102 Ibid., 349.
103 Ibid., 69.
104 Ibid., 70.
105 Ibid., 150–1.
106 George Jackson, 'Judson Church: Dance', Dance Heritage Coalition, 2012, http://www.danceheritage.org/treasures/judsonchurch_essay_jackson.pdf, 1 (accessed 11 July 2017).
107 Bottoms, *Playing Underground*, 150.
108 Michael Smith, quoted in ibid., 153.
109 Jerry Tallmer, quoted in ibid., 157.
110 Bottoms, *Playing Underground*, 157.
111 Michael Smith quoted in ibid., 157.
112 Ibid.
113 Bottoms, *Playing Underground*, 163.

114 David Vaughan, 'Al Carmines', in Billy J. Harbin, Kim Marra and Robert A. Schanke (eds), *The Gay and Lesbian Theatrical Legacy* (Ann Arbor: The University of Michigan Press, 2007), 86.
115 Lawrence Kornfeld, quoted in Bottoms, *Playing Underground*, 228.
116 Bottoms, *Playing Underground*, 253.
117 Al Carmines quoted in ibid., 274.
118 Bottoms, *Playing Underground*, 275.
119 Ibid.
120 Cindy Rosenthal, 'Ellen Stewart: La MaMa of Us All', *The Drama Review* 50 (2) (Summer 2006): 25.
121 Bottoms, *Playing Underground*, 89.
122 Jean-Claude van Itallie, quoted in ibid., 90.
123 Bottoms, *Playing Underground*, 91–2.
124 Ibid., 94.
125 Ibid., 97.
126 Ibid.
127 Rosenthal, 'Ellen Stewart', 14.
128 Ibid., 23.
129 Bottoms, *Playing Underground*, 267.
130 Ibid., 199.
131 Michael Smith, quoted in ibid., 201.
132 Richard Schechner, 'In Memory: Ringing the Bell for Ellen Stewart, 1919–2011', *The Drama Review* 55 (2) (Summer 2011): 10.
133 Bottoms, *Playing Underground*, 364.
134 Ibid., 365.
135 Zannie Giraud Voss and Glenn B. Voss with Ilana B. Rose and Laurie Baskin, *Theatre Facts 2015: A Report on the Fiscal State of the U.S. Professional Not-for-profit Theatre Field* (New York: Theatre Communications Group, 2016), http://www.tcg.org/pdfs/tools/TCG_TheatreFacts_2015.pdf (accessed 11 July 2017).
136 Richard Zoglin, 'Bigger than Broadway!', *Time*, 27 May 2003.
137 Wikipedia, 'Regional Theater in the United States', https://en.wikipedia.org/wiki/Regional_theater_in_the_United_States (accessed 11 July 2017).
138 Zeigler, *Regional Theatre*, 25.
139 Ibid., 17.
140 Margo Jones, quoted in ibid., 19.

141 Langston Hughes, quoted in Hatch, 'From Hansberry to Shange', 311.
142 O'Quinn, 'Going National'.
143 McNeil Lowry quoted in ibid.
144 O'Quinn, 'Going National'.
145 Zeigler, *Regional Theatre*, 185.
146 Ibid., 65.
147 Quoted in ibid., 68.
148 Zeigler, *Regional Theatre*, 69.
149 Quoted in O'Quinn, 'Going National'.
150 Zeigler, *Regional Theatre*, 75.
151 J. Wesley Zeigler, quoted in 'Regional Theater', *CQ Researcher*, n.d., http://library.cqpress.com/cqresearcher/document.php?id=cqresrre1969021200 (accessed 11 July 2017).
152 O'Quinn, 'Going National'.
153 Larry Neal, 'The Black Arts Movement', *Visions of a Liberated Future*, ed. Michael Schwartz (New York: Thunder's Mouth Press, 1989), 62.
154 John H. Bracey Jr, Sonia Sanchez and James Smethurst, 'Editors' Introduction', in *SOS – Calling All Black People: A Black Arts Movement Reader* (Amherst: University of Massachusetts Press, 2014), 8.
155 Ibid., 8–9.
156 LeRoi Jones, 'The Revolutionary Theatre', *Liberator*, July 1965.
157 Neal, 'The Black Arts Movement', 68.
158 Harold Cruse, *The Crisis of the Negro Intellectual* (New York: Quill, 1984), 74–5.
159 Amiri Baraka, *The Autobiography of LeRoi Jones* (Chicago: Lawrence Hill Books, 1984), 323.
160 Neal, 'The Black Arts Movement', 67.
161 Ed Bullins, *The Theme Is Blackness*, in *Twelve Plays and Selected Writings*, ed. Mike Sell (Ann Arbor, University of Michigan Press, 2006), 209.
162 Robert Macbeth, quoted in Hatch, 'From Hansberry to Shange', 393.
163 Ed Bullins, *In the Wine Time*, in *Twelve Plays and Selected Writings*, ed. Mike Sell (Ann Arbor, University of Michigan Press), 65.
164 Ibid., 63.

165 Williams, *Black Theatre*, 24.
166 Hatch, 'From Hansberry to Shange', 393–4.
167 August Wilson, quoted in Cliff Frazier, 'In the Beginning: Concept East', *Black Masks*, July/August 2007, http://www.blackmasks.com/features_frazier.html (accessed 19 May 2017).
168 Frazier, 'In the Beginning'.
169 Hatch, 'From Hansberry to Shange'. 399.
170 Ron Milner, *Who's Got His Own*, in Woodie King and Ron Milner (eds), *Black Drama Anthology* (New York: Meridian, 1971), 145.
171 Barbara Ann Teer, 'We can be what we were born to be', *New York Times*, 7 July 1968.
172 James Edward Smethurst, *The Black Arts Movement: Literary Nationalism in the 1960s and 1970s* (Chapel Hill: University of North Carolina Press, 2005), 104.
173 Ibid., 104.
174 Ibid.
175 Williams, *Black Theatre*, 52.
176 Ibid., 51.
177 Ronald Reagan, quoted in Lundeana Marie Thomas, *Barbara Ann Teer and the National Black Theatre: Transformational Forces in Harlem* (New York: Garland Publishing, 1997), e-book, n.p.
178 Timothy Miller, *The 60s Communes: Hippies and Beyond* (Syracuse: Syracuse University Press), xiii–xiv.
179 Ibid., xxiv.
180 Paul Goodman, quoted in Bigsby, *Critical Introduction*, 63.
181 James M. Harding and Cindy Rosenthal (eds), 'Introduction', in *Restaging the Sixties: Radical Theaters and Their Legacies* (Ann Arbor: University of Michigan Press, 2006), 9.
182 For readers interested in exploring collective theatres in more detail, see Harding and Rosenthal, *Restaging the Sixties*.
183 Erika Munk, 'Only Connect: The Living Theatre and Its Audiences', in Harding and Rosenthal, *Restaging the Sixties*, 34.
184 Julian Beck, 'Storming the Barricades', in Kenneth Brown, *The Brig: A Concept for Theatre and Film* (New York: Hill and Wang, 1965), 3.
185 Munk, 'Only Connect', 35.
186 Ibid., 38.
187 Bigsby, *Critical Introduction*, 77.

188 Munk, 'Only Connect', 40.

189 Rosenthal 'The Living Theatre: Overview', in Harding and Rosenthal, *Restaging the Sixties*, 28–9.

190 Julian Beck, *Life of the Theatre* (New York: Limelight Editions, 1972), n.p.

191 Munk, 'Only Connect', 47.

192 Bigsby, *Critical Introduction*, 91–2.

193 Harding and Rosenthal, *Restaging the Sixties*, 29.

194 See the essays by Rosenthal, Munk and Alisa Solomon in Rosenthal and Harding, *Restaging the Sixties*.

195 Hatch, 'From Hansberry to Shange', 397.

196 Ibid.

197 Annemarie Bean, 'The Free Southern Theater: Mythology and the Moving Between Movements', in Harding and Rosenthal, *Restaging the Sixties*, 273

198 Richard Schechner, quoted in Jan Cohen-Cruz, 'Comforting the Afflicted and Afflicting the Comfortable: The Legacy of the Free Southern Theater', in Harding and Rosenthal, *Restaging the Sixties*, 289.

199 Fannie Lou Hamer, quoted in Bean, 'The Free Southern Theater', 273.

200 Bean, 'The Free Southern Theater', 274.

201 Hatch, 'From Hansberry to Shange', 399.

202 Rosenthal, 'The Free Southern Theater: Overview', in Harding and Rosenthal, *Restaging the Sixties*, 265.

203 Bean, 'The Free Southern Theater', 272.

204 Ibid., 281.

205 Ibid.

206 Bottoms, *Playing Underground*, 55.

207 Robert Patrick, quoted in Darren Blaney, '1964: The Birth of Gay Theater', *The Gay and Lesbian Review*, 29 December 2013, http://www.glreview.org/article/1964-the-birth-of-gay-theater/ (accessed 8 May 2017).

208 Blaney, '1964: The Birth of Gay Theatre'.

209 Ibid.

210 Terry Miller, 'Unexpected Shocks: An Interview with Lanford Wilson', *New York Native*, 3–16 December 1984, 31–2.

211 Lanford Wilson, *The Madness of Lady Bright*, in *The Rimers of Eldritch and Other Plays* (New York: Noonday Press, 1967), 75.

212 Ibid., 80.
213 Blaney, '1964: The Birth of Gay Theatre'.
214 Ibid.
215 Patrick, *The Haunted Host*, quoted in ibid.
216 Blaney, '1964: The Birth of Gay Theatre'.
217 David Patrick Stearns, quoted in Ellis Nassour, 'Mart Crowley Revisits The Boys', *TotalTheater.com*, September 2003, http://www.totaltheater.com/?q=node/331 (accessed 8 April 2017).
218 *Making the Boys*, [film] Dir. Crayton Robey. USA: First Run Features, 2011.
219 Patrick Healy, '"The Band" Helped Writers Find their Beat', *New York Times*, 7 March 2010, http://www.nytimes.com/2010/03/07/theater/07influence.html (accessed 12 July 2017).
220 Mart Crowley, *The Boys in the Band*, in *The Band Plays* (Los Angeles, Alyson Books, 2003), 10.
221 Ron Tavel, *The Life of Lady Godiva*, in *Theatre of the Ridiculous*, revised and expanded edn, ed. Bonnie Marranca and Gautam Dasgupta (Baltimore: Johns Hopkins University Press, 1998), 39.
222 Ibid., 39–40.
223 Bottoms, *Playing Underground*, 225.
224 Ibid., 217–18.
225 Ibid., 218.
226 John Vaccaro quoted in ibid. 215.
227 Penny Arcade, quoted in Legs McNeil and Gillian McCain, *Please Kill Me: The Uncensored Oral History of Punk* (New York: Grove Press, 1997), 91.
228 Leee Childers, quoted in ibid., 92.
229 Bottoms, *Playing Underground*, 216.
230 Ibid., 229.
231 Ibid., 227.
232 Tavel, quoted in ibid.
233 Charles Ludlam, quoted in ibid.
234 Childers in *Please Kill Me*, 88.
235 Charles Ludlam, *Ridiculous Theatre: Scourge of Human Folly: The Essays and Opinions of Charles Ludlam*, ed. Steven Samuels (New York: Theatre Communications Group, 1992).

236 Gerald Rabkin, 'Kenneth Bernard and John Vaccaro: A Collaboration', in Bonnie Marranca and Gautam Dasgupta (eds), *Theatre of the Ridiculous*, revised and expanded edn (Baltimore: Johns Hopkins University Press, 1998), 147.
237 Ibid., 152.
238 Bottoms, *Playing Underground*, 236.
239 Esther Kim Lee, *A History of Asian American Theatre* (Cambridge: Cambridge University Press, 2006), 7.
240 Ibid., 8.
241 Quoted in ibid., 26.
242 Yuko Kurahashi, quoted in ibid., 27.
243 Lee, *A History of Asian American Theatre*, 27–8.
244 Ibid., 44.
245 Ibid,. 45.
246 Ibid., 29.
247 Ibid., 35, 26.
248 Jorge Huerta, 'From the Margins to the Mainstream: Latino/a Theater in the U.S.', *Studies in 20th and 21st Century Literature* 32 (2): 466.
249 Ramón H. Rivera-Servera, 'Theater', *Oxford Bibliographies: Latino Studies*, 19 March 2013, http://www.oxfordbibliographies.com/view/document/obo-9780199913701/obo-9780199913701-0066.xml (accessed 12 July 2017).
250 Nicolás Kanellos, 'Hispanic Theatre in the United States: Post-War to the Present', *Latin American Theatre Review* 25 (2) (Spring 1992): 198.
251 John Bell, 'Luis Valdez', in Gabrielle H. Cody and Evert Sprinchorn (eds), *The Columbia Encyclopedia of Modern Drama* (New York: Columbia University Press, 2007), 1415.
252 Huerta, 'From the Margins to the Mainstream', 468.
253 Yolanda Broyles-González, 'Re-Constructing Collective Dynamics: El Teatro Campesino from a Twenty-First Century Perspective', in Harding and Rosenthal, *Restaging the Sixties*, 222.
254 Huerta, 'From the Margins to the Mainstream', 469.
255 Diana Taylor, quoted in ibid., 468.
256 Tomás Ybarra-Frausto, quoted in Jorge Huerta, 'The Legacy of El Teatro Campesino', in Harding and Rosenthal, *Restaging the Sixties*; and Broyles-González, in ibid., 227.

257 Luis Valdez, *Los Vendidos*, *Early Works: Actors, Bernabe and Pensamiento Serpentino* (Houston: Arte Público Press, 1990).
258 Broyles-González, 'Re-Constructing Collective Dynamics'.
259 'Our History', El Teatro Campesino, n.d., http://elteatrocampesino.com/our-history/ (accessed 12 July 2017).
260 Nicolás Kanellos, *Hispanic Literature in the United States: A Comprehensive Reference* (Westport, CT: Greenwood Press, 2003), 273.
261 Ibid., 274.
262 Ibid.

3 Edward Albee

1   Edward Albee and Philip C. Kolin, *Conversations with Edward Albee* (Jackson: University Press of Mississippi, 1988), 49.
2   William J. Clinton, *Public Papers of the Presidents of the United States: William J. Clinton 1996* (Washington: National Archives and Records Administration, 1998), 2178.
3   Edward Albee, *Stretching My Mind* (New York: Carroll & Graf Publishers, 2005), 1.
4   Mel Gussow, 'A Voice of His Own: Albee's Epiphany at 30', *New York Times*, 25 July 1999, Books sec., http://www.nytimes.com/1999/07/25/theater/theater-a-voice-of-his-own-albee-s-epiphany-at–30.html (accessed 26 June 2015).
5   Edward Albee, *The Collected Plays of Edward Albee,* vol. 1 (Woodstock: Overlook Press, 2004), 14.
6   Gussow, 'A Voice of His Own.'
7   Rose A. Zimbardo, 'Symbolism and Naturalism in Edward Albee's *The Zoo Story*', *Twentieth Century Literature* 8 (1) (1962): 10–17.
8   Albee, *Collected Plays*, vol. 1, 40.
9   Jerry Tallmer, 'From the Archives . . . *The Voice* Reviews Edward Albee's *The Zoo Story* and Samuel Beckett's *Krapp's Last Tape*', *The Village Voice*, 8 July 2009.
10 Ibid.
11 Mel Gussow, *Edward Albee: A Singular Journey* (New York: Simon & Schuster, 1999), 129.
12 Tim Treanor, 'Edward Albee Interview', *DC Theatre Scene*, 7 February 2009.

13 Albee, *Collected Plays*, vol. 1, 86.
14 Philip C. Kolin, 'Albee's Early One-Act Plays: A new American playwright from whom much is to be expected', in *The Cambridge Companion to Edward Albee*, ed. Stephen J. Bottoms (Cambridge: Cambridge University Press, 2005), 27.
15 Ben Brantley, 'A Double Bill, Both Heavy on the Bile', *New York Times*, 2 April 2008.
16 Albee, *Collected Plays*, vol. 1, 101–2.
17 C. W. E. Bigsby, *A Critical Introduction to Twentieth-Century American Drama*, vol. 2 (Cambridge: Cambridge University Press, 1985), 262.
18 Gussow, *Edward Albee*, 22.
19 Martin Esslin, *The Theatre of the Absurd*, 3rd edn (Harmondsworth: Penguin Books, 1980), 23.
20 Ibid., 403.
21 Albee, *Stretching My Mind*, 9.
22 Ibid., 21.
23 Bruce J. Mann, 'Interview with Edward Albee', in *Edward Albee: A Casebook*, ed. Bruce J. Mann (New York: Routledge, 2003), 130.
24 Richard Schechner, 'Who's Afraid of Edward Albee?', *The Tulane Drama Review* 7 (3) (1963): 7–10.
25 Albee, *Stretching My Mind*, 12.
26 Matthew Roudané, '*Who's Afraid of Virginia Woolf*: Toward the Marrow', in *The Cambridge Companion to Edward Albee*, ed. Stephen J. Bottoms (Cambridge: Cambridge University Press, 2005), 41.
27 Edward Albee, *Who's Afraid of Virginia Woolf* (London: Vintage Books, 2001), 45.
28 Albee and Kolin, *Conversations with Edward Albee*, 52.
29 C. W. E. Bigsby, 'Who's Afraid of Virginia Woolf? Edward Albee's Morality Play', *Journal of American Studies* 1 (2) (1967): 257.
30 Gussow, *Edward Albee*, 159.
31 Albee, *Collected Plays*, vol. 1, 423.
32 Harold Clurman, *The Collected Works of Harold Clurman: Six Decades of Commentary on Theatre, Dance, Music, Film, Arts and Letters*, ed. Marjorie Loggia and Glenn Young (New York: Applause Books, 1994), 588.
33 Philip Roth, 'The Play That Dare Not Speak Its Name', *The New York Review of Books*, 25 February 1965.

34 Stephen Bottoms and Edward Albee, 'Borrowed Time: An Interview with Edward Albee', in *The Cambridge Companion to Edward Albee*, ed. Stephen J. Bottoms (Cambridge: Cambridge University Press, 2005), 233.
35 Gussow, *Edward Albee*, 213.
36 Ibid., 230.
37 Stanley Kauffman, 'Funless Games at George and Martha's: Albee's "Virginia Woolf" Becomes a Film', *New York Times*, 24 June 1966.
38 Gussow, *Edward Albee*, 260.
39 Edward Albee, *A Delicate Balance* (New York: Overlook Duckworth, 2013), 13.
40 Craig Lucas and Edward Albee, 'Edward Albee by Craig Lucas', *BOMB Magazine* 38, Winter 1992.
41 Edward Albee, *The Collected Plays of Edward Albee*, vol. 2 (Woodstock: Overlook Duckworth, Peter Mayer Publishers, Inc., 2005), 262.

4 Amiri Baraka

1 Amiri Baraka [LeRoi Jones], '"What Williams Means to Me": Four Contemporary Playwrights Weigh in on the Writer's Legacy', *American Theatre*, September 2011: 40–41.
2 Amiri Baraka [LeRoi Jones], 'The Black Arts Movement', in *The LeRoi Jones/Amiri Baraka Reader,* edited by William J. Harris (New York: Thunder's Mouth, 2000), 504.
3 Amiri Baraka, 'LeRoi Jones: An Interview on *Yugen*' by David Ossman, 6–7.
4 Hettie Jones, *How I Became Hettie Jones* (New York: E. P. Dutton, 1990), 222.
5 Amiri Baraka, *The Autobiography of LeRoi Jones* (Chicago: Lawrence Hill Books, 1997), 378.
6 *In Motion: Amiri Baraka* (1998), [Film] Dir. St Clair Bourne. Chicago: Facets Video, Videocassette (VHS), 60 mins.
7 Amiri Baraka, 'Preface to the Reader', in *The LeRoi Jones/Amiri Baraka Reader*, ed. William J. Harris and Amiri Baraka (New York: Thunder's Mouth, 2000), xi.
8 H. Jones, *How I Became Hettie Jones*, 133.

9   Ibid.
10 Baraka, *Autobiography*, 127.
11 Ibid., 177–8.
12 LeRoi Jones [Amiri Baraka], 'Notes for a Speech', in *Preface to a Twenty Volume Suicide Note* (New York: Totem Press, 1961), 47.
13 Baraka, *Preface to a Twenty Volume Suicide Note*, 13–14.
14 Baraka, *Autobiography*, 231.
15 Ibid.
16 Ibid., 223.
17 Ibid., 230.
18 *In Motion*.
19 Baraka, *Autobiography*, 251.
20 LeRoi Jones, *The Eighth Ditch (Is Drama)*, in *The System of Dante's Hell* (New York: Grove, 1965), 79–91; Baraka, *Autobiography*, 275.
21 José Esteban Muñoz, 'Cruising *The Toilet*: LeRoi Jones/Amiri Baraka, Radical Black Traditions, and Queer Futurity', in *Cruising Utopia: The Then and There of Queer Futurity* (New York: New York University Press, 2009), 84.
22 LeRoi Jones [Amiri Baraka], *The Baptism*, in *The Baptism & The Toilet* (New York: Grove, 1967), 9.
23 Ibid., 16–17.
24 Ibid., 29.
25 Debra L. Edwards, 'An Interview with Amiri Baraka', in *Conversations with Amiri Baraka*, ed. Charlie Reilly (Jackson: University Press of Mississippi, 1994), 151.
26 Muñoz, 'Cruising *The Toilet*', 84.
27 H. Jones, *How I Became Hettie Jones*, 180.
28 LeRoi Jones [Amiri Baraka], *The Toilet*, in *The Baptism & The Toilet* (New York: Grove, 1967), 62.
29 C. W. E. Bigsby, 'The Theatre and the Coming Revolution,' in *Conversations with Amiri Baraka*, ed. Charlie Reilly (Jackson: University Press of Mississippi, 1994), 131.
30 Ibid.
31 Komozi Woodard, 'Amiri Baraka, the Congress of African People, and Black Power Politics from the 1961 United Nations Protest to the 1972 Gary Convention,' in *The Black Power Movement: Rethinking*

the Civil Rights–Black Power Era, ed. Peniel E. Joseph (New York: Routledge, 2006). 61.

32 LeRoi Jones [Amiri Baraka], 'The Revolutionary Theatre', in *Home: Social Essays* (New York: William Morrow, 1966), 214.

33 Baraka, *Autobiography*, 175.

34 Ibid., 279.

35 Ibid.

36 Dora Apel, *Imagery of Lynching: Black Men, White Women, and the Mob* (New Brunswick: Rutgers University Press, 2004), 239.

37 Muñoz, 'Cruising *the Toilet*', 83, 85.

38 Joe LeSueur, *Digressions on Some Poems by Frank O'Hara* (New York: Farrar, Straus and Giroux, 2003), 246, 118.

39 Edwards, 'An Interview with Amiri Baraka', 150.

40 Judy Stone, Baraka, 'If It's Anger . . . Maybe That's Good: An Interview with LeRoi Jones', in *Conversations with Amiri Baraka*, ed. Charlie Reilly (Jackson: University Press of Mississippi, 1994), 11.

41 Woodard, 'Amiri Baraka, the Congress of African People, and Black Power Politics', 67–8.

42 Amiri Baraka [LeRoi Jones], 'Introduction', in *The Motion of History and Other Plays* (New York: William Morrow, 1978), 12.

43 Amiri Baraka, *A Recent Killing*. Black Drama – 1850 to Present, *North American Theatre Online*, Alexander Street (2005), accessed 1 October 2013 [no longer extant in database].

44 Baraka, *Autobiography*, 173, 144, 166.

45 Baraka, *A Recent Killing*, 81, 83.

46 Ibid., 80.

47 Baraka, *Autobiography*, 168.

48 Baraka, *A Recent Killing*, 61, 63, 68.

49 Baraka, 'Introduction'. *The Motion of History*, 12.

50 Ibid.

51 Theodore R. Hudson, 'A Conversation between Imamu Amiri Baraka and Theodore R. Hudson,' in *Conversations with Amiri Bara*ka, ed. Charlie Reilly (Jackson: University Press of Mississippi, 1994), 76.

52 Jerry Gafio Watts, *Amiri Baraka: The Politics and Art of a Black Intellectual* (New York: New York University Press, 2001), 336.

53 Amiri Baraka, 'Who Killed Our Little Shani? Our Youngest Child, Our Baby . . . Who Killed Amina & Amiri Baraka's Little Shani?' *The*

Blacklisted Journalist, 96 (1 September 2003), http://www.blacklistedjournalist.com/column96.html (accessed 26 July 2017).

54 Muñoz, 'Cruising *The Toilet*', 95.
55 H. Jones, *How I Became Hettie Jones*, 206.
56 Mike Sell, 'The Drama of the Black Arts Movement', in *A Companion to Twentieth-Century American Drama*, ed. David Krasner (Malden, MA: Blackwell Publishing, 2005), 265.
57 LeRoi Jones [Amiri Baraka], *Dutchman*, in *Dutchman and The Slave: Two Plays by LeRoi Jones* (New York: Morrow-Quill, 1964), 34.
58 Ibid., 37–8.
59 Susan Sontag, 'Going to the Theater, Etc.', In *Against Interpretation and Other Essays* (New York: Farrar, Straus and Giroux, 1966), 152, 156.
60 Charlie Reilly, 'An Interview with Amiri Baraka', in *Conversations with Amiri Baraka* (Jackson: University Press of Mississippi, 1994), 255.
61 Charles D. Peavy, 'Myth, Magic, and Manhood in LeRoi Jones' *Madheart*,' in *Imamu Amiri Baraka (LeRoi Jones): A Collection of Critical Essays*, ed. Kimberly W. Benston (Englewood Cliffs, NJ: Prentice-Hall, 1978), 168.
62 Anna Maria Chupa, *Anne, the White Woman in Contemporary African-American Fiction: Archetypes, Stereotypes, and Characterizations* (New York: Greenwood, 1990), 27.
63 L. Jones, *Dutchman*, 14.
64 Werner Sollors, *Amiri Baraka/LeRoi Jones: The Quest for a 'Populist Modernism'* (New York: Columbia University Press, 1978), 129.
65 Ibid.
66 H. Jones, *How I Became Hettie Jones*, 138.
67 Baraka, *Autobiography*, 208, 210, 212, 277.
68 Reilly, 'Interview with Amiri Baraka', 257.
69 Baraka, *Autobiography*, 250.
70 Ibid., 291.
71 Ibid., 280.
72 Ibid., 258.
73 Ibid., 288.
74 H. Jones, *How I Became Hettie Jones*, 138, 220.
75 LeRoi Jones [Amiri Baraka], *The Slave*, in *Dutchman and The Slave: Two Plays by LeRoi Jones* (New York: Morrow-Quill, 1964), 126, 118.

76 Ibid., 105, and Amiri Baraka [LeRoi Jones], 'Poem for HalfWhite College Students', in *The LeRoi Jones/Amiri Baraka Reader*, ed. William J. Harris and Amiri Baraka (New York: Thunder's Mouth, 2000).
77 L. Jones, *The Slave*, 105, 109, 127.
78 Ibid., 57.
79 Amiri Baraka [LeRoi Jones], *Selected Plays and Prose of Amiri Baraka/LeRoi Jones* (New York: William Morrow, 1979), dedication page.
80 Lawrence P. Neal, 'The Development of LeRoi Jones,' in *Imamu Amiri Baraka (LeRoi Jones): A Collection of Critical Essays*, ed. Kimberly W. Benston (Englewood Cliffs, NJ: Prentice-Hall, 1978), 27.
81 Baraka, *Autobiography*, 311.
82 L. Jones, 'The Revolutionary Theatre,' 210–11.
83 Ibid., 210, 212.
84 Ibid., 211, 214–15.
85 Baraka, *Autobiography*, 326.
86 Ibid., 295.
87 Ibid., 307.
88 Ibid., 328–9.
89 Ibid., 298, 309.
90 Ibid., 310.
91 Hudson, 'A Conversation between Imamu Amiri Baraka and Theodore R. Hudson', 76.
92 Sell, 'The Drama of the Black Arts Movement', 265.
93 L. Jones, 'The Revolutionary Theatre,' 210.
94 LeRoi Jones [Amiri Baraka], 'Introduction', in *Four Black Revolutionary Plays: All Praises to the Black Man* (Indianapolis: Bobbs-Merrill, 1969), vii.
95 Baraka, 'The Black Arts Movement,' 504.
96 L. Jones, 'The Revolutionary Theatre,' 215, 214.
97 Amiri Baraka, *Experimental Death Unit #1*, in *Four Black Revolutionary Plays: All Praises to the Black Man* (Indianapolis: Bobbs-Merrill, 1969), 13, 15.
98 Sandra G. Shannon, 'Amiri Baraka on Directing,' in *Conversations with Amiri Baraka*, ed. Charlie Reilly (Jackson: University Press of Mississippi, 1994), 234.
99 Baraka, *Experimental Death Unit #1*, 6.

100 Ibid., 10.
101 Ibid., 14.
102 Cornel West, *Race Matters* (Boston: Beacon, 1993), 84.
103 Frantz Fanon, *Black Skin White Masks*, trans. Charles Lam Markmann (New York: Grove, 1968), 165.
104 Leslie Catherine Sanders, *The Development of Black Theater in America: From Shadows to Selves* (Baton Rouge: Louisiana State University Press, 1988), 134.
105 Amiri Baraka, *A Black Mass*, in *Four Black Revolutionary Plays: All Praises to the Black Man* (Indianapolis: Bobbs-Merrill, 1969), 30–32.
106 Ibid., 32.
107 Ibid., 33.
108 Ibid., 35.
109 Ibid., 38.
110 Ibid., 39.
111 Ibid.
112 Amiri Baraka, 'Kimako Baraka (1936–1984) Lanie Poo: Her Life, Her Death, Our World!!!', in *Eulogies* (New York: Marsilio, 1996), 50.
113 Baraka, *Autobiography*, 379.
114 Hudson, 'A Conversation between Imamu Amiri Baraka and Theodore R. Hudson,' 72.
115 Amiri Baraka, *Great Goodness of Life: A Coon Show*, in *Four Black Revolutionary Plays: All Praises to the Black Man* (Indianapolis: Bobbs-Merrill, 1969), 41.
116 Ibid., 43.
117 Ibid., 46, 54.
118 Ibid.
119 Ibid., 45.
120 Ibid., 48–9.
121 Ibid., 50.
122 Ibid., 58–9.
123 Ibid., 60, 62.
124 Ibid., 62.
125 Ibid., 63.
126 Joyce A. Joyce, 'Interviews with Amiri Baraka, Askia Touré, and Sonia Sanchez', in *Black Studies As Human Studies: Critical*

Essays and Interviews (Albany: State University of New York Press, 2005), 139.

127 Henry C. Lacey, *To Raise, Destroy, and Create: The Poetry, Drama, and Fiction of Imamu Amiri Baraka (LeRoi Jones)* (Troy, NY: Whitston, 1981), 143.

128 Peavy, 'Myth, Magic, and Manhood', 168.

129 Susan Stone-Lawrence, '"A Simple Knife Thrust": The Complicated Power of Purgative Ritual in *Madheart*', *Continuum: The Journal of African Diaspora Drama, Theatre, and Performance* 1 (2) (January 2015), http://continuumjournal.org/index.php/all-issues/current-issue-amiri-baraka/32-volumes/issues/vol–1-no–2-content/articles-1-2/85-a-simple-knife-thrust-the-complicated-power-of-purgative-ritual-in-madheart (accessed 26 July 2017).

130 Joyce, 'Interviews with Amiri Baraka, Askia Touré, and Sonia Sanchez', 137, 135.

131 Baraka, *Autobiography*, 353.

132 Sanders, *The Development of Black Theater*, 165.

133 Kimberly W. Benston, *The Renegade and the Mask* (New Haven: Yale University Press, 1976), 222.

134 Sollors, *Amiri Baraka/LeRoi Jones*, 214–15.

135 Peavy, 'Myth, Magic, and Manhood', 168, 169.

136 Beth McCoy, 'A Nation's Meta-Language: Misogyny in Amiri Baraka's *Dutchman* and *The Slave*', in *Staging the Rage: The Web of Misogyny in Modern Drama*, ed. Katherine H. Burkman and Judith Roof (Cranbury, NJ: Associated University Presses, 1998), 60.

137 Amiri Baraka, *Madheart: (A Morality Play)*, in *Four Black Revolutionary Plays: All Praises to the Black Man* (Indianapolis: Bobbs-Merrill, 1969), 70.

138 Ibid., 75.

139 Ibid., 81–2.

140 Joyce, 'Interviews with Amiri Baraka, Askia Touré, and Sonia Sanchez', 139.

141 Baraka, *Madheart*, 81–2.

142 Ibid., 81.

143 Ibid., 83–4.

144 Baraka, 'Introduction', *Autobiography*, xiv.

145 Cheryl Clarke, 'The Failure to Transform: Homophobia in the Black Community,' in *Home Girls: A Black Feminist Anthology*, ed.

Barbara Smith (New Brunswick: Rutgers University Press, 2000), 197.
146 Baraka, *Madheart*, 76.
147 Baraka, *Autobiography*, 306, 338.
148 Amiri Baraka, 'Why No J-E-L-L-O?', in *Four Black Revolutionary Plays: All Praises to the Black Man* (Indianapolis: Bobbs-Merrill, 1969), 89.
149 Amiri Baraka, *J-E-L-L-O* (Chicago: Third World Press), 9.
150 Ibid., 33.
151 Baraka, *Autobiography*, 382.
152 Baraka, 'Introduction', *The Motion of History*, 12.
153 Amiri Baraka, *Rockgroup*, *The Cricket: Black Music in America* (December 1969): 41.
154 Ibid.
155 Ibid.
156 Baraka, 'Introduction', *The Motion of History*, 12.
157 Amiril Baraka, *Slave Ship*, in *The Motion of History and Other Plays* (New York: William Morrow, 1978), 137.
158 Ibid., 139.
159 Ibid., 140.
160 Ibid., 142.
161 Ibid.
162 Ibid., 144.
163 Ibid., 145.
164 Baraka, 'Introduction', *The Motion of History*, 11.
165 Ibid.
166 Harry J. Elam, Jr, *Taking It to the Streets: The Social Protest Theater of Luis Valdez and Amiri Baraka* (Ann Arbor: University of Michigan Press, 1997), 107.
167 Ibid., 124.
168 Val Ferdinand [Kalamu ya Salaam], 'A Report on Black Theatre in America: New Orleans,' *Negro Digest*, April 1970: 28.
169 Ibid., 29.
170 Ibid., 28.
171 Elam, *Taking It to the Streets*, 122.
172 Davi Napoleon, *Chelsea on the Edge: The Adventures of an American Theater* (Ames: Iowa State University Press, 1991), 67.

173 Elam, *Taking It to the Streets*, 78.
174 Ibid., 78, 89–90.
175 Clive Barnes, 'The Theater: New LeRoi Jones Play' [review of Chelsea Theatre Center production of *Slave Ship*], *New York Times*, 22 November 1969: 46.
176 Amiri Baraka, *Arm Yrself or Harm Yrself* (Newark: Jihad, 1967).
177 Amiri Baraka, *Home on the Range*, in *A Sourcebook of African-American Performance: Plays, People, Movements*, ed. Annemarie Bean (London: Routledge, 1999), 32–40.
178 Amiri Baraka, *Police*, in *A Sourcebook of African-American Performance: Plays, People, Movements*, ed. Annemarie Bean (London: Routledge, 1999), 40.
179 Amiri Baraka, *Black Power Chant,* Black Drama – 1850 to Present, *North American Theatre Online*, Alexander Street (2005), accessed 14 March 2017.
180 Amiri Baraka, *Board of Education*, Black Drama – 1850 to Present, *North American Theatre Online*, Alexander Street (2005), accessed 14 March 2017, 3, 14.
181 Amiri Baraka, *Junkies Are Full of (Shh . . .)*, Black Drama – 1850 to Present, *North American Theatre Online*, Alexander Street (2005), accessed 14 March 2017.
182 Kimberly W. Benston, 'Preface', in *Baraka: The Renegade and the Mask* (New Haven: Yale University Press, 1976), xviii.

5 Adrienne Kennedy

1 Adrienne Kennedy, *People Who Led to My Plays* (New York: Theatre Communications Group, 1987), 69.
2 Ibid., 123.
3 Ibid., 120.
4 Ibid., 119.
5 Howard Stein, 'Interview with Michael Kahn', in *Intersecting Boundaries: The Theatre of Adrienne Kennedy*, ed. Paul Bryant-Jackson and Lois Overbeck (Minneapolis: University of Minnesota Press, 1992), 194.
6 Howard Stein, 'Interview with Gaby Rodgers', in Bryant-Jackson and Overbeck, *Intersecting Boundaries*, 201.
7 Wolfgang Binder and Adrienne Kennedy, 'A *MELUS* Interview: Adrienne Kennedy', *MELUS* 12 (3) (Fall 1985): 102.

8   Stein, 'Interview with Michael Kahn', 191.
9   Margaret B. Wilkerson, 'Diverse Angles of Vision', in Bryant-Jackson and Overbeck, *Intersecting Boundaries*, 73.
10 Stein, 'Interview with Michael Kahn', 192.
11 Paul Carter Harrison et al., 'Personal Perspectives on Adrienne Kennedy', *Modern Drama* 55 (1) (Spring 2012): 90.
12 Olga Barrios, 'From Seeking One's Voice to Uttering the Scream: The Pioneering Work of African American Women Playwrights Through the 1960s and 1970s', *African American Review* 37 (4) (Winter 2003): 612.
13 Quoted in Harrison et al., 'Personal Perspectives on Adrienne Kennedy', 93.
14 Binder and Kennedy, 'A *MELUS* Interview', 108.
15 Quoted in Harrison et al., 'Personal Perspectives on Adrienne Kennedy', 91.
16 Stein, 'Interview with Michael Kahn', 195–6.
17 Ibid., 196.
18 Binder and Kennedy, 'A *MELUS* Interview', 103.
19 Ibid.
20 Ibid., 104.
21 Quoted in Harrison et al., 'Personal Perspectives on Adrienne Kennedy', 91.
22 Paul K. Bryant-Jackson and Lois More Overbeck, 'Adrienne Kennedy: An Interview', in *Intersecting Boundaries: The Theatre of Adrienne Kennedy* (Minneapolis: University of Minnesota Press, 1992), 4.
23 Quoted in Harrison et al., 'Personal Perspectives on Adrienne Kennedy', 91.
24 Binder and Kennedy, 'A *MELUS* Interview', 104.
25 Ibid., 104, 166.
26 Howard Stein, 'An Interview with Gerald Freedman', in Bryant-Jackson and Overbeck, *Intersecting Boundaries*,191.
27 Harrison et al., 'Personal Perspectives on Adrienne Kennedy', 91.
28 Adrienne Kennedy, *Deadly Triplets: A Theatre Mystery* (Minneapolis: University of Minnesota Press, 1990), ix.
29 Binder and Kennedy, 'A MELUS Interview', 104.
30 Ibid.
31 Quoted in Harrison et al., 'Personal Perspectives on Adrienne Kennedy', 97.

32 Kennedy, *The Owl Answers*, *The Adrienne Kennedy Reader* (Minneapolis: University of Minnesota Press, 2001), 42.
33 Ibid.
34 Ibid., 30.
35 Binder and Kennedy, 'A *MELUS* Interview', 105.
36 Quoted in Harrison et al., 'Personal Perspectives on Adrienne Kennedy', 97.
37 Paul K. Bryant-Jackson, 'Kennedy's Travelers in the American and African Continuum', in Bryant-Jackson and Overbeck, *Intersecting Boundaries*, 55.
38 Kennedy, *Funnyhouse of a Negro*, *The Adrienne Kennedy Reader* (Minneapolis: University of Minnesota Press, 2001), 25–6.
39 Lois Overbeck, 'The Life of the Work: A Preliminary Sketch', in Bryant-Jackson and Overbeck, *Intersecting Boundaries*, 27.
40 Kennedy, *Deadly Triplets*, 104.
41 Ibid., 116.
42 Overbeck, 'The Life of the Work', 26.
43 Ibid., 32.
44 Kennedy, *Deadly Triplets*, 107.
45 Stein, 'Interview with Michael Kahn', 191–2.
46 Philip C. Kolin, 'Revisiting *Funnyhouse*: An Interview with Billie Allen', *African American Review* 41 (1) (Spring 2007): 169.
47 Paul Bryant-Jackson and Lois Overbeck. 'Interview with Billie Allen,' in *Intersecting Boundaries*, 223.
48 Overbeck, 'The Life of the Work', 30.
49 Ibid., 29.
50 Ibid., 30.
51 Binder and Kennedy, 'A *MELUS* Interview', 107.

6 Jean-Claude van Itallie

1 John Lahr, *Up Against the Fourth Wall: Essays on Modern Theatre* (New York: Grove Press, 1970), 105.
2 Jean-Claude van Itallie, 'A Letter' preceding *The Serpent* in *America Hurrah and Other Plays* (New York: Grove Press, 1978), 12. Note that each play in this collection has separate pagination.

3. Arthur Sainer, *The New Radical Theatre Notebook* (New York: Applause Books, 1997), 9.
4. Jean-Claude van Itallie, *The Playwright's Workbook* (New York: Applause Books, 1997), 139.
5. Scott Proudfitt, 'Shared Space and Shared Pages: Collective Creation for Edward Albee and the Playwrights of the Open Theater', in Kathryn Mederos Syssoyeva and Scott Proudfitt (eds), *A History of Collective Creation* (New York: Palgrave Macmillan, 2014), 161.
6. Jean-Claude van Itallie, *War*, in *Five Short Plays* (Baltimore: Penguin, 1967), 113; *War* 114.
7. Stephen J. Bottoms, *Playing Underground: A Critical History of the 1960s Off-Off-Broadway Movement* (Ann Arbor: University of Michigan Press, 2004), 5.
8. Van Itallie, 'A Letter', 12.
9. Gene Plunka, *Jean-Claude van Itallie and the Off-Broadway Theatre* (Newark: University of Delaware Press, 1999), 14.
10. In 1966, van Itallie gave a talk at a UNESCO meeting in Budapest that showed considerable practical knowledge about how TV was made at the time, as well as an awareness of how the audience experience differed in theatre, film and television. For more see Jean-Claude van Itallie, 'The Adaptation of Theatre Plays to the Media of Television and Films', unpublished report presented at a UNESCO round table meeting on 'The sound-track in the cinema and television' held in Budapest in September 1966, Jean-Claude van Itallie Papers, Kent State University.
11. Bottoms, *Playing Underground*, 85.
12. Ibid., 90.
13. Proudfitt, 'Shared Space and Shared Pages', 159.
14. Ibid., 161.
15. Marshall McLuhan, *Understanding Media: The Extensions of Man* (New York: McGraw Hill, 1964), 9.
16. Joseph Chaikin, *The Presence of the Actor* (New York: Theatre Communications Group, 1991), 54.
17. Robert Pasolli, *A Book on the Open Theater* (New York: The Bobbs-Merrill Company, Inc., 1970), 53.
18. Ibid.
19. Pasolli, *A Book on the Open Theater*, 36.
20. Rhea Gaisner, 'Jean-Claude van Itallie: Playwright of the Ensemble: Open Theater', *The Serif* 9(4) (Winter 1971): 14.

21 Pasolli, *A Book on the Open Theater*, 12.
22 Eileen Blumenthal, *Joseph Chaikin: Exploring at the Boundaries of Theater* (New York: Cambridge University Press, 1984), 105.
23 Pasolli, *A Book on the Open Theater*, 47.
24 Jean-Claude van Itallie, 'Playwright and the Ensemble', transcript of a lecture delivered at the University of Connecticut at Storrs, March 1969, Jean-Claude van Itallie Papers, Kent State University, 19.
25 Ibid., 8
26 Pasolli, *A Book on the Open Theater*, 39.
27 Chaikin, *The Presence of the Actor*, 12.
28 Ibid,. 73.
29 Jean-Claude van Itallie, *Almost Like Being*, in *War and Four Other Plays* (New York: Dramatists Play Service, 1967), 141.
30 Ibid., 135.
31 Van Itallie, 'The Adaptation of Theatre Plays', 2–3.
32 Jean-Claude van Itallie, *I'm Really Here*, in *War and Four Other Plays* (New York: Dramatists Play Service, 1967), 47.
33 Ibid., 48–9.
34 Bottoms, *Playing Underground*, 182.
35 Jean-Claude van Itallie, 'Playwright at Work: Off Off-Broadway', *The Tulane Drama Review* 10 (4) (1966): 157.
36 Plunka, *Jean-Claude van Itallie*, 86, 87.
37 Chaikin, *The Presence of the Actor*, 105.
38 Plunka, *Jean-Claude van Itallie*, 85.
39 Ibid.
40 Jean-Claude van Itallie, 'A Reinvention of Form', *The Drama Review* 21 (4) (December 1977): 67.
41 Jean-Claude van Itallie, *Interview*, in *America Hurrah and Other Plays* (New York: Grove Press, 2001), 41–2.
42 The original, unpublished typescript of *Pavane* is kept in the Billy Rose Theatre Collection at the New York Public Library. For Terry's role in developing transformations, see her plays *Calm Down Mother* (1964) and *Keep Tightly Closed in a Cool, Dry Place* (1965), and Kerstin Schmidt, 'Megan Terry and Rochelle Owens: Transformation and Postmodern Feminism', in *The Theater of Transformation: Postmodernism in American Drama* (Amsterdam: Editions Rodopi 2005), 129–72.
43 Van Itallie, *Interview*, 40.

44 Pasolli, *A Book on the Open Theater*, 18
45 Van Itallie, *Interview*, 51.
46 Ibid., 46.
47 Ibid., 47.
48 Jean-Claude van Itallie, *TV*, in *America Hurrah and Other Plays* (New York: Grove Press, 2001), 61.
49 Robert Brustein, 'Introduction' to *America Hurrah*, in Jean-Claude van Itallie, *America Hurrah and Other Plays* (New York: Grove Press, 2001), 7.
50 Van Itallie, 'The Adaptation of Theatre Plays', 8.
51 Van Itallie, *TV*, 84.
52 Ibid., 87.
53 Ibid., 66.
54 Ibid., 134.
55 Marshall McLuhan, quoted in ibid., 57.
56 Jean-Claude van Itallie, *Motel*, in *America Hurrah and Other Plays* (New York: Grove Press, 2001), 135.
57 Ibid.
58 Van Itallie, 'Playwright at Work', 154.
59 Antonin Artaud, *The Theater and Its Double*, translated by Mary C. Richard (New York: Grove, 1994), 123.
60 Van Itallie, *Motel*, 135.
61 Quoted in ibid., 134.
62 Alfred Jarry, 'Preface', in *Ubu Roi*, translated by Beverly Keith and G. Legman (New York: Dover, 2003), 3.
63 Van Itallie, *Motel*, 139.
64 Ibid., 137.
65 Ibid.
66 Jean-Claude van Itallie, 'Should the Artist Be Political in His Art?' *New York Times*, 17 September 1967, D3.
67 Ibid.
68 Ibid.
69 Brustein, 'Introduction', 9.
70 Ross Wetzsteon, 'Theatre: *America Hurrah*, Three Views of the U.S.A.', *Village Voice*, 10 November 1966, cited in Bottoms, *Playing Underground*, 184.

71 Walter Kerr, 'The Theater: A Whisper in the Wind', *New York Times*, 7 November 1966.
72 See John Houchin, *Censorship in the American Theatre in the Twentieth Century* (New York: Cambridge University Press, 2003), 192.
73 Walter Kerr, 'New Techniques', *New York Times*, 27 November 1966.
74 Brustein, 'Introduction', 5.
75 Pasolli, *A Book on the Open Theater*, 108.
76 Plunka, *Jean-Claude van Itallie*, 105.
77 Pasolli, *A Book on the Open Theater*, 118.
78 Blumenthal, *Joseph Chaikin*, 134.
79 Chaikin, 'From the Director', in Jean-Claude van Itallie, *The Serpent*, in *America Hurrah and Other Plays* (New York: Grove Press, 2001), 8.
80 Blumenthal, *Joseph Chaikin*, 107.
81 Chaikin, *The Presence of the Actor*, 62–4.
82 Van Itallie, *The Serpent*, 22.
83 Lahr, *Up Against the Fourth Wall*, 159; Plunka, *Jean-Claude van Itallie*, 107.
84 Blumenthal, *Joseph Chaikin*, 120.
85 Chaikin, *The Presence of the Actor*, 101.
86 Plunka, *Jean-Claude van Itallie*, 108.
87 See van Itallie, *The Serpent*, 32.
88 Ibid., 33.
89 Ibid.
90 Ibid., 35.
91 Blumenthal, *Joseph Chaikin*, 126; van Itallie, *The Serpent*, 36.
92 Van Itallie, *The Serpent*, 38.
93 Ibid., 49; Van Itallie, 'Should the Artist Be Political in His Art?'
94 Lahr, *Up Against the Fourth Wall*, 160.
95 Jean-Claude van Itallie, 'From the Playwright', *The Serpent*, in *America Hurrah and Other Plays* (New York: Grove Press, 2001), 6.
96 Proudfitt, 'Shared Space and Shared Pages', 166.
97 See, for example, the description of the apple-eating in Blumenthal, *Joseph Chaikin*, 116–17.
98 Plunka, *Jean-Claude van Itallie*, 114.

99 Blumenthal, *Joseph Chaikin*, 126.
100 Chaikin, *The Presence of the Actor*, 106–7.
101 Pasolli, *A Book on the Open Theater*, 121.
102 Blumenthal, *Joseph Chaikin*, 147.
103 Van Itallie, 'From the Playwright', 7.
104 Van Itallie, 'A Letter', 12.
105 Walter Kerr, 'Cain-Abel Puzzle at Open Theater Rooted in Genesis', *New York Times*, 9 February 1969.
106 Martin Duberman, 'Theater '69', *Partisan Review* 36 (3) (1969): 499.
107 Van Itallie, 'Playwright and the Ensemble', 6.
108 Van Itallie, 'Playwright alone (how to organize a play)', transcript of a lecture delivered at the University of Connecticut at Storrs, March 1969, Jean-Claude van Itallie Papers, Kent State University, 5.
109 Ibid., 6.

Documents

1 Herbert Blau, *The Impossible Theater, a Manifesto* (New York: Collier Books, 1967), 3–4.
2 Ed Bullins, 'The So-Called Western Avant-Garde Drama', *Liberator* (December 1967); reprinted in *Black Expression*, ed. Addison Gayle Jr (New York: Weybright and Talley, 1969).
3 D. H. Melhem, 'Revolution: The Constancy of Change: An Interview with Amiri Baraka', *Black American Literature Forum* 16 (3) (1982): 95, doi:10.2307/2904344.
4 Blau, *Impossible Theater*, 11.
5 Henrik Eger, 'The Other Brick Road: Robert Patrick reflects on 50 years of Off-Off-Broadway and gay theater', *Broad Street Review*, 10 August 2014, http://www.broadstreetreview.com/theater/robert-patrick-reflects-on–50-years-of-off-off-broadway-and-gay-theater# (accessed 27 July 2017).
6 Michael Nolan, 'R. G. Davis Interview by missionlocal', UC Berkley School of Journalism Mission Local, YouTube, November 2013, https://www.youtube.com/watch?v=2EkGM51gRIg (accessed 27 July 2017).
7 Charles Ludlam and Gautam Dasgupta, 'Interview: Charles Ludlam', *Performing Arts Journal* 3, no. 1 (1978): 75, doi: 10.2307/3244993.

8   Larry Neal, 'The Black Arts Movement', *The Drama Review/TDR* 12 (4) (1968): 1–2, doi: 10.2307/1144377.
9   Kimberly W. Benston, 'Amiri Baraka: An Interview', *Boundary 2* 6 (2) (1978): 316, doi:10.2307/302321
10 Blau, *Impossible Theater*, 19.
11 Ludlam and Dasgupta, 'Interview: Charles Ludlam', 78–9.
12 Marvin X, 'Interview with Ed Bullins', *ChickenBones: A Journal*, 13 November 2006, http://www.nathanielturner.com/interviewwithedbullinsbymarvinx.htm (accessed 27 July 2017).
13 Blau, *Impossible Theater*, 8–9.
14 Bev Ostroska, 'Interview with Ellen Stewart of La Mama Experimental Theatre Club, December 9, 1989', *Journal of Dramatic Theory and Criticism* 6 (1) (Fall 1991): 105.
15 Dan Isaac and Brooks Riley, 'Charles Ludlam/Norma Desmond/Laurette Bedlam: An Interview', *The Drama Review/TDR* 13 (1) (1968): 116, doi: 10.2307/1144442.
16 Julian Beck, *The Life of the Theatre: The Relation of the Artist to the Struggle of the People* (San Francisco: City Lights, 1974), 45.
17 Nolan, 'R. G. Davis Interview by missionlocal'.
18 Judith Malina, *The Diaries of Judith Malina 1947–1957* (New York: Grove Press, 1984), 169.
19 Margo Jones, *Theatre-in-the-Round* (McGraw-Hill, 1951), 3–4.
20 Blau, *Impossible Theater*, 13.
21 Ludlam and Dasgupta, 'Interview: Charles Ludlam', 70.
22 William Flanagan, 'Edward Albee, The Art of Theater No. 4', *The Paris Review* 39 (Fall 1966), https://www.theparisreview.org/interviews/4350/edward-albee-the-art-of-theater-no-4-edward-albee (accessed 27 July 2017).
23 Arthur Sainer, *The New Radical Theatre Notebook* (New York: Applause, 1975), 47.
24 Ludlam and Dasgupta, 'Interview: Charles Ludlam', 69–70.
25 Beth Bagby, 'El Teatro Campesino Interviews with Luis Valdez', *The Tulane Drama Review* 11 (4) (1967): 79, doi: 10.2307/1125139.
26 Beck, *The Life of the Theatre*, 7.
27 Sainer, *The New Radical Theatre Notebook*, 61.
28 Jones, *Theatre-in-the-Round*, 7–8.
29 Ludlam and Dasgupta, 'Interview: Charles Ludlam', 73.

30 Beck, *The Life of the Theatre*, 10.
31 Lorraine Hansberry, *To Be Young, Gifted, and Black*, adapted by Robert Nemiroff (Caedmon, 1971), 118–20.
32 David Savran, *In Their Own Words: Contemporary American Playwrights* (New York: Theatre Communications Group, 1992), 54.
33 Malina, *Diaries*, 192.
34 Flanagan, 'Edward Albee'.
35 Ludlam and Dasgupta, 'Interview: Charles Ludlam', 80.
36 Jerry Tallmer, 'From the Archives . . . The Voice Reviews Edward Albee's The Zoo Story and Samuel Beckett's Krapp's Last Tape, 1960', *Village Voice*, 8 July 2009, https://www.villagevoice.com/2009/07/08/from-the-archives-the-voice-reviews-edward-albees-the-zoo-story-and-samuel-becketts-krapps-last-tape–1960/ (accessed 27 July 2017).
37 LeRoi Jones, 'To Survive "The Reign of Beasts"', *New York Times*, 16 November 1969, section 2, https://timesmachine.nytimes.com/timesmachine/1969/11/16/issue.html (accessed 27 July 2017).
38 Adrienne Kennedy, *People Who Led to My Plays* (New York: Theatre Communications Group, 1996), 125.

BIBLIOGRAPHY

Critical and historical sources on the United States in the 1960s

Allyn, David. *Make Love Not War: The Sexual Revolution: An Unfettered History*. New York: Little, Brown and Company, 2000.

Andrew, John A. *The Other Side of the Sixties: Young Americans for Freedom and the Rise of Conservative Politics*. New Brunswick, NJ: Rutgers University Press, 1997.

Baldwin, James. *The Fire Next Time*. New York: Dial Press, 1963.

Belgrad, Daniel. *The Culture of Spontaneity: Improvisation and the Arts in Postwar America*. Chicago: University of Chicago Press, 1998.

Bodroghkozy, Aniko. *Groove Tube: Sixties Television and the Youth Rebellion*. Durham, NC: Duke University Press, 2001.

Branch, Taylor. *Pillar of Fire: America in the King Years, 1963–1965*. New York: Simon & Schuster, 1998.

Brown, Elaine. *A Taste of Power: A Black Woman's Story*. New York: Pantheon Books, 1992.

Caute, David. *The Year of the Barricades: A Journey Through 1968*. New York: Harper & Row, 1988.

D'Emilio, John. *Sexual Politics, Sexual Communities: The Making of a Homosexual Minority in the United States, 1940–1970*. Chicago: University of Chicago Press, 1998.

Dickstein, Morris. *Gates of Eden: American Culture in the Sixties*. New York: Basic Books, 1977.

Duberman, Martin. *Stonewall*. New York: Plume, 1994.

Echols, Alice. *Daring to be Bad: Radical Feminism in America, 1967–1975*. Minneapolis: University of Minnesota Press, 1989.

Echols, Alice. *Shaky Ground: The '60s and Its Aftershocks*. New York: Columbia University Press, 2002.

Frank, Thomas. *The Conquest of Cool: Business Culture, Counterculture and the Rise of Hip Consumerism*. Chicago: University of Chicago Press, 1997.

Friedan, Betty. *The Feminine Mystique*. New York: Dell, 1963.

Gitlin, Todd. *The Whole World is Watching: Mass Media in the Making and Unmaking of the New Left.* Berkeley, CA: University of California Press, 1980.
Gitlin, Todd. *The Sixties: Years of Hope, Days of Rage.* New York: Bantam Books, 1987.
Hallin, Daniel C. *The 'Uncensored War': The Media and Vietnam.* New York: Oxford University Press, 1986.
Harrington, Michael. *The Other America: Poverty in the United States.* New York: Macmillan, 1969.
Harrison, Cynthia. *On Account of Sex: The Politics of Women's Issues, 1945–1968.* Berkeley: University of California Press, 1988.
Hold, Judith. *Rebirth of Feminism.* New York: Quadrangle Books, 1971.
Isserman, Maurice, and Michael Kazin. *America Divided: The Civil War of the 1960s.* New York: Oxford University Press, 2000.
Jackson, Kenneth T. *Crabgrass Frontier: The Suburbanization of the United States.* New York: Oxford University Press, 1985.
Jameson, Fredric. *Postmodernism, or, The Cultural Logic of Late Capitalism.* Durham, NC: Duke University Press, 1991.
Joseph, Peniel E. *Waiting 'Til The Midnight Hour: A Narrative History of Black Power in America.* New York: Holt, 2007.
Joseph, Peniel E., ed. *The Black Power Movement: Rethinking the Civil Rights–Black Power Era.* New York: Routledge, 2006.
Karnow, Stanley. *Vietnam: A History.* New York: Viking Press, 1983.
Katsiaficas, George. *The Imagination of the New Left: A Global Analysis of 1968.* Boston: South End Press, 1987.
Klatch, Rebecca E. *A Generation Divided: The New Left, the New Right, and the 1960s.* Berkeley: University of California Press, 1999.
Marable, Manning. *Race, Reform and Rebellion: The Second Reconstruction in Black America, 1945–1982.* Jackson: University Press of Mississippi, 1984.
Mark, Charles Christopher. *Reluctant Bureaucrats: The Struggle to Establish the National Endowment for the Arts.* Dubuque, IA: Kendall/Hunt, 1991.
Miller, Timothy. *The 60s Communes: Hippies and Beyond.* Syracuse: Syracuse University Press, 1999.
O'Neill, William L. *Coming Apart: An Informal History of America in the 1960s.* Chicago: Quadrangle Books, 1971.
Perry, Paul. *On the Bus: The Complete Guide to the Legendary Trip of Ken Kesey and the Merry Pranksters and the Birth of the Counterculture.* New York: Thunder's Mouth Press, 1990.
Podhoretz, Norman. *Why We Were in Vietnam.* New York: Simon & Schuster, 1982.
Sale, Kirkpatrick, and Eric Foner. *The Green Revolution: The American Environmental Movement, 1962–1992.* New York: Hill & Wang, 1993.

Smethurst, James Edward. *The Black Arts Movement: Literary Nationalism in the 1960s and 1970s*. Chapel Hill: University of North Carolina Press, 2005.
Spigel, Lynn, and Michael Curtin, eds. *The Revolution Wasn't Televised: Sixties Television and Social Conflict*. New York: Routledge, 1997.
Steigerwald, David. *The Sixties and the End of Modern America*. New York: St Martin's Press, 1995.
Stephens, Julie. *Anti-Disciplinary Protest: Sixties Radicalism and Postmodernism*. Cambridge: Cambridge University Press, 1998.
Stevens, Jay. *Storming Heaven: LSD and the American Dream*. New York: Atlantic Monthly Press, 1987.
Watson, Steven. *The Birth of the Beat Generation: Visionaries, Rebels and Hipsters, 1944–1960*. New York: Pantheon Books, 1995.
Weiss, Jessica. *To Have and to Hold: Marriage, the Baby Boom, and Social Change*. Chicago: University of Chicago Press, 2000.
Whalen, Jack, and Richard Flacks. *Beyond the Barricades: The Sixties Generation Grows Up*. Philadelphia: Temple University Press, 1989.
Yablonsky, Lewis. *The Hippie Trip*. New York: Pegasus, 1968.

Critical and historical sources on US theatre in the 1960s

Atkinson, Brooks. *Broadway*, rev. edn. New York: Macmillan, 1974.
Banes, Sally. *Greenwich Village 1963: Avant-garde Performance and the Effervescent Body*. Durham, NC: Duke University Press, 1993.
Beck, Julian. *Life of the Theatre: The Relation of the Artist to the Struggle of the People*. New York: Limelight Editions, 1972.
Bigsby, C. W. E. *A Critical Introduction to Twentieth-Century American Drama, Vol. 3. Beyond Broadway*. Cambridge: Cambridge University Press, 1985.
Blau, Herbert. *The Impossible Theater: A Manifesto*. New York: Collier Books, 1967.
Blumenthal, Eileen. *Joseph Chaikin: Exploring at the Boundaries of Theatre*. New York: Cambridge University Press, 1984.
Bottoms, Stephen J. *Playing Underground: A Critical History of the 1960s Off-Off-Broadway Movement*. Ann Arbor: University of Michigan Press, 2004.
Brecht, Stefan. *The Bread and Puppet Theatre*. Two vols. London: Methuen, 1988.
Brecht, Stefan. *Queer Theatre*. London: Methuen Drama, 1982
Broyles-González, Yolanda. *El Teatro Campesino: Theater in the Chicano Movement*. Austin: University of Texas Press, 1994.

Brustein, Richard. *The Third Theatre*. New York: Alfred A. Knopf, 1969.
Chaikin, Joseph. *The Presence of the Actor*. New York: Theatre Communications Group, 1991.
Fichandler, Zelda. 'Theatres or Institutions?', *Theatre 3* (September 1970): 110.
Grant, Mark N. *The Rise and Fall of the Broadway Musical*. Boston: Northeastern Press, 2004.
Guthrie, Tyrone. *A New Theatre*. New York: McGraw-Hill, 1964.
Harbin, Billy J., Kim Marra and Robert A. Schanke, eds. *The Gay and Lesbian Theatrical Legacy*. Ann Arbor: University of Michigan Press, 2007.
Harding, James M., and Cindy Rosenthal, eds. *Restaging the Sixties: Radical Theaters and Their Legacies*. Ann Arbor: University of Michigan Press, 2006.
Harding, James M., and Cindy Rosenthal, eds. *The Sixties, Center Stage: Mainstream and Popular Performances in a Turbulent Decade*. Ann Arbor: University of Michigan Press, 2017.
Hill, Errol G., and James V. Hatch. *A History of African American Theatre*. Cambridge, MA: Cambridge University Press, 2003.
Huerta, Jorge A. *Chicano Theater: Themes and Forms*. Tempe, AZ: Bilingual Press, 1981.
Jones, Margo. *Theatre-in-the-Round*. New York: Rinehart, 1951.
Kanellos, Nicolás, and Jorge A. Huerta. *Nuevos Pasos: Chicano and Puerto Rican Drama*. Los Angeles: Players Press, 1989.
King, Woodie, Jr. *Black Theater: The Making of a Movement*. San Francisco: California Newsreel, 1978.
Kirby, Michael. 'The New Theatre', *Tulane Drama Review* 10 (2) (1965): 23–43.
Lee, Esther Kim. *A History of Asian American Theatre*. Cambridge: Cambridge University Press, 2006.
Little, Stuart W. *Off-Broadway: The Prophetic Theatre*. New York: Coward, McCann, and Geoghegan, 1972.
Malina, Judith. *The Enormous Despair*. New York: Random House, 1972.
Napoleon, Davi. *Chelsea on the Edge: The Adventures of an American Theater*. Ames: Iowa State University Press, 1991.
Novick, Julius. *Beyond Broadway: The Quest for Permanent Theatres*. New York: Hill and Wang, 1968.
Pasolli, Robert. *A Book on the Open Theatre*. New York: Bobbs-Merrill, 1970.
Payne-Carter, David. *Gower Champion: Dance and the American Musical Theatre*, ed. Brooks McNamara and Steve Nelson. Westport, CT: Greenwood Press, 1999.
Poggi, Jack. *Theater in America: The Impact of Economic Forces, 1870–1967*. Ithaca, NY: Cornell University Press, 1968.

Poland, Albert, and Bruce Mailman. *The Off Off Broadway Book: The Plays, People, Theatre*. New York: The Bobbs-Merrill Company, Inc., 1972.
Prince, Harold. *Contradictions: Notes on Twenty-Six Years in the Theatre*. New York: Dodd, Mead, 1974.
Rosenthal, Cindy. *Ellen Stewart Presents: Fifty Years of La MaMa Experimental Theatre*. Ann Arbor: University of Michigan, 2017.
Sainer, Arthur. *The New Radical Theatre Notebook*. New York: Applause, 1975.
Samuels, Steven, ed. *Ridiculous Theatre: Scourge of Human Folly: The Essays and Opinions of Charles Ludlam*. New York: Theatre Communications Group, 1992.
Savran, David. *In Their Own Words: Contemporary American Playwrights*. New York: Theatre Communications Group, 1992.
Schechner, Richard. *Environmental Theater*. New York: Applause, 1994.
Sell, Mike. *Avant-Garde Performance and the Limits of Criticism*. Ann Arbor: University of Michigan, 2005.
Sell, Mike. 'The Drama of the Black Arts Movement', in David Krasner (ed.), *A Companion to Twentieth-Century American Drama*. Malden, MA: Blackwell Publishing, 2005.
Stone, Wendell C. *Caffe Cino: The Birthplace of Off-Off-Broadway*. Carbondale, IL: Southern Illinois University Press, 2005.
Thomas, Lundeana Marie. *Barbara Ann Teer and the National Black Theatre: Transformational Forces in Harlem*. New York: Garland Publishing, 1997.
Tytell, John. *The Living Theatre: Art, Exile, and Outrage*. New York: Grove Press, 1995.
Williams, Mance. *Black Theatre in the 1960s and 1970s: A Historical-Critical Analysis of the Movement*. Westport, CN: Greenwood Press, 1985.
Young, Harvey, ed. *The Cambridge Companion to African American Theatre*. Cambridge: Cambridge University Press, 2013.
Zeigler, Joseph Wesley. *Regional Theatre: The Revolutionary Stage*. Minneapolis: University of Minnesota Press, 1973.

The playwrights

Edward Albee

Plays

Albee, Edward. *The American Dream. The Collected Plays of Edward Albee, Volume 1: 1958–1965*. New York: Overlook Press, 2008.

Albee, Edward. *The Ballad of the Sad Café. The Collected Plays of Edward Albee, Volume 1: 1958–1965*. New York: Overlook Press, 2008.
Albee, Edward. *Box and Quotations from Chairman Mao Tse-Tung. The Collected Plays of Edward Albee, Volume 2: 1965–1977*. New York: Overlook Press, 2008.
Albee, Edward. *The Death of Bessie Smith. The Collected Plays of Edward Albee, Volume 1: 1958–1965*. New York: Overlook Press, 2008.
Albee, Edward. *A Delicate Balance. The Collected Plays of Edward Albee, Volume 2: 1965–1977*. New York: Overlook Press, 2008.
Albee, Edward. *Everything in the Garden. The Collected Plays of Edward Albee, Volume 2: 1965–1977*. New York: Overlook Press, 2008.
Albee, Edward. *Fam and Yam. The American Dream, The Death of Bessie Smith, Fam and Yam: Three Plays by Edward Albee*. New York: Dramatists Play Service, 1989.
Albee, Edward. *Malcolm. The Collected Plays of Edward Albee, Volume 1: 1958–1965*. New York: Overlook Press, 2008.
Albee, Edward. *The Sandbox. The Collected Plays of Edward Albee, Volume 1: 1958–1965*. New York: Overlook Press, 2008.
Albee, Edward. *Tiny Alice. The Collected Plays of Edward Albee, Volume 1: 1958–1965*. New York: Overlook Press, 2008.
Albee, Edward. *Who's Afraid of Virginia Woolf? The Collected Plays of Edward Albee, Volume 1: 1958–1965*. New York: Overlook Press, 2008.

Recommended sources

Albee, Edward. *Stretching My Mind*. New York: Carroll & Graf Publishers, 2005.
Albee, Edward, and Philip C. Kolin. *Conversations with Edward Albee*. Jackson: University Press of Mississippi, 1988.
Bottoms, Stephen J., ed. *The Cambridge Companion to Edward Albee*. Cambridge: Cambridge University Press, 2005.
Gussow, Mel. *Edward Albee: A Singular Journey*. New York: Simon & Schuster, 1999.
Mann, Bruce, ed. *Edward Albee: A Casebook*. New York: Routledge, 2003.
Roudané, Matthew C. *Understanding Edward Albee*. Columbia: University of South Carolina Press, 1987.
Solomon, Rakesh H. *Albee in Performance*. Bloomington: Indiana University Press, 2010.
Zinman, Toby. *Edward Albee*. Ann Arbor: University of Michigan Press, 2008.

Amiri Baraka

Plays

Baraka, Amiri. *Arm Yrself or Harm Yrself*. Newark: Jihad, 1967.

Baraka, Amiri. *A Black Mass*. In *Four Black Revolutionary Plays: All Praises to the Black Man*, 17–39. Indianapolis: Bobbs-Merrill, 1969.

Baraka, Amiri. *Black Power Chant*. Black Drama – 1850 to Present, *North American Theatre Online*, Alexander Street (2005), accessed 14 March 2017.

Baraka, Amiri. *Board of Education*. Black Drama – 1850 to Present, *North American Theatre Online*, Alexander Street (2005), accessed 14 March 2017.

Baraka, Amiri. *Death of Malcolm X*. Black Drama – 1850 to Present, *North American Theatre Online*, Alexander Street (2005), accessed 14 March 2017.

Baraka, Amiri. *Experimental Death Unit #1*. In *Four Black Revolutionary Plays: All Praises to the Black Man*, 1–15. Indianapolis: Bobbs-Merrill, 1969.

Baraka, Amiri. *Great Goodness of Life: A Coon Show*. In *Four Black Revolutionary Plays: All Praises to the Black Man*, 41–63. Indianapolis: Bobbs-Merrill, 1969.

Baraka, Amiri [LeRoi Jones]. *Home on the Range*. In *A Sourcebook of African-American Performance: Plays, People, Movements*, edited by Annemarie Bean, 32–40. London: Routledge, 1999, originally published in 1968.

Baraka, Imamu Amiri. *J-E-L-L-O*. Chicago: Third World Press, 1970.

Baraka, Amiri. *Junkies Are Full of (Shh. . .)*. Black Drama – 1850 to Present, *North American Theatre Online*, Alexander Street (2005), accessed 14 March 2017.

Baraka, Amiri. *Madheart: (A Morality Play)*. In *Four Black Revolutionary Plays: All Praises to the Black Man*, 65–87. Indianapolis: Bobbs-Merrill, 1969, originally published in 1968.

Baraka, Amiri [LeRoi Jones]. *Police*. In *A Sourcebook of African-American Performance: Plays, People, Movements*, edited by Annemarie Bean, 40–45. London: Routledge, 1999, originally published in 1968.

Baraka, Amiri. *A Recent Killing*. Black Drama – 1850 to Present, *North American Theatre Online*, Alexander Street (2005), accessed 1 October 2013 [no longer extant in database].

Baraka, Amiri. *Rockgroup*. The Cricket: Black Music in America (December 1969): 41–43.

Baraka, Amiri. *The Sidney Poet Heroical*. Black Drama – 1850 to Present, *North American Theatre Online*, Alexander Street (2005), accessed 1 October 2013.

Baraka, Amiri [LeRoi Jones]. *Slave Ship*. In *The Motion of History and Other Plays*, 129–50. New York: William Morrow, 1978.

Jones, LeRoi. *Dutchman*. In *Dutchman and The Slave: Two Plays by LeRoi Jones*, 1–38. New York: Morrow-Quill, 1964.

Jones, LeRoi. *The Eighth Ditch (Is Drama)*. In *The System of Dante's Hell*, 79–91. New York: Grove, 1965, originally published in 1961.

Jones, LeRoi. *The Slave*. In *Dutchman and The Slave: Two Plays by LeRoi Jones*, 39–88. New York: Morrow-Quill, 1964.

Jones, LeRoi. *The Baptism*. In *The Baptism & The Toilet*, 7–32. New York: Grove, 1967.

Jones, LeRoi. *The Toilet*. In *The Baptism & the Toilet*, 33–62. New York: Grove, 1967.

Poetry

Baraka, Imamu Amiri. *Black Magic*. New York: Bobbs-Merrill Co., 1969.

Baraka, Imamu Amiri. *It's Nation Time*. Philadelphia: Third World Press, 1970.

Jones, LeRoi. *Preface to a Twenty Volume Suicide Note*. New York: Totem, 1961.

Jones, LeRoi. *The Dead Lecturer: Poems*. New York: Grove, 1964.

Fiction

Baraka, Amiri [LeRoi Jones]. *The System of Dante's Hell*. New York: Evergreen/Grove, 1966.

Non-fiction

Baraka, Amiri. *The Autobiography of LeRoi Jones*. Chicago: Lawrence Hill Books, 1997.

Baraka, Imamu Amiri. *Raise Race Rays Raze: Essays Since 1965*. New York: Random House, 1971.

Jones, LeRoi. *Blues People*. New York: William Morrow & Company, 1963.

Jones, LeRoi [Amiri Baraka]. *Home: Social Essays*. New York: William Morrow & Company, 1966.

Jones, LeRoi. *Black Music*. New York: Da Capo Press, 1968.

Recommended sources

Benston, Kimberly W. *Baraka: The Renegade and the Mask*. New Haven: Yale University Press, 1976.
Benston, Kimberly W., ed. *Imamu Amiri Baraka (LeRoi Jones): A Collection of Critical Essays*. Englewood Cliffs, NJ: Prentice-Hall, 1978, originally published in 1966.
Elam, Harry J., Jr. *Taking It to the Streets: The Social Protest Theater of Luis Valdez and Amiri Baraka*. Ann Arbor: University of Michigan Press, 1997.
Hudson, Theodore R. *From LeRoi Jones to Amiri Baraka: The Literary Works*. Durham, NC: Duke University Press, 1973.
In Motion: Amiri Baraka. [Film] Dir. St Clair Bourne. Chicago: Facets Video, 1998. Videocassette (VHS), 60 min.
Jones, Hettie. *How I became Hettie Jones*. New York: E. P. Dutton, 1990.
Lacey, Henry C. *To Raise, Destroy, and Create: The Poetry, Drama, and Fiction of Imamu Amiri Baraka (LeRoi Jones)*. Troy, NY: Whitston, 1981.
Reilly, Charlie, ed. *Conversations with Amiri Baraka*. Jackson: University Press of Mississippi, 1994, originally published in 1970.
Sollors, Werner. *Amiri Baraka/LeRoi Jones: The Quest for a 'Populist Modernism'*. New York: Columbia University Press, 1978.
Watts, Jerry Gafio. *Amiri Baraka: The Politics and Art of a Black Intellectual*. New York: New York University Press, 2001.

Adrienne Kennedy

Plays

Kennedy, Adrienne. *Funnyhouse of a Negro*. *The Adrienne Kennedy Reader*. Minneapolis: University of Minnesota Press, 2001.
Kennedy, Adrienne. *The Owl Answers*. *The Adrienne Kennedy Reader*. Minneapolis: University of Minnesota Press, 2001.
Kennedy, Adrienne. *A Lesson in Dead Language*. *The Adrienne Kennedy Reader*. Minneapolis: University of Minnesota Press, 2001.
Kennedy, Adrienne. *A Rat's Mass*. *The Adrienne Kennedy Reader*. Minneapolis: University of Minnesota Press, 2001.
Kennedy, Adrienne. *Sun*. *The Adrienne Kennedy Reader*. Minneapolis: University of Minnesota Press, 2001.
Lennon, John, Adrienne Kennedy and Victor Spinetti. *The Lennon Play: In His Own Write*. New York: Simon & Schuster, 1965.

Prose

Kennedy, Adrienne. 'Because of the King of France.' In *The Adrienne Kennedy Reader*. Minneapolis: University of Minnesota Press, 2001.

Kennedy, Adrienne. *Deadly Triplets: A Theatre Mystery*. Minneapolis: University of Minnesota Press, 1990.

Kennedy, Adrienne. *People Who Led to My Plays*. New York: Theatre Communications Group, 1996.

Recommended sources

Binder, Wolfgang, and Adrienne Kennedy, 'A MELUS Interview: Adrienne Kennedy', *MELUS* 12 (3) (Fall 1985).

Brown, E. Barnsley. 'Passed Over: The Tragic Mulatta and (Dis)Integration of Identity in Adrienne Kennedy's Plays', *African American Review* 35 (2) (2001): 281–95. doi:10.2307/2903258.

Bryant-Jackson, Paul, and Lois Overbeck. *Intersecting Boundaries: The Theatre of Adrienne Kennedy*. Minneapolis: University of Minnesota Press, 1992.

Curb, Rosemary K. 'Fragmented Selves in Adrienne Kennedy's "Funnyhouse of a Negro" and "The Owl Answers"', *Theatre Journal* 32 (2) (1980): 180–95. doi:10.2307/3207111.

Diamond, Elin. 'Rethinking Identification: Kennedy, Freud, Brecht', *The Kenyon Review* 15 (2) (1993): 86–99. http://www.jstor.org/stable/4336842.

Effiong, Philip U. *In Search of a Model for African-American Drama: A Study of Selected Plays by Lorraine Hansberry, Amiri Baraka, and Ntozake Shange*. Lanham, MD; Plymouth: University Press of America, 2000.

Harrison, Paul Carter, Edward Albee, Robert Brustein, Ishmael Reed, Evan Yionoulis, Marcus Stern, June Pyskacek, Evangeline Morphos, Estelle Parsons and Gerald Freedman. 'Personal Perspectives on Adrienne Kennedy', *Modern Drama* 55 (1) (Spring 2012).

Kolin, Philip C. *Understanding Adrienne Kennedy*. Columbia: University of South Carolina Press, 2005.

Posnock, Ross. *Color and Culture: Black Writers and the Making of the Modern Intellectual*. Cambridge, MA: Harvard University Press, 1998.

Thompson, Deborah. 'The Fiction of Postmodern Autobiography: Adrienne Kennedy's People Who Led to My Plays and Deadly Triplets', *MELUS* 22 (4) (1997): 61–76. doi:10.2307/467989.

Jean-Claude van Itallie

Plays

Van Itallie, Jean-Claude. *Almost Like Being. War and Four Other Plays*. New York: Dramatists Play Service, 1967.
Van Itallie, Jean-Claude. *America Hurrah. America Hurrah and Other Plays*. New York: Grove Press, 2001.
Van Itallie, Jean-Claude. *The Hunter and the Bird. War and Four Other Plays*. New York: Dramatists Play Service, 1967.
Van Itallie, Jean-Claude. *I'm Really Here. War and Four Other Plays*. New York: Dramatists Play Service, 1967.
Van Itallie, Jean-Claude. *The Serpent. America Hurrah and Other Plays*. New York: Grove Press, 2001.
Van Itallie, Jean-Claude. *War. America Hurrah and Other Plays*. New York: Grove Press, 2001.
Van Itallie, Jean-Claude. *Where Is the Queen? War and Four Other Plays*. New York: Dramatists Play Service, 1967.

Recommended sources

Blumenthal, Eileen. *Joseph Chaikin: Exploring at the Boundaries of Theater*. New York: Cambridge University Press, 1984.
Gaisner, Rhea. 'Jean-Claude van Itallie: Playwright of the Ensemble: Open Theater', *The Serif* 9 (4) (Winter 1971).
Pasolli, Robert. *A Book on the Open Theater*. New York: Bobbs-Merrill, 1970.
Plunka, Gene. *Jean-Claude van Itallie and the Off-Broadway Theatre*. Newark: University of Delaware Press, 1999.
Proudfitt, Scott. 'Shared Space and Shared Pages: Collective Creation for Edward Albee and the Playwrights of the Open Theater'. In Kathryn Mederos Syssoyeva and Scott Proudfitt (eds), *A History of Collective Creation*. New York: Palgrave-Macmillan, 2014.
Schmidt, Kerstin. *The Theater of Transformation: Postmodernism in American Drama*. Amsterdam: Editions Rodopi, 2005.
Van Itallie, Jean-Claude. 'Playwright at Work: Off Off-Broadway', *The Tulane Drama Review* 10 (4) (1966): 154–8. doi: 10.2307/1125217.

Web resources (compiled by Mike Vanden Heuvel)

General

Doollee Database of Modern Playwrights (post-1956): http://www.doollee.com/
Theatre Communications Group: http://www.tcg.org/ (Their website is American Theatre: http://www.americantheatre.org/)
American Theatre Web: http://www.americantheaterweb.com
Theatre History on the Web: http://www.videoccasions-nw.com/history/jack.html

New York theatre

The Broadway League: https://www.broadwayleague.com/
The Internet Broadway Database: http://www.ibdb.com/
The Playbill New York City Theatre Database: http://www.playbillvault.com/index.html
The Broadway Database: Off-Off Broadway: http://www.broadwayworld.com/off-off-broadway/
The Off Off Broadway Review: http://www.oobr.com/

Regional/resident/university theatre

American Alliance for Theatre and Education: http://www.aate.com/
American Association of Community Theatre: http://www.aact.org/
University/Resident Theatre Association: http://urta.com/

INDEX

Aaron, Joyce 204
Abbott, George 230, 234
absurdism 41–2, 49, 78, 94, 99, 104–6, 186
Achebe, Chinua 153
Actors' Equity 43, 45, 62, 66, 213
Actors Studio 129, 164, 260
Actor's Workshop 43–4, 64–5, 243, 250
AfriCOBRA 7
After the Fall 37, 43, 236
AIDS crisis 51
Ailey, Albert 39
Albee, Edward 42, 46, 71, 81, 92–121, 132, 158, 160, 162–166, 182, 213, 216, 224, 233, 235, 236, 238, 253, 256, 259
  American Dream, The 99–101, 103–4
  Ballad of the Sad Café, The 42, 118, 235
  Broadway, response to 94, 105, 120, 253
  Delicate Balance, A 42, 98, 101, 106, 110, 114–18, 238, 239
  and European absurdism 94, 98
  Playwrights Unit 46
  Sandbox, The 99–100
  and Schneider, Alan 99
  and Theatre of the Absurd 42, 104–5
  Tiny Alice 112–14, 236
  Who's Afraid of Virginia Woolf? 42, 71, 95, 105–12, 115, 117, 119, 233, 234, 258–9
  Zoo Story, The 93–9, 104, 110, 117, 120, 121, 216, 224, 258–9
Alberghetti, Anna Maria 233
Albertson, Jack 237
Alda, Alan 39
Aldredge, Theoni V. 229
Aldredge, Tom 220
Alexander, Jane 226, 241
Alexander, Ross 60, 61
Alfred, William 225
Algarín, Miguel 90
Allen, Billie 164, 176, 177
Allen, Seth 220
Allen, Woody 40
Allers, Franz 232
Alley Theater 64, 65
Almost Like Being 182, 187, 190–2
America Hurrah 181, 193–204, 205
American Dream, The 99–101, 103–4
American Independent Party 29
American National Theater and Academy (ANTA) 37, 43
American Place Theater 69
American Psychiatric Association 12
Anderson, Chester 9

Anderson, Eddie 'Rochester' 144–5
Andrews, Julie 33
Angelou, Maya 46
Anger, Kenneth 23
Animals, The 24
Annenberg, Walter 20
Anouilh, Jean 231, 232
Apollinaire, Guillaume 57
Arcade, Penny 83
Arden, John 42, 225
Ardolino, Emile 223
Arenal, Julie 35
Arena Stage 64, 65
Arkin, Alan 223, 227, 228, 234
Armstrong, Louis 33
Armstrong, Will Steven 233
Aronson, Boris 35, 38, 227, 228, 239, 241
Artaud, Antonin 44, 75, 84, 138, 183, 186, 199–200, 250, 253
Ashberry, John 46
Ashcroft, Peggy 49
Ashe, Arthur 78
Ashley, Elizabeth 233
Asian American Political Alliance 85
Asian American theatre 84–7
Association of Producing Arts (APA) 49–50, 217, 219, 224
Atkinson, Brooks 36, 48, 50, 216
Atkinson, Ti-Grace 11
Atlantic Records 24
At the Foot of the Mountain 79
Auberjonois, René 242
AUDELCO Black theatre Excellence Award 73
Auden, W.H. 74
avant-garde 22, 26, 45, 243–4, 246, 253–4, 258
Ayler, Albert 137, 149

Babbs, Ken 26
baby boom 3, 15, 22
Bacall, Lauren 228, 242
Bacharach, Burt 227
Baez, Joan 23
Bailey, Pearl 34
Baker, Joan 58
Balcony, The 48–9, 215, 216
Baldwin, James 6, 39, 130, 164, 184
Ballard, Lucinda 233
Ball, William 217
Balls 61
Balsam, Martin 240
Bancroft, Anne 43, 230
Bandit, Sierra 84
Baraka, Amina (Sylvia Robinson) 7, 124, 125, 139
Baraka, Amiri (LeRoi Jones) 30, 40, 46, 47, 67, 68, 79, 98, 123–50, 158, 172, 178, 244, 247, 259
Baptism, The 128, 135
Beat period 127
Black Arts Repertory Theatre/School 68, 136–9, 144
Black Mass, A 139–40
black nationalism 137, 247, 259
Bullins, Ed, influence on 68
Cohen, Hetti Roberta 127, 133–4
Dutchman 47, 68, 119, 125, 132–7, 143–4, 149, 165, 172, 218
Experimental Death Unit #1 138–9
Great Goodness of Life: A Coon Show 140–2
Hansberry, Angela 40
homosexuality 128, 130, 132, 145
J-E-L-L-O 144–5
later works 148–50

Living Theatre 46
Madheart 142–4
Recent Killing, A 131, 135
'Revolutionary Theatre, The' 67, 130, 132, 137
Rockgroup 145
Spirit House 7, 74, 141, 146, 149, 244
Slave Ship 145–8, 223
Sidney Poet Heroical, The 145
Toilet, The 129
writing, periods of 125
Baraka, Kimako 140, 141
Baraka, Ras 149
Barer, Marshall 49
Barnes, Clive 35, 38, 41, 94, 148, 177
Barr, Richard 46, 119, 164, 182, 224, 234
Barrios, Olga 159
Barry, Paul 39
Bart, Lionel 234
Bay, Howard 231, 238
Beach Boys, The 24
Bean, Annemarie 77
Beard, James 17
Beast Story, A 159, 166, 170–1, 179
Beatles, The 19, 23, 25, 33, 173
Beaton, Cecil 231, 242
Beatty, Warren 21–2
Beck, Julian 74–6, 120, 186, 215, 218, 222, 255, 257
Beckett, Samuel 41, 55, 61, 77, 93, 94, 98, 99, 100, 104, 119, 154, 199, 216, 217, 218, 258
Bedford, Brian 219, 227, 228
Behan, Brendan 217, 224, 231
Belafonte, Harry 18, 78, 145
Belgrad, Daniel 52
Belgrave, Cynthia 40, 46
Benjamin, Harry 12
Benny, Jack 144–5

Benston, Kimberly 143, 150
Benton, Robert 21
Bergman, Ingmar 21
Berkeley, Busby 54
Bernard, Kenneth 83, 84
Bernhardt, Melvin 223
Bernhardt, Sarah 253
Besoyan, Rick 224
Bigsby, C.W.E. 36, 75, 76, 110
Billington, Michael 174, 175
Billy Rose Theatre 86
Biltmore Theatre 35
Black Armed Guard 7
Black Arts Alliance 142
Black Arts Movement 2, 7, 17, 26, 40, 52, 63, 67–73, 78, 90, 132, 137, 142, 145, 158–61, 169, 172, 173, 246–7
Black Arts Repertory Theatre/ School 68, 136–9, 144
Blackburn, Clarice 220
Black Cat Tavern 13
Black Communications Project 148
Black Horizon Theatre 65
Black House 69
Black Mass, A 139–40
Black Mountain College 134
Black Orpheus 153
Black Panther Party 7–8, 18, 26, 29, 68–9, 143
Black Power 26, 69, 123, 125, 132, 136, 138, 144, 146, 149, 246–67,
Black Student Union 30, 142
Blacks: A Clown Show, The 46–7, 49, 93, 216
Black Theatre Alliance Award 70
Blaney, Darren 80, 81
Blau, Herbert 43, 44, 166, 243, 247, 248–9, 252
blues 24, 25–6, 39, 77, 132, 164, 184,

Blues for Mr Charlie 39, 164, 184
Blumenthal, Eileen 188, 206
Bock, Jerry 34, 236
Bogdanovich, Peter 21
Boleyn, Anne 167
Bolt, Robert 232, 233
Bond, Edward 86
Bond, Julian 78
Bond, Sudie 217
Bonnard, Robert 221
Bonnie and Clyde 2, 21–2
Booker T and the MGs 25
Borderlands Theater 88
Bottoms, Stephen 51, 60, 61, 62, 63, 82, 83
Bovasso, Julie 222
Boyd, Reverend Malcolm 71
Boyle, Sarah Patton 184
Boys in the Band, The 81–2, 222, 226
Bradford, Alex 40
Brakhage, Stan 22
Brando, Marlon 23, 260
Brassi, Rossano 191
Bread and Puppet Theater 60, 74
Brecht, Bertolt 35, 42–4, 74–5, 88, 186, 229, 233
Brennan, Eileen 215
Brig, The 75–6, 218
British Invasion 25
Brittan, Robert 39
Broadside Press 7
Broadway 2, 31, 32–45, 49, 50, 51, 66, 67, 85, 87, 89, 90, 93, 94, 99, 100, 105, 106, 113, 114, 116, 118, 119, 120, 121, 178, 182, 213, 226, 229–42, 249–50, 251, 255–6, 258
Brook, Peter 89, 238
Brooks, Gwendolyn 47
Brooks, Mel 40
Brooks, Richard 162

Brookes, Jacqueline 218
Brooklyn Academy of Music 148
Brown, Elaine 26
Brown, James 23, 26
Brown, Helen Gurley 8–9
Brown, H. Rap 8
Brown, James 23, 26
Brown, John Mason 42
Brown, Kenneth 75–6, 218
Brown, Rita Mae 11
Brown, Tony 71
Brown Berets 88
Browne, Roscoe Lee 39, 46, 48
Bruns, Philip 218
Brustein, Robert 37, 160, 197, 202, 204
Bryant, Hazel 40
Bryden, Ronald 42
Buckley, William F. 2
Bullins, Ed 40, 46, 47, 68–70, 98, 158, 226, 243, 248
Bureau of Labor Statistics 5
Burnett, Carol 19, 49
Burns, David 234
Burrows, Abe 232, 233
Burton, Richard 21, 114, 231
Bush, Prescott 99
Bye Bye Birdie 33, 231, 232

Cabaret 33, 35, 238, 239
Caesar, Sid 40
Caffe Cino 31, 52–4, 55, 59, 60–1, 62, 79–82, 185, 219
Caldwell, Ben 70
Caldwell, Zoë 36, 66, 228, 238, 240
Calloway, Cab 34
Cambridge, Godfrey 46, 216
Campbell, Joseph 205
Camus, Albert 41, 70
Capote, Truman 53
Carlino, John Lewis 225
Carlos, John 29–30
Carlson, Marvin 43, 44

Canobianco, Dominique 138
Carmines, Al 57–60, 219, 221, 226, 227
Carroll, Beeson 223
Carroll, Diahann 233
Carroll, Vinnette Justine 40, 217
Caruana, Jerry 53
Cash, Johnny 23
Cash, Rosalind 48
Cassidy, Jack 236
Castro, Fidel 129
Cazale, John 222
Chaikin, Joseph 42, 181–2, 183, 185, 186–90, 204–7, 210, 211, 213, 218, 219, 228
Champion, Gower 33, 231, 232, 236, 240
Channing, Carol 34, 235
Chanel, Coco 34
Chaney, James 7
Channing, Carol
Charba, Mari-Claire 220
Charles, Martha 70
Charles, Martie 70
Chaucer, Geoffrey 166
Chavez, Cesar 1, 18
Chayefsky, Paddy 230, 232
Chekhov, Anton 66
Chelsea Theatre Center 223
Cherry Lane Theatre 45, 132, 137
Chin, Frank 86
Child, Julia 17
Childers, Leee 83, 84
Childress, Alice 48, 154, 157, 173
Childs, Lucinda 58
Chin, Frank 87
Chisholm, Shirley 10
Chong, Ping 87
Chupa, Anna Maria 133
Ciccone, Oscar 90
Cino, Joe 52–4, 80, 185
Circle in the Square 45, 48–9, 154, 162–4, 260

Cienfuegos, Lucky 90
Cieślak, Ryszard 228
Civil Rights Act of 1964 7, 10, 29, 173
civil rights movement 5–8, 12, 15, 19–20, 24, 26, 70, 77, 246
Claiborn, Craig 17
Clarenbach, Kathryn F. 10
Clark, Joseph S. 18
Clarke, John 129
Clarke, Cheryl 144
Clarke, Shirley 23
Cleage, Pearl 48
Cleveland Playhouse 64
Clift, Montgomery 49
Clinton, Hillary Rodham 30
Clurman, Harold 36, 43, 113, 119
Coca, Imogene 40
Coco, James 216, 222, 226
Cocteau, Jean 53
Cohen, Alexander H. 42
Cohen, Hettie Roberta 127, 133–4
Coleman, Ornette 26
Coleman, Shepard 236
Colón, Miriam 89–91
Coltrane, John 23, 26
Columbia Broadcasting System (CBS) 20, 184
Columbia University 27–8, 153, 168
Combahee River Collective 11
Comden, Betty 240
Comics Code Authority 2
Compton, Gardner 223
Compton's Cafeteria Uprising 13
Concept East Theatre (CET) 47, 70–2
Connection, The 31, 41, 46, 75–6, 215, 216
Connor, Eugene 'Bull' 6
Consumer Bill of Rights 18
Cook, Ralph 55–6, 63

Cooke, Sam 25–6
Cooper, Gary 190
Coppola, Francis Ford 21
Corman, Roger 21
Corzatte, Clayton 217
counterculture 3, 9, 12, 58
Counter Intelligence Program (COINTELPRO) 7
Country Joe and the Fish 25
Courtney, C.C. 229
Coward, Noël 53
Cowen, Ron 226
Cronkite, Walter 19, 20
Cronyn, Hume 49, 66, 115, 235
Crosby, Stills, and Nash 24
Crowley, Mart 46, 81–2
Cruse, Harold 68, 129
Cryer, Gretchen 222, 229
Cugat, Xavier 26

Dahdah, Robert 53, 54
Dailey, Irene 225
Dale, Grover 227
Dale, Dick 24
Dale, Michael 33
Daley, Richard J. 28
Dalí, Salvador 83, 252
Dames at Sea 54, 227
Daniels, William 216
Danner, Blythe 242
Darion, Joe 237
Dave Clark Five 25
David, Jean 222
David Merrick Arts Foundation 240
Davidson, Gordon 227
Da Vinci, Leonardo 175
Davis, Bette 36
Davis, Ossie 39
Davis, R.G. 31, 245, 250
Day, Dennis 145
De Niro, Robert 21
Dean, James 23

De Beauvoir, Simone 41
Decker, Lindsey 219
Dee, Ruby 39
Delcorte, George T 50
Delicate Balance, A 42, 98, 101, 106, 110, 114–18, 238, 239
Democratic National Convention (1968) 25, 28
Demme, Jonathan 21
De Martin, Imelda 225
De Niro, Robert 21
Dennis, Sandy 234, 235
Dent, Tom 78
De Priest, Margaret 219
De Pury, Marianne 194
Derby, Doris 77
Dewhurst, Colleen 48, 50, 217, 228, 231
Dews, Peter 241
Dhiegh, Khigh 216
Di Prima, Diane 127, 128
Di Prima, Dominique 127, 135
Diamond, Selma 40
Diggers 17
Diller, Phyllis 34
Dine, Jim 57
Dittman, Dean 219
Dixon, Billie 221
Dodd, Johnny 53, 54, 55, 220
Doors, The 25
'Doris' Plays 182, 187, 190–3
Douglas, Emory 26, 143
Douglas, Melvyn 230
Drama Desk's Vernon Rice Award 59, 69, 72, 204, 213, 224–9
Drama Review, The (*TDR*) 70
Drexler, Rosalyn 51, 57, 58–9
Driver, Donald 226
DRUM magazine (Janus society) 12
Duay, Grant 56
Duberman, Martin 77–8, 212

DuBois, W.E.B. 150, 153
Dukakis, Olympia 42, 218
Duncan, Sandy 228
Dunn, Joseph H. 220
Duquette, Adrian 232
Duquette, Tony 232
Dutchman 47, 68, 119, 125, 132–7, 143–4, 149, 165, 172, 218
Duvall, Robert 219
Dyne, Michael 237
Dvonch, Frederick 230
Dylan, Bob 24

East Coast Homophile Organization (ECHO) 12
East End Theatre 165
East West Players (EWP) 85–7
Eastwood, Mary 10
Ebb, Fred 227, 239
Ebert, Joyce 218
Ed Sullivan Show, The 19, 25
Edinburgh Fringe Festival 42
Edwards, Debra L. 128
Edwards, Gus 48
Ehrlichman, John 8
Einstein, Bob 20
Elam, Harry J. Jr 148
Eliason, James 61
Elder, Lonne III 39, 48, 227, 228
Eliot, T.S. 74
Ellen Stewart Theatre 63
Elliot, Stephen 228
Epstein, Alvin 221
Equal Pay Act 10
Equal Rights Amendment 11
Erdman, Jean 218
Eskow, Jerome 217
Esslin, Martin 104–5
Evers, Medgar 6–7, 77, 141
Eyen, Tom 51, 53

Fabray, Nanette 34
Faderman, Lillian 15

Fantasticks, The 33, 45, 224
Fair Packaging and Labeling Act 18
Fair Play for Cuba Committee 124
Fanon, Frantz 139, 140, 152, 172, 173
fast food 16–17
Federal Bureau of Investigation (FBI) 7, 11, 128, 140
Federal Theatre Project 64
Feibleman, Peter 39
Feiffer, Jules 222
Fellini, Federico 21
feminism 9–11
Feuer, Cy 232
Fichandler, Nina 64
Fiddler on the Roof 33, 34, 35, 236, 237
Field, Crystal 59
Field, Ron 228, 229, 239, 242
Finnerty, Warren 215
Firehouse Theater 187
First World War 249
Flanagan, Neil 80, 221
Flicker, Theodore J. 216, 224
Floating Bear 127, 128
folk rock 23–4
Food and Drug Administration 18
Ford Foundation 39, 43, 47, 50, 62, 64, 65, 69, 78, 86, 205, 245
Ford, Nancy 222, 229
Foreman, Richard 223
Forensic and the Navigators 55–6, 221
Fornés, María Irene 51, 57, 59, 79, 94, 219, 258
Fortune 220
Fortune Society 222
Fosse, Bob 235, 238
Foster, Gloria 218, 220, 225
Foster, Paul 51, 53, 60–1, 61–2
Four Tops, The 24
Frampton, Hollis 22

Frankel, Gene 46–7, 215
Franklin, Aretha 23
Franklin, J.e. 70
Frazier, Clifford 71
Frechtman, Bernard 216
Freddie Redd Quartet 31, 75
Freedman, Gerald 160, 166, 169–70, 216
Freedom Farm Corporation 18
Free Play for Cuba Committee 129
Free Southern Theater 52, 77–9, 147–8, 166
Freedom Riders 1, 6–7,
free love 9
Free Southern Theater 52, 77–9
Freeman, Al Jr 39
French, Arthur 48
Frey, John 29
Friedan, Betty 10–11, 39
Friedkin, William 81
Friedman, Gary William 222, 229
Friel, Brian 237, 241
Fugard, Athol 69
Fuller, Charles 48
Funny Girl 33–4
Funnyhouse of a Negro 151, 155, 157, 159, 161–5, 166, 168, 169, 171, 172, 173, 174, 176–7, 178, 179
Furth, George 229
Futz 63, 220, 227

Gabel, Martin 231
Gaisner, Rhea 187
Gans, Sharon 220
garage rock 25
Gardenia, Vincent 216, 223
Gardner, Herb, 233
Garen, Leo 134
Garland, Geoff 217, 224
Garrett, Jimmy 142
gay theatre 31, 52, 79–84
Gaye, Marvin 24

Geer, Ellen 66
Gelber, Jack 32, 41, 46, 75–6, 215, 216
Gelbart, Larry 40, 234
General Strike for Peace, 1961 75
Genet, Jean 41, 46–7, 48–9, 93, 98, 104, 114, 215, 216, 258
George, Nathan 222, 227
Getz, Stan 26
Gide, André 53
Gibson, William 43, 230, 231
Gilberto, Astrud 26
Gilberto, João 26
Gillespie, Dizzy 26
Gilroy, Frank 46, 217, 236, 237
Ginsberg, Allen 14, 23, 127, 130
G.I. Bill 3
girl groups 24
Gleason, Jackie 230
Glide Memorial Church 13
Godard, Jean-Luc 21
Goldoni, Carlo 86
Goldwater, Barry 2
Goodman, Andrew 7
Goodman, Paul 59, 73, 205, 207
Goodman Theatre 64
Gordone, Charles 51, 222, 227, 228
Gordy, Berry 24
Gorilla Queen, The 59, 83
Gorman, Cliff 222
Gorman, Mari 221
Gould, Harold 223
Goulet, Robert 240
Graduate, The 2, 22
Grant, Lee 218
Grant, Mark 33, 35
Grant, Micki 40
Grateful Dead, The 24
Green, Adolph 240
Greenidge, Kirsten 157, 160
Greensboro sit-ins 26
Gregory, Andre 223
Grey, Joel 34, 239

Grimes, Frank 228
Grimes, Tammie 228, 231, 242
Grimké, Angelina Weld 154
Grizzard, George 66
Grooms, Red 57
Grosbard, Ulu 219, 225
gross national product (of the US) 3
Grotowski, Jerzy 62, 228
Guare, John 46, 98, 221
Guggenheim Fellowship for Creative Writing 70, 165
Guinness, Alec 235
Gunn, Moses 48, 221
Guthrie Theater 65, 66–7
Guthrie, Tyrone 49, 66

Hackett, Joan 216, 224
Hadler, Walter 55, 56
Hagen, Uta 49, 234
Hailey, Oliver 224
Haimsohn, George 54, 227
Hair 35–6, 51, 63, 213, 226, 241
Hall, Peter 42, 239
Hambleton, T. Edward 49
Hamer, Fannie Lou 18, 77
Hamilton, William 184
Hamlet 49, 66, 136, 159, 184, 227, 235
Hammerstein, Oscar 31, 32, 192, 232
Hanan, Stephen Mo 34
Hancock, John 221
Hancock, Sheila 41
Hanisch, Carol 10
Hanley, William 224
Hansberry, Lorraine 31, 38–40, 46–7, 173, 230, 237, 257–8
Harding, James 74
Hardy, Joseph 226, 228, 242
Harnick, Sheldon 34, 236
Harrington, Michael 4

Harris, Barbara 217, 224, 239
Harris, Bill 71
Harris, Julie 241
Harris, Neal 70
Harris, Rosemary 217, 219, 238
Harrison, George 25
Harrison, Paul Carter 48, 158
Hart, Lois 11
Harvard University 182, 212
Hatch, James 217
Haunted Host, The 80, 81
Havel, Vaclav 221, 223
Hawkins, Cornell Wallace 152
Hawkins, Etta 152
Hayakawa, S.I. 30
Haydn, Joseph 167
Hayes, Helen 93, 226
Hayman, Lillian 240
Hays, David 48, 216
Heaven, Lily 198
Heeley, Desmond 240
Heffernan, John 216
Hellman, Lillian 230, 231
Hello, Dolly! 34, 228, 235, 236, 247
Hendrix, Jimi 23, 25
Henritze, Bette 221
Hepburn, Katharine 34
Herman, Jerry 235
Hill, Arthur 234
Hinnant, Bill 226
hippies 3, 29, 246
Hoffman, Dustin 22, 48, 219, 225, 227
Holbrook, Hal 238
Holgate, Ronald 241
Holland, Anthony 223
Holm, Ian 42, 239
Holt, Will 222, 229
Holy Modal Rounders 55
Home Movies 57, 58–9, 219, 225
Hong, James 85–6
Hooker, John Lee 26

INDEX

Hooks, Bobby Dean 39
Hooks, Robert 39, 47
Hoover, J. Edgar 7
Hopper, Dennis 21
Horovitz, Israel 46, 221, 222, 226
Hose and Heels Club *see* Phi Pi Epsilon
Houghton, Norris 49
Houseman, John 49
housing boom 15
Howard, Ken 242
Howard University 126, 135
Huang, El 85
Hudson, Ernie 71
Hudson, Theodore R. 140, 141
Huerta, Jorge 88
Hughes, Langston 7, 65
Humphrey, Hubert 28
Hunt, Peter 241
Hurd, Gale Anne 21
Hurst, David 218
Hurston, Zora Neale 154
Hutton, Bobby 29

Ichioka, Yuji 84
Iko, Momoko 86
Inge, William 36, 37, 53, 99
Internal Revenue Service 74
International Hotel 85
Ionesco, Eugène 41, 93, 101, 104, 120, 154, 231, 258,
Irving, Jules 43–4, 70, 166
Iwamatsu, Mako 85, 86
Ito, Teiji 216
It's Alright to be a Woman Theatre 79
Iwamatsu, Mako 85

Jacobs, Jane 16
Jack Benny Show, The 144–5
Jackson, Anne 218
Jackson, C. Bernard 217
Jackson Five, The 24

Jackson, George 58
James, Hal 240
James, Skip 26
Jarry, Alfred 200–1
jazz 25, 26, 31, 52, 68, 70, 75, 77, 136, 137, 149
Jedd, Gerry 216
Jefferson Airplane 24, 25
Jihad Press 145
Jorgensen, Christine 12
Johnson, Bumpby 137
Johnson, James Weldon 133
Johnson, Luci Baines 198
Johnson, Lyndon B. 4, 20, 27–8, 137
Johnson, Virginia E. 8
Jones, Coyette Leroy 126
Jones, Hettie *see* Cohen, Hettie Roberta
Jones, James Earl 46, 217, 219, 225, 226, 241
Jones, Landon 3
Jones, Kellie 134
Jones, LeRoi *see* Baraka, Amiri
Jones, Lisa 134
Jones, Margo 251, 255
Jones, Sondra Lee *see* Baraka, Kimako
Jones, Tom 45, 224
Jorgensen, Christine 12
Joseph, Jeff Weiss 57, 221, 222
Joyce, Joyce A. 142
Judson Art Gallery 57
Judson Dance Theater 57, 58
Judson Memorial Church 60
Judson Poets' Theater 52, 57–60, 63, 79, 83, 218
Juliá, Raúl 90

Kadogo, Aku 71
Kael, Pauline 22
Kahn, Michael 154, 155, 156, 160, 163, 164, 176

Kander, John 239
Kanellos, Nicolás 87
Kanfer, Stefan 22
Kaprow, Allan 31, 52
Karamu House 47, 65, 154
Karenga, Maulana 125, 143
Karnilova, Maria 237
Katz, Leon 59
Kazan, Elia 37, 43, 49, 156
Keach, Stacy 220, 226, 228
Kennedy, Adam 153
Kennedy, Adrienne 46, 47, 56, 98, 151–80, 259,
  African American identity 151–2, 157–8
  African diaspora 151, 171, 178
  Albee, Edward 158, 162–5
  Black Arts Movement 158–61, 169
  Cities in Bizique
    Beast Story, A 159, 166, 170–1, 179
    Owl Answers, The 155, 162, 165–7, 169–71, 172, 176, 179
    Circle in the Square 154, 162, 163, 260
  critical reception 155–7, 164–5, 169, 170–1, 175–8
  Deadly Triplets 175
  early life 152–3, 260
  Evening With Dead Essex, An 178
  Funnyhouse of a Negro 151, 155, 157, 159, 161–5, 166, 168, 169, 171, 172, 173, 174, 176–7, 178, 179
  Ghana 153–4
  He Brought Her Heart Back in a Box 180
  influences on 154–6
  Kennedy, Joseph, marriage to 153

Kuntu Drama: Plays of the African Continuum 170
Lesson in Dead Language, A 171, 174–5, 178–9
Lennon Play, The 173–4
motherhood 153
Rat's Mass, A 171–3, 178, 179
Rockefeller Foundation grant 165
Sun: A Poem for Malcolm X Inspired by His Murder 175, 178
themes 156–8, 160–1, 168–9, 178–9
Williams, Tennessee 154–5
Kennedy Center Drama Prize 73
Kennedy, John F. 7, 19, 28, 110, 137, 206
Kennedy, Joseph C. 153
Kennedy, Joseph Jr 153, 173
Kennedy, Robert F. 18, 28
Kenny, Sean 235
Kenrick, John 32, 34
Kenyon, Neal 227
Kerr, Walter 46, 50, 177, 203, 212
Kesey, Ken 25
Kessler, Bruce 61
Kidd, Michael 230
Kiley, Richard 238
Kim, Willa 219, 229
King, Martin Luther Jr 6, 7, 29, 206
King, Woodie Jr 71, 145, 149
Kinks, The 25
Kiser, Terry 220
Kissman, Lee 55, 223
Klatch, Rebecca 3
Klein, Maxine 223
Koch, Ed 61
Konoshita, Junji 86
Kopit, Arthur 46, 217, 224, 242
Koprince, Susan 40
Kornfeld, Lawrence 57–9, 83, 218

Kotto, Yaphet 162
Koutoutkas, H.M. 51, 53, 54–5, 59, 220
Kramer, Larry 51
Krapp's Last Tape 93, 94, 98, 99, 216
Krauss, Ruth 59
Krone, Gerald 39, 47
Ku Klux Klan 6, 7, 141
Kumari, Surya 216
Kurosawa, Akira 21, 85
Kushner, Tony 81, 94

La Compañía de Teatro de Alburquerque 88
La MaMa Experimental Theatre Club 35, 52, 60–3, 120, 185, 213, 219, 221, 249
La Vigne, Robert 221
labour market 3, 5, 18
Lahr, Bert 235
Lahr, John 40, 181, 202, 207, 209
Langella, Frank 220, 227
Lansbury, Angela 34, 238, 241
Latino theatre 52, 63, 74, 87–90
Lappé, Frances Moore 17
Laurel, Alicia Bay 17
Lavender Menace 11
Lavin, Linda 227
Lawrence, Elliot 233
Layton, Joe 233, 241
League of Repertory Theatres 66
Lee, Esther Kim 84, 85, 87
Lee, Eugene 148
Lee, Ming Cho 227
Lee, Will 226
Leibman, Ron 223, 227, 228
Leigh, Mitch 237
Leighton, Margaret 233
Leigh, Vivian 234
Lém, Nguyễn Văn 27
Lennon, John 22, 25, 173–4
Lenya, Lotte 42

Lerner, Alan Jay 34, 192
LeSeur, Joe 130
Levy, Jacques 193, 203
LGBTQ rights 11–15, 79, 130, 132
Life magazine 66
Lights, Fred 60
Lincoln, Abbie 26
Lincoln Center Theater 16, 43–4, 70, 86, 87, 166
Lindsay, John 90
Link, Peter 229
Linklater, Kristen 205
Lipton, Michael 220
Little, Cleavon 48, 228, 242
Little, Stuart 45, 46, 49, 50,
Living Theatre, The 31, 41, 42, 46, 57, 74–6, 77, 120, 186, 212, 218, 222, 225, 250, 255
Lira, Agustín 88
Little, Cleavon 48, 228, 242
Livings, Henry 220
Livingston, Jock 216
Livingston, Robert 222
Loan, Nguyễn Ngọc 27
Loden, Barbara 236
Loewe, Frederick 192
London, Dorothy 227
London, Roy 207
Lorca, Federico García 74, 154, 155, 157
Los Angeles Free Press 2
Losey, Joseph 175
Loti, Elisa 216
Love, Barbara 11
Lowry, W. McNeil 31, 65, 245
Ludlam, Charles 51, 82, 83, 84, 223, 246, 248, 250, 252–3, 256, 259
Luke, Peter 226, 241
Lumumba, Patrice 124, 141, 152, 154, 171

INDEX

Mabou Mines 163
Macbeth, Robert 39, 69, 70
MacDermot, Galt 35, 226
Madden, Donald 49
Madden, Edward 210
Madhubuti, Haki 7
Madness of Lady Bright, The 53, 62, 80–1
Magee, Patrick 44, 238
Malcom X 7, 68, 124–5, 129, 134, 141, 152, 175, 178
Malina, Judith 74–6, 120, 186, 215, 218, 222, 250–1, 255, 258
Mamas and the Pappas, The 24
Mame 33, 34, 237, 238
Man of La Mancha 33, 237, 238
Manhoff, Bill 39
Mankiewicz, Joseph L. 21
Marasco, Robert 228, 242
Marat/Sade see The Persecution and Assassination of Jean-Paul Marat as Performed by the Inmates of the Asylum of Charenton Under the Direction of the Marquis de Sade
March on Washington for Jobs and Freedom 7, 23–4
Marchand, Nancy 216
Mar-Keys, The 24
Marcus, Frank 238, 239
Marcuse, Herbert 9
Margot Jones's Theatre '47 64
Mark Taper Forum 89
Marlowe, Christopher 180
Marqués, René 89
Marre, Mary 31, 34, 230
Martha and the Vandellas 24
Martin, Ernest H. 232
Martin, Mary 31, 34, 230
Martin, Steve 20
Martyrs Can't Go Home 86

Marvelettes, The 24
Marvin X 68, 69, 70
Mast, Gerald 35
Masters, William H. 8
Matthau, Walter 41, 233, 236,
Maxwell, Roberta 223
May, Elaine 228
Mayfield, Julian 129
MC5 25
McCarthy, Eugene 28
McCarty, Eddie 221
McCauley, Robbie 160
McCowen, Alex 226
McCoy, Beth 143
McDonald's 16–17, 83
McDowell, Roddy 230
McGovern, George 28
McLuhan, Marshall 186, 199
McMahon, Frank 228, 242
McNeil, Claudia 38, 39
Meacham, Anne 216
Mead, Taylor 218
Mednick, Murray 56, 223
Mee, Charles 55
Mekas, Jonas 22–3
Melfi, Leonard 46, 55, 56, 62, 119
Mercer, Marian 227, 241
Merkerson, S. Epatha 71
Merrill, James 46
Merlo, Frank 36
Merman, Ethel 33, 228
Merrick, David 34, 235, 240
Michaels, Frankie 238
Michaels, Sidney 233, 235
Midnight Cowboy 23
Mielziner, Jo 43
Miller, Arthur 36–8, 43, 66, 96, 154–6, 219, 225, 236, 239, 256
Miller, Robin 54, 227
Miller, Timothy 73
Milligan, Andy 60

Milner, Ron 69, 71
Minnelli, Liza 237
Miracles, The 24
Mishima, Yukio 86
Mississippi Free Press 77
Moiseiwitsch, Tanya 66, 227
Molière (Jean-Baptiste Poquelin) 66
Montez, Mario 82
Monroe, Marilyn 37
Moody, Howard 57
Moon, Marjorie 40
Moore, Jim 60
Moore, Melba 228, 242
Moore, Robert 226
Morath, Inge 37
Morningside Park 27
Morrow, Lance 26
Morse, Robert 223
Moscow Art Theatre 64
Mosel, Tad 231
Moses, Gilbert 77–8, 147, 148, 223
Mostel, Zero 34, 41, 231, 234, 237
Motown Record Corporation 24
movies of the decade 20–3
Motts, Robert T. 65
Muhammad, Elijah 139
Munk, Erika 75
Muñoz, José Esteban 128
music of the decade 23–6
Mysteries and Smaller Pieces 76

Nation of Islam 7, 17
National Association for the Advancement of Colored People (NAACP) 129
National Black Theatre 71–3, 249
National Conference on Black Power 146
National Endowment for the Arts 70, 205
National Endowment for the Humanities 205
National Farm Workers Association 1, 18
National Mobilization Committee to End the War in Vietnam 28
National Organization for Women (NOW) 10
National Theatre 37, 42, 174, 250–1
National Review magazine 2
Neal, Larry 67, 136, 142, 145, 246
Negro Ensemble Company (NEC) 39, 47–8, 221, 222, 226
Nelson, Claris 53
Nemiroff, Robert 39
NewArk 149
New Bowery Theatre 128
New Federal Theatre 145, 149
New Lafayette Theatre 39, 68–70, 72, 243
New York City Ballet 43
New York City Center 86
New York City Pan Asian Repertory Theatre 87
New York City Philharmonic 43
New York Drama Critics award 90
New York Poets Theatre 128
New York Pride Parade 13
New York Radical Women (NYRW) 10, 11
New York Shakespeare Festival 50–1, 64–5, 70, 89–90
New York State Council on the Arts 205
New York Times 66, 71, 83, 104, 106, 148, 177, 181, 201, 203
New York's Theatre for a New Audience 180
Neway, Patricia 230
Newman, David 21

Newman, Phyllis 233
Newport Folk Festival 24
Newton, Huey 29
Nicholas, Denise 78
Nichols, Mike 22, 41, 236, 237, 239, 240
Nichols, Peter 239, 240
Nicholson, Jack 21
Nichtern, Claire 236
Nietzsche, Friedrich 184
Nixon, Richard 2, 8, 18–19, 40
North Carolina Agricultural and Technical College 6
Noto, Lore 45
Nuevo Círculo Dramático, El 89–91
Nuevo Teatro Pobre de las Américas, El 74
Nurorican Poet's Café 90
Nusbaum, Jane C. 240
Nuyorican theatre 90

Obama, Barack 15
Obie Award 58, 59, 62, 65, 70, 72, 90, 94, 98, 132, 137, 165, 212, 215–23
O'Connor, Kevin 220, 225
Off-Broadway 45–51, 151
Off-Broadway Theatre Four 81
Off-Off Broadway 2, 31, 51–2
O'Hara, Frank 46, 127, 130
O'Horgan, Tom 35, 62–3, 185, 212, 220, 226, 227
Oh, Soon-Tek 86
Ohio State University 152
Old Vic Theatre 64
Olivier, Lawrence 174
O'Loughlin, Gerald S. 217
Om Theatre 222
Ondine 54
O'Neal, John 77
O'Neal, Ron 222, 227
O'Neill, Eugene 48, 93–4, 120

Ono, Yoko 22, 57
Open Theater 35, 52, 56, 74, 181–2, 183, 185, 186–90, 204–7, 211–13, 222
Oppenheimer, Joel 57
O'Quinn, Jim 67
Orbach, Jerry 46, 227, 241
Oriental Actors of America 86–7
Orton, Joe 41, 222
Osafemi, Olabumi 139
Osborne, John, 235, 237
O'Shea, Tessie 236
O'Sullivan, Michael 218
Osuna, Jess 220
Oswald, Lee Harvey 19, 209
Otrabanda 74
Ottley, Roi 126
Outer Critics Circle Award 204
Owens, Rochelle 51, 59, 63, 220, 227
Oyamo 70

Pacino, Al 221, 226, 241
Paddleford, Clementine 17
Page, Geraldine 48
Paley, William S. 20
Palmstierna-Weiss, Gunilla 238
Paper Bag Players, The 219
Papp, Joseph 35, 50–1, 63, 64, 89–90, 165–6, 169–70, 176, 226
Paradise Now 76
Paris Review, The 93
Parsons, Estelle 218
Partisan Review 212
Passloff, Aileen 58
Pasolli, Robert 187, 188, 190, 196, 211
Patrick, Robert 53, 79, 80, 245
Patterson, Charles 68
Patterson, James 218, 240
Patterson, William 68
Paul Revere and the Raiders 25

Payton-Wright, Pamela 223
Peaslee, Richard 205
Peavy, Charles D. 133, 142, 143
Pecheur, Bruce 84
Pekin Theatre 65
Peluso, Emanuel 220
Pendleton, Austin 223, 228
PEN International 37–8
Penn, Arthur 230
Pépin, Jacques 16, 17
Performance Group, The 35, 52, 74, 163, 212, 222
Pernick, Solly 235
Persecution and Assassination of Jean-Paul Marat as Performed by the Inmates of the Asylum of Charenton Under the Direction of the Marquis de Sade, The 44–5, 63, 237, 238
Personal Rights in Defense and Education (PRIDE) 13–14
Peter, Paul, and Mary 24
Peters, Bernadette 54, 227
Phoenix Theatre, The 49–50
Phi Pi Epsilon 12
Pill, The 9
Piñero, Miguel 90
Pinter, Harold 42, 104, 217, 218, 232, 238
Pirandello, Luigi 41, 217
Piscator, Erwin 74
Play-House of the Ridiculous, The 59, 82, 185
Playwrights Unit, The 46, 119, 132, 182
Plaza Suite 41, 239, 240
Pleasence, Donald 42, 226
Plowright, Joan 231
Plummer, Christopher 43
Plunka, Gene 210

Pocket Theater 193, 203
Poggi, Jack 32
Poitier, Sidney 38, 39, 145
Pollock, Jackson 252
Pop, Iggy 25
Pope, Peggy 221
Porter, Cole 192
Powell, Anthony 235
Present Stages 128
Presidential Commission on the Status of Women (PCSW) 10
Presley, Elvis 33
Preston, Robert 239
Previn, André 34, 39, 145
Price, The 38, 239
Prince, Harold 35, 228, 234, 236, 239
Prince, Virginia 12 (*see also Transvestia*)
prison-industrial complex 8
Proudfitt, Scott 185, 186, 210
Provincetown Playhouse 59, 94, 99
psychedelic rock 24–5
Public Theater 35, 51, 90, 166, 169, 226
Puerto Rican Traveling Theatre (PRTT) 90

Quayle, Anna 234
Quintero, José 45, 48
Quinto Festival 89
Quo, Beulah 85

Ra, Sun 137, 139
Rabb, Ellis 49, 217
Rabe, David 51
Rabkin, Gerald 84
Radio Free Dixie 7
Rado, James 35
Ragni, Gerome 35, 213
Rahman, Aisha 160
Rainer, Yvonne 58

Rambeau, David 71
Raisin in the Sun, A 31, 38–40, 46, 47, 230
Randall, Dudley 7
Rapson, Ralph 66
Rat's Mass, A 171–3, 178, 179
Rauschenberg, Robert 57
Rawlins, Lester 216
Rea, Oliver 66
Reagan, Ronald 2, 30, 73, 88
Redding, Otis 23, 24
Redford, Robert 22
Reed, Clarence 68
Reed, Ishmael 159
Reed, Kate 36
Reich, Wilhelm 9
Reid, Beryl 239
Reilly, Charles Nelson 233
Reilly, Clayton 47
Reiner, Carl 40
Reiner, Rob 20
Repertory Theatre of Lincoln Center 43–4, 70, 86–7, 166
Republican National Convention 30
residential theatre movement 63–5
Resnais, Alain 21
Revere, Anne 230
Revill, Clive 44
Ribman, Ronald 220
Richards, Lloyd 31, 38–9, 65
Richardson, Jack 46, 216, 224
Ridiculous Theatrical Company, The 223
Rigby, Harry 240
Rivas, Bimbo 90
Rivera-Servera, Ramón 87
Rivers, Larry 130
Rivieras, The 25
Roach, Max 26
Robard, Jason 48

Robbins, Jerome 165, 167, 175, 237
Robinson, Dorothy 71
Robinson, Sylvia *see* Baraka, Amina
Rochester *see* Anderson, Eddie
Rockefeller Foundation 62, 78, 165
Rodgers, Gaby 155
Rodgers, Mary 49
Rodgers, Richard 31, 32, 192, 232
Rodríguez, Roberto 89, 90–1
Roebling, Paul 217
Rogers, Ginger 34
Rogers, Paul 217
Rogoff, Gordon 186
Rolle, Esther 48
Rolling Stones, The 25
Roosevelt, Eleanor 10
Rosenthal, Cindy 60, 62, 74, 76
Ross, David 216
Ross, Diana 24
Roundtree, Richard 48
Rothlein, Arlene 58, 222
Routledge, Patricia 240
Royal Court Theatre 174–5, 203
Royal National Theatre 41–2
Royal Shakespeare Company (RSC) 44
Russ, Thomas Everett 126

Sab Shimono et al vs. the Repertory Theater of Lincoln Center 87
Sackler, Howard 226, 227, 241
Sainer, Arthur 182, 253, 255
Sainthill, Loudon 241
Salaam, Kalamu ya (Val Ferdinand) 147
Salvio, Robert 220
Sam and Dave 24
San Francisco Art Institute 31
San Francisco Asian American Theater Company 87

San Francisco Mime Troup 31, 74, 88, 222, 245
San Francisco State University 30, 85, 142
San Fransciso State College Black Student Union 30, 142
Sanchez, Sonia 30, 47, 68, 70, 136
Sanders, Leslie Catherine 139, 143
Sanders, Pharoah 26
Sandoval, Arturo 26
San Jose State College 87
Sands, Diana 39, 162, 164, 175, 218
Sankey, Tom 221
Sartre, Jean-Paul 41, 114
Satellite Records 24
Schary, Dore 231
Schechner, Richard 52, 63, 77, 78, 106, 163, 212
Scheider, Roy 221
Schisgal, Murray 46, 225, 236, 237
Schlichter, Joseph 205
Schlinsinger, John 23
Schneeman, Carolee 23
Schneider, Alan 41, 42, 99, 217, 234
Scofield, Paul 233
Scorsese, Martin 21
Scott, Bernard 57
Scott, George C. 41, 48, 217
Schmidt, Harvey 45, 224
Schweitzer, Albert 39
Screen Test 83
Sealy, Robert 61
Seattle Northwest Asian American Theatre 87
Second Story Players, The 221
Second World War 1, 3, 16, 32, 37, 39, 104
Selden, Albert 240
Seldes, Marian 218, 239
Serpent, The 56, 182, 183, 186, 194, 201, 202, 204–13, 222

Servicemen's Readjustment Act of 1944 *see* G.I. Bill
Schultz, Michael A. 221, 227
Schumann, Peter 60, 220
Schwerner, Michael 7
Scorpio Rising 23
Seal, Elizabeth 231
Sedgwick, Edie 82
Seale, Bobby 26, 68
Seeger, Pete 24
Segal, George 48
Serban, Andrei 62
Sell, Mike 132, 137
sexual revolution 8–9, 245
Shakespeare, William 49, 66, 166, 178
Shange, Ntozake 51, 160
Shantigar 213
Shaw, Robert 226, 241
Shelton, Gilbert 2
Shepard, Sam 46, 51, 53, 55–6, 94, 98, 119, 163, 185, 220, 221
Shepp, Archie 147
Sheridan Square Playhouse 45, 187, 193
Sherin, Edwin 227
Sherman, Hiram 240
Sherwood, Madeleine 218
Shevelove, Burt 234
Shirelles, The 24
Shriver, Sargent 137
Shumlin, Herman 235
Shumsky, Ellen 11
Sign in Sidney Brustein's Window, The 38, 237
silent majority 1, 2, 40
Sills, Stephanie 193
Silverman, Stanley 223
Simon and Garfunkel 22, 24
Simon, Josette 37
Simon, Neil 40–1, 235, 236, 237, 239, 240, 242

Sirhan Sirhan 28
Sklar, Roberta 205
Sollors, Werner 133, 143
Slave, The 68, 134–6
Smethurst, James 72
Smith, Jack 22–3, 82, 83
Smith, Michael 51, 54, 55, 56–7, 58, 63,
Smith, Oliver 41, 231, 232, 236, 237
Smith, Sharon 4
Smith, Tommie 29
Smothers Brothers Comedy Hour, The 20
Sondheim, Stephen 87, 229
Sontag, Susan 23, 133, 205, 207
Soyinka, Wole 153
Sound of Music, The 31, 230, 231
Spellman, A.B. 125, 145
Spinetti, Victor 174, 175
Spirit House 74, 141, 146, 149, 244
Spock, Benjamin 8
Spoerri, Daniel 57
Spolin, Viola 186, 189, 195
Springfield, Dusty 25
St James, Amanda 13
St. Mark's Playhouse 46–7, 49, 129, 134, 138
St. Mark's Poetry Project 56
Stadlin, Lewis J. 228
Stapleton, Maureen 41
Starkweather, David 53,
Starr, Ringo 25
Star Trek 85
Stax Records 24
Stein, Gertrude 57–60, 74, 218, 219, 221
Stein, Howard 156, 160
Sternhagen, Frances 219
Stevens, Roger L. 232
Stewart, Ellen 52, 60–3, 185, 249–50
Stewart, James 228

Stewart, Michael 235
Strasberg, Lee 129
Streisand, Barbra 34
Stone, Peter 227
Stone, Wendell C. 52
Stone-Lawrence, Susan 68, 79
Stonewall Inn uprising 2, 13–15
Stooges, The 25
Stoppard, Tom 41–2, 239, 240
Stratford Connecticut's American Shakespeare Festival 65
Stryker, Susan 12, 13
Stubblefield, Clyde
Student Nonviolent Coordinating Committee 77
Students for a Democratic Society 1
Styne, Jule 240
Su Teatro 88
Sullivan, Dan 83
Sun Ra Arkestra 72
Supremes, The 24
surf rock 24
Surtee, Robert 22
Sutherland, Eufua 153
Swados, Kim E. 46

Tallmer, Jerry 55, 58
Takei, George 85
Tandy, Jessica 49, 66, 115
Tarlow, Florence 59, 220
Taubman, Howard 34, 37, 44
Tavel, Ronald 57, 59, 82–4, 222
Taylor, Cecil 26
Taylor, Elizabeth 21, 114
Teatro Campesino, El 74, 87–9, 222, 254
Teatro Cuatro 90
Teatro Dallas 88
Teatro de la Esperanza 88
Teatro delle Arti 205
Teatro Repertorio Español 90
Teer, Barbara Ann 47, 58–9, 71–3, 225

television 2, 6–7, 15–20, 32–3, 40, 142, 185
Temptations, The 147
Terry, Megan 35, 51, 79, 119, 187, 195, 205, 222
Theater in the Street 220
Theatre '47 64, 251
Theatre '61 224
Theatre Communications Group *see* Ford Foundation
Theatre de Lys 45
Théâtre de Nations 89
Theatre for Ideas 220
Theatre Genesis 52, 54–6, 62, 120, 222
Theatre of the Ridiculous, The 52, 82–4
Theme is Blackness, The 69
Three Sisters, The 66
Third World Liberation Front 30
Third World Press 7
Thompson, Sada 219, 223, 228
Time magazine 19, 22–3, 26
Title VII *see* Civil Rights Act of 1964
Tony Award 36, 38, 41, 42, 95, 229–42
Torn, Rip 221
Tougaloo College Drama Workshop 77
Touré, Askia 68
Towers, Susan 225
Transvestia 12
Trashmen, The 25
Truffaut, Francois 21
Trump, Donald 3
Trungpa, Chögyam 213
Tulane Drama Review 77
Tumarin, Boris 224
Turman, Glynn 39
Twilight Crane 86
Tynan, Kenneth 42, 174
Tyson, Cicely 39, 46, 224

UCLA's Theatre Group 65
Uggams, Leslie 240
Umbra poetry group 78
United Artists 22
United Nations Educational, Scientific, and Cultural Organiation (UNESCO) 197
United States Food and Drug Administration (USFDA) 18
United States Supreme Court 5, 6
University of Connecticut 189
Urban Art Corps 40

Vaccaro, John 82–4, 185, 223
Valdez, Luis 87–90, 254
Van Ark, Joan 66
van Bemmel, Teddy 232
Vance, Nina 64
van Dyke, Dick 19, 33, 231
van Itallie, Jean-Claude 51, 52, 61, 119, 120, 181–213, 225
   Airplane: Its Passengers and Portents, An 188–9
   Almost Like Being 182, 187, 190–2
   American culture 202
   America Hurrah 193–204
      critical reception to 181, 201–5
      Interview (Pavane) 194–7
      Motel: A Masque for Three Dolls 199–201
      TV 197–9
   Caffe Cino 185
   Chaikin, Joseph 181–2, 186–90, 204–7
   'Doris' Plays
      Almost Like Being 182, 187, 190–2

I'm Really Here 182, 187, 190–2
  early life 182–4
  First Fool, The 189
  Genesis 204
  Girl and the Soldier, The 189
  Hobbies: Or Things are Fine with the Forbushers 184
  Hunter and the Bird, The 189
  I'm Really Here 182, 187, 190–2
  La Mama ETC 185
  later works 213
  language 183–4
  Look Up and Live 184
  McLuhan, Marshall 186
  Mystery Play 213
  'Odet's Kitchen' 188, 189
  Open Theater 181, 183–7, 221
  Picnic in Spring 188–9
  Playwright of the Workshop 186, 187, 193
  Playwrights Unit 185
  Serpent, The 56, 182, 183, 186, 194, 201, 202, 204–13, 222
    Chaikin, Joseph 204–7
    composition of 206–10
    critical reception 210, 212–13
    'Should the Artist Be Political in His Art?' 201, 208–9
  Struck Dumb 213
  Tibetan Book of the Dead: or How Not to Do it Again, The 213
  television writing 184–5
  Thoughts on the Instant of Greeting a Friend in the Street 189
  War 182–3
  Where is de Queen? 187
Vanguard 13

Variety 66
Vaughan, David 59
Vega, Cecilia 90
Vehr, Bill 254
Vernon Rice Award *see* Drama Desk Award
Vidal, Gore 230
Vietnam War 2, 20, 27–9, 56, 183–4, 197, 244, 246
Village Voice 61, 94, 98, 132, 169, 202, 212, 258–9
Vivian Beaumont Theater *see* Repertory Theatre of Lincoln Center
Voelpel, Fred 228
Voigt, Jon 23
Voting Rights Act 7, 29

Waiting for Godot 77
Walken, Christopher 228
Walker, Joseph A. 48
Walker, Zena 240
Wallace, George 28–9
Wallach, Eli 49, 218
Walter, Sidney 187
Walters, John 231
Ward, Douglas Turner 39, 46, 47, 48, 220, 225, 227
Warden, Jack 218
Wardle, Irving 175
Warhol, Andy 22, 54, 82–3
Warner Playhouse 85
war on drugs 8
war on poverty 4, 137
Warner Brothers 22
Warner, Jack 22
Waters, Muddy 26
Waugh, Evelyn 131
Weaver, Fritz 228, 242
Weber, Fredericka 223
Weill, Kurt 229
Weiner, Matthew 204
Weiss, Peter 44, 57, 237

Wenrich, Percy 210
Weinstock, Jack 232
Weiss, Peter 44, 63, 237, 238
Wesley, Richard 70, 158
West, Cornel 139
West, Jennifer 133
Westmoreland, General William 27
Wetzsteon, Ross 202
Weyand, Ronald 218
White Barn Theatre 166
Whitehead, Robert 232
White, Jane 219
White, Ruth 217
Who's Afraid of Virginia Woolf? 42, 71, 95, 105–12, 115, 117, 119, 232, 233, 234, 256, 258–9
Wilde, Oscar 79
Wilder, Clinton 46, 119, 164, 182, 224, 234
Wilder, Thornton 94–5, 98
Wilkerson, Margaret B 155–6, 170
Williams, Mance 69, 73
Williams, Robert F. 7, 129
Williams, Samm-Art 48
Williams, Tennessee 36, 37, 45, 48, 53, 74, 84, 94, 96, 120, 123, 154, 155, 156, 157, 175, 184, 232, 256
Williamson, Nicol 227
Willis, Ellen 11
Willis, Harold 225
Willman, Noel 233

Wilson, August 39, 65, 70, 120
Wilson, Doric 51, 53, 79
Wilson, Lanford 51, 53, 61, 62, 80–1, 185, 220, 221, 225
Winters, Shelley 36, 190
Wise, Jim 54
Wiseman, Joseph 227
Wittop, Freddy 229, 236
Wittstein, Ed 219
Wonder, Stevie 24
Woodstock Music and Art Fair 25
Wolden, Judd 39
Worth, Irene 236
Writers' Stage Theatre 128

Yale School of Drama 178
Yankowitz, Susan 229
Yeats, William Butler 200
York Playhouse 100
Youker, Timothy 52, 74, 181
Young, Harvey 38
Young American for Freedom 2
Youth International Party (Yippies) 28

Zapruder, Abraham 206
Zeigler, Joseph Wesley 64, 65, 66
Zeisler, Peter 66
Zindel, Paul 222, 229
Zipprodt, Patricia 48, 227, 237, 239
Zoo Story, The 93, 99, 104, 108, 110, 117, 120, 121, 216, 224, 258–9

www.ingramcontent.com/pod-product-compliance
Lightning Source LLC
Chambersburg PA
CBHW070012010526
44117CB00011B/1539